Trevor Marriott is a retired British Police murder squad detective who joined the service in 1970 and was soon promoted to the Criminal Investigation Department (CID), where he was involved in the investigation of numerous murders as well as assisting in the investigation of many other major crimes throughout his long and distinguished career. He is the author of *Jack the Ripper: The 21st Century Investigation*, and a new book on Jack the Ripper entitled *Jack the Ripper – The Secret Police Files*, to be published to mark the 125th anniversary of the Whitechapel Murders.

To contact the author, to arrange press and media interviews, speaking engagements or any other personal appearances please email tmarriott@btinternet.com or contact him via his website: www.trevormarriott.co.uk.

THE EVIL
WITHIN

THE EVIL WITHIN

A TOP MURDER SQUAD DETECTIVE
REVEALS THE CHILLING TRUE STORIES OF
THE WORLD'S MOST NOTORIOUS KILLERS

TREVOR MARRIOTT

JOHN BLAKE

Published by John John Blake Publishing
3 Bramber Court, 2 Bramber Road
London W14 9PB

www.johnblakepublishing.co.uk

www.facebook.com/Johnblakepub facebook
twitter.com/johnblakepub twitter

First published in paperback in 2013

ISBN 978 1 85782 798 9

British Library Cataloguing-in-Publication Data:
A catalogue record for this book is available from the British Library

Designed by www.envydesign.co.uk

Printed in the UK by CPI Group (Ltd), Croydon, CR0 4YY
9 7 5 3 1 2 4 6 8 10

Photographs reproduced with kind permission of PA

Paper used by John Blake Publishing are natural, recyclable products made
from wood grown in sustainable forests. The manufacturing processes conform
to the environmental regulations of the country of origin.

Every attempt has been made to contact the relevant copyright holders,
but some were unobtainable. We would be grateful if the appropriate
people could contact us.

This book is dedicated to the men and women of law enforcement agencies worldwide who strive relentlessly and fearlessly to make the streets of our towns and cities safe, and to bring to justice and eradicate the small minority of evil men and women who become known as serial killers – who prey on unsuspecting and helpless people, attacking, beating, torturing and mutilating them before finally murdering them.

Acknowledgements
Among others, I am very pleased to acknowledge the help and
support of: Elisabeth Wetsch; The Crime Library; Paul B Kidd;
Frances Farmer; Kathleen Ramsland; Mark Gado; Michael
Newton: Rachael Bell; Marylyn Bardsley; David Lohr; James
Card; Martin Strohmm; Alexander Gilbert; Patrick Bellamy;
www.crimezzz.net; and the entire team at John Blake Publishing.

CONTENTS

CHAPTER 9 UNITED KINGDOM

INTRODUCTION

The first recorded murder was the killing of Abel by his brother Cain. Since that early time, men and women alike have continued to commit murder. Many of these murders have been committed in the most brutal and horrific ways imaginable, showing no respect for human life. Throughout my time as a murder squad detective, I have seen first-hand the wanton slayings and butcheries committed by both men and women with warped, depraved and sadistic minds. The serial killers I have documented here – among the world's worst – all had the desire to maim, kill and mutilate their fellow men, women and children in the most callous and cold-blooded fashion imaginable. I hope that, like me, when you have become familiar with the victims in the chapters that follow, you will pause to reflect on the pain and suffering endured by all as they drew their last breath before succumbing to murder at the hands of despicable and cowardly monsters.

A question I am asked frequently is 'What defines a serial killer?' And what turns a normal human being into a killer who then progresses to become a serial killer? The term 'serial killer' was adopted by the FBI in the mid-1970s, following its investigation into a spate of killings by the same perpetrators. A

INTRODUCTION

serial killer is loosely defined as someone who commits three or more murders at the same or different locations, usually coupled with an emotionally-significant lapse of time (a 'cooling-off' period) between each death. This time between each murder could be days, weeks, months or even years. Many convicted serial killers are proven psychopaths, suffering from personality disorders, but they are not always psychotic and to an outside observer may appear quite normal.

Serial killers are driven by a variety of psychological urges, but primarily by the desire for power and sexual motivations. They often have feelings of inadequacy and rejection by society. Many were both physically and sexually abused at an early age and their crimes in later years seek to compensate for this and provide them with a sense of potency and often revenge, by giving them a feeling of power, both at the time they commit their murders and afterwards. They also revel in the knowledge that their actions bring terror and fear to communities. This adds to the sense of power.

Serial killers often begin fantasising about murder during, or even before, adolescence. This fantasy grows with them and they daydream compulsively about domination, submission and murder, usually with very specific elements to the fantasy that will eventually be made apparent in real crimes. Others initially take to reading stories about or looking at photographs in magazines that feature sadistic acts such as rape, torture and murder. They will later feel compelled to act out in real life what they have seen and read. They usually prey on victims from the lower social classes, such as vagrants or prostitutes, in addition to the vulnerable – young children and elderly people.

Early signs of such tendencies are often displayed in childhood, and include fire-starting, (setting fire to things to gain attention) and cruelty to animals, commonly referred to as 'zoo sadism'. Many children are cruel to animals, pulling the legs off spiders for example, but future serial killers often kill larger animals, such as dogs and cats, and frequently for solitary enjoyment rather than to impress peers. You will find this is a recurring theme in this book.

THE EVIL WITHIN

When apprehended, most serial killers will try to raise a defence of insanity and will plead not guilty on that basis, forcing the prosecution to prove that, at the time of committing the crimes, they were not suffering from a severe subnormality and knew the difference between right and wrong. With some serial killers, extensive premeditation combined with a lack of any obvious delusions or hallucinations that would hinder the defendant's ability to evade detection after committing multiple murders makes such a defence easily disproved. However, this tactic does allow the introduction of evidence about the killer's background that would normally be deemed inadmissible, for example a history of childhood abuse. It has been widely suggested that once a serial killer starts to kill they cannot stop.

With the modern forensic technology and DNA analysis now available to the police, more killers than ever before are being caught. Of course, any serial killer who kills on a regular basis is much more likely to be caught than one whose killings are less frequent.

There are four categories of serial killer: organised, disorganised, missionary and hedonistic. Some killers will show more than one type of characteristic, though usually one will dominate. Some killers descend from organised into disorganised behaviour as their killings continue. They will carry out careful and methodical murders at the start, but as their compulsion grows out of control and utterly dominates their lives, they become careless and impulsive.

Organised types plan their crimes methodically, usually abducting victims, killing them in one place and disposing of them in another. They will often lure the victims with ploys that appeal to their good nature. Others specifically target prostitutes, who are likely to go voluntarily with a serial killer posing as a customer. They are able to maintain a high degree of control over the crime scene and nowadays are usually forensically aware, knowing about the need to bury a body deep, or weighting it down to sink it in a river. They also follow their crimes in the media carefully and often take pride in their actions. The organised killer is usually socially adequate and has friends and lovers, perhaps even a wife and children. He is the type who, when captured, is most likely to be described by acquaintances as 'a really nice guy' who 'wouldn't hurt a fly'. Some serial killers go to lengths to make their crimes difficult to discover, such as falsifying suicide notes, or setting up innocent people to take the blame for their crimes.

Disorganised types tend, as a rule, to commit their crimes impulsively. They will murder when the opportunity arises, rarely disposing of the body but instead simply leaving it at the scene. They usually attack their victims without warning and will typically perform whatever they feel compelled to do once they have killed, for example necrophilia, mutilation and cannibalism. They rarely bother to cover their tracks but may still evade capture for some time because of a level of cunning that compels them to keep on the move. They are often socially inadequate with few friends, usually have a history of mental problems and are regarded by family and acquaintances as eccentric or even weird. They have little insight into the crimes they commit and they may even block out memories of the killings.

Missionary killers believe that their acts are justified on the basis that they are getting rid of a certain type of person, often prostitutes or members of a certain ethnic group, and are therefore doing society a favour. Missionary killers differ from other types of serial killer in that their motive is generally non-sexual.

A hedonistic killer kills for the sheer pleasure of it, although the particular aspect they enjoy will vary. Some may enjoy the 'chase' of hunting down a victim more than anything, while others may be primarily motivated by the act of torturing and abusing the victim while they are still alive. Others will kill their victims quickly and then in indulge in necrophilia with or cannibalism of the body. Usually there is a strong sexual aspect to the crime, even if it may not be immediately obvious; some killers obtain a surge of excitement that is not necessarily sexual.

So where does this urge to kill come from, and why is it so

powerful? If we were all to experience this urge, would we be able to resist it? Is it genetic, hormonal, biological or culturally conditioned? Do serial killers have any control over their desires? We all experience rage and inappropriate sexual instincts, yet most of us have some sort of internal 'cage' that keeps our inner monsters locked up. Call it morality or social programming; these internal blockades have long since crumbled in psychopathic killers. Not only have they let loose the monster within, they become virtual slaves to its beastly appetites and will kill and mutilate until they are finally caught and called to account for their crimes in a court of law. The phenomenon of serial murder is popularly regarded as a modern one but it can be traced back through history with some degree of accuracy.

Liu Pengli of China, cousin of Emperor Jing, was made king of Jidong in the sixth year of the middle period of Jing's reign, 144 BC. It was written that he would 'go out on marauding expeditions with 20 or 30 slaves or young men who were in hiding from the law, murdering people and seizing their belongings for sheer sport'. Although many of his subjects knew about these murders, they were afraid to go out of their houses at night; it was not until the 29th year of his reign that the son of one of his victims finally sent a report to the emperor. It was then discovered that he had murdered at least 100 people. The officials of the court requested that Liu Pengli be executed; however, the emperor could not bear to have his own cousin killed; Liu Pengli was instead made a commoner and banished.

In the fifteenth century, one of the wealthiest men in France, Gilles de Rais, is said to have abducted, raped and killed at least 100 young boys whom he brought to his castle as pages. The Hungarian aristocrat Elizabeth Báthory was arrested in 1610 and subsequently charged with torturing and butchering as many as 600 young girls. Like Liu Pengli, de Rais and Báthory were rich and powerful; therefore, although their crimes were known in their areas, they were not brought to justice for a long time. Chronicles of the times dealt largely with the affairs of the powerful; moreover, there was a lack of established police forces, at least in Europe, during those centuries. Therefore, there may have been many other classical or medieval serial killers who were either not identified or publicised.

Thug Behram, a gang leader of the Indian Thuggee cult of assassins, has frequently been described as the world's most prolific serial killer. According to numerous sources, he was believed to have murdered 931 victims by strangulation by means of a ceremonial cloth or *rumal*, which in Hindi means 'handkerchief', used by his cult between 1790 and 1830, thus holding the record for the most murders directly committed by a single person in history. In total, the Thugs as a whole were responsible for approximately two million deaths, according to Guinness World Records. The notoriety of the Thugs eventually led to the word 'thug' entering the English language as a term for ruffians, miscreants and people who behave in an aggressive manner towards others. Recent scholarship has cast doubt on the Thuggee cult and has suggested that the British Empire rulers in India were confused by the vernacular use of the term by Indians and may also have used fear of such a cult to justify their colonial rule.

Some historical criminologists have suggested that there may have been serial murders throughout history, but specific cases were not adequately recorded. Some sources suggest that medieval serial killers inspired legends such as those concerning werewolves and vampires.

CHAPTER 1

AUSTRALIA

DAVID AND CATHERINE BIRNIE

David Birnie (b. 1951) and Catherine Birnie (née Harrison, b. 1951) formed a Bonnie and Clyde relationship when they met in their early teens. During this early period, they were involved in a string of burglaries in Perth at shops and factory premises. This resulted in both of them spending some of their teenage years in separate reform schools. In 1984, their paths crossed yet again and, having formed a strong relationship, they got married. However, David became lost in a world of bizarre sexual fantasies to go with his insatiable sexual appetite.

On 6 October 1986, they changed from being petty thieves to becoming serial killers. On this day, they crossed paths with 20-year-old psychology student Mary Neilson, who visited the Birnie home. She had replied to an advertisement for the sale of tyres placed by David Birnie, who took advantage of the situation of a lone, unsuspecting female. After pulling a knife on her, they forced her into the bedroom of their house where she was chained to the bed and repeatedly raped. Catherine Birnie was present on this occasion, watching and taking photographs. They then placed the victim in David's vehicle and drove her to the Gleneagles National Park, some 34 miles south of Perth, where Birnie raped her yet

1

again before he finally strangled her with a nylon cord. All the time this was taking place Catherine was present, encouraging him. They both then took turns in slashing the body of the victim, apparently in order to prevent the body swelling up while decomposing in the shallow grave they had dug.

Fuelled by this violent act, they both had the desire to kill and mutilate again. On 20 October, they found their second victim, 15-year-old Susannah Candy, who was hitchhiking. They picked her up and drove her back to their home where they held her captive, raping and sexually abusing her over a period of several days. They even made her write letters to her parents indicating that she was safe and well. As with the previous victim, they drove her to the Gleneagles National Park where on this occasion Catherine Birnie strangled the victim, again burying her in a shallow grave.

Their third victim, who was in fact known to the Birnies, was 31-year-old air hostess Noelene Patterson. David and Caroline Birnie came across Noelene, whose car had run out of petrol. Instead of helping her, David Birnie abducted her at knifepoint and drove her back to their home where she was chained to the bed and raped over a three-day period. It was later suggested that because of her beauty David became infatuated with her. This made Caroline jealous and she apparently told David that Noelene must die, but David apparently would not accede to her request. However, he later relented and gave the victim an overdose of sleeping tablets, and then, while she was unconscious, he strangled her. As with the previous murders, they took the body of the victim to Gleneagles National Park where they buried it in a shallow grave.

On 4 November, they found their fourth victim. Again, as with the previous victim, they preyed on a lone female hitchhiker in the Perth area – Denise Brown, a 21-year-old computer operator. As before, they took their victim back to their home and for two days thereafter Denise Brown was repeatedly raped and sexually abused. Following this, they drove Brown to a pine plantation some 40 miles south of the city where she was again raped and then stabbed by David Birnie. Catherine watched and took photographs while this was happening. However, despite this savage attack on the victim she remained alive. Catherine then gave David a bigger knife, but despite inflicting more stab wounds on Brown she still remained alive. David Birnie then shattered her skull with an axe, which finally killed her. They buried the victim in another shallow grave.

The next intended victim would prove to be their downfall. On 9 November, they abducted a lone 16-year-old female hitchhiker named Kate Moir. As with the previous victims, she was taken to the Birnies' home and again chained and subjected to sexual abuse. However, the Birnies' luck was about to run out, as the following day the victim found herself unchained and apparently alone in the house. As a result, she managed to escape through a bedroom window. Badly bruised and half-naked, she staggered into a local shop and the police were called. She led them directly back to the Birnies' address where they arrested Catherine Birnie and then went to David Birnie's place of work to arrest him.

When questioned by police, the Birnies vigorously denied the girl's allegations. Instead, they claimed that she had been a willing party and had gone with them to smoke marijuana. Birnie admitted to having sex with the girl but maintained that he had not raped her. A search of the house found the girl's bag and a packet of cigarettes that she had had the common sense to conceal in the ceiling as proof positive that she had actually been there, but there was little else to prove the allegation of rape or to connect the Birnies with any of the other missing women.

Under more intense questioning, David Birnie finally confessed and calmly told the officer questioning him: 'It's getting dark. Best we take the shovel and dig them up. There are four of them.' When told of David's confession, Catherine Birnie finally confessed. They both agreed to take police to the bodies which were buried not far from the city.

On 3 March 1987, the Birnies appeared in court. They were both charged with four counts of murder and numerous connected offences. They pleaded guilty and were both sentenced to life imprisonment with a minimum of 20 years before parole. In relation to David Birnie, the judge expressed a hope that he would never be released from prison. That, however, may now not be the case with new challenges to life sentences under the Human Rights Act 1998.

David Birnie committed suicide at on 7 October 2005. He was found hanged in his cell. He had been due to appear in court the following day, charged with the rape of a fellow inmate.

At the time of writing, Catherine Birnie remains imprisoned in Bandyup Women's Prison. Her request to attend David's funeral was denied. She applied in 2007 but this was rejected. The Attorney General of Western Australia at the time, Jim McGinty, was against her ever being released.

Her case was due for review in January 2010, but on 14 March 2009, Christian Porter, the new Western Australian Attorney-General, revoked her non-parole period. She became only the third Australian woman to have her papers marked 'never to be released'. She appealed against this decision in 2010 but Porter rejected the appeal.

WILLIAM MACDONALD, AKA THE SYDNEY MUTILATOR

William MacDonald was born Allan Ginsberg, in Liverpool, England, in 1924. At the age of 19, he joined the army, where he was raped in an air-raid shelter by a corporal who threatened to kill him if he told anyone. When he was discharged from the army in 1947, psychiatrists diagnosed him as schizophrenic and his brother had him committed to a mental asylum in Scotland where he shared cells with raving lunatics and received shock treatment every day. After six months, his mother had him released and took him home. As he grew older, he became what was termed a 'practising' homosexual, openly soliciting men in public toilets and bars. He emigrated to Canada in 1949 and then to Australia in 1955, where he decided to start a new life, changing his name to William MacDonald.

AUSTRALIA

MacDonald's career as a murderer began in Brisbane in 1960 when he befriended Amos Hurst, 55. They started drinking together and then went back to Hurst's hotel room, where they sat on the bed and drank more beer. Hurst was almost unconscious when MacDonald strangled him. During the strangulation, blood spurted from his mouth all over MacDonald's hands. MacDonald punched him in the face and Hurst fell to the floor dead. MacDonald then calmly undressed Hurst and put him into bed. He washed the blood from his hands and arms and left. In the cold light of the day, realising what he had done, MacDonald feared arrest. When no police called on him, he began to relax and his luck held. While scouring a local paper five days later, he saw Hurst's name in the obituary column. It said he had died suddenly of a heart attack. What the papers didn't say was that while Amos Hurst's post mortem showed that he had died of a heart attack, it also revealed that the severe bruising on his neck suggested the possibility of death by strangulation; however, under the circumstances this could have been bruising from a fight or some other drunken misadventure. The case was closed.

MacDonald moved to Sydney in 1961 and continued to solicit men in toilets and bars. On 4 June 1961, McDonald met a homeless man, Albert Greenfield. They walked to a local swimming baths where they sat and talked. MacDonald's urge to kill Alfred Greenfield had been growing, but he controlled his urge until Greenfield had drunk all his beer and fallen asleep on the grass. MacDonald removed a knife from its sheath as he knelt over the sleeping Greenfield. He brought it down swiftly and buried the blade deep in his victim's neck. He then repeatedly stabbed Greenfield. The ferocity of the attack severed the arteries in Greenfield's neck. Blood was everywhere, but MacDonald had come prepared. He had brought a light plastic raincoat in his bag and had put it on before he attacked the unsuspecting Greenfield. MacDonald removed Greenfield's trousers and underpants, slicing the testicles and penis off at the scrotum with his knife. On leaving the scene, MacDonald stopped along the way and washed his hands and face under a tap. On the way home, he threw Greenfield's genitals into the harbour.

On Saturday, 21 November 1961, MacDonald purchased a bigger knife with a 6in blade. The urge to kill had again manifested itself. That night, MacDonald saw Ernest William Cobbin, 41, staggering towards him under the influence of drink. On the pretext of giving him more drink, MacDonald lured Cobbin to a nearby park where they sat in the public toilets and drank beer. MacDonald openly put on a raincoat from his bag and then took out the knife and thrust it into Cobbin's throat, severing his jugular vein. MacDonald inflicted several more cuts to the throat, which caused blood to spurt all over MacDonald's arms, face and raincoat. Despite his severe injuries, Cobbin tried to defend himself, but McDonald continued with his frenzied attack. MacDonald pulled Cobbin's trousers and underpants down, lifted his penis and testicles, sliced them off with his knife and put them in a plastic bag he had brought with him. When he had finished, he calmly took off his raincoat, wrapped his knife and the plastic bag in it, put them in his bag and walked out of the toilet, again stopping along the way to wash his hands under a tap.

On returning home, MacDonald washed the bloody contents of the plastic bag in warm water, put them in a clean plastic bag and took them to bed with him. The following day, he wrapped the plastic bag and its grisly contents, the knife and a brick in newspaper, tied them with string and threw them from the Sydney Harbour Bridge into the deepest part of the harbour. This time, there would be no evidence left lying around for the police to find.

On 31 March 1962, MacDonald claimed his fourth victim. That morning, he purchased another long-bladed sheath knife and packed it in his bag with his raincoat and a plastic bag. At 10pm, he came upon Frank McLean, who was very drunk and making his way along the road. MacDonald suggested they went somewhere quiet for a drink. As they turned a corner MacDonald attacked McLean, stabbing him in the throat. McLean attempted to defend himself but MacDonald continued to stab him repeatedly in the face. McLean fell to the ground and MacDonald took advantage of the situation, jumping on him and continuing his frenzied attack with the knife. He stabbed McLean in the head, neck, throat, face and chest until he was dead. Saturated in Frank McLean's blood, MacDonald dragged the body a few feet further into the lane, lowered his victim's trousers and proceeded to cut off McLean's genitals and put them in a plastic bag. On returning home, he washed the contents of the plastic bag in the sink and put them in a clean plastic bag. In the morning, he threw the incriminating evidence off Sydney Harbour Bridge. When he was found, Frank McLean was still alive. Unfortunately, he died a short time later from his wounds and without being able to give a description of his attacker to the police. By now, the investigating officers were of the belief that the murderer might be specifically targeting homosexuals.

In November 1962, MacDonald, using the name Allan Brennan, acquired a shop premises and for a time ran the small shop on his own. However, it wasn't long before he killed again. One night, MacDonald went to a bar in search of a potential victim. Here, he met 42-year-old James Hackett, a petty thief and down-and-out. MacDonald took Hackett back to his shop and they continued drinking until Hackett passed out on the floor. MacDonald pulled out a long knife and went to stab Hackett in the throat with the knife but it went straight through Hackett's neck. Hackett woke up and attempted to ward off further blows with his arms and hands. As he did this, MacDonald was cut with his own knife. This enraged MacDonald further and he unleashed a volley of blows with the knife, eventually killing Hackett with a wound to the heart. Bleeding profusely, MacDonald bandaged his hand and set about removing Hackett's genitals, but the knife was now blunt and bent from the ferocity of the attack. Too exhausted to go and get another one, he sat covered from head to foot in Hackett's blood, hacking away at Hackett's scrotum with the blunt and bent blade. He stabbed the penis several times and made some cuts around the testicles before finally giving up and falling asleep where he sat.

The following morning, MacDonald found himself covered in dry, congealed blood. He was still lying next to his victim. MacDonald was concerned that blood had seeped through the floorboards and dripped down onto the counters of his shop below. He cleaned himself up and went to the hospital, where he had some stitches put in his hand. It took MacDonald the whole day to clean up. The huge pools of blood on the lino couldn't be removed so he had to take all the flooring up, cutting it into smaller pieces and putting it in the dustbin. He also removed Hackett's blood-soaked clothes, for some reason leaving only the socks. He managed finally to drag the body down as far as the foundations. There he left it, together with Hackett's clothing. By now, he was starting to become agitated and panicky, realising the full horror of what he had done. He had only been able to remove some of the bloodstains and there was still blood all over the floorboards.

He decided to leave the city. He caught a train to Brisbane, where he took up lodgings in a boarding house. He changed his features by dyeing his greying hair black, growing a moustache and assuming the name of Allan MacDonald. Every day, he bought the Sydney newspapers expecting to read of the murder of Hackett and how police were looking for a man named Brennan in connection with the Mutilator Murders.

Shortly after he left, the police received a complaint of rancid odour emanating from the shop premises. Enquiries revealed that the owner had not been seen since 4 November. They entered the premises and found the naked and butchered Hackett concealed beneath the shop. At the time, the police believed that this victim was the new tenant, Brennan (MacDonald). The press reported that this victim was Allan Brennan (William MacDonald) and, on that basis, the police enquiry continued. However, that assumption later turned out to be false.

In April 1963, MacDonald returned to Sydney, a move that was to be his undoing. On 22 April 1963, a former co-worker of MacDonald spoke to him in the street. He told MacDonald about what the papers had reported and that he was supposed to have been murdered. The police were notified and a month later MacDonald was arrested while working under the name of David Allen. When interviewed, he confessed his identity and confessed to the murders, giving his motive as having being raped by homosexuals in his teenage years and having formed a hatred of them since then.

William MacDonald confessed to all the murders. He was charged with four counts of murder and he pleaded not guilty on the grounds of insanity. His trial, held in September 1963, was one of the most sensational the country had ever seen. When he gave evidence, the public hung onto every word of horror that he spoke. At one point, when he was describing how he cut off one of the victim's testicles and penis, a woman juror fainted. The jury found him guilty of four counts of murder.

There was one final twist to the tale. Despite MacDonald's insanity plea, the jury found him to have been sane at the time of the murders. He was sentenced to life imprisonment but was later transferred to a home for the criminally insane. He spent the next 16 years in that institution. In 1980, he was deemed sane enough to be sent back to a mainstream prison, where he volunteered to be isolated from the other prisoners. He is Australia's second-longest serving prisoner. In 2000, he declined a parole date hearing. He was quoted as saying, 'I am institutionalised now and I have no desire to go and live outside, I would not last five minutes. I have everything I could want in here.' He is, however, taken on the occasional day trip out.

IVAN MILAT, AKA THE BACKPACKER MURDERER

Between 1989 and 1992, on the Australian highway stretching

from Sydney to Melbourne, seven hitchhikers mysteriously disappeared. Two were Australian teenagers and five were European tourists in their early twenties, of whom two were British. The latter two's disappearances would lead to the discovery of Ivan Milat's murderous activities and his subsequent apprehension.

On 19 September 1992, a walker in the Belanglo State Forest just outside Sydney came across the remains of a grave containing two bodies, which were later identified as two missing British women, Joanne Walters and Caroline Clarke. Both had been savagely stabbed and shot and had probably been tied up prior to their deaths.

In October 1993, two further bodies were discovered. These were the young Australian couple, James Gibson and Deborah Everist. They were found buried in undergrowth in a forested area. Both had been brutally murdered. Further searches in that location revealed the body of one of the missing German backpackers, Simone Schmidl. A further search in the same location revealed the bodies of two more missing European backpackers, 21-year-old Gabor Kurt Neugebauer and his 20-year-old girlfriend, Anja Susanne Habschied. Both had vanished two years previously. Police revealed that both victims had been killed by multiple stab wounds. Habschied had been decapitated and her head used for target practice with a rifle. At this location, the police found spent cartridge cases, which were later connected to a weapon that they found. The investigation team deduced that the killer, or killers, spent more time with each victim as the crimes progressed. This fact indicated that, apart from being cruel and sadistic, the perpetrators were also cool, calculating and confident individuals.

Around the time of the disappearances, a young British backpacker by the name of Paul Onions was involved in an encounter with a passing motorist who picked him up while he was hitchhiking north. Onions stated that he had been picked up by an Australian male, who introduced himself as Bill and then pulled a gun on him. However, Onions managed to escape from the car and flag down another motorist, telling that motorist of the incident. The young backpacker was taken to a local police station where he gave his account. However, due to the fact that he had been unable to obtain the registration number of the vehicle in question, the police filed the report and apparently took no further action as they were unable to trace the vehicle or the man in question.

Several years later, still troubled by his experience and now aware of the bodies being found in the Australian outback, Onions called the Australian High Commission and was put in touch with the taskforce conducting the investigation in Australia. On 13 November 1993, he told the officer who answered the telephone the details of his attack in 1990 and was asked why he had not reported it then. When he replied that he had, he expected the officer to ask him where and when and the name of the officer he spoke to. Instead, he was thanked for the information and the call was terminated. When he didn't hear any more, he assumed that his report was of no value and did his best to forget about it.

The official search of the forest was suspended on 17 November 1993. No more bodies or additional evidence had been found. During the course of the ongoing police investigation, the motorist who had taken Mr Onions to the police station had been seen and re-interviewed. A further witness had mentioned the name of Ivan Milat as being a possible suspect; he was known to have a mania for guns. The police decided to visit the work premises of Ivan Milat, whose brother Richard coincidentally worked with him. Timesheets were requested for both men for the dates and times of the murders. Richard was found to have been working on every occasion. However, his brother Ivan had been away from work around the dates of the disappearances of the victims.

From this point on, Ivan Milat (b. 1943) was looked on as a suspect but the police did not have any evidence. A criminal record check revealed that Milat had previous convictions – in

1971 he had picked up two girls hitchhiking from Liverpool to Melbourne and had allegedly raped one of them. Both girls testified that he was armed with a large knife and carried a length of rope. He was later acquitted when the prosecution case was dismissed as unproven. As a result, the police closely scrutinised Milat's past history and his more recent lifestyle right through until 1994.

The search for evidence continued. Officers obtained records of all premises and vehicles that the Milat brothers had owned in the past. They found that three of the Milats owned a small property on the Wombeyan Caves road, 25 miles from Belanglo. In addition, one vehicle found was a silver Nissan Patrol four-wheel-drive that had been owned by Ivan Milat. The new owner was interviewed and showed police a bullet that he had found under the driver's seat. It was a .22 calibre and was later analysed and found to be consistent with cartridge cases found at one of the grave sites. Milat had sold the vehicle two months after the bodies of the two English girls had been discovered.

The police were still aware of Mr Onions' incident and statement. At the end of April, Paul Onions received an important telephone call from the Australian police asking him if he could fly to Sydney as soon as possible. He was totally confused. Why had it taken them so long? He was subsequently shown a video identification parade, which contained an image of Milat. Onions was left alone to view the images as many times as he liked. He was told to take his time. He felt strange. Four years had passed since the attack and here he was looking for the man who did it. He looked through the tape again and again. He then made a positive identification of Milat.

This identification gave the police sufficient grounds to arrest Milat on suspicion of the assault on Mr Onions and thereby give them the opportunity to execute search warrants at Milat's home address, where he was subsequently arrested along with his girlfriend. He remained at their house, having been handcuffed while the search commenced. The first item found in Ivan's house was a postcard. He was asked whom it was from. He replied that it was from a friend in New Zealand. It began with the words 'Hi Bill'. Ivan was asked if he was also known as 'Bill'. He replied, 'No, it must have been a mistake.' When a bullet was found in one of the bedrooms, police asked Ivan if he owned any firearms. He said that he didn't. When asked about the bullet, he said it was left from when he went shooting with his brother. The rooms were searched one at a time. In the second bedroom, two sleeping bags were found in a wardrobe. They were later identified as belonging to Simone Schmidl and Deborah Everist, two of the murder victims.

Milat was taken from the house to Campbelltown police station where he was questioned. During the interview, Milat was evasive and uncooperative. Following the interview, he was charged with the robbery and attempted murder of Paul Onions as a holding charge.

The search of Milat's house continued. Camping and cooking equipment that belonged to Simone Schmidl was found in the kitchen pantry. The police had hoped that they would find some evidence linking Milat to the murders, but were not prepared for the amount of identifiable property that was found. As the search continued, more identifiable items were found, such as a camera, which was later identified as belonging to one of the victims. A fully loaded Browning automatic pistol was found wedged under the washing machine.

At other locations connected to Milat, more evidence was found: rifles, shotguns, knives and crossbows, together with ammunition. Most of the camping gear belonging to the victims was found in these raids. Also found in a locked cupboard in the house of Ivan's mother was a long curved cavalry sword. To add more weight to the case, ballistics experts matched the spent cartridges found at some of the crime scenes to the Ruger .22 rifle that was found in Ivan Milat's home.

Ivan Milat was charged with the murders of the seven back-packers. It was almost a year before the case came to court. The sheer volume of evidence and the long list of witnesses meant it took weeks for the prosecution to present their case. During cross-examination of the prosecution witnesses, the defence tactics unfolded. Milat would be trying to convince the jury that he was not responsible for the murders but instead implied that his brothers, Richard and Walter, had committed the crimes and implicated him by planting the evidence at his house. Twelve weeks and 145 witnesses later, the prosecution closed their case. After Milat had presented his defence, the jury, after deliberating for three days, found him guilty on 27 July 1996.

For the attack on Paul Onions, he was sentenced to six years' imprisonment. For the remaining seven counts of wilful murder, he received a life sentence for each. The judge recommended that Ivan Milat remain in prison for the rest of his natural life. Milat is suspected of committing numerous other murders in which people have disappeared in similar circumstances but where no bodies have yet been discovered. He has still continued to protest his innocence in relation to his conviction for the seven aforementioned victims. However, it is hoped that one day Milat may choose to unburden his conscience. The search for clues to the missing victims and their bodies will continue in the hope that further evidence may then connect Milat to these horrendous crimes. This would at least give the families some consolation and the chance to grieve and to bury their loved ones.

Ivan Milat appealed against his convictions on the grounds that the quality of legal representation he had received was too poor, and therefore constituted a breach of his common law right to legal representation. The Appeal Court found that this was not the case and dismissed the appeal.

Since being imprisoned, Milat cut off his little finger with a plastic knife in January 2009, intending to send the severed digit to the High Court. Following this incident he was taken to hospital under high security, but later returned to prison after doctors decided it would not be possible to reattach the finger. This was not the first time Milat had injured himself while in prison, having swallowed various metal objects including razor blades and staples. He also went on hunger strike in 2011.

JAMES MILLER AND CHRISTOPHER WORRELL, AKA THE TRURO SERIAL MURDERERS

Between December 1976 and January 1977, seven young women in Adelaide were abducted and murdered during a 51-day period. All of the young women had previously been reported missing. Then, over a 12-month period between 1978 and 1979, the bodies were discovered in shallow graves in the bush.

James Miller (b. 1938) and Christopher Worrell (b. 1954) had been friends for many years. Both were petty criminals in their own right, and even served a term of imprisonment together. Miller was a homosexual and became infatuated with Worrell, who it would seem was the dominant force and also bisexual; his yearning for women seemed to overtake his male sexual desires according to the events that followed.

On the night of Thursday, 23 December 1976, Miller and Worrell were cruising around the city in their car. There were many young women about that night and Worrell told Miller to drive around the main block of the city centre while he went for a walk. Miller drove around for a short time and then he picked up Worrell and 18-year-old Veronica Knight at the front of the Majestic Hotel. Veronica had accepted the offer of a lift home. She lived at the nearby Salvation Army Hostel in Angus Street and had become separated from her friend while shopping at the City Cross Arcade.

On the way to her home, Miller talked her into going for a drive with them in the Adelaide foothills. Miller pulled the car off the road onto a small track and Worrell forced the girl into the back seat. Miller went for a walk to allow his friend some privacy and waited for half an hour before returning to the car. Worrell was sitting in the front seat and the girl was lying motionless on the floor in the back. She was fully dressed. Worrell told Miller that he had just raped and murdered the girl.

They then drove to Truro a few miles further on. They drove down a dirt track and pulled over next to a wooded area. When Miller resisted helping Worrell lift the body from the car, Worrell threatened him with the knife. They then disposed of the body.

On 2 January 1977, and in similar circumstances, Worrell picked up 15-year-old Tania Kenny, who had just hitchhiked up from Victor Harbour. Worrell had chatted her up in the street. They drove to Miller's sister's home on the pretext of picking up some clothes. After checking that no one was home, Worrell and Tania went into the house while Miller waited in the car. Eventually, Worrell came out to the car and asked Miller to come inside. From the look on Worrell's face, Miller knew that something was drastically wrong. In the children's playroom was Tania's body – she had been bound with rope and gagged with a piece of sticking plaster. She was fully clothed and had been strangled. Miller and Worrell had another violent argument. Worrell threatened to kill Miller if he didn't help him hide the body. They hid the body in a cupboard and returned later that night, putting the body in the car then driving to a remote location where they had been earlier in the day and had already dug a shallow grave. They buried Tania in the prepared grave. Miller later maintained that he helped bury the body because he didn't want to get his sister involved.

On 21 January 1977, a third young female victim met her death. The pair met 16-year-old student Juliet Mykyta at the Ambassador's Hotel in King William Street. She had just rung her parents to tell them that she was going to be a little late getting home and that they were not to worry. She was sitting on the steps of the hotel waiting for a bus at 9pm when Worrell offered her a lift. Miller drove to one of their usual spots and Worrell forced the girl into the back seat. Miller sat in the front, waiting to be told to leave. While he was sitting there, Worrell started to tie the girl up. She was struggling and crying but Worrell was too strong. Miller got out of the car and walked about 50m away. He later stated that he heard voices and turned to see the girl falling out of the car to the ground as if she had been kicked in the stomach. Worrell rolled her over with his foot, knelt on her stomach and strangled her with a length of rope. They placed the body back in the car and drove back to the Truro area. On this occasion, they didn't bury the body in a grave but simply covered it with branches and leaves. They took care to dispose of the body away from the previous victims. They then drove back to Adelaide.

On 6 February, Miller and Worrell picked up 16-year-old Sylvia Pittman as she waited for a train at Adelaide Station. They drove to another secluded area where, as soon as they arrived, Worrell told Miller to go for a walk. After half an hour, Miller returned to find the girl lying face down on the back seat with a rug over her. She had been strangled with her own tights. As with the previous victims, they then disposed of the body in a similarly remote area.

The following day, 7 February 1977, Worrell told Miller to pick him up at the Adelaide Post Office building at 7pm. With Worrell was 26-year-old Vicki Howell. Vicki was older than the others and Miller took a liking to her straight away. Vicki seemed to have a few worries and mentioned that she was separated from her husband. As they drove along, Worrell even had Miller stop the car so the girl could use the toilet. A little further on Miller stopped the car and, leaving the couple to chat, he went to the bushes to relieve himself. He returned a few minutes later on the pretext that he had forgotten his cigarettes. He was really checking to see if the girl was all right. She was nice. He didn't want Worrell to kill her.

Miller was still hoping that the woman would not be murdered and walked away into the bush. A short time later, Miller returned to the car to find Worrell kneeling on the front seat and leaning into the back. He was covering Vicki Howell's body with the blanket. She had been strangled. Again, they drove back to Truro and disposed of the body, hiding it under foliage.

Two days later, on 9 February, Miller and Worrell were

cruising in the centre of Adelaide when they spotted 16-year-old Connie Iordanides standing on the footpath. They did a U-turn, pulled up in front of the girl and asked if she wanted a lift. She accepted and sat in the front between the two men. Connie became frightened when the car headed in the opposite direction to where she wanted to go. Miller stopped at another secluded spot and Worrell forced the screaming girl into the back seat. Miller did nothing to help the girl and got out and walked away from the car. When he returned to the car, Connie Iordanides was dead. Worrell had strangled and raped her. She was on the back seat covered with a blanket. Again, Miller did as he was instructed and drove back to Truro and hid the fully clothed body under bushes.

On 12 February 1977, they committed their fourth murder in a week. In the early hours of that morning Miller and Worrell were again cruising the city when they picked up 20-year-old hitchhiker Deborah Lamb. Worrell suggested that they could take her where she wanted to go and the girl allegedly accepted the ride. They drove to the beach at Port Gawler. Miller left them alone and went for a walk. When he returned to the car, Worrell was standing in front of it, filling in a hole in the sand by pushing sand into it with his feet. The girl was nowhere to be seen. It was later to come out in court that this victim may have still been alive when buried in the sand.

On Saturday, 19 February 1977, in a cruel twist of fate and before the police had a chance to arrest and convict Christopher Worrell, he was killed in a road crash. Also in the car at the same time was a female, Deborah Skuse, who was also killed. James Miller escaped with a fractured shoulder. It would seem that she had been another intended victim.

At the funeral, Miller struck up a conversation with Worrell's girlfriend. During this conversation, he told her that Worrell had been killing young girls. It was not until almost two years later, when some of the victims' bodies were discovered, that she broke her silence, telling the authorities about the conversation she had

had with Miller. As a result, Miller was arrested and later charged with being involved with the murders of the seven women. However, he did assist in the recovery of the bodies of some of the victims.

At his trial in February 1980, Miller pleaded not guilty to seven counts of murder. His defence was that, although present, he had taken no part in the actual murders and therefore there was no joint enterprise. The jury did not agree with this defence, and on 12 March 1980, Miller was found guilty of six counts of murder. He was found not guilty of the murder of the first victim, Veronica Knight. The jury agreed that he had not known that Worrell intended to murder the girl. He was sentenced to life imprisonment.

In 1999, James Miller applied to have a non-parole period set in the hope that one day he might be released. On 8 February 2000, Chief Justice John Doyle of the South Australian Supreme Court granted Miller a non-parole period of 35 years from the date of his arrest.

On 21 October 2008, at the age of 68, Miller died of liver failure, a complication of hepatitis C. He also suffered from prostate cancer and lung cancer. At the time of his death he was one of the longest-serving prisoners in the state.

PETER DUPAS

By the time Peter Dupas (b. 1953) committed his first murder, he had a long history of violence towards women and many convictions for rape and connected sex crimes. Dupas is probably best described as the perfect sex predator. He was a man to whom ordinary people warmed, showing nothing on the outside of the evil that lurked within him. At the age of 15, he stabbed a neighbour with a knife. For this, he was given psychiatric treatment, and for many years afterwards continued to receive such treatment. However, in all this time, the authorities were never able to pinpoint any specific mental disorders.

It seemed that prison and attempts at rehabilitation had no

effect on Peter Dupas and a little more than two months after his release on 4 September 1979, after serving five years and eight months for raping a woman, he attacked four women over a 10-day period, leaving them traumatised for the rest of their lives. This time, he was equipped with what would become his signature. The first of these four attacks was the rape of a female in a public toilet. His next three intended victims managed to escape. However, one, an elderly woman, was stabbed in the chest as she tried to fight him off. His attempt at rape thwarted, he made off.

The police subsequently arrested Dupas and he made full and frank admissions to all the offences when interviewed. He told the police he was glad he had been caught. As for his motive, he cited an irresistible urge to attack women in this way. For these crimes, he received only a six-year prison sentence despite his previous convictions for similar offences.

He was released on 27 February 1985, after serving five years and three months, and it took only four days for him to reoffend, raping a 21-year-old female as she lay sunbathing at a local beach. Two men, to whom the victim had run following the rape, apprehended him nearby. While in custody for this offence, he was interviewed about a murder that had occurred 16 days earlier while he was on home leave from prison. Another lone female sunbather and mother of four, Helen McMahon, had been beaten to death in the sand dunes at Rye Back beach, only 2½ miles away from where Dupas had raped the female sunbather. He denied any knowledge of this offence. For this new offence of rape, he was sentenced to 12 years' imprisonment. While in prison, he underwent treatment to suppress his sex drive and also married a nurse.

He served seven years and was released in 1992 and, for the following 18 months, it would appear that Dupas had surpressed his sexual desires – but this turned out not to be the case. On 23 September 1993, he attacked a 15-year-old girl who was out horse riding. He was not able to carry out his plan, as the girl had the common sense to put her horse between herself and the attacking Dupas and managed to escape, as did Dupas. Once again, Dupas was a sexual time-bomb. On 3 January 1994, he struck again, attacking a 26-year-old female at Lake Eppalock in northwestern Victoria, as she sat on a public toilet. Dupas burst into the cubicle wearing a hood with eyeholes and pointing a knife at the woman's face. Dupas kept yelling for the woman to turn around and face the wall, but she resisted. The woman was cut badly on the hands as she fought to prevent her attacker from dragging her out of the toilet cubicle. Thwarted, Dupas abruptly stopped the attack, let the woman go and calmly walked away to his car. As Dupas sped off, the woman identified him to her fiancé. He happened to be an off-duty Australian Federal Police officer who, with friends, chased the estate car Dupas was driving. Dupas was apprehended after his car ran off into the bush on a dirt road. When he was searched, a pair of metal handcuffs was found in his pocket. When his vehicle was searched, police found a roll of insulation tape and a cache of the tools of the trade for a well-prepared travelling rapist: knives, a black balaclava, condoms, a roll of sticking plaster and, chillingly, a sheet of plastic and a shovel.

Despite all the circumstances surrounding this offence and what police saw as Dupas's meticulous planning of what looked to be a sexual abduction, murder and concealment of the body, the prosecution stated that there was insufficient evidence to proceed with an attempted rape charge. Consideration was given to a lesser charge of false imprisonment, to which he pleaded guilty and was sentenced to three years and nine months. He was released on 29 September 1996, to find his wife had left him. Dupas, it seems, suppressed his urges for almost 12 months. Then it is suggested that he once more unleashed his violent and sexual side with a vengeance.

On 4 October 1997, a local prostitute, Margaret Maher, was abducted and murdered. Her body was found in long grass on industrial land. She had been stabbed many times and her breasts had been grotesquely mutilated. Four weeks later, on 1 November 1997, Mersina Halvagis, 25, was attacked as she tended a grave at a cemetery. She was repeatedly stabbed and left to die. Coincidentally, the grave of Dupas's grandfather is only 300ft away from where Halvagis was murdered. At 6.30 am on New Year's Eve 1997, Kathleen Downes, a frail 95-year-old woman, was found stabbed to death in her room at Brunswick Lodge nursing home.

On 19 April 1999, another female, Nicole Patterson, a psychotherapist who worked from home, was found dead on her consulting-room floor. Patterson was naked from the waist down. Her clothes had been ripped and cut. An autopsy revealed that the 28-year-old had been dead since that morning. She had been stabbed 27 times. There were numerous defence wounds to both her hands. It was impossible to say whether she had been raped. Both of Patterson's breasts had been sliced off and were nowhere to be found at the murder scene. Patterson's mutilations were similar to those of Margaret Maher, murdered 18 months earlier. Her killer had been thorough. It appeared that he had attempted to clean up the crime scene before leaving. There were no fingerprints or footprints. The killer even took Patterson's purse, containing her driving licence and her mobile phone.

However, the killer had missed the most incriminating piece of evidence. Under clothing in the lounge, detectives found Patterson's appointment book. It contained a 9am appointment for a 'Malcolm' that morning and a mobile phone number written next to it. The police soon traced 'Malcolm' and he turned out to be a student who had no idea who Patterson was. He was asked if he had given his phone number to anyone recently. He then gave police a list of people to whom he had given his number. One of the names was Peter Dupas, for whom he had been doing casual work.

The investigating officers believed that the killer had used someone else's name to make an appointment and had given a false mobile number. Patterson advertised her business to clients in the local papers. Without this appointment, it would have been difficult to get into her house. Her killer had made an appointment under a false name for that morning using the false mobile phone number to avoid detection. What he didn't count on was police finding the appointment book.

Three days after the murder, police decided to arrest Dupas at his home address, which was only 30 minutes from where Patterson was murdered. Dupas had what appeared to be a fingernail scratch on his face. A search of the premises uncovered a bloodstained green jacket in a bundle of clothing in a workshop cupboard. Subsequent DNA testing linked this with Patterson's blood.

As the search continued, police found a black balaclava and a page from a local newspaper, which reported the murder of Patterson. The photo of Nicole Patterson in the article had been slashed. In a rubbish bin, they found torn-up pieces of newspaper, and when the pieces were put together, they formed a handwritten note with the words 'nine o'clock Nicci' and 'Malcolm' written on it. Other enquiries showed that on the day of the killing, Dupas was caught on video buying petrol near Patterson's home.

When interviewed, Dupas denied any knowledge of Patterson's death, suggesting that the police had planted the evidence. Peter Dupas was charged with the murder of Nicole Patterson and remanded in custody for trial, which took place in August 2000. He entered a plea of not guilty and still maintained that he was innocent and that the police had planted the evidence. However, the jury thought otherwise and duly found him guilty. He was sentenced to life imprisonment with a recommendation from the judge that it should be for the rest of his natural life, without the opportunity for release on parole.

Peter Dupas was later questioned about the unsolved murders of Margaret Maher, Mersina Halvagis, Helen McMahon and Kathleen Downes. He has denied any involvement and for the time being these crimes remained unsolved.

However, police then reopened the murder of Margaret Maher, a prostitute aged 40 who was last seen alive at midnight on 4 October 1997. Her body had been discovered under a cardboard box containing computer parts at 1.45pm. A black woollen glove was found near Maher's body, which police later confirmed contained DNA matching that of Dupas, who was already serving a life sentence without parole for the murder of Nicole Patterson. At the time of his arrest, police were able to obtain a DNA sample, linking him to the 1997 murder of Maher.

A post-mortem examination revealed Maher had suffered a stab wound to her left wrist, bruising to her neck, blunt force trauma to the area of her right eyebrow and lacerations to her right arm. Her left breast had been removed and placed into her mouth. At the time of Maher's murder, Dupas had been out of prison for just over a year after serving time for rape offences.

Dupas was charged and brought to trial and he pleaded not guilty. The trial lasted for three weeks, during which evidence was presented to the jury that the removals of Patterson's and Maher's breasts were so 'strikingly similar' as to be a signature or trademark common to both crimes, thereby identifying Dupas as the killer of both women. The jury, who were not told that Dupas was already serving a life term for the murder of Patterson, took less than a day to convict him of his second murder. Upon hearing the jury deliver the guilty verdict, Dupas claimed, 'it's a kangaroo court'.

On 16 August 2004, Dupas was convicted of the murder of Maher and sentenced to a second term of life imprisonment. On 25 July 2005, Dupas appeared in the Supreme Court of Victoria Court of Appeal to appeal his conviction for the murder of Maher on the grounds of;

- whether the judge erred in ruling that the facts of the mutilation of Patterson's body should have been admitted at trial
- whether the directions of the judge aimed at keeping the evidence of the Patterson murder discreet were sufficient

- whether the judge incorrectly directed the jury regarding the compression applied to the deceased's neck as one of three possible causes of death
- if the matters relied upon in the other grounds listed above did not result in a miscarriage of justice, their 'aggregate effect' did.

His appeal was dismissed.

PAUL DENYER, AKA THE FRANKSTON SERIAL KILLER

In the summer of 1999, Frankston, a small suburb of Melbourne, was almost brought to a standstill as a result of the violent murders of three young women. Over a seven-week period, three women aged 17, 18 and 22 were violently attacked, one in broad daylight. They were all repeatedly stabbed and slashed to death in frenzied attacks. During the same period, another 41-year-old woman was violently assaulted but managed to escape with her life.

The first murder was that of Elizabeth Stevens, aged 18. On Saturday, 12 June 1993, her partially clothed body was found in a local park a short drive from Frankston. The teenager had been reported missing the previous evening. Naked from the waist up, Elizabeth Stevens had had her throat cut, and there were six deep knife wounds to her chest, four deep cuts running from her breast to her navel and four more running at right angles forming a macabre criss-cross pattern on her abdomen. Her face had several cuts and abrasions and her nose was swollen, indicating that it had been broken. Her bra was up around her neck. A post-mortem revealed that she had not been sexually assaulted.

On the evening of 8 July 1993, 41-year-old bank clerk Rosza Toth was making her way home from work when she was violently attacked by a man who said he had a gun and tried to drag her into a nearby nature reserve. Toth put up a fight for her life, during which the man pulled out clumps of her hair and she bit his fingers to the bone on several occasions. She eventually fought the man off and, with torn stockings and trousers and no shoes, she managed to flag down a passing car as her assailant fled into the night. Rosza Toth had little doubt that had she not resisted so strongly she would most definitely have been murdered. Later that same evening, police had a report that 22-year-old Debbie Fream had gone missing after she drove to her local store. Four days later, her body was found by a farmer in one of his paddocks. She had been stabbed in the neck, head, chest and arms 24 times. She had also been strangled, but not sexually assaulted.

On the afternoon of 30 July, 17-year-old Natalie Russell was reported missing. Eight hours later, her body was found in the bushes beside a cycle track. Like the previous victims, she had been stabbed repeatedly about the face and neck and her throat had been cut. It appeared that the savagery in Natalie Russell's slaying was far worse than in the previous two victims. Natalie had not been sexually assaulted either.

Up until that time, the extensive police enquiries had proved negative. However, this time they were able to gather important evidence and information. A piece of skin, possibly from a finger, was found on the neck of the dead girl. It didn't belong to the victim; the only other possible explanation was that the killer had cut himself as he attacked the student and the sliver of flesh had attached itself by dried blood onto her skin. The other evidence was the sighting of a yellow Toyota Corona by a police officer on a road near the bike track at 3pm, the time the coroner estimated that Natalie Russell had been murdered. The observant police officer had written down its number from its registration tag (the Australian equivalent of a UK road fund licence) because the car had no number plates. Detectives fed the registration number into their computer. It matched up with a report from a postman who had spotted a man acting suspiciously, as if to avoid being seen, in the front seat of a yellow Toyota Corona.

Further enquiries revealed that this same car had been seen near to where Debbie Fream's body had been found. The police believed that three separate sightings of the same vehicle were too much of a coincidence. The car was registered to a Paul Charles Denyer (b. 1972). Police officers went straight to his home address. Denyer was out. They subsequently received information that he had now returned home and went back to his house. The spoke to Denyer and questioned him about his car. He told them that his car had no number plates but that he had a permit to drive it for 28 days while he made the necessary repairs. While questioning him, detectives noticed that he had cuts to his hands. They observed that from one cut, a piece of skin was missing, and they mentally noted that the missing piece could have resembled the piece of skin on Natalie Russell's body. Although he admitted to being in the vicinity of two of the murders at the time they were believed to have taken place, Denyer emphatically denied any knowledge of the killings. He offered weak excuses for being at the murder scenes, saying that his car had broken down near the place where Natalie Russell was murdered and that he was waiting to pick up his girlfriend from the train on the other occasion. He explained the scratches away by saying that he got his hands caught in the fan while working underneath the bonnet of the car. From this moment on, police believed that Denyer was the killer.

He was arrested and questioned at length. Denyer continued to protest his innocence up until the time the police requested a blood sample and a sample of his hair for a DNA test. After a short period of deliberation, he finally admitted killing all three women. Just before 4am on 1 August 1993, Paul Denyer began his confession to the murders of Elizabeth Stevens, Debbie Fream and Natalie Russell, and the attack on Rosza Toth. He told them that at around 7pm on the bleak, rainy evening of 11 June 1993, Elizabeth Stevens got off a bus on Cranbourne Road, Langwarrin, to walk the short distance to her home. Paul Denyer was waiting – but not for Elizabeth in particular; just someone to kill. Elizabeth Stevens just happened to be in the wrong place at the wrong time. Denyer followed the young student along the street in the driving rain and grabbed her from behind, telling her that he had a gun and that if she screamed or tried to run away he would kill her. He told detectives that the 'gun' he held in her back was in fact a piece of aluminium piping with a wooden handle. At 'gunpoint', Denyer marched the terrified girl to nearby Lloyd Park. Denyer's statement said in part: 'Walked in a bit of bush land beside the main track in Lloyd Park. Sat there, you know, stood in the bushes for a while just – I can't remember, just standing there I suppose. I held the "gun" to the back of her neck, walked across the track over towards the other small sand hill or something. And on the other side of that hill, she asked me if she could, you know, go to the toilet, so to speak. So I respected her privacy. So I turned around and everything while she did it and everything. When she finished, we just walked down towards where the goal posts are and we turned right and headed towards the area where she was found. I got to that area there and I started choking her with my hands and she passed out after a while. You know, the oxygen got cut off to her head and she just stopped. And then I pulled out the knife ... and stabbed her many times in the throat. And she was still alive. And then she stood up and then we walked around and all that, just walking around a few steps and then I threw her on the ground and stuck my foot over her neck to finish her off.'

The manner in which Denyer gave his confession chilled the detectives to the bone. It was devoid of emotion or remorse, almost flippant. When the detectives asked questions, they were answered in an almost condescending manner, as if Denyer was in complete control of the situation because he was the only one who knew what had actually happened. Denyer matter-of-factly described and demonstrated how he had pushed his thumb into Elizabeth Stevens's throat and strangled her. He made a stabbing motion, showing how he stabbed and slashed her throat. Then, to the astonishment of the detectives, he demonstrated for the video camera how Elizabeth Stevens's body had begun shaking and shuddering as she went through the death rattles before finally dying.

Denyer then told police how he had dragged Elizabeth Stevens's body to the drain and left it, where it was eventually found. He explained that the blade of the homemade knife he had used to stab Elizabeth had bent during the assault and had broken away from the handle. He dumped the pieces beside the road as he made his way from the murder scene. When asked why he had killed Elizabeth Stevens, Denyer replied: 'Just wanted ... just wanted to kill. Just wanted to take a life because I felt my life had been taken many times.'

Paul Denyer went on to tell of the events of the night of 8 July 1993. He told detectives that he had approached Rosza Toth from behind after he had seen her walking near Seaford station. He put a hand over her mouth and held a fake gun to her head with the other hand. Roszsa resisted strongly and bit his finger to the bone. The couple wrestled and she escaped from his grasp and ran out into the middle of the road, but none of the passing cars stopped. Denyer chased after her, grabbed her by the hair and said: 'Shut up, or I'll blow your fucking head off', and she nodded in agreement but again escaped and this time managed to flag down a passing car while Denyer fled. When asked what he intended to do to Rosza Toth, Denyer replied coolly: 'I was just gonna drag her in the park and kill her, that's all.' Denyer said that as well as the fake gun, he was carrying one of his homemade knives with a razor-sharp aluminium blade in his sock.

After the near-miss with Rosza Toth, Denyer went to the nearby railway station and casually boarded the Frankston-bound train. He got off at Kananook, the next station along, and crossed over the rail overpass bridge in search of another victim. Here he saw Debbie Fream get out of her car and go into the milk bar on the corner. Denyer said that while Debbie Fream was in the milk bar, he opened the rear door of her car, let himself into the back and closed the door behind him. He crouched in the back seat, listened as her footsteps came back to the car and she got in and drove away. 'I waited for her to start up the car so no one would hear her scream or anything,' Denyer said in his confession. 'And she put it into gear and she went to do a U turn. I startled her just as she was doing that turn and she kept going into the wall of the milk bar, which caused a dent in the bonnet. I told her to, you know, shut up or I'd blow her head off and all that shit.' Denyer said that he held the fake gun in her side.

The detectives asked Denyer if he had noticed anything in the back and he said that he had seen a baby carrier beside him in the back seat. Denyer must have known that he was about to kill a young mother. Obviously it made not the least scrap of difference to him. Denyer told Debbie Fream in which direction to drive. It was to an area that he knew well and where he knew he wouldn't be seen as he murdered her. 'I told her when we got there that if she gave any signals to anyone, I'd blow her head off, I'd decorate the car with her brains,' Denyer told the police. Denyer told her to stop the car near some trees and get out, and he pulled a length of cord from his pocket. 'I popped it over her eyes real quickly, so she didn't see it ... 'cos I was gonna strangle her. But I didn't want her to see the cord first. I lifted the cord up and I said: "Can you see this?" And she just put her hand up to grab it to feel it and when she did that I just yanked on it real quickly around her neck. And then I was struggling with her for about five minutes.' Denyer said that he strangled Debbie Fream until she started to pass out. He then drew the knife from his sock and repeatedly stabbed her about the neck and chest. When she fell limp at his feet, he set upon her with the knife, stabbing her many times in the neck and once in the stomach. 'She started breathing out of her neck, just like Elizabeth Stevens,' he told the detectives. 'I could just hear bubbling noises.' When asked if Debbie Fream put up any resistance, Denyer replied: 'Yeah, she put up quite a fight. And her white jumper was pulled off during that time as well. I just felt the same way I did when I killed Elizabeth Stevens.'

The detectives then asked Denyer what happened after he

had stabbed her round the chest and throat area. 'I lifted up her top and then ploughed the knife into her gut. I wanted to see how big her boobs were.' He said that when he saw Debbie's bare stomach he 'just lunged at it with the knife'. Satisfied that Debbie Fream was dead, Denyer dragged her body into a clump of trees and covered it over with a couple of branches he broke from the nearest tree. He then spent about five minutes looking for the murder weapon, which he had dropped after the killing, found it and put it in his pocket. He drove off in Debbie Fream's car, dumped it close to where he lived and walked home in time to ring his girlfriend Sharon at work and pick her up at the Kananook railway station.

The following morning, he brazenly returned to Debbie Fream's car, collected her handbag and the two cartons of milk, eggs, chocolate and a packet of cigarettes she had purchased from the milk bar the previous evening and took them home with him. The only thing of value he found in the purse was a $20 note. He emptied the milk down the sink, threw out the eggs and burnt the carton, as he considered this to be evidence that could be used against him. He then buried the dead woman's handbag in the nearby golf course and near the bike track where he would later kill Natalie Russell. Denyer then dismantled his homemade knife and hid the parts in the air vent in the laundry room of his apartment. 'Why did you kill her?' the detectives asked him. 'Same reason I killed Elizabeth Stevens. I just wanted to,' he replied.

His account of the murder of Natalie Russell chilled the officers to the bone and showed what a vicious and callous killer he was. What they were about to hear would shock them. Denyer's almost unbelievable confession to the murder of Natalie Russell would put him among the most despicable monsters Australia has ever known. Denyer had planned this next murder in advance. His intention was to abduct a young woman, any young woman, as she walked along the bike track. His intention was to drag his victim into the reserve and murder her. He had gone to his planned abduction spot earlier in the day and, with a pair of pliers, had cut three holes a few yards apart in the wire cyclone fence that ran between the bike track and the reserve. Each hole was cut big enough to fit him and his victim through into the cover of the tree-lined reserve. At about 2.30 that afternoon, he drove back to the start of the bike track and waited for a victim to enter on foot. His plan was to follow his victim and, as she approached a hole in the fence, he would grab her and take her through it and into the reserve. He was armed with a razor-sharp homemade knife and a leather strap, which he intended to use to strangle his victim. After a wait of about 20 minutes, he saw a girl in a blue school uniform come along the road and enter the bike track. He followed. 'I stuck about 10 yards behind her until I got to the second hole,' Denyer told the detectives. 'And just when I got to that hole, I quickly walked up behind her and stuck my left hand around her mouth and held the knife to her throat … and that's where that cut happened.' Denyer then indicated the cut on his thumb from which the piece of skin was missing. 'I cut that on my own blade.'

Denyer said that Natalie was struggling at first when he grabbed her but stopped when he told her that if she didn't he would cut her throat. The terrified girl then offered Denyer sex, which disgusted him as he clearly failed to see that Natalie must have realised that she was in the hands of the Frankston Serial Killer and would have done anything, even if it meant having sex with him, to save her life. 'She said "you can have all my money, have sex with me" and things – just said disgusting things like that, really,' Denyer told the detectives as he shook his head in revulsion at what he obviously interpreted as the schoolgirl's loose morals. Nothing could have been further from the truth. Upset, Denyer forced Natalie to kneel in front of him and held the point of the knife very closely over her eye. Then he forced her to lie on the ground and he knelt over her, holding her by the throat and still holding the point of the knife over her eye. When she struggled he cut her across the face. She somehow managed to stand up and started to scream. 'And I just said, "Shut up. Shut up. Shut up. Shut up." And, "If you don't shut up, I'll kill you. If you don't do this, I'll kill you, if you don't do that,"' Denyer told the detectives. 'And she said, "What do you want from me?" I said, "All I want you to do is shut up." And so when she was kneeling on the ground, I put the strap around her neck to strangle her and it broke in half. And then she started violently struggling for about a minute until I pushed her onto her back again – and pushed her head back like this and cut her throat.' Denyer then demonstrated how he had held Natalie Russell's head back. 'I cut a small cut at first and then she was bleeding. And then I stuck my fingers into her throat ... and grabbed her cords and I twisted them.' The detectives could hardly believe what they were hearing, but somehow managed to contain their abhorrence so that they could prompt him to continue with his confession of horror. 'Why'd you do that?' 'My whole fingers like, that much of my hand was inside her throat,' Denyer said as he held up his hand, indicating exactly how much of it he had forced into the wound in the schoolgirl's throat. 'Do you know why you did that?' the detective asked again. 'Stop her from breathing ... and then she slowly stopped. She sort of started to faint and then when she was weak, a bit weaker, I grabbed the opportunity of throwing her head back and made one big large cut which sort of cut almost her whole head off. And then she slowly died.'

'Why did you kill her?' the shocked detectives asked, just managing to hold themselves back from being physically ill. 'Just the same reason as before, just everything came back through my mind again. I kicked her before I left.' Denyer then told the stunned detectives that he had kicked Natalie Russell's body to make sure she was dead, slashed her down the side of her face with his knife and left her where she lay. As he walked back the way he had come in, his blood-soaked hands concealed in his pockets, Denyer saw two uniformed officers taking details from the registration sticker on his car, so he turned around and walked home the other way. At home, he washed his clothes and hid the murder weapon in his back yard. Denyer told the detectives that he had been stalking women in the Frankston area 'for years, just waiting for the right time, waiting for that silent alarm to trigger me off. Waiting for the sign.'

'Can you explain why we have women victims?' a detective asked Denyer. 'I just hate 'em.' The detectives said, 'I beg your pardon?' 'I just hate 'em,' Denyer repeated. 'Those particular girls,' asked the detective, referring to the victims, 'or women in general?' Denyer replied 'general'.

Paul Charles Denyer was charged with the murders of Elizabeth Stevens, Debbie Fream and Natalie Russell and the attempted murder of Rosza Toth, which was later changed to the lesser charge of abduction. At his trial, on 15 December 1993, he pleaded guilty to all charges. He showed no remorse for his crimes. During the trial, it emerged that his murderous intentions started at an early age when he regularly dissected his sister's teddy bears with a homemade knife and, when he was 10, he stabbed the family kitten and hung it from a tree in the back yard. Later on, while working at what would be his last place of employment, he allegedly slaughtered and dismembered two goats in a paddock next door.

He was sentenced to life imprisonment with no fixed non-parole period. He appealed to the Full Court of the Supreme Court of Victoria against the severity of his sentence and, on 29 July 1994, he was granted a 30-year non-parole period, making him eligible for parole in 2023.

During his imprisonment, Denyer has requested to be allowed to purchase and wear cosmetics, but this has been denied. He has sought to learn of the state government's policy on gender reassignment for prisoners and asked for evaluation to determine his suitability for such surgery, but this was rejected.

LEONARD FRASER

From the age of 15, Leonard Fraser (b. 1951) became involved in petty thefts, before going on to commit more serious offences of robbery and numerous offences of rape. The first of these rapes took place on the morning of 11 July 1974, just three weeks after he was released from prison. He accosted a young woman as she walked along a road in Sydney's outer western suburb of St Mary's and attacked her from behind. The MO (*modus operandi*) he used in committing this offence was unique to him and would turn out to be his signature, connecting him to a subsequent string of similar offences. The method he used on this occasion was that he physically took hold of the woman, forcing her arm up behind her back and forcing her down an embankment, where he raped her. Fraser believed that his victim had enjoyed him sexually assaulting her and, after getting back up, he held her hand as he walked her back up onto the roadway, before making off.

On 17 July, Fraser struck again. He went into a shop where a 20-year-old female was working alone. When she went into the back of the shop, he followed her and again took hold of her by forcing her hand up behind her back. Fortunately for his victim, someone came into the shop and Fraser fled before he was able to rape her. However, his sexual urges remained, and three days later he accosted a woman as she walked along a quiet road. He punched her in the face and forced her arm up against her back. As she struggled, she tried to remain calm, and by talking to him somehow convinced him that she was indeed in the mood for sex, and suggested that they go back to his house and have sex there. This ploy worked and Fraser walked the woman hand-in-hand back up onto the road and, as soon as she saw her chance, she broke free and fled to the nearest house and raised the alarm. Fraser was soon arrested. He had dropped his wallet, containing his birth certificate, at the scene of the last attack. When interviewed, he readily confessed to the series of attacks and to the surprise of the police he also confessed to another rape of a French tourist two years previously in Sydney.

Fraser was sentenced to a term of 22 years' imprisonment with a maximum seven-year non-parole period. He was released in 1981, having served seven years. However, in 1985 he struck yet again. In broad daylight he stalked, attacked and raped a 20-year-old woman on an isolated beach. He approached his victim from behind and held her arm up against her back. Referring to this MO, police were soon able to identify the attacker and Fraser was arrested. He was sentenced to a further 12 years' imprisonment. In sentencing Fraser, Justice Derrington said he regarded the prisoner as a dangerous man who preyed on women who were strangers and alone. 'They [the victims] would regard you as being the equivalent of a filthy animal,' he said. 'It [rape] is one of the worst forms of degradation on another human being you can think of and it deserves no sympathy whatever.' He was made to serve the full 12 years. Following his release from prison he managed to avoid further brushes with the law.

On 22 April 1999, nine-year-old Keyra Steinhardt disappeared on her way home from school. An eye-witness to the abduction told police that she saw a man catch up with the little girl and hit her from behind around the head. The child fell to the ground and the witness couldn't see her in the long grass but she saw her assailant fall on her and move as if he was raping her. Then the assailant ran off and returned shortly afterwards in a car, picking the little girl up, placing her in the boot and driving off. Sadly, the witness took 20 minutes to call the police. From the description given by the witness of the car, police were soon able to trace Fraser. Despite intense questioning, it was two weeks before Fraser finally confessed to the abduction and murder of Keyra and he then took police to her naked body. He had disposed of it in a thick bed of grass near the Rockhampton racecourse. Her throat had been cut and Fraser had draped her green school jumper over her torso. To further corroborate his confession, DNA samples taken from the blood and hair found in the trunk of Fraser's car matched that of Keyra Steinhardt. There was also another female's blood on the hinges of the boot and on a cigarette paper in the glove compartment. On 7 May, Fraser was charged with the rape and murder of Keyra Steinhardt.

Strangely enough, he pleaded not guilty at his trial. The court was told that due to the advanced decomposition of the girl's body, it was impossible to determine what the actual cause of death was or if she had been sexually assaulted. But the prosecution highlighted the damaging evidence of a tape recording of Fraser talking with another prisoner, in which he had asked the prisoner whether, on his release, he would go and dispose of a knife Fraser had hidden in his own apartment. The prosecution suggested that Fraser used this knife to stab and kill the young girl.

Leonard Fraser was found guilty of the abduction and murder of Keyra Steinhardt. 'Lone females in a public place, as is present in this case, were compelled by force and threats to go to a place where the risk of disturbance was less,' Justice Mackenzie said. 'The offence involved severe, indeed extreme, violence on a child. Fraser's story is that of a sexual predator of the worst kind.' Justice Mackenzie went on to say that he could see no reason to suppose that Fraser had any prospect of rehabilitation and sentenced him to an indefinite life sentence. Under new Queensland legislation enacted in 1997, an indefinite life sentence means that, unlike a life sentence where the prisoner could automatically apply for parole after 15 years, he must not only apply to the Parole Board but also to a Supreme Court judge before he can ever be released. Both would have to be satisfied that Fraser no longer posed a threat to the community before the indefinite order could be lifted. This sentence left Fraser in no doubt that he would spend the rest of his natural life in prison.

Police still believed that Fraser was responsible for other murders. A young schoolgirl and three other women had all gone missing without trace between September 1998 and April 1999. Natasha Ryan, 14, had disappeared on 2 September 1998, while on her way to school in the same area where Keyra Steinhardt was killed. Julie Dawn Turner, 39, had worked with Fraser for a couple of months in 1998 at a local abattoir. On 28 December 1998, Julie left a nightclub in the early hours of the morning, heavily under the influence of alcohol. She was last seen walking home alone. Beverly Leggo, 36, also had a connection with Fraser. They met at a local hostel where he was staying in 1997. She was last seen on 1 March 1999. Sylvia Maria Benedetti, 19, disappeared on 17 April 1999. Six days later while police were searching for the body of Keyra Steinhardt, who had disappeared the day before, they received a call to go to a derelict hotel that was in the process of being demolished. The demolition workers had made a grisly discovery. In one of the rooms, the carpet was soaked with blood and there was blood splattered all over the ceiling and walls. They also found bone fragments in the carpet. In a downstairs freezer, police found a pair of women's shoes submerged in filthy water. A forensic examination revealed that the blood was human and, given the spate of missing women in recent months, police had good reason to believe the blood to be that of one of the missing women. They soon matched the blood found in the room to that found in the boot of Fraser's car and to the missing woman, Sylvia Benedetti. Experts suggested that the attack had been so ferocious and savage that the victim had lost about four litres of blood, which was about as much as a woman the size of Sylvia Benedetti would have in her entire body. Police believed that Sylvia Benedetti was known to Fraser and was seen with him on the night before she disappeared.

Police now suspected that all four missing women had been murdered by Fraser, but knew that without their bodies or a confession they would not be able to charge him. Then they got lucky. Fraser started talking to his cell-mate, Alan Quinn, and confessed to the murders. Fraser said he killed Natasha Ryan by knifing her because she was pregnant by him. He then buried her body in a shallow grave. Fraser also said that he murdered Sylvia Benedetti and 'bled her like an animal' in a disused hotel and made a bloodied hand mark on the wall before smearing over it. Fraser also alleged that he had met Julie Turner in a shopping mall and was giving her a lift home. He then 'flogged into her' (attacked her) after she had slapped him when he put his hand on her leg. When confronted by detectives about the confessions, he confessed and volunteered to take them to where the bodies of Beverly Leggo and Julie Turner were hidden. A short time previously, skeletal remains had already been discovered in bush land. These were later identified as those of Sylvia Benedetti. Fraser was unable to lead police to where the rest of the remains were. Fraser was charged with those murders and brought back for trial.

During the trial, there was a sensational revelation when one of the alleged victims, 18-year-old Natasha Ryan, was discovered by police hiding in a cupboard at the home of her boyfriend, 26-year-old Scott Black. Having charged Fraser with her murder, the court directed the jury to find him not guilty. Natasha Ryan appeared in court as a defence witness and stated that she had never seen Leonard Fraser before. She said that on the day she was reported missing, her mother had dropped her off at school. She decided that she had had enough of school, had decided to run away and stay with Scott Black, and had been with him ever since.

The defence lawyers suggested that there was now a major doubt about some of the evidence provided by Alan Quinn, as he had stated that Fraser had confessed to Ryan's murder and given specific details as to how he carried out the crime. There was also doubt as to whether Fraser's subsequently recorded confessions were genuine or whether he had made them up. However, the prosecution soon negated these suggestions. One admission had been that Beverly Leggo was strangled with her black knickers and a bra. Fraser made this admission three days before forensic scientists revealed that that was indeed how she had died. Fraser also said that where Julie Turner had been murdered he had abandoned a pair of her sandals. A subsequent search found a sandal and Julie Turner's bra.

On 9 May 2003, Fraser was found guilty of the murders of

Sylvia Benedetti and Beverly Doreen Leggo and the manslaughter of Julie Dawn Turner. The verdict of manslaughter meant that the jury believed that Fraser did not intend to kill Julie Turner. Fraser stood silent and red-faced in the dock and then yawned and stretched his hands behind his head as the verdicts were handed down. He was sentenced to life imprisonment.

On 31 December 2006, Leonard John Fraser died in his sleep aged 55 in the secure unit at Princess Alexandra Hospital. He had been in the hospital since Boxing Day 2006, when he had suffered a cardiac arrest.

JOHN WAYNE GLOVER, AKA THE GRANNY KILLER

John Wayne Glover (b. 1932) was in his late fifties when he became one of the most despised and despicable murderers in the annals of Australian crime history. His warm and friendly personality disguised a monster lurking within. Glover was a petty thief with a gambling habit and a number of minor convictions for sexual offences against women. In 1989, in the North Shore suburb of Sydney, he started to prey on poor, frail, defenceless old ladies, initially robbing them. With his later victims, he brutally murdered them and then stole their money.

His first non-fatal attack on an elderly woman was on 11 January 1989, when an 84-year-old woman was walking along a quiet road. On seeing her, he parked his car and approached her, punched his unsuspecting victim in the face and stole her handbag and its contents. On 1 March 1989, he found his second victim, Gwendoline Mitchelhill, who was walking along with a stick. Glover went back to his car and armed himself with a hammer. Then he slowly followed the old lady back to her accommodation and, as she entered, he came up behind her and repeatedly hit her over the head and body with the hammer. After stealing her purse, he made off. She died from her injuries a short time later.

Two months then passed before another old lady fell victim to Glover. On 9 May, Glover was out on his own when he saw Lady

Winifreda Ashton walking slowly towards him in a red raincoat with the aid of a walking stick. Glover followed her into the foyer of her apartment building where he attacked her, again using his hammer. Later evidence revealed that the frail Lady Ashton put up an incredible fight for her life. After rendering her unconscious, Glover removed her tights and strangled her with them. He did not sexually assault her. Then, as if in respect for the dead woman, Glover laid her walking stick and shoes at her feet before stealing her handbag. The police now knew that they were dealing with a homicidal maniac and not just an ordinary mugger.

By now, Glover had gained confidence but also became complacent and more brazen. Police received complaints of old ladies confined to their beds in nursing homes being sexually assaulted. These crimes would turn out to have been committed by Glover, who worked as a pie salesman delivering to many nursing homes. On one occasion, Glover visited one such home. He made his way upstairs and into a bedroom where he lifted the dress of an elderly woman and fondled her private parts. He then went to another old lady's room where he put his hand down the front of her nightdress and stroked her breasts. The terrified woman cried out. Staff spoke to Glover but he was not detained. The staff did report the incident to the police who, at this time, failed to make any connection between these incidents and the murders. And so Glover continued to commit other non-fatal attacks on old ladies.

On 8 August 1989, Glover attacked elderly Effie Carnie in a quiet street and stole her groceries. On 6 October, again in a nursing home, he passed himself off as a doctor and put his hand up the dress of an elderly female patient. The old lady called for help but Glover escaped. At no time while committing these non-fatal assaults was he ever identified. By the time the police did make a connection, Glover had gone on to commit several more murders of old ladies.

On 18 October 1989, Glover came upon 86-year-old Doris Cox slowly making her way home. He walked with her into the secluded stairwell of her accommodation, attacking her from behind by smashing her face into a brick wall. She collapsed at his feet. After finding nothing worth stealing, he left her for dead and went home. However, she survived. When spoken to by the police, she was not able to give an accurate description of her attacker, but nevertheless the police prepared an identikit picture. Unfortunately, it turned out to be nothing like Glover and for a time this impeded the police enquiry. Their worst fears were realised on 2 November with the murder of another old lady, 85-year-old Margaret Pahud. She was killed in identical fashion to the previous victims by being hit over the head with a blunt instrument as she walked home. Her handbag was also missing. Within hours of the murder of Margaret Pahud, they had the report of a second victim. Glover had called at a nursing home in the early afternoon in his capacity as pie salesman. On his way through the garden, he struck up a conversation with 81-year-old Olive Cleveland, who was sitting on a bench reading. When she got up and walked towards the main building, Glover grabbed her from behind and forced her into a secluded area, dragging her to the ground. He repeatedly slammed her head onto the concrete before he removed her tights and knotted them tightly around her neck. Glover then made off with money from her handbag. Unbelievably, no one connected this murder with the attack on an elderly lady at the same nursing home only six months earlier. There were no clues; the murderer vanished into the afternoon.

The police now knew they were dealing with a dangerous serial killer who had to be caught. As a result, a $20,000 reward was offered for information on him. After cross-checking statements, one distinct description kept appearing in relation to several of the murders. The police finally realised that they had been looking for the wrong type of man based on the identikit and previous description given. But still Glover continued his killing spree.

On 23 November 1989, Glover spotted 92-year-old Muriel

Falconer struggling down the street with her shopping. He returned to his car, collected his hammer and gloves and followed her to her front door. As Falconer was partially deaf and blind, she did not notice Glover slip through the door behind her with his gloves on and his hammer raised. He silenced her by holding his hand over her mouth as he hit her repeatedly about the head and neck. As she fell to the floor, he started to remove her tights but she regained consciousness and cried out. Glover struck her again and again with the hammer and only when he was satisfied that she was unconscious did he remove her undergarments and strangle her with them. He searched her purse and the rest of the house before he left, taking with him cash and his hammer and gloves in a carrier bag. A neighbour discovered Falconer's body the following afternoon. Forensic experts found a perfect footprint in blood on the carpet, their first solid clue since the investigation had started, but they still needed a suspect for comparison purposes.

The major break came when Glover again became careless. On 11 January 1990, he called at the Greenwich Hospital for an appointment with the administrator. Afterwards, Glover dressed in his blue-and-white salesman's jacket and, carrying a clipboard, walked into one of the wards, where four very old and very sick women lay in their beds. He approached Daisy Roberts, who was suffering from advanced cancer, asking if she was losing any body heat, then pulled up her nightgown and began to indecently assault her. Mrs Roberts became alarmed and rang the buzzer beside her bed. A sister at the hospital answered the call and found Glover in the ward; she called out and Glover ran from the ward. She chased him and took down the registration of his car as he sped off. She notified the police. Staff at the hospital was able to identify and name Glover from previous visits on his pie round. But it would be a further three weeks before the incident reached the investigating officers involved in the murders. Now armed with the information, detectives confirmed Glover's name with his employers. They rang him at home and asked him to come to the police station at 5pm the following day. When he hadn't turned up by 6pm, police called his home where his wife told them that he had attempted suicide and was in hospital. Police went to the hospital but Glover was too sick to be interviewed. Staff at the hospital handed police a suicide note that included the words 'no more grannies'. The police still had not made the connection between the nursing home assaults and the murders. Eventually though, the connection was made and Glover suddenly became the prime suspect in all the murders. Due to the lack of direct evidence, they decided not to arrest him but instead kept him under 24-hour surveillance. During this time, his conduct was exemplary.

On 19 March 1990, at 10am, police saw him call at the home of a lady-friend, Joan Sinclair; they saw him spruce himself up in the rearview mirror. He went to the door and was let in. The watching police had no reason to believe that it was anything other than a social visit. At 1pm, there was no sign of Glover nor any sign of life from the house. The police became concerned. At 5pm, all was still quiet, and at 6pm, deciding that all was not well, the police decided to enter the house. As they entered, they noticed pools of blood. With guns drawn, they silently moved from room to room. They saw a hammer lying in a pool of drying blood on the mat. As they peered further around the doorway, they saw a pair of women's knickers and a man's shirt covered in blood. Then a woman's body came into view. Joan Sinclair's blood-splattered head was wrapped in a bundle of blood-soaked towels. She was naked from the waist down and her tights were tied around her neck. Her genitals had been mutilated. But where was her attacker? They continued searching and found Glover unconscious and naked, lying in the bath. One wrist was slashed and there was a strong smell of alcohol. They found he was still alive. He was taken to hospital and, after recovering, told the police of the final chapter in the Granny Murders.

Glover had known Joan Sinclair for some time and they were extremely fond of each other in a platonic way. However, after he entered the house he got his hammer out of his briefcase and struck Mrs Sinclair about the head with it. He then removed her tights and strangled her with them. He rolled her body over onto the mat, wrapped four towels around her massive head wound to stem the flow of blood and then dragged her body across the room, leaving a trail of blood. When he had done that he ran a bath, swallowed a handful of Valium with a bottle of Vat 69, slashed his left wrist and lay in the bath to die. During his interview, he was asked 'why?' And he kept giving the same answer: 'I don't know. I just see these ladies and it seems to trigger something. I just have to be violent towards them.'

He was charged with murdering the six elderly women. His wife Gay and their two daughters, both in their late teens, were stunned. There had never been the slightest indication that the man they loved as husband and father was the infamous Granny Killer. At his trial in November 1991, John Wayne Glover pleaded not guilty to six counts of murder on the grounds of diminished responsibility, claiming that he had been temporarily insane when he carried out the murders. The jury did not agree and it took them just two and a half hours to find that Glover was both sane and guilty.

Justice Wood sentenced Glover to six life terms of imprisonment, and said in summary: 'The period since January 1989 has been one of intense and serious crime involving extreme violence inflicted on elderly women, accompanied by the theft or robbery of their property. On any view, the prisoner has shown himself to be an exceedingly dangerous person and that view was mirrored by the opinions of the psychiatrists who have given evidence at his trial. I have no alternative other than to impose the maximum available sentence, which means that the prisoner will be required to spend the remainder of his natural life in jail. It is inappropriate to express any date as to release on parole. Having regard to those life sentences, this is not a case where the prisoner may ever be released pursuant to order of this court.'

THE EVIL WITHIN

In September 2005, John Wayne Glover, the Granny Killer, hanged himself in his prison cell.

ARCHIBALD MCCAFFERTY, AKA MAD DOG

Before turning to murder, Archibald McCafferty (b. 1951) was already known to the police. By the age of 24, he had 30 previous criminal convictions involving theft and stealing cars, but no convictions for serious violence. This, however, changed following his marriage. He took to drinking and taking drugs and subjected his wife to a series of violent assaults. As a result of this, he received treatment at various psychiatric hospitals. More mental problems were soon to befall McCafferty. His young baby died while sleeping in bed with his mother. The death was investigated and a coroner recorded the death as accidental. Janice McCafferty, while sleeping, had rolled over onto the baby and suffocated it. Archibald McCafferty did not agree with the verdict and made accusations that his wife had murdered their son. Was the death of his son all that McCafferty needed to tip him over the edge? It was a question about which psychiatrists in the future would sharply disagree. Certainly the tragedy of his son's death played constantly on his already troubled mind. But did it light the fuse of the dynamite that was about to explode? McCafferty took to getting tattooed, until almost his entire body was covered with more than 200.

So affected was he by the loss of his son, he believed that to avenge the death seven people must die, seven being a significant number to his troubled mind. His wife had bricks thrown through her window with notes attached, which were obviously from McCafferty. The first note read: 'You and the rest of your family can go and get fucked because anyone who has anything to do with me is going to die of a bad death. You know who this letter is from so take warning. Bill is the next off the rank. Then you go one by one.' It was signed 'you-know-who'. The man referred to as Bill was Bill Riean, the boyfriend of Janice's mother. The second note read: 'The only thing in my mind is to kill your mother and Bill Riean. This is not a bluff because I'm that dirty on all of you for the death of my son but I can't let it go at that. I have a matter of a few guns so I am going to use them on you all for satisfaction so beware.'

On 24 August 1973, the first day of the inquest into the death of his son, the killing started. A week earlier, McCafferty had formed a gang from an odd assortment of teenagers along with Carol Ellen Howes, a 26-year-old woman with whom he was living. McCafferty had met her and 16-year-old Julie Ann Todd when he was a patient at a psychiatric centre. The rest of the gang was made up of Michael John (Mick) Meredith and Richard William (Dick) Whittington, two 17-year-olds McCafferty had met in a tattoo parlour a few days earlier. Mick and Dick had a couple of rifles. The sixth member of the gang was 17-year-old Donald Richard (Rick) Webster, whom McCafferty had met only days earlier. Led by McCafferty, the gang chose their first victim, 50-year-old George Anson, who, on the evening of 24 August 1973, was spotted by the gang as he staggered down the street towards his home after drinking heavily at a local bar. The gang was in a stolen Volkswagen. Anson was far too drunk to put up a fight. They dragged him into a side street. McCafferty kicked Anson repeatedly in the head and about the body. McCafferty later stated that he heard voices for the first time, saying 'Kill seven. Kill seven. Kill, kill, kill... ' As a result, McCafferty pulled out a knife and plunged it into Anson's back and neck seven times. McCafferty gave the dying man one final kick in the face before running back to the car. One of the gang, Rick Webster, was not happy about what had happened and voiced his concern to McCafferty. This would later prove to be Webster's demise.

Still hearing voices telling him to kill seven, McCafferty and his gang planned another crime en route to the cemetery to visit the grave of his son. They dropped Julie Todd and Mick Meredith off to pose as hitchhikers. The plan was that as soon as a car stopped they would force the driver to the cemetery at gunpoint and then rob him. Moments later, a car pulled into the cemetery and stopped about 150yd from the graveside. In the car were Julie Todd and Mick Meredith. They were holding 42-year-old Ronald Neil Cox at gunpoint. Cox had felt sorry for the two kids hitchhiking in the rain and had stopped to give them a lift. McCafferty left the graveside and ran over to them. Ronald Cox was forced to lie face down in the mud while McCafferty and Meredith held rifles to the back of his head. Cox begged for his life as the voices in McCafferty's head spurred him on. Ronald Cox was still begging for his life, telling them that he was the father of seven children. Although he had no way of knowing, this was a fatal mistake. On hearing the word 'seven', McCafferty and Meredith each shot Ronald Cox through the back of the head.

After the killing of Cox, the gang members returned home. But McCafferty could still hear the voices telling him to 'kill seven' and he told two of his gang to go out and find him another victim. In the early hours of the following morning, 24-year-old driving instructor Evangelos Kollias picked up Julie Todd and Dick Whittington as they hitchhiked along the road. Once in the car, Whittington produced a .22 rifle from under his coat. They forced Kollias into the back seat and told him to lie on the floor while Julie drove the car back to the flat. McCafferty then took over. They went out in the victim's car with McCafferty driving. They all knew that McCafferty had murder on his mind. Kollias was told to lie low, as they did not want him to see where they were going. Assured that he would come to no harm, Kollias lay on the back floor and went to sleep. McCafferty's plan was to kill Kollias then drive his car to where his wife, Janice McCafferty, her mother and her mother's boyfriend were. Killing them would make the total six. The seventh victim was to be one of his own gang, Rick Webster. McCafferty felt that Webster was likely to betray him to the police. McCafferty told Whittington to kill Kollias. As Kollias woke up in the back of the car, Whittington held the sawn-off .22 rifle to his head and pulled the trigger, killing him instantly. McCafferty told Whittington to shoot Kollias again to make sure he was dead. Whittington fired another bullet into the dead man's head. They then dumped the body in a deserted street nearby. Unfortunately McCafferty's plan backfired and, thankfully, saved the lives of more potential victims. There was not enough petrol in the car to get to where the other intended victims lived so McCafferty aborted the plan for that night.

During a conversation Webster had with another gang member he found out that McCafferty intended to kill him. The plan was to wait for him to come out of his workplace then to shoot him. Webster saw them waiting outside his workplace and called the police, who arrested McCafferty, Meredith and Whittington. The police found an arsenal of weapons in the men's possession. On the way to the police station, McCafferty confessed to the murders.

At his trial in February 1974, McCafferty pleaded not guilty to three counts of murder on the grounds of insanity. His five co-accused – Todd, Howe, Meredith, Whittington and Webster – all pleaded not guilty to the same charges. Mick Meredith and Dick Whittington were found guilty of the murders of Ronald Cox and Evangelos Kollias and each sentenced to 18 years in prison. Richard Webster was found guilty of the manslaughter of Cox and sentenced to four years in prison. Julie Todd was found guilty of murdering Cox and Kollias and sent to prison for 10 years. On 20 May 1974, having just turned 17, she was found hanged in a bathroom at a detention centre. Carol Howes was found not guilty on all counts. Eight months pregnant with McCafferty's child when the verdict was handed down, Howes made a passionate promise from the dock to McCafferty. 'I'll wait for you Archie,' she sobbed. 'No matter what, I'll always be waiting for you with our child.'

The jury returned a verdict of guilty against McCafferty on all counts and dismissed his claims that at the time of the murders he had been insane. He was sentenced to three life sentences. All the time he was in prison, he kept telling people of his need to kill four more people and that he would do so if ever released. Even locked away, he was a problem prisoner for the authorities. Police believe that he was a member of the secret 'murder squad' that acted as judge, jury and executioner behind the walls of Parramatta Jail in 1981. They believe the squad was responsible for four murders within the prison. In September 1981, Archie was charged with the murder of Edward James Lloyd, who was stabbed to death in his cell. Archie's co-accused, Kevin Michael Gallagher, was eventually found guilty of the murder.

It was proved that McCafferty was present while the murder took place and, though he strenuously denied the charges, he was found guilty of manslaughter and given a further 14 years. McCafferty protested his innocence and appealed against the sentence, claiming that he had been framed. To prove it, he named those who were responsible. This automatically made him an outcast within the prison system. For his own protection, he was transferred from one jail to the next in search of a permanent home.

In November 1981, McCafferty was found in his cell with 10 foil-wrapped packages containing heroin, for which he received a three-year sentence. The prison authorities were also aware that there was a price on his head for giving evidence against other prisoners.

As no parole period had been given, it was clear that he would spend the rest of his life behind bars, but he kept applying for parole. In October 1991, his application for parole was heard before Mr Justice Wood. The judge granted him a 20-year parole period dating from 30 August 1973. He became eligible for release on parole on 29 August 1993. After many years, his anger had subsided and he was looked on as a model prisoner. Was this for real or was he playing games with the authorities? In any event, he convinced the parole board, who agreed that he was indeed a changed man who was no longer a danger to society and decided that he would be released on parole. The only condition of the parole was that Archie would be deported. On 1 May 1997, he was sent back to his native Scotland, where he had several minor brushes with the law and was given two years' probation for threatening to kill police officers.

On 21 July 2002, McCafferty was arrested in New Zealand for failing to declare his criminal convictions when he arrived in the country. McCafferty was believed to be on the first leg of a secret journey back to Australia, and he was voluntarily deported back to Scotland immediately. At the time of writing he is still resident in Scotland living under an assumed name.

CHAPTER 2
CANADA

PAUL BERNARDO AND KARLA HOMOLKA

Paul Bernardo (b. 1964) and Karla Homolka (b. 1970) became known as the Ken and Barbie Murderers due to the fact that they resembled the Barbie and Ken children's dolls. When the couple first met in 1987, he was an accountant and she worked in a veterinary clinic. As soon as they met, she became infatuated and obsessed with him to the point that she would do anything and everything to retain his love, even to the point of murder. At first, she did not know that he possessed a warped and evil mind and had a history of violence and sex crimes. This would soon re-emerge in their relationship. When she did find out, she encouraged his sadistic sexual behaviour.

Between 1987 and 1992 in Scarborough, a Toronto suburb in which he lived, Bernardo committed a series of rapes and sexual assaults on 13 women. His *modus operandi* was simple. He would loiter around bus stops in sparsely populated areas and wait for unsuspecting women to get off a bus and start to walk away. He would then grab his victims from behind and pull them to the ground, where he anally raped them and, after performing oral sex on them, he would simply let them go.

Karla knew exactly what Paul was doing and encouraged him.

One victim even remembered seeing a woman with the rapist with what appeared to be a video camera in her hand. The police at the time took no notice of this part of the victim's evidence. However, they did believe that all the attacks had been the work of the same man. It would not be until 1990 that the police finally decided to publish an identikit picture that the victims had agreed upon as being a likeness of their attacker.

That picture, plus the $150,000 reward, initiated a wealth of information. It wasn't long before Paul Bernardo's name came to the notice of the police. He was visited by the police and elected to give voluntary DNA samples. These samples, along with 230 samples from other suspects, were sent to the forensic laboratory. Only five of the samples had a similar DNA make-up to the attacker. Paul Bernardo was one of those five. His sample was resubmitted for additional testing in April 1992. By that time, Bernardo had stopped raping women. There was not the urgency there had been two years earlier when the attacks were in progress and so the samples and forensic examination were treated as non-urgent.

When Bernardo and Homolka first met, Karla was not a virgin and this played on Bernardo's mind. He told her that to make up for this, she should allow him to take the virginity of her younger sister, Tammy. But he said it must be done without her knowledge and he wanted to film it. Without even contemplating what he was suggesting, Karla agreed and obtained some sedatives from the clinic where she worked.

The day of 23 December 1990 was a day that would end in tragedy. On this day, all the family members were together at Karla's home. Bernardo began plying young Tammy with drinks laced with the sedatives. It wasn't long before she passed out. When the other family members went up to bed, Karla and Paul started on Tammy. Karla first held a rag containing an anaesthetic over Tammy's face. Bernardo then proceeded to rape her, filming the act at the same time. Then he ordered Karla to carry out sexual acts on her sister. While this was taking place,

Tammy regained some form of consciousness and was violently sick. Karla tried to put her in the recovery position and clear her throat but it was too late. Tammy had choked to death on her own vomit. Now faced with a dilemma, they dressed her, hid the drugs and camera and called an ambulance. Everybody was led to believe that Tammy had died from accidentally choking on her vomit with no other factors involved.

Bernardo vented his anger on Karla. He told her that she would still have to find another girl to take the place of Tammy. Karla knew of one girl who was very similar in appearance to her dead sister, called Jane. Karla invited Jane round to the house that she and Bernardo were now sharing. Karla plied her with drinks, again laced with sedatives. It wasn't long before Bernardo arrived home and saw the sleeping Jane. He and Karla then set about sexually abusing the unconscious girl. First, Karla committed sexual acts on the girl, which were filmed by Bernardo. Then Bernardo raped her both vaginally and anally; Karla filmed those acts. The following morning, Jane had no idea what had happened.

After their marriage, Bernardo had started smuggling cigarettes across the border and needed to use stolen number plates to disguise his frequent visits across the American–Canadian border. It was the need for these number plates that brought him into contact with his first murder victim, Leslie Mahaffy, aged 14. On the night of 14 June 1991, while cruising around one night looking for plates to steal, he saw Leslie walking along on her own. At knifepoint he forcibly abducted her, taking her back to his home. He took her inside and, while Karla slept, he began to videotape Leslie naked and blindfolded. Eventually, Karla woke up and joined Paul, who told her how he wanted her to make love to Leslie, filming every moment like he was a director making a movie. After she had finished, Bernardo raped Leslie viciously and brutally. As a result, Leslie died. Her body was dismembered and taken to a local lake where the body parts were tied to concrete blocks and discarded.

However, on 29 June 1991, a man and his wife were canoeing on the lake when they came across a concrete block with some pieces of what they believed were animal flesh encased in it. They later went back to the spot and, with the help of a fisherman, pulled out the concrete block and looked at it closely. Inside the block was the calf and foot of a young woman. The remaining body parts were later recovered.

On 16 April 1992, another teenager, Kristen French, was abducted from a car park. Karla had lured the pretty girl over to their car on the pretext of asking directions. When Kristen stood by the car looking at Karla's map, Paul forced the girl into the back seat with his knife. Kristen, who was a bright, intelligent girl, did everything she could to cooperate with this depraved couple and their outrageous and humiliating demands. She believed that cooperation was her only chance of survival. The ordeal became worse and worse. The more she cooperated, the more sadistic Bernardo became. While holding her captive and with the camera running, Bernardo urinated on her and also attempted to defecate on her without success. He held her captive for several days before killing her and dumping her body in a ditch. This time, they didn't cut the body up, and as a result the police didn't connect the two murders. On 30 April 1992, Kristen's naked body was found in the ditch.

In late 1992, Bernardo started becoming violent towards Karla and she reported him to the police. She eventually moved into a refuge away from him. His name again came to the notice of the murder squad officers who were aware that, because the DNA samples from the previous rapes had not yet been examined, he had not been cleared. After visiting him and talking to him, they decided to put him under surveillance. In early February 1993, when the police investigation intensified, the police wanted to interview Karla. They also wanted to fingerprint her and question her about a Mickey Mouse watch in her possession that was very similar to Kristen French's watch. She realised that the police had linked the rapes to the murders.

But Karla did not confess to the police. Instead, she told her uncle that Bernardo was the rapist and a murderer. He in turn consulted an attorney, who advised Karla to sit and wait to see what transpired.

In February 1994, Bernardo was arrested for both the rapes and the murders. His DNA had been positively matched to the rapes. On 19 February, police executed search warrants at the home address of Paul and Karla and found a wealth of evidence. Bernardo had a written description of every one of the rapes. The police also found a home video that showed Karla participating in lesbian acts with two other women.

Karla's legal team then went to the Attorney General's office with what they had and set out to plea-bargain. It was discussed that Karla would get 12 years in prison for being involved in the murder of the two victims, but the sentences would be served concurrently. This would mean she would serve only 12 years and would be eligible for parole in three years with good behaviour. It was even agreed that no objections to parole would be made. Arrangements would be made for her to serve out her sentence in a psychiatric hospital instead of prison. All of this would be in return for her giving evidence against Bernardo.

Her separate trial took place on 28 June 1993. In the interim period, a psychiatric report on her had been prepared. The sentence she received was as agreed. But her greatest test was yet to come when she would come face to face with Bernardo in court. This didn't happen for almost two years due to legal arguments. These revolved around the videotapes of the rapes and murders, which Bernardo had given to his defence lawyer in the belief that the prosecution would not be able to obtain them and use them in evidence. However, the prosecutors knew of the tapes from Karla and had secretly recorded Bernardo's lawyer's conversations with him. Eventually, the pressure increased on his lawyer, who felt obliged to withdraw from representing Bernardo and in doing so turned the tapes over to the prosecutors and withdrew from the case. A new legal team was appointed to represent Bernardo.

In May 1995, the trial began and the damning videotapes became crucial to the prosecution. On 1 September 1995, Bernardo was found guilty of the kidnappings, rapes and murders of Leslie Mahaffy and Kristen French, and the death of Tammy Homolka. He was sentenced to life imprisonment, eligible for parole after 25 years. He subsequently lodged an appeal.

As they each served their sentences, the hostility between the couple grew stronger. Bernardo prepared for his appeal in 2000, while Karla made plans for her pending parole in 2001. Bernardo was unsuccessful in his appeal against his conviction, citing legal issues.

Due to her bad behaviour while serving her sentence, Karla was not paroled as expected after three years, and a recommendation was put forward that she should serve a further four years. Bernardo had launched a second appeal, which was also rejected. He is still behind bars in one of Canada's toughest maximum-security prisons where he is locked up for 23 hours a day to protect him from attacks by other prisoners.

On 8 March 2001, Karla Homolka was officially denied parole. The cited grounds for the refusal were: 'The board is satisfied that, if released, you are likely to commit an offence causing the death of or serious harm to another person before the expiration of the sentence you are now serving.'

Her case, however, would be reviewed each year up until July 2005, when her sentence ended. Prior to her eventual release, Karla took on a new identity. Changing her name to Karla Teale and altering her appearance, when finally released she tried to blend back into society, but for some time after she was hounded by the press who regularly traced her whereabouts, despite the fact that she repeatedly changed her name.

On 9 February 2007, it was reported that Karla Homolka had found a new partner and had given birth to a baby boy.

THE EVIL WITHIN

WAYNE BODEN, AKA THE VAMPIRE RAPIST

Wayne Boden (b. 1948) became known as the Vampire Rapist after his distinctive MO of biting his female victims' breasts. He was responsible for a two-year reign of terror in a suburb of Montreal, where after stalking his female victims he attacked, raped and murdered them in a perverted and sadistic manner.

On 23 July 1968, Norma Villancourt, a 21-year-old teacher, was found dead in her apartment. She had been raped and strangled, her breasts savaged with bite marks. Police found no sign of a struggle. Twelve months elapsed before the killer struck again. Shirley Audette had been strangled and her body had been dumped at the rear of an apartment complex in West Montreal. Though fully clothed when found, she had also been raped and the police found bite marks on her breasts.

On 23 November, Marielle Archambault left work in company with a young man she addressed as 'Bill'. When she did not arrive at work the following morning, Marielle's employer went to see if she was ill. He found her dead body on the floor of her apartment living room. She had been raped and her breasts had been savaged with teeth marks. The police found a crumpled photograph on the floor, identified as 'Bill'.

On 16 January 1970, the killer struck again, murdering Jean Way, 24, in her apartment. Way's boyfriend found her naked body on the sofa; she had been subjected to bite marks on her breasts. As before, police officers could find no sign of a struggle. It was not until 1971 that the killer struck again, this time 2,500 miles away in Calgary. His victim was Elizabeth Pourteous, a teacher, reported missing from work on 18 May. Her apartment manager was called and he found her body on the bedroom floor. Raped and strangled, she had also suffered the by-now-familiar bite marks on her breasts. A forensic examination revealed a broken cufflink near the body. Police were given details of a young man she had been seen with on the night she died. He was driving a blue Mercedes. A friend of the victim told police that Pourteous had recently started dating a new acquaintance named 'Bill'.

CANADA

On 19 May 1971, a police officer found the Mercedes car parked near the murder scene. Wayne Boden was arrested half an hour later, walking towards the car. He told police that he had moved from Montreal a year earlier, admitted seeing Elizabeth Pourteous on the night she died and identified the cufflink as his own. The final major piece of evidence was from a forensic orthodontist, who compared a cast of Boden's teeth with bite marks on the victim. This was the first such case where this type of evidence was used in North America. He was found guilty of the murder in Calgary and then returned to Montreal where he confessed to the other murders. At his trial he was sentenced to life imprisonment. He was also suspected of the murder of Norma Vaillancourt, a student aged 21 who was murdered on 23 July 1968. However, in 1994 another man, Raymond Sauve, was convicted of this crime. Wayne Boden died at Kingston Regional Hospital, Montreal, on 27 March 2006 of natural causes after being confined in hospital for six weeks.

CLIFFORD OLSON

By the age of 17, Clifford Olson (b. 1940) had amassed 83 convictions including possession of stolen property, possession of firearms, forgery, obtaining property by false pretences, fraud, parole violation, theft, burglary, robbery and escaping from lawful custody. By the age of 41, he had spent only four years of his adult life as a free man. He was a petty but persistent offender.

It was late afternoon on 17 November 1980 when 12-year-old Christine Weller was out cycling in one of the outer suburbs of Vancouver. She had been with friends in a local shopping centre and was on her way home. Sadly, she never arrived. On Christmas Day, a man walking his dog along a dike found her brutalised body at the back of a refuse dump. Christine had multiple stab wounds in the chest and abdomen and had been throttled with a belt. Christine's death would turn out to be the first in a series of murders of at least 10 more youngsters of both sexes between the ages nine and 18, all from the same area.

Thursday, 16 April 1981 was the date of the second murder. Colleen Marian Daignault, a 13-year-old girl, had told her grandmother that she would be home about 4pm, after spending the night at a girlfriend's house. Around 1pm, while she waited at a bus stop, a car pulled up beside her. She was abducted and was never seen alive again. For some reason, the police treated her as a runaway until 17 September, when her skull and skeletal remains were found in a forest near the American border. Just five days after Colleen's disappearance, a 16-year-old boy went missing.

Daryn Todd Johnsrude disappeared from a shopping centre on Wednesday, 22 April 1981. On 2 May, Daryn's battered body was found crumpled at the bottom of a rocky embankment. He had died from repeated hammer blows to the head. The police were at this point unsure whether the three murders were connected as the ages and sexes of the victims had varied.

On Tuesday, 19 May 1981, Sandra Lynn Wolfsteiner, a pretty, hazel-eyed brunette, went to visit her boyfriend for lunch. The sixteen-year-old made her way to the highway to hitchhike to where her boyfriend worked. She was seen getting into a silver-grey, two-door car driven by a male. Her body was later found hidden in dense bush. She had been hit over the head and her skull crushed. But again, the police were left with no major clues to work with.

On the morning of Sunday, 21 June 1981, Ada Court became the next victim. Ada caught a bus to meet her boyfriend but never reached her destination. That night, a witness saw a man with a pick-up truck bending over a female who was slumped on the floor. The witness went over and, on speaking to the male, realised something was wrong and decided to flee. However, Olson knew he had been seen and chased after the witness, who managed to elude him. Olson then disposed of the body deep in the forest. It would later come to light that the killer's vehicle had been stuck in the mud at least twice while disposing of two bodies. In one case, he even called a tow truck. For some reason, though, the witness didn't report this incident to the police for almost two months.

The turning point in the case came with the disappearance of nine-year-old Simon Partington on Thursday, 2 July 1981. He disappeared only a short distance from where the first victim, Christine Weller, had last been seen alive. Sadly, he was to be the sixth victim of the killer: he was strangled. By now, there was a public outcry with the disappearance of so many young children. However, all the media attention did not deter the killer, and on Thursday, 9 July 1981, Judy Kozma, a 15-year-old girl, became his next victim. She disappeared on the way to an interview.

On Thursday, 23 July 1981, Raymond King became another victim of the killer. Two days later, on 25 July, Judy Kozma's body was found. She had been raped and strangled. The frequency of the killings had now increased. On that same day, Sigrun Arnd, a young German student, disappeared. She was battered to death with a hammer. Two days later, on Monday, 27 July 1981, 15-year-old Terri Lyn Carson also went missing. She was raped and strangled.

During the enquiries the police conducted, one name kept being mentioned – Clifford Olson – but at the time he was just one of many names the police had been given. They did at one point put Olson under surveillance, but lifted this when they believed he knew he was being watched, and they did not have any evidence against him. The police then came up with a simple plan – to speak to Olson informally as part of the overall enquiry. This conversation would be secretly recorded and an offer of a reward mentioned for any information about the murders or disappearances. If Olson was the murderer, and he thought he could make some money from that fact, it was possible that he might go back to the crime scenes in order to retrieve some physical evidence. Or, if he was not the murderer or knew who the murderer was, then maybe he would tell the police. Out of the blue, Olson said he wanted to be paid $3,000 a month. In exchange, he claimed he would provide information about the disappearances.

On 30 July, the killer struck again, abducting and murdering 17-year-old Louise Chartrand. Her body was later found in a shallow grave. She had died from multiple head injuries caused by her skull being smashed with a blunt object. The police began following Olson yet again. This was not easy, as he appeared to adopt anti-surveillance techniques. However, they persisted and were soon rewarded. They followed Olson, who took the ferry over to Vancouver Island and, after burgling two houses, pulled over to the side of the road to pick up two young women hitchhiking. The police continued to follow the car, which turned onto a dirt road, and decided to make their move. Police cars pulled across the entrance to the road to block the car's retreat. Further down the road, into open country, they could see three people standing beside the car passing a bottle around, and they could hear Olson. They moved closer. Olson was heard telling one of the women to take a walk. Olson spotted the police emerging from the undergrowth, sprinted back to the car, and roared back the way he had come, but he was arrested at the roadblock. The women were confused, but safe. Olson claimed they had only stopped so he could relieve himself.

The police could only charge Olson with impaired and dangerous driving, but they impounded his rental car and searched it. They found a green address book with the name of one of the victims, Judy Kozma.

A decision was then taken to arrest Olson for the murders. When he was arrested, only three bodies had been discovered and identified. The police did not yet know exactly how many children had been murdered. He was later charged with the murder of Judy Kozma and he made a full confession to this murder. He then shocked police by wanting to make a financial deal with them, which he called 'Cash for Bodies', involving the other disappearances and murders. He offered to give officers the details and locations of 11 bodies in return for a payment of $100,000. The first body he would give up as a show of good faith. The police agreed to this but it was not made public at the time in order not to prejudice his right to a fair trial. This deal was met with a mixed reaction among the police.

In a period of nine months, Olson killed 11 times. There were also four other murders for which he was suspected but not tried. The fact that he killed both girls and boys hindered the investigation. In the 1980s, the phenomenon of serial killers was poorly understood. Police relied too heavily on their experience in dealing with paedophiles, wrongly assuming that cases were not linked because the victims were of different sexes and ages. It is now known that paedophiles who prey on pre-pubescent children usually have no gender preference, while those preying on older children focus on one gender or the other, not both.

Clifford Olson was brought to trial on 11 January 1982. He initially pleaded not guilty but after three days changed his plea to guilty. He was sentenced to life imprisonment with a recommendation that he should never be granted parole. The families of the victims took legal steps to try to recover the $100,000, which had gone to Olson's wife, whom he had married in May 1981 and who had also fathered his child. After lengthy legal arguments, she was allowed to keep the money.

In Canada, people convicted of first-degree murder are eligible for parole after a maximum of 25 years. Olson reached this limit and applied for parole on 18 July 2006, but was denied it. Under Canadian law, Olson is now entitled to make a case for parole every two years. However, parole was not to be, and he died of cancer in September 2011 aged 71.

ROBERT WILLIAM PICKTON, AKA THE PIG FARM KILLER

Between 1983 and 2001, almost 60 women disappeared from a drug-ridden neighbourhood of Vancouver. It is believed that most were either addicts or prostitutes. During that period of time, Robert Pickton (b. 1949) lured these women to his pig farm in Port Coquitlam, near Vancouver. There it is alleged that he killed them, butchered the bodies and then disposed of the remains both on the farm and at an animal waste rendering plants to which he had access. The police were not to discover the extent of his killings until much later, as many of the women who disappeared had no families and most were never officially reported as missing. Vancouver police began their review of missing women by going even further back to 40 unsolved disappearances of local women, dating from 1971. They came from all walks of life and all parts of Vancouver, but the search for a pattern narrowed the area of disappearances to the same part of Vancouver.

Throughout the enquiry, many names came to the notice of the police. Among these were the Pickton brothers. The pig farm where they lived had been used for illegal raves and parties frequented by local prostitutes. Robert Pickton also had a conviction for attacking a woman with a knife at his farm and was known to visit the area where prostitutes plied their trade. Despite this, police chose not to keep him under closer scrutiny. The worrying factor for the police was that if these missing women had been murdered, where were the bodies, as none had come to light?

On 7 February 2002, the police finally got the break they were looking for. Robert Pickton had been arrested on a charge of possessing illegal firearms and his farm was searched thoroughly by a forensic team. As a result of DNA evidence they found at the farm, he was re-arrested on 22 February, this time facing two counts of first-degree murder of two missing persons, Sereena Abotsway and Mona Wilson, who had vanished three years previously. Syringes linked by DNA to Abotsway were located in the trailer, as were inhalers with her name on in a rubbish bin outside the trailer. The heads, hands and feet of Abotsway were found in April 2002 in buckets that were inside a freezer in a workshop. Wilson's skull, hands and feet were found on 5 May 2002.

Pickton had made no admissions and further DNA evidence from the farm identified three more missing women, Jacqueline McDonell, Heather Bottomley and Dianne Rock, adding three more murder charges to the list. A sixth murder charge for another woman, Andrea Joesbury, was filed against Pickton six days later when her head, hands and feet were found in April 2002 in buckets inside a freezer in a workshop.

In the adjacent pig slaughterhouse, jewellery was found in the outbuilding and identified as belonging to Joesbury. A tool mark expert examined various reciprocating saws and blades seized from the building, but he was unable to say conclusively that the blades had been used to cut three bisected human skulls identified as Joesbury, Abotsway and Wilson. A seventh murder charge was filed against Pickton when the jawbone of Brenda Wolfe was found on his farm.

In a motor home on the property, a blood spatter expert deduced that a mattress found inside had been the scene of a major blood-letting event and that marks indicated that something had been dragged from the rear of the vehicle to the front. Forensic experts tested 235,000 items taken from the property, in an effort to collect and identify human DNA.

The public were by now asking difficult questions about the actions of the police. Why had the searches of Pickton's property in 1997 and 1998 failed to uncover any evidence? More to the point, how could he have abducted and murdered additional victims between 1999 and 2001, when he should have been under police surveillance?

Pickton was charged with four more murders on Wednesday, 2 October 2002, making a total of 15. He indicated his intention to plead not guilty to all charges and a trial date was set for November 2002, but detectives and forensic experts were not finished with their search of the farm. They indicated that it could take up to another year for the full examination to be completed, and the trial date was put back to 2005. As the examination continued, more female victims were linked to

Pickton's farm, making a total of 30 women whose remains have been found there. Some have not been possible to identify. Police found human body parts in freezers used to store unsold meat. They also discovered remains in a wood chipper, with the victims' bodies turned into pig feed. It was suggested that there was a possibility that the human remains from some of Pickton's victims may have been mixed with pork meat and processed for human consumption.

The trial of Robert Pickton finally opened in Vancouver on 22 January 2007 when he pleaded not guilty to murdering 26 women. These charges were later reduced from 26 to six by the judge to assist the jury and with regard to the intended length of trial. All 26 women Pickton was charged with killing were on a list of 65 women missing from Vancouver's Downtown Eastside between 1978 and 2001. The remaining six charges related to the following victims:

Sereena Abotsway, 29, who was reported missing by her stepmother on 22 August 2001. Forensic evidence showed she had been shot with a .22 calibre handgun. Her dismembered head, hands and feet were found in a freezer on 4 April 2002 inside Pickton's workshop.

Mona Wilson, 26, who disappeared from the Downtown Eastside in November 2001. Her partial remains were found on 4 June 2002 during the Pickton farm search. Her blood was also found in Pickton's motor home, parked behind his workshop. She also had been shot.

Andrea Joesbury, 22, who was reported missing by her doctor on 5 June 2001. Her dismembered head, hands and feet were found in the same freezer as Abotsway's remains on 4 April 2002.

Brenda Wolfe, 32, who was last seen on 1 February 1999, but wasn't reported missing until 25 April 2000. Police found skeletal remains – her jawbone – and five of her teeth in the soil and debris beside the slaughterhouse where Pickton killed and butchered pigs.

Georgina Papin was last seen in March 1999, aged 34. Police

found several of her hand bones in the slaughterhouse. DNA testing matched the bones to Papin. A witness would also testify that her body was hanging on a meat hook at the farm and that Pickton was seen skinning the body.

Marnie Frey, aged 25, was reported missing on 30 August 1997. Her partial remains, including a jawbone, were found buried outside the slaughterhouse on 23 August 2002.

It is alleged that all the victims were murdered at Pickton's pig farm, which came to be known as 'Piggy Palace'. At the opening of the trial, the jury were told they would hear evidence about what was found on Pickton's property, including skulls cut in half with hands and feet stuffed inside. The remains of another victim were stuffed in a refuse sack in the bottom of a rubbish bin, and her bloodstained clothing was found in the trailer in which Pickton lived. Part of one victim's jawbone and teeth were found in the ground beside the slaughterhouse, and a .22 calibre revolver and dildo containing both his and a victim's DNA were in his laundry room. In a videotaped recording played for the jury, Pickton claimed to have attached the dildo to his weapon as a makeshift silencer. Other items found were boxes of .357 Magnum handgun ammunition, night-vision goggles, two pairs of fox-fur-lined handcuffs, a syringe with blue liquid inside, (later identified as screenwash) and 'Spanish Fly', an aphrodisiac.

In addition, the police had videotape of Pickton's friend Scott Chubb saying that Pickton had told him a good way to kill a female heroin addict was to inject her with screenwash. During interviews, a second tape was played for Pickton, in which an associate named Andrew Bellwood said Pickton mentioned killing prostitutes by handcuffing and strangling them, then bleeding and gutting them before feeding them to pigs. However, defence lawyer Peter Ritchie said the jury should be sceptical of Chubb and Bellwood's credibility as witnesses.

By this time, the police had obtained witness statements from a friend of Pickton, who stated that he saw Pickton skinning the body of Georgina Papin, who was hanging on a meat hook at the farm. Other damning testimony came from an undercover police officer who had been put in a cell with Pickton. The officer, who cannot be identified under a court order, told the 12-member jury that he had posed as a man who was facing attempted murder charges and had gained the trust of Robert Pickton during their incarceration in February 2002. Pickton had told the undercover officer that he had killed 49 women and was caught before he could reach his goal of 50. The cell, which they shared, was set up for audio and video recording.

The defence case was formulated around the premise that the prosecution witnesses were not credible – all were drug addicts with previous criminal convictions. The defence also went to great lengths to suggest to the jury that another person had planted the remains of the victims.

The jury retired on 30 November to deliberate on all the charges against Pickton after hearing evidence from 128 witnesses over a 10-month period. On 9 December 2007, the jury returned to court to deliver its verdict. When the foreman of the jury announced the first verdict of not guilty on the charge of the first-degree murder of Sereena Abotsway there were gasps and screams from within the public gallery from relatives of the victims, but these quickly subsided when the foreman then announced they found Pickton guilty of second-degree murder. The jury foreman also announced that Pickton was guilty of second-degree murder for the killings of the five other women: Georgina Papin, Andrea Joesbury, Marnie Frey, Brenda Wolfe and Mona Wilson. The verdict reflected the fact that the jury believed Pickton intended to kill the women but that the murders were not planned. A conviction for first-degree murder requires the jury to find that the murders were planned and deliberate.

Canada does not have the death penalty, but second-degree murder automatically carries a mandatory life sentence, and so the judge asked the members of the jury whether they wished to make a recommendation on how long Pickton should serve before being eligible for parole – between 10 and 25 years – but they made no recommendation.

The case was then adjourned for the judge to hear submissions from the Crown and defence on the appropriate parole ineligibility period in this case. The Crown indicated it would urge the judge to impose the maximum 25 years before Pickton could be considered for parole. Killers convicted of two or more murders are not eligible to be considered for early parole under the so-called 'faint hope clause' after serving at least 15 years.

On 11 December 2007, the trial judge Justice Williams sentenced Pickton to life imprisonment on all six charges. In sentencing Pickton, he told him he would have to serve 25 years of a life sentence before he could apply for parole. This is the maximum sentence that can be imposed for second-degree murder. Justice Williams said: 'Mr Pickton's conduct was murderous and repeatedly so. I cannot know the details of what happened. I know this: each of these women were [sic] murdered and their remains were dismembered. What happened to them was senseless and despicable. There is nothing I can say to adequately express the revulsion the community has with regards to these killings.'

Following sentencing, Pickton's defence lawyers lodged an appeal against his conviction. Pickton still stood accused of first-degree murder in the deaths of 20 other women and is suspected of killing many more.

On 7 January 2008, there was another twist in the Pickton case. In a surprise announcement, Attorney General Wally Oppal announced that the Crown, on behalf of the criminal justice branch, had also lodged an appeal with the Court of Appeal against the six convictions against Pickton, despite the maximum sentence he received. Oppal said at a press conference that the Crown believed Pickton was guilty of first-degree murder. 'The Crown's position has always been this was a proper case for first-degree murder and that a certain amount of the evidence excluded went to that,' he said. In its application to appeal to the Court of Appeal, the Crown said that the judge had made several errors in law. Among those errors was improperly instructing the jury. The Crown maintains that the jury should have been told they could find Pickton guilty of planning and deliberation if they held him responsible for the dismemberment and disposal of victims' remains. Oppal said the Crown filed an appeal because Pickton had also lodged an appeal that, if granted, would allow him another trial but this time on second-degree murder charges only. The Crown would be asking for the Court of Appeal to order a new trial to hear all 26 counts of first-degree murder, stating that the trial judge, Justice James Williams, had erred when he severed the counts to hear only six of the charges.

On 30 March 2009 Pickton began his appeal against the six counts of second-degree murder in the British Columbia Court of Appeal. His defence lawyers were asking the court to grant a retrial on the second-degree murder charges. The appeal was heard by three senior judges.

The appeal hearing concluded on 11 April. Following lengthy deliberations on Thursday 27 June the Appeal Court finally announced its decision. In a two-to-one decision, it rejected Pickton's appeal of his second-degree murder convictions. Due to the verdict not being unanimous, this left the door open for Pickton to make a further appeal to the Supreme Court. Pickton's lawyer Gil McKinnon later confirmed the appeal would go ahead based on dissenting reasons by one of the Appeal Court judges Justice Ian Donald.

Justice Donald said in his written reasons that the original trial judge had not instructed the jury on the issue of aiding and abetting and how it might apply to the Pickton case. He said he would have ordered a new trial. The two other judges rejected defence claims that there were numerous errors in the trial judge's instructions to the jury and found the verdict safe.

However, Justice Donald disagreed and concluded that there was 'a misdirection amounting to a serious error of law'. Much of the appeal arguments surrounded a question from the jury on the sixth day of deliberations, and how the trial judge handled the question. Jurors wanted to know if they could find Pickton guilty if they found that he acted indirectly in the murders.

The judge accepted the Crown's position on the question and re-instructed the jury, telling jury members that if they found that Pickton had shot three of his alleged victims, or was otherwise an active participant in the killings, then they could find him guilty.

'The trial judge did not provide the jury with an instruction on the law of aiding and abetting,' Donald wrote. 'In my opinion this was an error of law.'

Following a lengthy appeals process, on 30 July 2010, the Supreme Court of Canada rendered its decision, dismissing Pickton's appeal and affirming his conviction. The argument that Pickton should be granted a new trial was unanimously rejected by the justices of the Supreme Court of Canada.

A spokesman for the Crown announced that the prosecution of Pickton on the 20 other murder charges would likely be discontinued. 'In reaching this position,' the spokesman said, 'the crown has taken into account the fact that any additional convictions could not result in any increase to the sentence that Mr Pickton has already received.'

Families of the victims had varied reactions to this announcement. Some were disappointed that Pickton would never be convicted of the 20 other murders, while others were relieved that the gruesome details of the murders would not be aired in court.

CHAPTER 3

GERMANY

JOACHIM KROLL, AKA THE RUHR CANNIBAL

In 1955, at the age of 22, Joachim Kroll (b. 1933) committed his first rape, and then went on to murder that same year. His first victim was a 19-year-old blonde he met as she was walking along the road. He invited her to walk with him into the woods, apparently promising her something, and then attempted to kiss her. When she struggled against him, he dragged her into a barn and stabbed her in the neck, then raped her. To make certain she was dead, he strangled her. He also used a long-bladed knife to disembowel her. An autopsy indicated that while he had raped her in a frenzy, this mutilation had occurred post-mortem. Her body was discovered five days after she went missing.

Twelve months elapsed before Kroll killed again. His victim was 12-year-old Erika Schuletter: he raped and killed her. In 1959, after moving to Duisburg, Kroll killed two women in quick succession, in different towns. By now, he had the thirst for more blood. On 16 June, he accosted Klara Tesmer as she walked near some fields. He hit her hard on the head. She continued to struggle as he tried to remove her clothing and they slipped together down the embankment. He grabbed her by the throat to keep her from resisting and throttled her until she no longer moved. He undressed her and raped her motionless body. The more women he killed, the more brutal and horrific his actions became.

On 26 July 1959, he came across Manuela Knodt, aged 16. After raping and strangling her, he stripped her of clothing, then, using his long-bladed knife, he removed pieces of flesh from her thighs and buttocks, which he took home, cooked and ate. He had also masturbated over her, leaving a significant deposit of semen on her face and pubic area. This led police to suspect, wrongly, that more than one person had attacked her.

By now, Kroll believed he could commit the perfect crime. The MO he used made him believe there were few risks. He would take a train or bus to an area that seemed isolated and then he would get out and walk until he spotted a lone female. By now, it was 1962 and he was still active. One of his victims in that year was a 12-year-old girl, Barbara Bruder. She was on her way to a playground near her home in Burscheid, near Hamburg. He spotted her and dragged her into a field where he raped and strangled her. Her remains were never found. During that year he murdered several other young girls in similar fashion. With some of them he again removed pieces of their flesh, taking them home and eating them. Because he was travelling from town to town, the police failed to form any direct link between the murders. In one case a local man came under the suspicion of the police and when he was found hanged they believed the killer had committed suicide.

Three years passed before Kroll was to kill again, then, on 22 August 1965, he approached a courting couple in their car near a lake outside Duisburg. Twenty-five-year-old Hermann Schmitz was with his girlfriend, Rita. Kroll snuck up on the car and used his knife to puncture a tyre to draw Schmitz outside. He had already planned to render Schmitz incapable of defending his girlfriend. He pounced, stabbing Schmitz several times directly in the heart. However, Schmitz's girlfriend reacted immediately, jumping into the driver's seat and sounding the horn. She started the car and tried to drive off, striking Kroll with the car. This panicked him and he made off, though sadly her boyfriend died from the attack. Following this, Kroll committed no further murders until 13 September 1966, when he came upon 20-year-old Ursula Rohling. He met her in a park, talked with her and then dragged her into the bushes, where he strangled and raped her. Her body was found two days later.

Kroll then changed his MO. On 22 December 1966, he abducted five-year-old Ilona Harke. He took her by train to Wuppertal where he made her walk with him until he found a ditch. There he forced her head into the water until she stopped struggling. He then also removed pieces of flesh from her body, taking them home, cooking and eating them. About six months later, Kroll tried to murder again, but this time he was disturbed and almost caught. In June 1967, he met a 10-year-old girl by the name of Gabriele on a park bench. Kroll had some pornography with him. He persuaded the girl to accompany him to a meadow, where he promised to show her a rabbit, but instead he flashed his book of erotic pictures. She tried to run away, but he detained her, pulling her into a secluded area where he started to strangle her. However, a nearby coalmine sounded its siren for a change of shifts. Kroll panicked when he looked up and saw some of the miners walking nearby. He fled, leaving the girl for dead. However, she was found still alive and taken to a hospital, where she remained in a coma for more than a week. On waking, she told her parents what had happened, but they declined to report the incident at the time, perhaps afraid that her attacker would return.

In 1969 and 1970, Kroll murdered two more young victims in similar fashion. Ten months later, he followed 13-year-old Jutta Rahn as she alighted from a train in Breitscheid and started to walk home through a wooded area. He raped and strangled her. Then, in 1976, he raped and strangled 10-year-old Karin Toepfer. By now, he was becoming complacent and he was tired of travelling. It was then that he committed murder in his own domain.

On 3 July 1976, in Laar, a town outside Duisburg, four-year-old Marion Ketter vanished from a playground. It was her disappearance that finally led to the arrest of Kroll, and would finally end his 21 years of deviant, grisly murders. Kroll was living in the town and became known as Uncle Joachim to the children who played near his apartment block. He would befriend them, giving them sweets. He lived alone, but had a collection of dolls and always bought the latest electronic gadgets. He kept dolls specifically for the girls, whom he liked. But what the local residents didn't know was that he was a sadistic sexual predator living among them.

Shortly after Marion Ketter went missing, one of Kroll's neighbours met him in the building. The neighbour was going to use the toilet. Kroll told the neighbour not to use it because it was blocked. When asked what it was blocked with, Kroll replied: 'With guts'. The neighbour didn't believe him and went to look. He saw that the bowl was blood-red and had a foul odour. Looking more closely, the neighbour believed he could see some sort of skin tissue floating to the top. What he saw did resemble guts and he was puzzled as to why anyone would dispose of meat down the toilet. He immediately called the police, who sealed it off as a crime scene. The bowl was removed and the contents poured into a bucket. To their shock they found what appeared to be body parts: lungs, kidneys, intestines and a heart, together with pieces of flesh.

Kroll was then arrested and when interviewed confessed to 13 murders and one attempted murder. However, due to the passage of time, police were unable to provide sufficient evidence on all charges and he was only charged with eight murders and one other attempt. In April 1982, he was finally given nine life sentences. However, on 1 July 1991, at the age of just 58, Joachim Kroll died from a heart attack in his prison cell.

PETER KÜRTEN, AKA THE DÜSSELDORF VAMPIRE

Like so many other serial killers, Peter Kürten (b. 1883) was involved in lesser crimes before turning to murder. By the age of 16, he was stealing and had run away from home. He was soon to receive the first of 27 prison sentences, which would last 24 years of his life. The crimes were petty at first – mostly stealing food and clothing.

In 1899, Kürten began living with an ill-treated, masochistic prostitute twice his age. His 'education' was thus completed and he transferred his inherent sadistic impulses from torturing animals to human beings. He took to crimes of burglary, entering rooms in bars and taverns while the owners were working.

On 25 May 1913, having entered a bar intending to steal and while searching the rooms, he came upon a 10-year-old girl sleeping in one of the rooms. Kürten seized the girl by the neck and strangled her with both hands. The child struggled for some time before lapsing into unconsciousness. He then drew her head over the edge of the bed and penetrated her genitals with his fingers. He had a small, sharp pocketknife with him and he held the child's head and cut her throat. This was to be the first of many vicious and savage murders, which would later bring terror to the residents of Düsseldorf.

In 1921, Kürten married and for a time resisted the urge to kill, but he was later to return to Düsseldorf and wreak havoc. Around 9 February 1929, he abducted an eight-year-old girl, Rosa Ohliger. He stabbed her body 13 times and also inflicted stab wounds to her vagina, as well as ejaculating over her. He then made an unsuccessful attempt to burn the body, and it was later found under a hedge. He was later to reveal that he got a thrill from ejaculating over the dead bodies.

Only five days after the murder of Rosa Ohliger, a 45-year-old mechanic named Rudolf Scheer was found stabbed to death on a road in the Düsseldorf suburb of Flingern. He had 20 knife wounds, including several in the head. On the following day, Kürten returned to the scene of his attack and even spoke with a detective at the murder scene. Although suspicious, the policeman clearly had no reason for concern and so spoke frankly about the crime: a fantastic cameo episode, which was confirmed during the trial by the detective in question.

On 21 August, Kürten attacked and stabbed three people. None was fatally injured. By now, he was taking enormous risks. On the night of 23 August 1929, hundreds of people were enjoying the annual fair in the ancient town of Flehe. At around 10.30pm, two foster sisters, five-year-old Gertrude Hamacher and 14-year-old Louise Lenzen, left the fair and started walking through the adjacent allotments to their home. Kürten saw them and followed them along a footpath. He stopped the children and asked whether Louise would run an errand for him. She agreed and ran back towards the fairground. Kürten then strangled the second girl before cutting her throat. Louise returned a few moments later and was dragged off the footpath before being strangled and decapitated.

The following afternoon, he accosted a girl and tried to persuade her to have sex with him. When she said 'I'd rather die' he answered 'die then' and stabbed her. However, she survived and was able to give a good description of her assailant. He then raped and battered to death a young girl named Ida Reuter in September and, on 12 October, murdered a servant girl named Elizabeth Dorrier by beating her to death. This was followed by hammer attacks on two other women, both on 25 October. On 7 November, he abducted five-year-old Gertrude Albermann. He stabbed her 35 times and strangled her. Following this, he sent a letter and a map to a local newspaper setting out where the body could be found. The period between February and May 1930 saw him continue to carry out non-fatal attacks. By now, terror had gripped the residents of Düsseldorf and Kürten was now dubbed the Vampire – but he was still roaming free to kill.

On 14 May 1930, Maria Budlick left the city of Cologne in search of work in nearby Düsseldorf. On the platform at Düsseldorf station, she was accosted by a man who offered to show her the way to a girls' hostel. After walking for a short distance, he started to lead her towards the park. She suddenly remembered the newspaper stories of the murderer and refused to go any further and they started to argue. Kürten, who happened to be passing by, heard the argument and intervened. Eventually, the first man left her alone with Kürten, who then offered to let her stay in his room. They went back to his room and she suddenly said she did not want sexual intercourse and asked if he knew where there was somewhere else she could sleep. The pair went by tram to Worringerplatz and walked deep into the Grafenberger Woods. Here, Kürten grabbed her with one hand by the neck and asked whether he could have her. They had sex and then he took her back to the station. He did not kill her because he knew that a policeman had seen him with her at the station. In the meantime, she had written a letter to her friend back home detailing the attack. Her friend then informed the police. It took only a short time for the police to trace Budlick. She remembered Kürten's address and three days later took the police to his apartment. At the time, Kürten was not at home, but when he arrived back, he entered the house and began climbing the stairs towards her. He looked briefly startled, but carried on to his room and shut the door behind him. A few moments later, he left the house with his hat pulled down over his eyes, passing the two plainclothes policemen standing in the street, and disappeared around a corner. He was now of the belief that his arrest was imminent.

Kürten went to find his wife and confessed everything to her. She, on his instructions, went to the police to tell all. He had told her that she could then claim the high reward put out for the arrest of the Vampire. She had arranged to meet her husband outside a local church at 3pm. By that time, the whole area had been surrounded and, as Kürten appeared, he smiled at the officers and offered no resistance.

When interviewed, he confessed to 79 attacks and detailed almost every one. However, the police looked on this confession with scepticism, as they did not have enough evidence to substantiate all of them. As a result, he was charged with only nine murders and seven attempted murders. His trial opened on 13 April 1931.

A special shoulder-high cage was built inside the courtroom to prevent his escape and behind it were arranged some of the grisly exhibits of the Kürten 'museum'. There were skulls of his victims and body parts displaying the injuries inflicted by the killer, each meticulously presented in chronological order. Knives, rope, scissors and a hammer were on show, along with many articles of clothing and a spade he had used to bury one woman. He initially pleaded not guilty and retracted his confession. He said he had confessed to the crimes only to secure the reward for his wife. However, two months into his trial he changed his plea to guilty again.

Kürten told the court his motive for these crimes had been that he wanted to take revenge on society for the wrongs he had suffered in prison. The judges asked him if he had a conscience, and Kürten replied 'I have none. Never have I felt any misgiving in my soul; never did I think to myself that what I did was bad, even though human society condemns it. My blood and the blood of my victims will be on the heads of my torturers. There must be a Higher Being who gave in the first place the first vital spark to life. That Higher Being would deem my actions good since I revenged injustice. The punishments I have suffered have destroyed all my feelings as a human being. That was why I had no pity for my victims.' Inevitably the question of his sanity, and his legal responsibility, became a major issue of the trial. It was decided by experts that he was not criminally insane and was therefore responsible in law for his crimes. The jury found him guilty and he was sentenced to death by guillotine.

On 2 July 1932, Peter Kürten went to his death at a guillotine erected in the yard of the Klingelputz Prison. Kürten expressed his last earthly desire on the way to the yard: 'Tell me,' he asked the prison psychiatrist, 'after my head has been chopped off, will I still be able to hear, at least for a moment, the sound of my own blood gushing from the stump of my neck?' He savoured this thought for a while, and then added 'That would be the pleasure to end all pleasures.'

CHAPTER 4

JAPAN

TSUTOMU MIYAZAKI, AKA THE LITTLE CHILD MURDERER

Miyazaki's premature birth left him with deformed hands, which were permanently gnarled and fused directly to the wrists, necessitating him to move his entire forearm in order to rotate the hand. As a result of this deformity, he was ostracised at school and consequently kept to himself.

Miyazaki would turn out to be a murderer influenced by pornography and anime. As a teenager, he became a loner who devoured fantasy and comic books. Highly sexed, he moved into the world of child pornography, collecting videos. He also had a craving for horror films.

He committed his first murder at the age of 26 and his first victim was four-year-old Mari Konno, on 22 August 1988. He took her into a park, photographed her and strangled her. He then undressed her and left her naked body in the hills near his home, taking her clothing with him. He allowed the corpse to decompose. He later returned to the body and chopped off the hands and feet, which he then took home and kept in his wardrobe. These were recovered on his arrest. He charred the remaining bones in his furnace, ground them into powder and sent them to the victim's family in a box, along with several of her teeth, photos of her clothes and a postcard reading: 'Mari. Cremated. Bones. Investigate. Prove.'

Undetected, he went on to kill again. In October the same year, he saw Masami Yoshizawa, aged seven, walking by herself. He enticed the girl into his car and drove to the location of his first murder, where the skeletal remains of his first victim still laid undiscovered. He strangled the little girl and then he sexually abused the body, taking the girl's clothing with him when he left the scene.

On 12 December, Miyazaki murdered another four-year-old girl, Erika Nanba. Again enticing her into his car, he photographed her before strangling her and dumping her body. For the next few months he kept a low profile. He believed he might have been seen at the murder location. In the interim period, Erika's body was found and witnesses described the car they had seen in the area. The police also learnt that each of the families of the three murdered girls had received strange phone calls: always, the caller remained silent. They also received gruesome postcards with letters cut from magazines to form words such as 'cold' and 'death'.

On 6 June 1989, Miyazaki abducted Ayako Nomoto, aged five, from a park after he'd taken photographs of her. Having strangled the girl, he took the body home. Then he dismembered the corpse, consumed some of the flesh and disposed of the remains in a cemetery. The body was soon discovered and quickly identified. He then made his first mistake. In July 1989, he approached two sisters and lured one away. The other ran home to get help. Their father went to where Miyazaki had last been seen and caught him in the act of photographing the child's genitals. At the same time, the police arrived as he ran to his car. When questioned, he confessed to killing the four children. In the end, Miyazaki was found to have multiple personality disorder and schizophrenia, but was nevertheless deemed sane. He was sentenced to death by hanging. Following an appeal, that sentence was upheld early in 2006. He was finally executed by hanging on 17 June 2008.

CHAPTER 5

RUSSIA

VLADIMIR BRATISLAV, AKA THE BEAST OF LYSVA

Vladimir Bratislav's reign of terror started in 1997 in Lysva, a town in the mid-Urals with a population today of 65,000 inhabitants. He stalked the parks and nightclubs, and in March 1997 he raped and killed his first victim. One week later, he struck again. This time, his victim was a woman who was jogging in the park, early in the morning. He overpowered her and raped her, and bit her breasts, before eventually strangling her. Bratislav was the son of a prosperous working manager who, ironically, offered a reward to anyone who could give any information about the case. Bratislav's brother was a member of the Russian civil army, the militia. Vladimir sometimes went along with his brother and other policemen in search of the serial killer. However, between March and July he committed two more murders in similar fashion.

On the night of 28 July 1997, Bratislav took his fourth victim, Elena Lyzhina, who had made the mistake of making eye contact with him. He waited for her, raped her and then savagely attacked her eyes in a vicious frenzy which left her permanently blind. On 4 August, he struck again, laying in wait for Olga Kosenko until she left a nightclub early in the morning. She was later found raped and strangled. His next two victims were women he knew. On 17 August, he started attacking 18-year-old Anna Marakulina from behind, until he realised that he knew her. At first, he tried to make his attack seem like a joke, but she didn't believe him, so he raped her and beat her about the head until she was dead. Five days later, he killed another girl he knew, 17-year-old Maria Shetsova. Again, he waited outside a night club and then suggested they go for a walk. In a nearby park, he overpowered and strangled her. He bit her breasts and pushed a wooden stick into her mouth. One week later, he successfully attacked Alvira Kanzeparova. He raped and strangled her and tore out her eyes. However, his next intended victim would lead to his arrest.

On 10 June 1998, he attacked Natalya Mezentseva, but for some strange reason, instead of killing her, he only took her handbag and ran off. Natalya recognised him and called the police. At first, they thought it had been nothing more than a theft, but several days later, another woman was assaulted in the park in similar circumstances and severely beaten. When Natalya drove with some police officers around the park, she saw Bratislav, recognised him, and he was arrested.

When questioned, Bratislav admitted the murders and told police he had committed many more than the 10 he was subsequently charged with. He claimed that he only wanted to rob his victims of their jewellery, though he never actually sold any. He said he had to kill them once they had seen his face. He could not explain the fact that he didn't sell the jewellery. He also claimed that he raped and mutilated his victims to distract the police. He said that he removed their eyes to ensure that they would not identify him. He raped and killed only those women who wouldn't cooperate. Psychiatrists have since concluded that his atrocities stemmed from a humiliating sexual experience in his teenage years. When he was 14, an older woman rejected him, and as a result he couldn't sustain an erection. At trial he was found guilty and sentenced to life imprisonment.

THE EVIL WITHIN
ANDREI CHIKATILO, AKA THE ROSTOV RIPPER

Andrei Chikatilo (b. 1936) had a traumatic childhood. His older brother died in a famine and the body had been cannibalised by starving neighbours. During World War II, Chikatilo had many fantasies involving leading German captives into the woods and executing them, a scenario that would later have parallels with his murders.

If the grisly death of his brother were not bad enough, Chikatilo grew up short-sighted and half-blind, and suffered from a sexual dysfunction that began in adolescence and rendered him periodically impotent. Though he married in the early 1960s and fathered two children, Chikatilo persisted in believing that he had been blinded and castrated from birth, a condition that later fuelled morbid fantasies of violent revenge.

His first sexual encounter came when he was 15. He jumped on a young girl and wrestled her to the ground, ejaculating as she struggled in his grasp. This incident helped to foster in him a lifelong association between sex and violent aggression.

In 1978, at the age of 42, Chikatilo committed his first documented murder. On 22 December, he lured a nine-year-old girl to an old shed and attempted to rape her. When the girl struggled, he stabbed her to death, inflicting 22 wounds on her body. He ejaculated during the process of knifing the child. He threw her body into a river, where she was found on Christmas Eve. From then on, he was only able to achieve sexual arousal and orgasm through stabbing and slashing women and children to death. Russian justice was swift but often inaccurate. A young man, Alexsandr Kravchenko, a paroled sex offender, was arrested and later tried and executed for this particular murder.

Chikatilo did not murder again until 1982. His next victim was 17-year-old Larisa Tkachenko, who was cutting class in Rostov when Chikatilo approached her and persuaded her to join him in the nearby woods for sex. She made the grave mistake of laughing at his failure to perform, whereupon Chikatilo strangled her, biting at her throat, arms and breasts. He bit off one of her nipples and swallowed it in a frenzy then forced a large stick into her vagina.

Chikatilo claimed his third victim on 12 June 1982. Twelve-year-old Lyuba Biryuk was lured from the village of Zaplavskaya. He stabbed her 40 times in the woods, and her wounds included mutilation of the eyes, which would become a standard Chikatilo trademark. More than a year elapsed before her skeletal remains were found in July 1983. In the meantime, Chikatilo claimed three more victims, including his first male victim, nine-year-old Oleg Podzhidaev. While Oleg's body was never found, we know from Chikatilo's subsequent confession that the child was emasculated; his genitals were carried from the murder scene, in what became another signature of Andrei Chikatilo's crimes.

During that year Chikatilo killed seven times. He established a pattern of approaching runaways and young vagrants at bus or railway stations and enticing them to leave. He took his victims on a short journey to a nearby forest each time before murdering them. By this time, he had also started to take out the eyes of his victims as well as mutilating the bodies and removing organs.

In June 1983, he murdered four more adult females – prostitutes or homeless women who could be lured with promises of alcohol or money. Chikatilo usually attempted intercourse with these victims, but was often unable to get an erection, which would send him into a murderous fury, especially if the woman mocked his inability to perform. He would achieve orgasm only when he stabbed the victim to death. The child victims were of both sexes and Chikatilo would lure them away with his friendly, talkative manner by promising them toys or sweets. By this time, the police had found six bodies but their attempts to apprehend the killer had failed.

On 22 February 1984, Chikatilo was charged with stealing a roll of linoleum from his workplace. Seven months later, with that case still pending, he was arrested for licentious behaviour in public, after policemen watched him accosting women at the

Rostov bus station. Chikatilo was sentenced to 15 days imprisonment on that charge, but he remained in jail for the next three months, while detectives questioned him about the murders. Cleared of suspicion when his blood type (A) inexplicably failed to match the semen found on the bodies, Chikatilo was finally convicted of the linoleum theft in December 1984. He was sentenced to a year in jail, but a sympathetic judge gave him credit for time served since his September arrest and Chikatilo was freed on the spot.

By the end of 1984, police believed the same killer was responsible for at least 24 murders. The police posted extra patrols and plainclothes officers at many public transport stops. Chikatilo found new work and kept a low profile. He did not kill again until August 1985, when he murdered two women in separate incidents. He committed no further murders until May 1988 when, on a business trip to the Ukraine, he killed a young boy whose body was discovered in the woods not far from a train station. He had been buggered and his orifices were stuffed with dirt. He also bore numerous knife wounds and a blow to the skull, and his penis had been cut off. Chikatilo went on to kill again in July and September of that year.

In 1988, Chikatilo resumed his killing, this time away from the Rostov area where he knew there was a large police presence. He murdered a woman in Krasny-Sulin in April 1989 and went on to kill another eight people that year, including two victims in Shakhty. Again, there was a long period between killings, then he murdered seven boys and two women between January and November 1990. The discovery of one of the bodies near Leskhoz station led to increased police patrols. On 6 November 1990, Chikatilo killed and mutilated Sveta Korostik. He was stopped by police returning from the murder scene but allowed to go. However, a report on this suspicious encounter returned Chikatilo's name to the investigation. On 20 November 1990, after police again observed his suspicious behaviour, he was arrested and interrogated, finally confessing his crimes.

Between 30 November and 5 December 1990, Chikatilo confessed to 56 murders. Three of the victims had been buried and could not be found or identified, so Chikatilo was not charged with these crimes. The number of crimes Chikatilo confessed to shocked the police, who had listed only 36 killings in their investigation. A number of victims had not been linked to the others because they were murdered far from Chikatilo's other killing fields, while others had not been linked because they were buried and not found until Chikatilo led the police to their shallow graves subsequent to his arrest.

After being deemed sane, Chikatilo finally went to trial on 14 April 1992. During the trial, he was famously kept in a cage in the centre of the courtroom; it was constructed for his own protection from the relatives of the deceased. The trial ended in July and sentencing was adjourned until 15 October when he was found guilty of 52 of the 53 murders and sentenced to death. His execution took place on 15 February 1994. He was shot in the back of the head with a single bullet.

ALEXANDER PICHUSHKIN, AKA THE CHESSBOARD KILLER

In July 2003, citizens of Moscow were gripped by fear when, in a short space of time, 10 women were murdered. By September there were two more murders, fuelling anxieties that a serial killer was at large. All the victims were young and had been attacked while walking home alone. All had either been strangled or had their throats cut. Soon a series of murders in another part of the city would cause even more panic among the residents of Moscow.

This second series of murders involved elderly victims who were attacked and murdered by a killer wielding a heavy metal instrument, which he used to crush their skulls. At the time, the police suspected that there were two different serial killers at work due to the two different profiles of victims and the two different killing methods used. As time progressed, the police remained clueless as to the identity of either killer or any possible motives.

It was not until June 2006 that the police finally made a breakthrough that would lead to the arrest and conviction of a killer who had been active since 1992. In June 2006, Moscow police investigated the murder of a 36-year-old female supermarket worker, Marina Moskalyova. Her body had been found in a local park near where she worked. Police enquiries at her home uncovered a note she had left her son, telling him that she was going out with a male co-worker by the name of Alexander Pichushkin (b. 1964). The note also contained his phone number. Police obtained CCTV footage from a train, which showed Pichushkin walking with the victim.

The police arrested Pichushkin at the apartment where he lived with his mother. He initially denied his involvement, but after he was shown the CCTV footage he started to confess, not only to the murder for which he was under arrest, but to other murders as far back as 1992. Following his confessions, he led police to some of the locations where he had hidden bodies. During the interviews that followed, he claimed to have murdered up to 62 people. He told police that his ultimate goal was to surpass the death toll of another Russian serial killer, Andrei Chikatilo, whose official murder count was 53. Pichushkin intended to kill 64 victims, to match the number of squares on a chessboard, which is why he became known as the Chessboard Killer.

He told police that with regard to the murder of Marina Moskalyova he had taken a risk, but stated that he had been in the mood for murder that night, so he just did it. During further interviews, he told investigators that he often targeted the elderly. He would invite his intended victim to drink with him in a secluded area of the park and, once they were drunk, he would crush their heads with a hammer or a metal pipe, then either leave them where they were or dispose of the bodies by dumping them in a sewer pit, sometimes alive but too inebriated to save themselves.

In his 2006 confession, televised to prove that it was not coerced, Pichushkin described his first murder, way back in 1992 when he was a teenager. (Coincidentally, this was the same year that Chikatilo was tried and convicted.) Pichushkin's first victim was a young boy whom he'd pushed out of a window. Police had questioned Pichushkin but saw the case as suicide. It was nine years before he committed his next murder in 2001, and quickly achieved serial killer status with the slaying of many elderly people in a local park. He believed that he managed to evade detection because most of his victims were homeless people with no one to report them missing. Three survived his murder attempts, however, and one of them later identified Pichushkin as the perpetrator.

Following his arrest, Pichushkin was medically assessed and deemed fit to stand trial. He was charged with 49 murders and three attempted murders. At the 15-minute preliminary hearing on 13 August 2007, from a glass cage, he asked to be tried by a jury rather than before a panel of judges. His request was granted. The date set for the trial was 13 September 2007, and it would be open to the public. Pichushkin had admitted to 63 murders. However, the police had found no evidence to support a number that high, although when they searched Pichushkin's home they found a drawing of a chessboard on which he had placed dates for 62 of the 64 squares.

Following a lengthy trial, Pichushkin was found guilty of 49 murders and was sentenced to life in prison with the first 15 years to be spent in solitary confinement. When asked by the judge if he understood his sentence, Pichushkin replied 'I'm not deaf. I understood.' To this day, the other series of murders committed in 2003 remain unsolved.

CHAPTER 5

SOUTH AFRICA

MOSES SITHOLE, AKA THE ABC MURDERER

As with many serial killers, the absence of a father figure in childhood coupled with rejection by his mother perhaps led Moses Sithole (b. 1964) to form a hatred for women that, in later years, would turn him into one of South Africa's most notorious serial killers.

His notoriety began on 4 January 1995, when the body of a semi-naked woman was found in a field. She was severely decomposed and was never identified. A second body was found on 9 February. She was completely naked, with her clothes placed on top of her chest and weighted down with rocks. Her fingerprints were later used to confirm her identity as 20-year-old Nuku Soko, who had been missing since January.

On the morning of 6 March, construction workers digging a ditch in Atteridgeville arrived to find a woman's breast protruding from the soil. They uncovered the body of Sara Matlakala Mokono. She was 25, and had disappeared three days earlier on her way to meet someone who had offered her work.

On 12 April, another body was discovered in Atteridgeville. This woman's hands had been tied behind her back with her bra. She had been strangled with a ligature. Although her clothes were recovered in the surrounding area, her knickers were missing. She was later identified as Letta Nomthandazo Ndlangamandla, aged 25.

On 13 May, 29-year-old Esther Mainetja's body was found in a cornfield near Hercules in Pretoria West. She was naked from the waist down and she had been strangled. She had last been seen the previous evening as she left a café for home.

On 13 June, Francina Nomsa Sithebe, aged 25, was found propped up against a tree. Although she was wearing a dress, closer examination revealed that her knickers and handbag strap had been tied around her neck and then around the tree.

On 16 June, Elizabeth Granny Mathetsa's naked body was discovered in Rosslyn, an industrial area about nine miles to the northwest of Pretoria. She was 19 years old, and had last been seen alive on 25 May.

On 22 June, a body was found in Rosherville. The victim had been raped and strangled and her identity documents were found nearby. She was 32-year-old Ernestina Mohadi Mosebo.

On 24 June, Nikiwe Diko's body was found in Atteridgeville. She had been missing since 7 April, when she went for a job interview. Wild dogs had eaten most of her body. Her hands had been tied together with her knickers. Police only managed to find her skull the following day, 40yd from her torso. Her tights had been tied around her neck and wound so tightly with a stick that bone fragments were embedded in the material. A stick had also been rammed into her vagina. Her husband identified her by the wedding ring on her finger.

On 17 July 1995, police got the break they had been searching for. A man who lived in a caravan in Beyers Park, Boksburg, had watched a man and a woman walk into the grassland some distance from his caravan. He had spoken to them, telling them that they could not go too far because of a fence around the land. The man stated that he knew the area. After a while, they disappeared from view. However, he kept on watching. Sometime later, the man re-emerged by himself and ran off. The resident went into the field, where he found the body of Josephine Mantsali Mlangeni. She was 25 years old and a mother of four, and had gone to meet someone about possible employment. The following day, Granny Dimakatso Ramela, 20, was found in Pretoria West. Lying face down, she was fully clothed and had been strangled. She had disappeared on 23 May.

On 30 May, Mildred Ntiya Lepule, 28, was taken to Pretoria by her husband to meet a man about a job offer, and was not seen alive again. Her body was found on 26 July in a canal near the Bon Accord Dam near Onderstepoort, nine miles north of Pretoria. In the coming weeks, detectives would come to know this area well. Lepule's tights had been used to strangle her and her knickers had been pulled up over her face. Between 8 and 30 August, the bodies of five more victims were discovered, three of whom had been killed in similar fashion.

Between 15 and 17 September 1995, in a field at the Van Dyk Mine near Boksburg, South African police discovered 10 more bodies in various stages of decomposition within a 300yd radius. A crime scene investigation and forensic tests showed that the murders had all the hallmarks of the serial killer who had been responsible for raping and murdering women over the past year.

These victims were Makoba Tryphina Mogotsi, 26, who went missing on 15 August. Nelisiwe Nontobeko Zulu, also 26, last seen on 4 September on her way to search for a job. Amelia Dikamakatso Rapodile, 43, disappeared on 7 September after she left her place of work, Johannesburg International Airport, in the company of a man who had promised her a better job. She was found with her hands tied behind her back to her neck with her tights. Her bank card had been used to withdraw money three times later on the night of her disappearance in Germiston.

Monica Gabisile Vilakazi, 31, left her grandmother's house on 12 September to look for work. Hazel Nozipho Madikizela, 21, was found with her hands tied to her neck with her underwear. She had last been seen by her parents in Germiston. Tsidi Malekoae Matela was identified more than a year later, in

November 1996. Originally from neighbouring Lesotho, she was 45 years old when she died. The other four women could not be traced and identified.

The police now offered a reward equivalent to £50,000 for information leading to the arrest of the killer. They even used an FBI profiler in an attempt to gain more information. They had now established that they had three separate crime scenes all used by the same killer of the 27 known victims, and that his MO was to lure his victims to go with him on the pretext of helping them find employment. They believed that he must have been confident in his manner and dressed in a smart fashion.

From the Boksburg crime scene, police recovered a handbag belonging to one of the victims, Amelia Rapodile. Tracing her last known movements, they learnt from her friends that she had made an appointment with a man named Moses Sithole on 7 September, the day on which she had disappeared. Detectives also found an application form for Sithole's Youth against Human Abuse organisation, in which he had offered Amelia a position. A telephone number on the form led them to Wattville, an area southeast of Boksburg. There they interviewed Moses' sister, who told them he did not live there and that she did not know where he was. When they went back and spoke to friends of the other victims, Sithole's name kept cropping up. He was now becoming of great interest to police.

Despite all the media coverage, the killings continued. Twenty-year-old Agnes Sibongile Mbuli disappeared on her way to meet a friend. Her body was found on 3 October at Kleinfontein train station near Benoni.

On 13 October, the police decided to take a positive step. They published the name and photograph of Moses Sithole in all the newspapers, hoping that someone would come forward with information about him. However, the next day, a woman's body was found at the Village Main Reef Mine near Johannesburg. Her shoelaces had been used to bind her neck to a tree. She has never been identified.

Following Sithole's picture appearing in the papers, he contacted his sister's husband Maxwell and said that he needed a gun. He arranged to meet Maxwell at the Mintex factory in Benoni, where Maxwell worked. Maxwell informed the police of Sithole's request. The police decided that one officer would act as a security guard at the factory and that when Sithole arrived an attempt would be made to arrest him, with other officers secreted nearby. Sithole arrived at the factory and asked for Maxwell. The other guards, who knew nothing of the plan, told the police officer to go and fetch Maxwell, but he refused because he didn't want to leave Sithole. This made Sithole suspicious and he ran off. The police officer followed him into a dark alley. He identified himself as a police officer, yelling at Sithole to stop, and finally fired two warning shots. But Sithole would not heed the warnings. It is alleged that Sithole turned and came at the police officer with an axe in his hand, forcing the officer to shoot him in the stomach and the leg. He was taken to hospital and survived.

When interviewed, Sithole initially refused to answer any questions until a female detective entered the room. Then he began describing some of his crimes and masturbated while he did so. He then said that he chose the murder locations before he chose the victims and that he only killed the pretty ones. He caught them with his hands around the neck and strangled them. He placed stockings around their necks and did not like the sight of blood. He forced the women to look down while he raped and killed them and masturbated as he watched them die. However, he would later go on to retract these confessions, stating that the police had forced them out of him by giving him details of the murders. He had, according to the police, declined legal assistance during the initial interviews. However, he did take the police to the locations where he had murdered and buried the bodies. He was later charged with 38 murders.

Following psychiatric evaluation, Sithole was deemed sane and fit to stand trial on 21 October 1996. He stood trial for 38 murders and the rapes of 40 women. He had already been convicted of a previous rape in 1989 and had served part of a six-year sentence. Despite the evidence against him, he pleaded not guilty and a lengthy trial ensued.

On 3 December 1996, the prosecution produced a video that had been recorded in prison shortly after his arrest and contained his confession to murders he had committed. Fellow inmates in Boksburg Prison had made the video; these were Charles Schoeman, Jacques Rogge and Mark Halligan – former police officers who had been involved in a £315,000 diamond robbery in Amanzimtoti in 1995. They had also murdered an accomplice.

Rogge met Sithole in the infirmary, where the former slept because of his diabetes. Sithole asked Rogge if he could steal some pills so that he could commit suicide, but first he wanted to tell his story. Schoeman, Rogge, Halligan and Sithole all signed a contract, agreeing to share the profits from the sale of the story. Sithole's share was to go to his daughter. He is heard disputing the number of murders he was charged with, saying that he killed only 29 women.

On 4 December 1997, almost 12 months after the trial began, Mr Justice David Curlewis found Moses Sithole guilty on 40 charges of rape, 38 charges of murder and six charges of robbery. It took three hours to read the verdict and judgment was deferred until the following day. Then Judge Curlewis sentenced Sithole to a total of 2,410 years in prison. He received 12 years for each of the 40 rapes, 50 years for each of the 38 murders and another five years for each of the six robberies. These sentences would not run concurrently and the judge recommended no possibility of parole for at least 930 years. The judge said 'I do not take leniency into account. What you did was horrible.' The judge also stated that he would have had no trouble imposing the death penalty, had it still been a viable option. He did not have the necessary faith in the prison authorities nor the parole boards to hand down life sentences. That would have meant that Sithole would be eligible for parole in 25 years. The judge said 'I want to make it clear that Moses Sithole should stay in jail for the rest of his life.'

STEWART WILKEN, AKA BOETIE BOER

Like many other sexual predators and serial killers, Stewart Wilken (b. 1966), when finally apprehended, revealed a life of torment in which he was sexually abused and buggered as a young boy. He began smoking drugs at the age of eight and was forced to eat his food out of a dog bowl. As with all serial killers, there was a deep psychological motive underlying his choice of victims. He had two failed marriages and could not hold down a relationship with a woman, so he turned to prostitutes for more than sexual gratification.

Normally, a serial killer will target a specific type of person or a group of people. Wilken was different. He killed two different types of victims: adult female prostitutes and young adolescent boys, in and around the town of Port Elizabeth. By the beginning of 1997, at least eight people had already been murdered, the police believed by one person. These murders went back to 1990. The police had no clues as to the identity of the killer, but this was soon to change.

On Wednesday, 22 January 1997, a 12-year-old boy disappeared. His mother was initially not concerned, as the boy frequently stayed over at his grandmother's house in nearby Missionvale, walking distance from their home in Algoa Park. However, when he did not arrive home by Thursday evening, she became uneasy. On the Friday morning, she went to the grandmother's house, only to hear that her son had left for home on Wednesday.

The police investigation showed that the boy had been at his mother's house on Wednesday afternoon, after which he had played with a friend at a nearby park. The friend said that he had to go and buy milk for his parents and later saw the boy with a man called Stewart Wilken in Dyke Way. Wilken asked the boy where he was going and the boy said that it was none of his business. Both the boy and his mother knew Wilken, and Wilken had even lived at his mother's for a while after he had had some marital problems. The police then started to enquire about Wilken. They found that Wilken's daughter had also gone missing in 1995 and that there were two charges of buggery being investigated against him. Like the missing boy, Wilken's daughter was last seen in his company. The buggery charges had been filed by his parents-in-law in connection with the two sons of his second wife, Victoria.

Wilken was traced and arrested on 28 January 1997 and when questioned appeared genuinely concerned about the missing boy and eager to help. He admitted that he had indeed been with the missing boy on that Wednesday, but that he knew nothing about his disappearance. Wilken stated that he had spent the night at a female friend's house. Strangely, he was released from custody before they checked out his alibi, which soon turned out to be false. He was re-arrested on 31 January 1997.

The police knew that they had no direct evidence but tried to make Wilken think that they had. They straightaway told him that they 'knew' he had killed the two children and that he had revisited the location of the bodies to fantasise and commit necrophilia – and the trick worked. Wilken confessed to both murders, In fact, he had returned to the decomposing body of the boy that very morning to have sex with it. When questioned about the murder of his daughter, he told police he took her to a garden filled with fairy-tale figures such as dwarves. It was a place where he used to play as a child. Here, he strangled her. He removed her clothes and stayed with her lifeless body, talking to it and sleeping next to it at night. When the body had decomposed, he covered the skeleton with a tarpaulin. He placed her clothes next to him, as if they were still being worn. He denied having any sexual interaction with his daughter, before or after her death. As far as the murder of the young boy was concerned, Wilken stated he had met the boy in the park, whereupon the boy allegedly asked Wilken about sex. Wilken took the boy to an open field on the outskirts of the park. He told the boy to take off his clothes and proceeded to perform fellatio on him. Then he told the boy to lie on his back and buggered him. At this point, he stated, the boy began to cry and resisted. Then Wilken began to strangle him. As the boy drew his last breath, Wilken ejaculated. Wilken then showed police where both bodies were hidden and the remains were recovered.

The police conducted another interview with Wilken, believing that he may have more to confess. Despite the fact that they had no more specific crimes to talk to him about, they tried the same ploy. This time, they told him they knew there were more bodies hidden. Again, their tactics proved fruitful. Wilken, out of the blue, indicated there were at least 10 more victims. He then made a full confession to his lawyer, describing the crimes in explicit detail. This confession kept the police busy for months, trying to locate the crime reports pertaining to the crimes Wilken had described.

Wilken's first confirmed victim was murdered in February 1990 – 15-year-old Monte Fiko. He was a homeless street child, of which there were many in South Africa. Wilken buggered the boy and then strangled him. On 3 October 1990, after an argument with his first wife, Wilken picked up a prostitute, Virginia Gysman, at Russell Road. She was 25. He paid her and took her to Dagbreek Primary School, where they had sex. He then buggered her. When she complained, he strangled her with her clothing and ejaculated as she died. He left her body in the schoolyard.

On 10 January 1991, Wilken picked up another prostitute, Mercia Papenfus, 37, at the Red Lion Hotel and they went to St George's Park. When Mercia demanded her payment before intercourse, Wilken flew into a rage and strangled her. Then he buggered her and left her body in the park.

On 21 October 1991, Wilken met a 14-year-old street boy, who apparently agreed to have sex with him for money. Wilken took the boy to St George's Park. The boy wanted his money, which angered Wilken. The boy tried to flee, but Wilken overpowered him and buggered him, ejaculating as he strangled his victim. In 1993, sometime between June and September, Wilken met another young street child and solicited him. They went to the river valley of Target Kloof, where Wilken buggered and strangled the boy. He hid the body in the ravine.

On 27 July 1995, Wilken again killed a prostitute. Her name was Georgina Boniswa Zweni, aged 42. He buggered and strangled her but was still filled with lust and proceeded to mutilate her vagina and anus with a knife. The forensic pathologist testified at Wilken's trial that the wound was star-shaped and it appeared as if the assailant had 'stuck in the knife, pulled it out, stuck it in and pulled it out'. In all, he counted at least 20 stab wounds, which included a cluster of five next to her navel. He characterised it as 'a wild knife stabbing'. Wilken also cut off her nipples and ate them at the scene. Her clothing was thrown into a fishpond.

On 25 May 1996, he again murdered a prostitute, 22-year-old Katriena Claassen, at the Albany Road interchange. They went down to the beach. Wilken forced a plastic bag down her throat to keep her from screaming. He buggered and strangled her. Somewhere between May and August 1996, he met another street child, whom he took to Fort Frederick. After the boy masturbated him, Wilken told the boy to undress and buggered him. The boy threatened to tell the police and Wilken strangled him, hiding the body afterwards.

Wilken told police that he would return to the bodies of the boys he had killed. He rubbed vinegar and butter on the boys' feet to hide their scent from the police dogs. He rolled up pieces of newspaper and inserted these into their anuses to keep the maggots out, so that he could commit necrophilia. He said he liked to face his victims while buggering them so that he could watch their faces as he strangled them. He referred to their last moments when their eyes would bulge, their lips swell and their tongues protrude from their mouths. It was at this moment that he would ejaculate.

THE EVIL WITHIN

On 20 February 1998, Wilken was found guilty on seven counts of murder and two of buggery, including the murder of his daughter. On 23 February 1998, Stewart Wilken was sentenced to seven terms of life imprisonment. Mr Justice Jansen said that Wilken had to be removed from the community. If the death penalty had still been available in South Africa, he would have imposed it. He made mention that throughout the trial Wilken had shown neither emotion nor remorse.

CHAPTER 7
SOUTH KOREA

YOO YOUNG CHEOL

Yoo Young Cheol (b. 1970) committed his first crime in 1987 and from then on led the life of a petty criminal, in and out of prison. By 2002, he had fourteen criminal convictions, one of which was for rape, and he had spent a total of 11 years in prison.

On the morning of 24 September 2003, Cheol rode the subway to Apgujeong-Dong Station, the most affluent district in Seoul. He had devised a plan for robbery and murder and was armed with a 6in bladed knife and a homemade hammer, which he had used to kill dogs and cats. He was looking for a church. Once he spotted one, he searched nearby for an expensive-looking house, something that would indicate that its owners were wealthy. It didn't take him long to find one. However, the occupants were at home; a 72-year-old man and his 68-year-old wife. Cheol attacked them both, stabbing the man in the throat and then hitting his wife over the head with the hammer. He decided not to take any items in an effort to confuse the police.

On 9 October, Cheol took the subway to Bulgwang Station and then a taxi to Gugi Tunnel. He walked until he found a church and then an expensive-looking house in the adjacent affluent neighbourhood. He noticed that there was no security system and that it had an inner garden surrounded by a wall. Cheol watched the movement of people inside through the window and then climbed the wall wearing gloves. He landed in some fine gravel and walked over it, careful of noise, with his homemade hammer in his hand. As he entered the house, he was confronted by the first of his victims, an 85-year-old woman. He smashed her over the head with the hammer. Cheol then came across a 60-year-old female. He asked her if there were more people in the house. She said that her husband and son were upstairs. Cheol hit her over the head several times with his hammer before moving upstairs. He confronted the 35-year-old son and forced him to kneel down. Cheol then hit him over the head several times and left him for dead. He looked around for the other man but couldn't find him. While searching the house, Cheol found a safe and scattered various contents around to disguise the crime scene as a robbery. He cleaned his footprints with a towel. Then he walked back to the Gugi Tunnel and took a taxi back to Bulgwang Station and the subway back home.

On 16 October, Cheol travelled by subway to the Samsung neighbourhood of the Gangnam district, known as one of Seoul's wealthier areas. He walked around until he found a church, and then saw a house with a big garden and a surrounding wall that bordered a narrow alley. It was around 1pm. As before, he went over the wall wearing gloves and approached the front door. At that same moment, a 69-year-old woman, the owner of the house, came out to fetch the post. As she went back inside, Cheol followed her into the house. He threatened her with his knife and asked if she was alone. No one else was there. He dragged her into the bathroom and hit her over the head, crushing her skull with his homemade hammer. Before leaving, he again scattered items in the master bedroom to confuse the police, and he wiped the bloodstains off his shoes and cleaned the smeared footprints from the floor. He left the house and walked to Gangnam Ward Office Station.

SOUTH KOREA

On 18 November, in the morning, Cheol took the subway to Hanseong University Station. While looking for a house near a church, he noticed a small police station in an alley and decided it would be a prime place to commit his crimes because the residents would perceive the area as safe. He theorised that their guard would be down because of the nearby police station. Again, it was a house in a nice neighbourhood in Hyehwa-Dong, and it had a surrounding wall and a small garden within. As with his previous crimes, he looked for quick ways to escape in case of trouble and watched the house for movement. He cleared the back wall wearing gloves and used a gas pipe to climb down. A baby cried from inside the house, so he knew at least two people were home. He entered through the front door and then went up to the second floor, but didn't find anyone. As he was coming down the stairs, the 53-year-old female housekeeper saw him and asked who he was. Brandishing his knife, he ordered her into the master bedroom. There he found the owner of the house, an 87-year-old man, lying on his bed. Cheol immediately smashed his skull. Terrified, the housekeeper held the baby tight but Cheol prised the infant from her arms. He put the baby on the sofa and covered it with a blanket, then bludgeoned the housekeeper's head with his hammer.

Cheol rummaged through the house and found a safe on the second floor. He used a golf club and pruning shears to break it open. In the process, he cut himself. Worried that the police could track him with a DNA test, he set fire to the room. Covered in blood, he snatched a black jacket, put it on and left the house. He watched the house from a distance for 30 minutes, unable to see any flames. A woman who looked like a family member entered the house and that was enough. Cheol left the scene, not remembering whether he took a bus or taxi, and not realising that he had left behind a set of footprints and his image captured from behind on a CCTV camera.

In January 2004, Cheol got lucky. He was arrested for a theft at a sauna and held briefly at the Sodaemun police station. The police did not check his details, which would have connected him to the murders, but instead dealt with him as a petty criminal and released him.

On 6 February, he took a taxi to the Imoon-Dong neighbourhood, intent on killing again. He approached a 25-year-old female, in front of a restaurant 20yd from a busy four-lane road, thinking that she looked like a prostitute. He asked her where she was going, showed her a forged police ID card and asked her to go to a bar with him, but she refused and called him a crazy bastard. She tried to run away and, almost reaching the restaurant door, she fell down screaming for help. Cheol stabbed her five times in the chest. No longer was he interested in lethal rages against the rich, he now had a hatred of young, attractive prostitutes – and this forced him to change his MO.

In March, he called a phone-sex parlour and had a woman sent over to his apartment. When she arrived, he hit her head with his hammer and then cut her body up into 18 pieces. He didn't even have to leave his house except to dispose of the body. He hauled the dismembered woman to a small mountain trail behind Seogang University and buried her there. He was now on a high, having realised that his new killing method was even easier than before. He was sold some Viagra tablets and when he found out they were fake, he abducted the seller, murdered him, cut up his body and placed the pieces in the van, subsequently setting it alight.

Between early April and mid-July 2004, Cheol murdered 10 women and dismembered their bodies, later disposing of the body parts. He knew of a bushy hillside and headed there each time with a loaded backpack. Each body required two trips. He buried the human remains in shallow graves and, later on, he marked them to avoid burying bodies in the same spot. All were women from the sex trade whom he had called on chat lines to arrange for them to come to his apartment. He never had sex with any of them for fear of leaving his DNA – he was very forensically aware. He saved the victims' mobile phones so he could avoid using his own number for later calls. Cheol also shaved off the skin of the victims' fingertips. In South Korea, all citizens have a national identification number and are fingerprinted by the government.

On Thursday, 15 July, Cheol was arrested for assaulting a prostitute in southern Seoul. The police had no idea that they had captured the killer. He feigned epileptic twitches and they removed his handcuffs during interrogation. When they weren't paying attention, Cheol escaped. However, he was eventually re-arrested after he arranged to meet a prostitute and her pimp became suspicious and contacted the police. He very quickly confessed to all his crimes, leading police to where he had buried the body parts of his victims.

Although he had confessed, the police struggled to corroborate his story. The only evidence they had was what he told them and the dead bodies pointed out by him. From particles of human flesh taken from the hammer, DNA tests matched some of the recovered victims. By measuring his feet, police were able to determine that the footprints left at the Hyehwa-Dong scene were his. Cheol informed the police that he had kept a written record of each killing but it was not found in the search of his apartment and nothing on his computer hard drive revealed anything useful. Cheol also kept changing his story. He told police that he had murdered 26 people, six more than the original 20 he had confessed to. He went to court charged with 21 counts of murder, along with burglary, impersonating a police officer, arson and improperly disposing of bodies.

Cheol first appeared in court on 6 September and admitted his guilt. He described how he had dismembered the corpses and said that he had killed two more people in addition to the 21 counts he was charged with. The trial dragged on and on, mainly because Cheol kept refusing to appear in court. On 13 December, the trial finally came to an end and the court found him guilty and sentenced him to death by hanging.

THE EVIL WITHIN

He lodged an appeal against the death sentence but his appeal was turned down, and at the time of writing was on death row, awaiting execution.

CHAPTER 8

THE USA

ALBERT DESALVO, AKA THE BOSTON STRANGLER

Between 14 June 1962 and 4 January 1964, 13 single and respectable women in the Boston area were victims of either a single serial killer or possibly several killers. At least 11 of these murders were attributed to the killer who came to be known as the Boston Strangler. Of these 11, six of the victims were between the ages of 55 and 75. Two possible additional victims were 85 and 69 years of age. The remaining five victims were considerably younger, ranging in age from 19 to 23. All of these women were murdered in their apartments; they all had been sexually assaulted and were strangled with articles of their own clothing. There were no signs of forced entry and either the women knew their assailant or had been confident enough to let him in.

The dates of the murders are as follows:

14 June 1962: Anna E. Slesers, 55, was found dead in her apartment by her son. She was lying naked in the bathroom with the cord from her robe around her neck. She had been sexually assaulted.

30 June 1962: 68-year-old Nina Nichols was found murdered in her apartment at 1940 Commonwealth Avenue in the Brighton area of Boston. She was found with her legs spread wide open,

and her housecoat and slip pulled up to her waist. Two of her own nylon stockings were tied tightly around her neck in a bow. She too had been sexually assaulted; blood had been found in her vagina. The time of death was estimated to be around 5pm. The apartment looked as if it had been burgled; every drawer had been pulled open, and possessions lay scattered on the floor. The killer had gone through her address book and her post for some unknown reason, although later it was determined that nothing had been taken. Later that same day, Helen Blake met a similar death sometime between 8pm and 10pm. The 65-year-old divorcée had been strangled with one of her nylons. Her brassiere had been looped around her neck, over the stockings, and tied in a bow. Both her vagina and anus had been lacerated, but there was no trace of semen. She was found lying face down and naked on her bed, with her legs spread wide apart. Her apartment had also been thoroughly ransacked. It appeared as though two rings that she was wearing had been pulled from her fingers and taken. The killer had also tried unsuccessfully to open a metal strongbox and a footlocker.

19 August: 75-year-old Ida Irga, a very shy and retiring widow, fell victim to the Strangler. She was found two days later in her apartment at 7 Grove Avenue in Boston's West End. As with the other deaths, there was no sign of forced entry. She was found lying on her back on the living-room floor wearing a light brown nightdress, which was torn, completely exposing her body. There was a white pillowcase knotted tightly around her neck. Her legs were spread approximately 5ft from heel to heel, her feet were propped up on individual chairs and a standard bed pillow was placed under her buttocks, in what was described as an obstetrical position, and she had died of manual strangulation. Dried blood covered her head, mouth and ears. She, too, had been sexually assaulted but again there was no trace of semen.

20 August 1962: a 67-year-old nurse named Jane Sullivan was found murdered in her apartment at 435 Columbia Road in

Dorchester, across town from where Ida lived. She had apparently been dead for some 10 days before she was found. Police found her on her knees in her bath with her feet up over the back of the bath and her head underneath the taps. She too had been strangled with her own nylons. It was difficult to tell whether she had been sexually assaulted, due to the decomposition of the body. However, there were bloodstains on the handle of a broom, leading officers to believe this may have been inserted into her vagina. There was no sign of forced entry to the property, nor was the apartment ransacked.

5 December 1962: Sophie Clark, a 21-year-old student at the Carnegie Institute of Medical Technology, was found by her two room-mates in the apartment they shared at 315 Huntington Avenue in the Back Bay area, a short distance from Anna Slesers's apartment (the first victim). Sophie was found naked; her legs were also spread wide apart. She had been strangled with three of her nylon stockings, which had been knotted and tied very tightly around her neck. Her half-slip had also been tied around her neck. There was evidence of sexual assault and this time the police found traces of semen on the rug near her body. There was no sign of a forcible entry, but Sophie had been very security-conscious and had insisted on having a second lock on the apartment door. She was so cautious that she even questioned friends who came to the door before she let them in. Despite this, her killer had somehow convinced her to let him in. There were signs that she had put up a fight with the killer. Her time of death was calculated as 2.30pm. This crime left the police puzzled – there were marked differences between Sophie's murder and the others. Sophie was young; all the previous victims had been elderly. Semen had been found this time but none had been found at any of the previous murders. Was this the same killer? Or was there a copycat killer at work? Police questioned another female resident living in the same building who mentioned that at around 2.20pm a man had knocked on her door and said that the building superintendent had sent him to see about painting her

apartment. He then told her that he'd have to fix her bathroom ceiling and complimented her on her figure. He asked her if she had ever thought of modelling. When she put her finger to her lips, the man became angry. His character seemed to change completely. She told him her husband was sleeping in the next room. The man then stated that he had got the wrong apartment and left. She described him as between 25 and 30 years old, of average height and with honey-coloured hair, wearing a dark jacket and dark green trousers. Was this Sophie's killer? It was quite probable, as the building superintendent had not sent a workman to any part of the building and this coincided with the time that Sophie Clark was murdered.

31 December 1962: 23-year-old Patricia Bissette, a secretary for a Boston engineering firm, was found dead. She had failed to turn up for work and her boss went to look for her. Her apartment was locked, so he climbed through a window into the apartment. He found her lying face up in bed with the covers drawn up to her chin; it looked as if she was asleep. When he pulled the covers back he could see that she had several stockings knotted and interwoven with a blouse tied tightly around her neck. There was evidence of recent sexual intercourse and it was later revealed that she was in an early stage of pregnancy. There had been some damage to her rectum. The killer had made a search of her apartment.

8 May 1963: Beverly Samans, a pretty 23-year-old student, missed her Wednesday night choir practice at the Second Unitarian Church in Back Bay. Her friend went to her apartment and opened it with the key she had given to him. On opening the door, the friend saw Beverly lying directly in front of him on a sofa bed, her legs spread apart. Her hands had been tied behind her with one of her scarves. A nylon stocking and two handkerchiefs tied together were tied and knotted around her neck. A cloth had been placed over her mouth. Under it, a second cloth had been stuffed into her mouth. It appeared that Beverly had been strangled, but she had, in fact, been killed by the four

stab wounds to her throat. She had sustained 22 stab wounds in all, 18 of which were in a bull's-eye design on her left breast. The ligature around her neck was like a necktie and was not tied tightly enough to strangle her. A bloody knife was found in her kitchen sink. She had not been raped either by man or by object, nor was any semen present in her body. It was estimated that she had been dead approximately 48–72 hours and had probably been killed between late Sunday evening and Monday morning.

8 September 1963: Evelyn Corbin, a pretty 58-year-old divorcée, was found murdered. She had been strangled with two of her nylon stockings. She lay across the bed, face up and naked. Her knickers had been stuffed into her mouth as a gag. Around the bed were lipstick-marked tissues that had traces of semen on them, and semen was also found in her mouth but not in her vagina.

25 November 1963: 23-year-old Joann Graff was raped and murdered in her apartment. Two nylon stockings had been tied in an elaborate bow around her neck. There were teeth marks on her breast. The outside of her vagina was bloody and lacerated. At 3.25pm, a tenant living above her had heard footsteps in the hall. His wife had been concerned that someone had been sneaking around, so he went to the door and listened. When he heard a knock on the door of the apartment opposite his, he opened his door to find a man of about 27 with pomaded hair, dressed in dark green slacks and a dark shirt and jacket. 'Does Joan Graff live here?' he asked, mispronouncing Joann's name. The tenant told him that Joann lived on the floor below. Moments later, he heard the door open and shut on the floor beneath him and assumed that Joann had let the man into her apartment. Ten minutes later, a friend telephoned Joann, but there was no answer. The morning before Joann's death, in the apartment down the hall from Joann's, a woman had heard someone outside her door. Then she saw a piece of paper being slipped under her door. She watched, mesmerised, as it was moved from side to side soundlessly. Then suddenly the paper vanished and she heard footsteps. The description of this man

was similar to the one who had been seen and spoken to in the apartment block where Sophie Clark was found murdered on 5 December 1962.

4 January 1964: Two young women came home after work to their apartment. They were horrified to find their new room-mate, 19-year-old Mary Sullivan, murdered in the most grotesque and shocking fashion. Like the other victims, she had been strangled: first with a dark stocking; over the stocking a pink silk scarf tied with a huge bow under her chin; and over that, another pink-and-white flowered scarf. A 'Happy New Year' card had been placed against her feet. She had been left in a sitting position on the bed, with her back against the headboard. Thick liquid that looked like semen was dripping from her mouth onto her exposed breasts. A broomstick handle had been inserted almost 4in into her vagina.

Despite all the murders, police had no evidence or any clues as to the identity of the killer or killers and a Strangler taskforce was formed. Its enquiries revealed a series of strange sexual offences that had occurred in the same area some two years previously. These offences had been committed by a man who would knock on the doors of apartments occupied by young, attractive women. He would tell them he was from a modelling agency and ask if they were interested in becoming models. He would then ask if he could take their measurements. He then left each time, telling them that someone from the agency would be in touch. All the details were, of course, false. Police subsequently arrested a man for these offences – Albert DeSalvo, who was 29 at the time. He was sentenced to 18 months' imprisonment and was released two months before the first murder in 1962.

In November 1964, DeSalvo was arrested again on a more serious charge relating to an offence that had taken place on 27 October, when a woman who was in her bed suddenly found a man in her room holding a knife. The man had put the knife to her throat and threatened to kill her if she made a sound. He stuffed her underwear in her mouth and tied her in a spreadeagle position to the bedposts with her clothes. He kissed her and fondled her, then apologised before fleeing. Police arrested DeSalvo and the woman later identified him on an identity parade. DeSalvo was released on bail. His photo and details were circulated to other police forces and soon calls came in from Connecticut where police were seeking a male sexual predator they called the Green Man, because he wore green work trousers. This offender had assaulted four women in one day in different towns in Connecticut.

DeSalvo was arrested yet again at his home and in front of his wife, who told him to confess to whatever he had been responsible for. It appeared that DeSalvo heeded her advice and, when interviewed, admitted to breaking into 400 apartments and a couple of rapes. He had allegedly assaulted some 300 women in a four-state area. The police were also aware of DeSalvo's tendency to exaggerate and tell lies. This was borne out by the police not having the reported crimes to corroborate his admissions. They attributed this to the fact that a lot of the women had not reported the crimes.

DeSalvo was detained at the state medical hospital for mental assessment. At the hospital, he was put in the same ward as another murderer, George Nasr, with whom he became close friends.

In March 1965, DeSalvo confessed to his lawyer that he was responsible for all 11 of the strangulation murders, in addition to two other deaths of women who had apparently died of heart failure before he could strangle them. It would appear that while in custody he had realised that he was likely to spend many years in prison. He had been thinking about his wife's future and her financial security and considered the financial rewards that his story could bring. DeSalvo and Nasr got together and discussed the reward the police were offering for information leading to the arrest and conviction of the killer. They discussed the possibility of DeSalvo admitting to the stranglings; Nasr would tell the police about DeSalvo and then they would split the reward money between them. DeSalvo believed that he would not receive the death penalty, so the plan was agreed. DeSalvo contacted his lawyer and made the confessions to him.

DeSalvo's lawyer was unsure what to do with the confession his client had given him. His priority was to satisfy himself that DeSalvo had actually committed the murders. He obtained some information about the murders from the police that only the killer would have known about. He went to visit DeSalvo a second time on 6 March 1965. DeSalvo mentioned that a detective had come to take his palm print the day before. His lawyer knew that he had to work fast if he was going to be able to protect his client, so he recorded a lengthy interview with DeSalvo. After hearing the confession in great detail, he believed that DeSalvo was the killer. The lawyer then went to the police and played the tape to them with the voice disguised. This was in an attempt to plea-bargain to avoid DeSalvo receiving the death penalty. Finally, this was agreed and DeSalvo made a full confession to the police. However, many people connected to the police and to DeSalvo still had their doubts. Some of the evidence did not point to DeSalvo. Cigarette butts had been found at some of the crime scenes, yet DeSalvo did not smoke. The witness descriptions of the workman seen and spoken to did not match DeSalvo.

Another important factor that suggested DeSalvo was not the killer was that police had taken two female witnesses to secretly view him in the prison hospital, with one being the only woman to survive an encounter with the Strangler. Police were hoping that the women would positively identify DeSalvo. What the police had not foreseen was that they would identify someone totally different – George Nasr. The women posed as visitors in the prison's visiting room. Nasr was the first to enter the room to meet with a prison social worker. He glanced at one of the women then immediately took a second look. She was disturbed by his presence and wondered if she knew him, or vice versa. At that moment, DeSalvo came in and sat down. Straightaway, the woman realised DeSalvo was not her attacker. She had been shown his photograph previously and was unsure then; now she was positive. She later made a revelation to police, stating that she believed that the other man she had seen that day, George Nasr, looked like her attacker but she could not be 100 per cent sure. The second female witness also failed to identify DeSalvo but, having seen Nasr, believed he was the man who had called at her apartment posing as a workman.

Despite these doubts and relying totally on DeSalvo's confession, the legal wrangling continued. In the interim, on 10 January 1967, Albert DeSalvo was tried on the original charges relating to the Green Man offences. DeSalvo's legal team explained that they hoped to convince a jury to find him not guilty by reason of insanity. They would attempt to use the 13 murders he had committed as the Boston Strangler to show the extent of his insanity in this trial. To do this, they would attempt to get evidence to support his confession and its corroboration by the police. However, the ploy failed and he was deemed sane enough to stand trial. The jury subsequently found DeSalvo guilty on all counts and sentenced him to life in prison without any hope of psychiatric help. DeSalvo was not charged at that time with any of the murders attributed to the Boston Strangler.

In November 1973, Albert DeSalvo, while serving out his life sentence, was stabbed to death in the prison hospital. The night before he was murdered, he had telephoned his doctor and asked to meet him urgently, apparently very frightened. The doctor promised to meet with him the following morning, but DeSalvo was murdered that night. He had also asked a reporter to meet him that same night, and was going to reveal the identity of the Boston Strangler. DeSalvo had asked to be placed in the hospital under special lock-up about a week before. According to the doctor: 'Something was going on within the prison and I think he felt he had to talk quickly.' DeSalvo had indicated that there were people in the prison, including guards, who were not happy with him. Following his death, the doctor remarked that somebody must have had to leave an awful lot of doors open, because for anyone to get to DeSalvo there were several guards to go past. But the reality is that someone did get through and stuck a knife into Albert DeSalvo's heart sometime between the evening check and the morning. Prison officials believed that DeSalvo's death was related to his involvement in drugs. Three men were later tried, but twice the trials ended in hung juries.

Since DeSalvo's death, there have been lingering doubts as to whether he was the Boston Strangler, so much so that the relatives of DeSalvo and of one of the victims, Mary Sullivan, joined forces in 2000 to have Sullivan's remains exhumed for DNA testing, not available in the 1960s. In his confession, DeSalvo said he had strangled Mary Sullivan with his hands. In fact, she had been strangled with her own clothing. DeSalvo also claimed to have raped her when evidence proved that she was sexually assaulted with a broomstick. A forensic scientist who took part in an autopsy arranged by the families said that experts were unable to find the effects of a blow DeSalvo claimed to have inflicted on Sullivan. Also, the families said DeSalvo claimed to have left a knife and a sweater at the murder scene, but neither was found. Tests were also conducted on samples of hair, semen and tissue taken from Sullivan's exhumed body. The Attorney General's office reviewed the Sullivan case but has continually refused the families access to evidence because it considers the case unsolved.

In October 2000, a judge ordered the two sides to try to work out a compromise but the Boston authorities have been less than cooperative. Jerry Leone, chief of the Massachusetts Attorney General's criminal bureau, said that if evidence does point to someone other than DeSalvo as Sullivan's killer, it doesn't necessarily cast doubt on all the other Boston Strangler murders and doesn't mean the other cases will be re-investigated. 'We are looking into the Sullivan case because it's the only case that has any evidence that can be used in a viable prosecution right now,'

Leone said. On the other hand, DeSalvo's brother Richard believes that if it is proven that his brother didn't kill Mary Sullivan, it raises a serious question about who really killed the other victims. On Friday, 26 October 2001, the body of Albert DeSalvo was exhumed and taken to a forensic laboratory for examination. An autopsy was conducted on the remains, attempting to prove DeSalvo's innocence of the murders and, possibly, to identify his killer. On Thursday, 31 December 2001, it was confirmed that DNA evidence taken from Mary Sullivan's remains did not provide a match to Albert DeSalvo. A forensic scientist confirmed that they had found DNA evidence and that the evidence does not and cannot be connected to Albert DeSalvo. The scientist did make it clear that the evidence only cleared DeSalvo of sexual assault. To this day, the fight for the truth goes on.

The murders attributed to the killer known as the Boston Strangler are known the world over and even now, over 35 years since the suspicious death in prison of the prime suspect, there is still a mystery surrounding the case.

ROBERT BERDELLA, AKA THE KANSAS KILLER

In Kansas City over the Easter weekend of 1988, police received a report of a naked man running down the road. When the police came upon the man, they were startled and slightly amused. As they drew closer, they saw that he was totally naked and wearing a dog collar with a red lead attached. The naked man could barely talk and his foot appeared to be injured. His eyes were swollen and red, and he seemed to be having trouble seeing in the daylight. When the officers asked him what had happened, it was clear that he was distressed and visibly shaken. A witness told the police that the man had jumped out of the window of a house across the street. The naked man was Chris Bryson, and he initially told the police a lie about what had happened to him. He told them he had been picked up in a pick-up truck by a man and a woman who had taken him to a house and held him captive.

However, he would later retract that statement as facts emerged to show that there had only been one man and that Bryson was in fact a male prostitute.

The man who picked up Bryson on 29 March was called Bob – an older and taller man than Bryson. They drove to a house. Inside, the house was a mess. Junk was piled up in several rooms and it smelt strongly of dogs. Bob invited Bryson to go upstairs. As Bryson reached the top landing, he was hit from behind on the back of the head. He tried to turn and defend himself, but he felt the prick of a needle in his neck and knew that Bob was injecting him with something; he couldn't fight. Bryson couldn't move and he blacked out.

When Bryson came round he found himself gagged and on a bed, spreadeagled and tied to the bedposts. He had no clothes on and he had no idea how much time had elapsed. He passed out again and when he came round he found that he had a dog collar around his neck. Bob had been sexually abusing him while he had been unconscious and placing drops in his eyes, which caused him great pain. On waking again, he was subjected to more physical torture of the worst kind. Bob had attached an electrical device to Bryson's testicles and thigh, and he felt a sudden strong jolt of electricity going through his lower body. The pain was excruciating, and he gave out a muffled scream. He saw a flash of light and heard a whirring sound. He realised that Bob was taking pictures of him in these humiliating, involuntary poses. By now, Bryson had realised that he was in the hands of a sexual sadist and that he had to try to escape or risk being killed. For the next four days, Bryson was kept a prisoner at the house, alternately drugged, bound, tortured with shocks and sexually assaulted. He was always tied to the bed with the dog collar and lead even when a hand or foot was freed. Bob sometimes injected his throat with drain cleaner and sometimes hit Bryson with an iron bar. Bob also warned Bryson that others before him had died for misbehaviour. To prove this, he showed Bryson photographs of men who looked deceased. They might have been just sleeping, but Bryson could not tell.

However, Bob made one mistake. He tied Bryson's hands in front of him rather than to the bed and, once Bob was gone from the house, Bryson managed to get free and escape. After Bryson told his story to the police, they decided to go and arrest the man they had by then identified as Robert Berdella (b. 1949). He was not at home when the police called so they waited for him to return. When he did, they immediately arrested him on suspicion of sexual assault and asked if he would sign a consent form to allow them to search his home.

Berdella asked for an explanation and refused the police entry to his house without a warrant. He was arrested and taken to the police station without his house having been searched. However, the police soon returned with a warrant and commenced a search. The upstairs bedroom was just as Bryson had described it, with a bed and a television. On the bed were some burnt ropes, which Bryson said he had set light to with discarded matches to free himself, and some bindings tied to the bars on the headboard. Near the bed was a homemade electrical device, plugged in, with wires that led to the bed. The police also found syringes on a tray on a table, prepared and ready, along with a bottle of eye drops and a bottle of what appeared to be a liquid drug. Pornographic magazines were scattered on the floor. The police also found a collection of audiotapes, together with what appeared to be a log or notebook full of scribbled notes that looked like code, and photographs of men who appeared to be asleep. In another room, police found a box of Polaroid photos of Bryson, who appeared to be frightened and suffering. They catalogued everything methodically, unaware that the investigation was soon going to escalate. When they searched Berdella's bedroom the police found two human skulls and two envelopes containing human teeth. One skull was identified as being human, the second a fake. The teeth were believed to have come from the skull and belonged to a young male. By now, a full forensic team was combing the house for evidence.

Police found even more photographs around the house, along with more written records, and a wallet with a man's name in it that was not Berdella's – it turned out to belong to a missing person. Newspaper articles about another missing man were discovered on a table. Even worse, a fresh area of cement had been poured in the basement's concrete floor. By this time, Berdella had been arrested on suspicion of murder. Inside a cupboard, officers found a bag containing human vertebrae. All around the house, they found pieces of paper on which the names of men were written, as well as a man's passport. A thorough police check showed that Berdella had been investigated in 1985, three years earlier, over the disappearance of two young men: Jerry Howell, 19, who went missing in July 1984, and James Ferris, 25, who vanished in September 1985, after Berdella had been seen with both men before their disappearances.

In order to detain Berdella while they continued to search, the police charged him with nine holding charges with regard to Bryson. He was not granted bail. The forensic search then focused on Berdella's back yard, especially when it appeared that one area had recently been dug up. On opening up the ground, they found a human head with tissue and hair still clinging to it, as well as a vertebra. It became of prime importance to ascertain whether the skull had belonged to any of the men whose names and possessions had been found in the house, or other men who had been reported missing. A chainsaw seized from the house was taken for analysis. The analysts found traces of human blood, hair and flesh. They unearthed more vertebrae but no other bones.

Forensic tests on the skulls revealed that both belonged to specific men whose presence in Berdella's house could be proven by other means – items that belonged to them, logs of what Berdella had done to them in which he had sometimes written names, and photographs. One skull was that of a young man named Robert Sheldon. The skull found in the ground was identified as having belonged to Larry Pearson.

As a result, Berdella was charged with Pearson's murder, and in a bid to avoid the death penalty, Berdella pleaded guilty to killing him. Prosecutors were caught off-guard, but they decided to accept this. At that time, the second skull had not yet been identified. They hoped they could bring more charges later. Berdella admitted that he had killed Larry Pearson by asphyxiation. He had placed a plastic bag over his head, secured it with a rope and let him die. He acknowledged that he had been aware of what he was doing and that it was wrong.

The judge deferred judgment at this time. In the meantime, police had been able to identify the body of Sheldon using dental records. This time, prosecutors were ready for his defence team's tactics. They notified the court in advance that they were seeking the death penalty, while Berdella indicated his intention to plead not guilty. Berdella's attorneys offered a deal: Berdella would make a full confession, giving detectives the details of his sadistic crimes and naming names, in exchange for life in prison and for the police dropping their efforts to seize his house. Prosecutors decided to accept the deal and preparations were made to record everything that Berdella revealed. In a small conference room in the basement of the Kansas City jail, under oath, Berdella described what he had done; the confession took up 717 pages. His said his crime spree had begun four years earlier in 1984. All the victims had been abused and all had died inside his house.

The first victim was Jerry Howell; they'd had a sexual relationship for a couple of months. Berdella picked Howell up on the evening of 4 July and took him home, where he fed the young man a variety of tranquillisers. When Howell passed out, Berdella buggered him repeatedly. He used a carrot or cucumber to continue to assault him and then bound him to keep him at the house. Berdella went to work and returned that evening to repeat the assault. He injected Howell with several substances to keep him subdued and beat him with a metal rod. At about 10pm,

Howell died. Berdella claimed that this had surprised him. He had not expected this turn of events and he figured that Howell must have accidentally inhaled his own vomit, as a result of the drug consumption. Berdella knew he had to get rid of the body but before he could dismember it he had to drain out the blood. He hung the body upside down by the feet. Then he took it down and used kitchen knives to cut it into manageable pieces. For some parts, he used his chainsaw. To dispose of Howell, he placed the pieces in bags. He then casually left the bags outside for the dustman to take away.

The next victim was Robert Sheldon, who had stayed at Berdella's house several times. On 10 April 1985, he was taken captive by Berdella, who subjected him to the same atrocities to which he had subjected Howell. However, this time Berdella added something – an injection of Drano (drain cleaning fluid) into the left eye. The idea was to permanently blind Sheldon to make him a more manageable captive. Berdella also mutilated Sheldon's hands with various implements. At one point, a visitor came to the house and, fearing that Sheldon might be heard, Berdella put a bag over his head and suffocated him, ending his four days of torture. Berdella cut Sheldon up in the bath and put the pieces out with the rubbish yet again. He kept the head in a freezer for a few days and then buried it in his back yard.

Two months passed before Berdella killed again. His victim this time was Mark Wallace, who was killed quickly after being given electric shock torture. In September, Walter Ferris was imprisoned and, after being injected and tortured, also died. His body, like the others before him, was cut up into pieces and put out with the rubbish for the dustman. The last murder victim was Larry Pearson, a male prostitute, whom Berdella said he had met in spring 1987. He held Pearson captive towards the end of June. Pearson was more cooperative than the other men, so Berdella did not have to use as much pressure on him. Berdella said that he kept Pearson around as a sex slave for about six weeks. He even thought of putting the dog collar on him first, before he had used it on Bryson. But Pearson decided to try fighting back. Berdella knocked him out to subdue him, and he died. Berdella also kept Pearson's head in the freezer. During his confession, he stated that he had dug up Sheldon's head and replaced it in the ground with Pearson's. Taking the skull inside, he had removed the teeth and placed the skull in the wardrobe.

On 19 December 1988, Berdella pleaded guilty to five more murders. To four of them, he pleaded guilty to second-degree murder, but for Robert Sheldon he accepted the charge of first-degree murder. He was sentenced to life imprisonment. On 8 October 1992, Berdella died in prison of a heart attack. For his four years of crimes against other men, he had served just four years in prison.

ANGELO BUONO AND KENNETH BIANCHI, AKA THE HILLSIDE STRANGLERS

In October 1977, the city of Los Angeles was thrown into a state of panic following a series of unexplained murders of young women. The police dubbed the killer the Hillside Strangler, simply because the bodies of the murder victims were dumped on hillsides on the outskirts of LA.

On Sunday, 20 November 1977, police were called to see the body of a young naked girl, Kristina Weckler, a 20-year-old student who had been found in the hills between Glendale and Eagle Rock. There were ligature marks on her wrists, ankles and neck, blood was oozing from her rectum and there were bruises on her breasts. Police also noticed two puncture marks on her arm, but no signs of the needle tracks that would indicate she was a drug addict. The initial police reaction was that the girl had been murdered elsewhere and that whoever dumped the body must have known the area.

That same day, police were alerted to the bodies of two girls that had been found on the other side of the same hillside area. The girls were Dolores Cepeda, 12, and Sonja Johnson, 14, both of whom had been missing for about a week from St Ignatius

School. The bodies were in an advanced state of decomposition and were maggot-infested. Both girls had been strangled. They were last seen getting off a bus and going over to a large two-ton sedan truck to talk to someone seated in the passenger seat. If this vehicle were connected to the murders, it would confirm police suspicions that there could have been two killers, probably both men.

On 23 November, the body of Jane King, 28, was found, this time near the Golden State Freeway. Her maggot-infested body was estimated to have been there for some two weeks. She had been strangled like the others, but it was not clear whether she had been raped or not. She had gone missing on 8 November.

The killer or killers struck again that same month on 29 November around Glendale's Mount Washington area. The naked body of Lauren Wagner, an 18-year-old student, was found lying partially in the street. Her body bore the same ligature marks on her ankles, wrists and neck, which the police had come to associate with the aptly named Hillside Strangler. However, there were other aspects of the murder that officers had not seen in the previous murders. They noticed that she had burns on her hands. There was also something else that was different, a shiny trace of some sticky substance. If this substance was semen or saliva, there was the possibility that the killer's blood group could be determined. Tests on semen found in the earlier victims had revealed nothing.

The police came up with an eye-witness to Lauren's abduction. The middle-aged female witness lived in the house next to which Lauren's car had been parked and had seen Lauren pull over to the kerb at around 9pm. Two men had pulled up in a car alongside her. There was some kind of disagreement and Lauren ended up in the car with the two men. The witness described the men's car as large and dark with a white top. One of the men had dragged Lauren from her car into his. She heard Lauren cry out, 'You won't get away with this!' The witness described the men: one was tall and young with acne scars; the other one was Latin-looking, older and shorter with bushy hair. She was certain that she would be able to identify them again. The police were a little unsure about what the witness told them. The descriptions and overheard conversation seemed too good to be true considering the distance she had been from the abduction. However, this female witness was now terrified – prior to the police arriving to talk to her, she had received a mysterious phone call from a man with a New York accent who, in no uncertain terms, told her to keep quiet about what she had seen.

By now, the police had formed an elite taskforce and it looked closely at other similar murders that had occurred before this series. On 17 October 1977, a prostitute called Yolanda Washington had been raped and strangled. Her naked body had been dumped near the Forest Lawn cemetery.

On 31 October, the naked body of a woman was found on the roadside. Bruises on her neck showed that she had been strangled. Police found marks on her wrists and ankles as well as her neck. Her body had started to decompose. On one of her eyelids was a small piece of light-coloured fluff that forensic experts seized. It did not appear that she had been murdered where the body was found. The police had great difficulty in trying to identify the body. They believed it to be that of a young prostitute, Judy Miller. A witness said he had seen Judy Miller leave the Fish and Chips restaurant at 9pm on the evening before she was found dead.

A week later, on the morning of Sunday, 6 November 1977, the naked body of Lisa Kastin, 21, a waitress who worked at the Healthfair restaurant near Hollywood and Vine, was found. Lisa had last been seen leaving the Healthfair restaurant just after 9pm on the night she was murdered. She had been strangled and there was evidence of rape, but not buggery.

In mid-December, police were called to a steep hillside on Alvarado Street where they found the body of Kimberly Diane Martin, another prostitute working under the cover of a modelling agency. Kimberly Martin's last client had directed her to apartment 114 at 1950 Tamarind, which turned out to be vacant. The murderer's call was traced to a pay phone in the lobby of the Hollywood public library.

No more murders occurred until 16 February 1978, when 20-year-old Cindy Hudspeth was murdered. Her strangled and brutalised body was found in the boot of her car, which had been pushed off a cliff. The murder had all the hallmarks of the previous killings, and the police now had a lead. Cindy lived in the same area of Glendale as one of the other victims, Kristina Weckler. The police believed that the killer or killers might live in the same area. This, however, was the only lead they had to pursue – and then, all of a sudden, the murders ceased.

It was not until December 1979 that the police had to dust the files down and review them all once more. On 12 January 1979, the police in Bellingham, Washington, were told that two female students were missing. The two room-mates, Karen Mandic and Diane Wilder, were not the type of people to take off irresponsibly without telling anyone, so when Karen didn't show up for work, her boss became worried. He remembered that she had accepted a house-sitting job in a very wealthy bayside neighbourhood from a security-guard friend of hers. Police contacted the security firm, which in turn called the security guard to ask him about the supposed house-sitting job for one of the company's clients. The security guard claimed he knew nothing about it and had never heard of the two missing women. The security guard had told his employer that he had been at a sheriff's reserve meeting the night the two women disappeared.

When police found out that the security guard had not been at the sheriff's reserve meeting as he had told his employer, they decided to contact the security guard directly. They found him to be a friendly young man who had missed the sheriff's meeting because it was about first aid, a subject with which he was familiar. At that time, they had no cause to disbelieve the man, as all they had were two missing persons. It wasn't long before the missing girls both turned up dead. Their bodies were found inside an abandoned car in some woods. Both had been strangled. Other bruises suggested that they had been subjected to savage assaults. A full forensic examination was carried out.

Police decided to arrest the security guard, a man named Kenneth Bianchi (b. 1955). They wanted to try to keep him in custody while awaiting the forensic results. This was made easy as stolen property from sites he had been guarding was found at his house. They also ascertained from Los Angeles that Bianchi had resided in the Glendale area at the time of the murders there. Jewellery found in Bianchi's home matched the description of jewellery that was worn by two of the victims: Kimberly Martin's ram's horn necklace and Olanda Washington's turquoise ring. They now believed they had either the killer or one of the killers responsible for the Los Angeles stranglings. Police also discovered that Bianchi and his cousin Angelo Buono (b. 1934), who still resided in Los Angeles, had both come to the notice of police in Los Angeles for incidents involving young girls, where they had been impersonating police officers and trying to entice young girls into their car. They suspected that Buono might be the second killer.

While Bianchi languished in custody, he hatched a cunning defence plan. He would try to convince the authorities that he was suffering from a personality disorder and therefore insane. There followed protracted discussions between the defence and the prosecution with regard to the issue of insanity. The prosecution would not accept this plea. The outcome was that a deal was offered to Bianchi. If he pleaded guilty to the Ashington murders and to some of the Hillside Strangler murders, he would get life with the possibility of parole and he would be allowed to serve his sentence in California, where the prisons were supposedly more bearable than in Washington. In return, Bianchi was to agree to testify against Angelo Buono. He agreed.

Bianchi was then questioned at length about the murders and the involvement of Angelo Buono. Bianchi told officers that he and Angelo had pretended to be policemen, with fake police badges.

Most of the victims were prostitutes, so it had been easy to convince them to get into the car. The hillside areas used to dispose of the victims were used because Buono knew them well. An important moment in the interview came when Bianchi was asked what type of material had been used to blindfold Judy Miller. Kenneth thought that it was foam that Angelo used in his car upholstery business. The little piece of fluff that forensic experts had found on the dead girl's eyelid could be just the kind of corroborating evidence they needed to convict Buono. Police had been puzzled by the murder of Kristina Weckler, but Bianchi told them the grisly story. He described how she was brought out to the kitchen and put on the floor, then her head was covered with a bag. A pipe from the new stove, which wasn't yet fully installed, was disconnected, put into the bag and then turned on. There may have been marks on her neck because a cord was put around it with a bag and tied to make a more complete seal. It took about an hour and a half of suffering before she died of asphyxiation.

Bianchi was finally brought to trial and sentenced to two life sentences in the state of Washington. He was immediately transferred to California, where he was sentenced to additional life terms. He would serve 35 years in Californian prisons and additional time in Washington.

Angelo Buono was finally arrested on 22 October 1979. Police found his wallet, which clearly showed the outline of the police badge. However, things were not going well for the police. Bianchi by this time had started to change his story; he realised that the prisoners had a code of conduct that they should not inform on each other. Rough justice could be dealt out if these rules were broken. But Bianchi also had another plan, which he hoped might secure his freedom.

Bianchi had a girlfriend, Veronica Crompton, who was supposedly writing a play about a female serial killer. She wanted desperately to talk with Bianchi to better understand the mind of a murderer. Bianchi saw his opportunity to manipulate Veronica to his own advantage. He made a startling proposal, which he told her would lead to him spending his life with her. He asked her to go to Bellingham, the scene of the Ashington murders, and strangle a girl to make it look as if the same man who had killed Karen Mandic and Diane Wilder had killed her. Bianchi even suggested that Veronica plant semen on the murdered girl. Blinded by love, Veronica agreed. Bianchi was a non-secretor, which meant that in the days before DNA testing, his blood type could not be determined from his semen. Safe in this knowledge, he supplied Veronica with some of his semen in a plastic glove.

Veronica went to Bellingham and, fuelled by drink and drugs, she lured a woman to her motel room for a drink. Veronica lunged at the woman with a cord and tried to strangle her, but the woman was too strong and knocked her over. This brought Veronica to her senses. She aborted the plan and went back to California. On arriving back, she created a hysterical disturbance at the airport and then went on to send the police an audiotape with a letter telling them that they had arrested an innocent man for the Hillside murders and pointed to the recent strangling attempt to prove that the real culprit was still at large. It did not take the police very long to link Veronica to the attempted strangling and the airport disturbance.

By now, the evidence the police needed to corroborate Bianchi's confession implicating Buono had been obtained. The fibres found on Judy Miller's eyelid and Lauren Wagner's hands came from Angelo's house and upholstery shop. Animal hairs stuck to Lauren's hands were from the rabbits that Angelo raised. In addition to the imprint of a police badge on his wallet were appropriate puncture marks from where the badge had been pinned. Two witnesses had also positively identified Buono in a photo identification procedure.

Angelo Buono was charged with the murders and a number of connected offences and brought to trial. Before the trial started, the judge agreed to sever the charges in respect of the unconnected offences, allowing Buouno to be tried on just the murder charges.

It was anticipated that during the trial the prosecution would introduce evidence relating to the connected offences.

Bianchi was called to give evidence on 6 July 1981 against his cousin, Buono. He made an effort to convince the court that they should not use his evidence. He stated that he may have faked the multiple personality disorder, but he didn't know whether he was telling the truth or not when he said that Angelo was involved in the murders. In fact, he didn't think he himself was involved in any of the killings either. This put the prosecution case in jeopardy and they made an application for the charges against Buono to be dropped. The judge, however, would not agree and believed that there was still enough evidence for a jury to decide.

In spring 1983, Buono finally stood trial. The jury did not begin deliberating until 21 October and, after much discussion, finally came to agreement on 31 October 1983. They found him guilty of the murder of Lauren Wagner. After more deliberation on 3 November, they found him not guilty of the murder of Yolanda Washington. More deliberating took place and they found him guilty of the murders of Judy Miller, Dolores Cepeda, Sonja Johnson, Kimberly Martin, Kristina Weckler, Lisa Kastin, Jane King and, finally, Cindy Hudspeth. Under Californian law at that time, as a 'multiple murderer', Buono faced either the death penalty or life in prison without possibility of parole. The jury spared him the death penalty and he was sentenced to life imprisonment. The judge was not happy. He said: 'Angelo Buono and Kenneth Bianchi subjected various murder victims to the administration of lethal gas, electrocution, strangulation by rope and lethal hypodermic injection. Yet the two defendants were destined to spend their lives in prison, housed, fed and clothed at taxpayers' expense, better cared for than some of the destitute law-abiding members of our community.'

On 21 September 2002, at Calipatria State Prison, Angelo Buono, 67, was found dead in his cell. He was believed to have died from heart failure.

WILLIAM BONIN, AKA THE FREEWAY KILLER

At the age of eight, William Bonin (b. 1947) was arrested for stealing car number plates, and he soon ended up in a juvenile detention centre. It was there that older boys sexually abused him. After leaving high school, Bonin joined the US Air Force and served in the Vietnam War as a gunner, picking up a medal for good conduct.

In 1969, after a very brief marriage that ended in divorce, Bonin moved to California. At the age of 23, he was arrested for sexually assaulting young boys. He was imprisoned and released in 1975 but was soon arrested again and imprisoned for raping a 14-year-old boy. David McVicker was hitchhiking when Bonin offered a ride. Bonin asked the boy for sex and pulled out a gun, drove to a remote area and raped him. Bonin then proceeded to choke the boy with his own T-shirt, the same method he would use to kill some of his later victims. However, when McVicker cried out, Bonin released him and apologised for choking him.

The first victim Bonin murdered was named Marcus Grabs, a 17-year-old hitchhiker who was last seen hitchhiking on 5 August 1979. Bonin and a friend, Vernon Butts, picked up Marcus, buggered him and stabbed him more than 70 times. Grabs's naked body was found a short time later with a yellow nylon rope around his neck. An electrical cord was wrapped around one ankle.

Three weeks after Grabs's naked body was found, a 15-year-old, Donald Hyden, was found dead and mutilated in a rubbish bin near a freeway. Bonin and Butts had struck again. Hyden was raped and strangled with a ligature. His throat had also been slashed and an attempt had been made to castrate him. On 12 September 1979, the body of David Murillo, 17, was found near the same freeway. He had disappeared while riding his bike to the cinema three days earlier. His skull had been crushed. He had also been buggered and strangled with a ligature.

No more bodies were discovered until December 1979, when the body of Frank Fox, 17, was found in a similar condition to the previous victims, near another freeway. On the morning of 3 February 1980, Bonin and another accomplice, Gregory Matthew Miley, were cruising the highways when they saw 15-year-old Charles Miranda. They picked up the young man, drove around and parked the van. Bonin then buggered the boy and urged Miley to do the same, but Miley was unable to sustain an erection. Frustrated by this, he raped the boy with a blunt object. Bonin then strangled the boy with his own shirt, using a tyre lever to twist the shirt like a tourniquet around his neck. They then dumped the body in a Los Angeles alley, where it was later found. Bonin then suggested they went hunting for another victim. A few hours later, they abducted, raped and killed James McCabe who, aged 12, was the youngest victim.

Between 14 March and 29 April 1980, six other teenage boys went missing. All were found dead near freeways, and all had been murdered in an identical fashion. But now the police got the break they had been needing. A 17-year-old youth, William Pugh, was arrested for stealing a car. He told police that Bonin had boasted he was the Freeway Killer. Bonin was now the prime suspect, but where was he?

On the morning of 2 June 1980, Bonin and another accomplice, James Munro, picked up 19-year-old Steven Wells, who agreed to accompany them back to the apartment they were sharing so they could have sex. Bonin and Wells had sex and Bonin offered Wells $200 if he would allow himself to be tied up. Wells agreed. After Wells was bound, Bonin began to assault him. Munro then supposedly went into another room and allegedly took no part in the murder of Wells that followed. After Wells was killed, both Bonin and Munro took the body and dumped it.

Bonin was now under police surveillance, which paid dividends. On 11 June, they arrested him in the act of assaulting a 15-year-old boy – he had been in the process of buggering the teenager in his van. Tape and rope similar to that used to bind some of the victims was found in the van, as well as a scrapbook of the Freeway Killer stories.

When interviewed, Bonin readily admitted to abducting and killing 21 boys and young men. Police also suspected him of committing up to 15 other murders. He was eventually charged with 14 of the murders to which he admitted. He expressed no remorse and said, 'I couldn't stop killing. It got easier each time.'

On 5 January 1982, Bonin was found guilty on all 14 charges and sentenced to death. However, he spent many years on death row before the execution was finally carried out. On 23 February 1996, Bonin was executed by lethal injection. He was the first person to be executed by this method in Californian penal history.

Bonin's main accomplice, Vernon Butts, was charged with being involved in six of the murders, but he hanged himself while awaiting trial. Gregory Miley and James Munro were given sentences of 25 years to life imprisonment and 15 years to life, respectively, after pleading guilty to being involved in one murder each. Both men are still in prison. Munro has tried to appeal, claiming that he was tricked into accepting a plea-bargain. William Pugh was sentenced to six years for manslaughter.

The bodies of young men and boys continued to be found along the freeways of southern California after Bonin's arrest, leading police to believe at first that he had other accomplices who were still active. However, these later murders turned out to have been committed by Randy Steven Kraft, who acted entirely separately from Bonin but who happened to have a similar MO. In fact, there was also a third freeway killer, Patrick Kearney, who abducted young men from the freeways of southern California during the 1970s. The three independent killers may have claimed up to 130 victims between them.

KEITH HUNTER JESPERSON, AKA THE HAPPY FACE KILLER

In Portland, Oregon, on Tuesday evening, 23 January 1990, pretty 23-year-old Taunja Bennett was to be the first victim of 35-year-old Keith Jesperson (b. 1955), who befriended her in a local bar. After striking up a conversation and plying her with drinks, Jesperson invited her back to his house, where they had sex. However, following this, Jesperson started arguing with Taunja and started to hit her about the face and head with brute force. He was over twice her size, weighing 240lb. When Taunja attempted to fight back and defend herself against this giant of a man, he placed one of his massive hands around her throat and grabbed a rope with his other hand. Without even taking the time to think about his actions, Jesperson wrapped the rope around Taunja's neck, pulled it tight and strangled her, watching the life slowly leave her body. When she ceased to struggle and her body became limp, he let her partially naked body slump to the floor. For a man who had just killed another person for the first time, he remained calm. Leaving her at his house, he drove back to the bar and sat around drinking and talking to anyone who would listen to him, presumably to establish an alibi for himself. After a few more beers, Jesperson drove back to the house and placed Taunja's lifeless body in the front seat of a friend's car. He drove for a while then found a secluded and dark place to dispose of the body. He pulled her body out of the car and threw it down an embankment, where it was found several days later.

Meanwhile, Jesperson was just a step away from fulfilling his childhood dream of becoming a policeman. However, after being initially accepted he sustained an injury and was rejected as a result. This may have been what finally tipped him over the edge and turned him into a vicious serial killer.

Rejected by the police, Jesperson took up work as a truck driver on long-haul journeys. Over a year elapsed until July 1992, when he would kill again. This time, his victim was an unidentified female whose body was found on 30 August, approximately 10 miles over the state border in California. Investigators believed that she had been dead for a number of weeks. She was never formally identified, although Jesperson would later state that her name was Claudia. The following month, the body of Cynthia Lynn Rose, 32, was found along

Highway 99, also in California. She too had been dead for some time and her death was initially listed as a drug overdose.

Instead of keeping a low profile, Jesperson did the complete opposite. He began writing letters to a newspaper in Oregon, claiming responsibility for Rose's murder as well as others. In one letter, he had claimed that Rose was a prostitute he had picked up and murdered. He signed his letters with a smiling 'happy face', which is how he came to be known as the Happy Face Killer. The letters were given to the police but there was no evidence as to who the writer was. However, it wasn't long before a pattern emerged in the killer's MO.

Laurie Ann Pentland, 26, became the next victim. Laurie's body was found in November 1992 behind a shop in Salem, Oregon, 50 miles south of Portland. She had been strangled. Again, there were no leads save for the method used by the killer. In July 1993, another unidentified female body was discovered in California by the side of a truck stop. The woman had been dead for only a couple of days when her body was found and a County Coroner listed her death as a drug overdose. Her case would eventually be reopened and looked at as a murder, after Jesperson wrote another letter to the newspaper as the Happy Face Killer, referring to the victim as a 'street person'.

On 14 September 1994 in Florida, and again by the side of a busy road, the skeletal remains of what would be known as victim number six were found. Again, the victim was not identified despite extensive police enquiries. It was believed she had been approximately 40 years old at the time of her death. Victim number seven soon followed, 21-year-old Angela Subrize of Oklahoma City, whose body was found soon after that of the previous victim. Many who knew her did not even realise she was missing, as she moved about the country on a regular basis.

Jesperson was soon to make his first mistake. It wasn't until victim number eight was found that the net started to close on him. This time, he murdered someone he knew instead of a complete stranger. Julie Ann Winningham, 41, from

Washington, was believed to have been murdered on 10 March 1995, just a few miles east of Vancouver. Like the others, she had been strangled and her naked body had been dumped over an embankment alongside a busy road. Julie's friends and relatives knew that she had been seeing Jesperson and gave the police his details.

As a result, the police started to investigate Jesperson more closely. They found that he was a truck driver who travelled the length and breadth of North America. Knowing his connection with Julie Ann Winningham, they traced him to New Mexico, where he was detained and spoken to in relation to Winningham's murder; however, the police had to release him as they had no evidence to hold him on.

Jesperson now believed it was only a matter of time before he was caught and so he wrote letters to his brother and one to his children confessing to murdering a woman in his truck, and adding that he had killed eight more. He then telephoned the police and made a confession over the phone. He was arrested and charged with the murder of Julie Ann Winningham.

Victim number seven was found following his arrest after he had boasted about killing a female he picked up in Wyoming in September 1995. He described a specific tattoo of Tweety Pie that she had on her ankle. Based on this information, Nebraska highway patrolmen found the remains of Angela Subrize, where she had been lying in tall grass for several months, probably since early January. Badly decomposed, most of her skin had decayed and investigators were able to identify her only after examining pelvic X-rays and finding the tattoo of Tweety Pie that was still visible on one of her ankles, one of only a few identifying marks that remained on her body. Jesperson was then charged with her murder. This time, if convicted, he would face the death penalty. In an effort to avoid this, he offered to provide information in relation to other murders. This offer was rejected.

Police had now also been able to connect Jesperson to the other murders by comparing his handwriting on the letters he had sent to the newspapers. While awaiting trial, he indicated he might well have killed up to 160 people, but he would later retract all of these confessions.

In October 1995, Jesperson was brought to trial for the murder of Julie Ann Winningham. He pleaded guilty and was sentenced to life imprisonment. Following this, he was extradited back to Oregon. On Thursday, 2 November 1995, after waiving all of his rights, he pleaded guilty to the murder of Taunja Bennett. This sentence gave Jesperson the chance to avoid the death penalty in Wyoming. The Oregon sentence made potential death penalties in other states less likely and Jesperson knew it.

However, there was another Oregon case involving Jesperson that had yet to come to court. This was the murder of 23-year-old Laurie Ann Pentland. Jesperson had now been forensically linked to her murder through DNA and also by the letters. Jesperson was again sentenced to life in prison in Oregon, with a 30-year minimum term before parole eligibility. Following his sentencing in Washington, he was transferred to the Oregon State Penitentiary to begin serving consecutive sentences. If he remains alive to complete his sentences in Oregon, he will be transferred to the Washington State Penitentiary to begin serving his life sentence there.

However, in 1997, more than two years later, the State of Wyoming finally succeeded in extraditing Jesperson for trial for the murder of Angela Subrize. For the next few months, there were many legal arguments. Jesperson stated that he would change his story regarding the jurisdiction in which he had killed Angela. At one point, he said that he had killed her in Wyoming and at another point he claimed that he had killed her in Nebraska. Eventually a deal was struck. Jesperson agreed to plead guilty to murdering Angela Subrize in Wyoming if prosecutors would agree not to seek the death penalty against him.

As a result, on 3 June 1998, Jesperson was sentenced to life in prison and it was ordered that the sentence would run consecutive to the two life sentences in Oregon and the life sentence in Washington, leaving little doubt that he would die in prison. It remains to be seen whether any other jurisdictions, such as the states of Florida or California, will prosecute Jesperson for murders that he confessed to in those states, both of which still have the death penalty.

ROBERT LEROY ANDERSON

Monday, 29 July 1996 was destined not to be an ordinary day for the Streyle family of Canistota, South Dakota. It was their son Nathan's second birthday and they looked forward to celebrating later that evening. Piper Streyle, 28, was preparing to take Nathan and her daughter, Shaina, three, to their babysitter before going to work. Her husband Vance, 29, had left earlier to go to work.

Around 9.30am a man forced his way into the Streyles' mobile home while Piper, Shaina and Nathan were still there. A violent struggle occurred between Piper and the man, which the children witnessed. The intruder then abducted Piper, leaving Shaina and Nathan alone, utterly traumatised by what they had seen. Friends later found them after frantic phone calls. As a result of what the children said, the police were called. Three days after Piper's abduction, her husband remembered an important piece of information, which he told to the police. It would prove to be the break they were looking for and would lead to the identification of one of South Dakota's most sadistic sexual murderers.

Streyle told the police about a man he remembered visiting their home several days prior to his wife's disappearance. He recalled that a balding man in his twenties named Rob Anderson had come to their trailer at around 7.30am on 26 July to enquire about enrolling his kids into the Streyles' Bible camp for children, which they operated every July. He claimed that Anderson seemed startled to see him, as if he didn't expect him to be home. Once Anderson overcame his initial surprise, he briefly asked about the camp. Vance referred him to Piper, who explained that the camp was over for the summer but suggested he sign his kids up for the next year. Anderson agreed and wrote down his name and telephone number before leaving.

The police immediately began investigating the information Vance gave them. Their new suspect was 26-year-old Robert Leroy Anderson, a maintenance man at the John Morrell & Co. meat-packing plant.

A number of witnesses told police that they had seen a black Bronco truck in the vicinity of the Streyles' mobile home on the day Piper went missing. One of the witnesses was a highway worker who told investigators that he saw a black Bronco approximately three times that day, once at around 9.45am, a second time approximately one hour later and a final time at about 12.30pm. A neighbouring couple told police that at around 11.45am on the day in question they saw a black Bronco close to the Streyles' home. The neighbours saw the truck again about one hour later. It was stationary in the front of the driveway and they saw a man wearing a baseball cap and jeans coming out of the Streyles' home.

On 30 July, police contacted Anderson and asked him to go voluntarily to the police station to be interviewed, which he did. During approximately eight hours of videotaped questioning, Anderson calmly admitted to going to the Streyles' trailer four days earlier. Even though he hadn't established an alibi for 29 July, he did tell police that he had returned to the Streyles' house that day to ask permission to use the archery range on their property, but no one answered the door so he left. Anderson denied knowing anything about the abduction of Piper or her whereabouts.

While the police were interrogating Anderson, they examined his blue Bronco and his home. During the search, they would find what would prove to be some of the most crucial incriminating evidence against Anderson in respect of other crimes. Sadly, it would not lead to Piper's whereabouts. In fact, she was never found. The police discovered several receipts for duct tape, black water-based tempera paint, paintbrushes and a bucket, most of which had been purchased a few days prior to and on the day Piper went missing.

Police suspected that the paint was used to disguise Anderson's Bronco, and these suspicions would prove to be correct. They called in experts to analyse the paint on the truck more closely. Samples were taken and chemically tested. They found that the Bronco had been painted with the same material bought by Anderson around 29 July. The paint used was a kind that could be easily applied and washed off.

Inside the vehicle, even more incriminating evidence was discovered. The police found a wooden platform that had holes drilled into it. It was believed that it had been made as a restraining device – a person's ankles and hands could be tied to metal hoops that were strategically inserted into the board. The platform had been sized to fit perfectly into the back of the truck. The forensic team also found hairs attached to the wooden platform, and these were identified as Piper's. Moreover, a dirty shovel, furniture-moving straps, weeds, a toolbox and dog hairs similar to those of the Streyles' dog were also discovered in the truck. It was becoming increasingly clear that there was more to Anderson than met the eye.

At Anderson's home, police found a pair of jeans in his laundry basket, stained with what appeared to be blood. The jeans were taken away for analysis. It was found that the DNA structure of the blood did not match that of Anderson or his family. It was believed to be Piper's blood. They also found semen stains on the jeans but they were not able to match them genetically to Anderson because they had such a limited specimen to test. During the search, a set of handcuff keys was found, but Anderson emphatically denied that he owned a pair of handcuffs. After lengthy questioning, and due to the lack of evidence at that time, he was released.

In the interim period, police carried out photo identification parades in which a photo of Anderson was included among others of similar description. One of Piper's children identified him as the man who had abducted their mother; Piper's husband identified him as being the man who had come to discuss the Bible classes. These positive identifications gave police the evidence they needed to press charges against Anderson.

On 2 August 1996, Anderson was arrested on two counts of kidnapping. The police were unable to charge him with murder because they lacked the evidence of a body. In September of that year, the police launched a massive search for Piper and any other evidence that might convict Anderson of murder. They wanted to ensure that he would serve the maximum sentence for his crime, and employed the help of hundreds of volunteers who searched the wooded area around the Big Sioux River. During the hunt for evidence, several significant items were discovered. Half of a shirt torn down the middle with the logo 'Code Zero' was found. It was the same shirt Piper had been wearing on the day she disappeared. A man picked up the other half of the black-and-white striped shirt on 29 July on a road near Baltic. He initially thought it was a referee shirt, yet when he discovered it wasn't he threw it in the back of his car and forgot about it. He later gave it to the police when he realised the shirt's significance. Near the Big Sioux River, where part of the shirt had been found, was a roll of duct tape with human hairs attached to it. The hair was later analysed and found to be consistent with samples taken from Piper's hairbrush. Moreover, the duct tape taken from the scene matched the roll recovered from Anderson's truck two months earlier. More gruesome physical evidence was discovered around the river, which included several lengths of rope and chains, eyebolts, a vibrator and a half-burnt candle. It was believed that the items had been used to torture Piper. They also presented clear evidence that Anderson was a sexual sadist.

In May 1997, Anderson was tried and found guilty of kidnapping Piper. He was eventually sentenced to life imprisonment in South Dakota State Penitentiary. However, it would not be the only charge for which he would be convicted.

One of Anderson's friends, Jamie Hammer, came forward and spoke to the police and gave them new information regarding Anderson's sexually sadistic and predatory behaviour. They learnt that Piper was not his only victim. Hammer said that as far back as high school he was aware of Anderson's obsession with torturing and murdering women. Hammer was intrigued by the idea and the two often discussed ways in which to commit the perfect crime. As their conversations progressed and grew more detailed over time, so did their fantasies. It wasn't long before the two men decided to act them out. Hammer and Anderson actually planned abducting a woman together. They placed sharp objects on the road and then waited for a victim to drive by, run over the sharp objects and get a flat tyre. It was then that they planned to attack the unsuspecting female. Hammer didn't know it, but Anderson had already pre-selected a victim named Amy Anderson, 26 (no relation to Anderson himself).

In November 1994, Amy was on her way home from a friend's house near Tea, South Dakota. As Anderson had planned, her car tyre was punctured. She pulled off the road to change it. As she reached into her boot to get the spare tyre, Anderson grabbed her and carried her off the road towards a wooded area. Luckily, Amy managed to break free and flag down a passing car that stopped to pick her up.

The attempted kidnapping of Amy remained unsolved until the arrest of Anderson, when it was brought once again to the fore. Amy was able to identify Anderson in a police line-up, but he would never stand trial for the crime. Instead, another friend of Anderson named Glen Marcus Walker would take the blame. He had also been involved with Anderson and Hammer in Amy's unsuccessful abduction. Several years later, during his trial, Walker pleaded guilty to the offence. However, it would not be the only crime he would admit that he committed with Anderson. Police discovered that even before Amy was attacked, Anderson and Walker had committed another, more gruesome, crime. In 1991, while working together, they devised a plan to abduct and kill a female worker from where they worked, Larisa Dumansky. On 26 August, Anderson approached Larisa in the car park at their place of work. He abducted her at knifepoint and ordered her into his vehicle. Then Anderson and Walker drove Larisa to Lake Vermillion. When they arrived at the lake, Walker watched as Anderson dragged Larisa out of the car and raped her several times. Larisa pleaded desperately for her life but Anderson ignored her. Anderson suffocated her with duct tape and then buried her remains under a bush. At the time of Larisa's death she was six weeks pregnant. Walker later told police he was not involved in the murder and led them to where her body had been buried. When they dug up her remains, they were puzzled as to why there were only half of her remains in the grave – but would only find the answer several months later.

While in prison, Anderson shared a cell with Jeremy Brunner, who contacted the Attorney General's office in August 1997 with information about Anderson's crimes. He told them that Anderson bragged excessively and in great detail about the murders of Piper and Larisa during the week in which they shared a cell. Brunner told the authorities that Anderson admitted he was a serial killer and that he kept trophies of his victims at his grandmother's house. He even gave the precise location of the items. He said Anderson had hidden them between the ceiling and the wall of his grandmother's basement. The items included a ring and a necklace belonging to Piper and Larisa, as well as his gun. Anderson told Brunner that he believed Walker might tell the authorities about the murders. Anderson told him that he had a feeling that if Walker were ever arrested he would reveal the location of Larisa's body.

In order to prevent the police from discovering Larisa's identity if she was ever found, which could link the murder to him, Anderson decided to remove her skull and teeth from the shallow grave. He then threw them from the car window as he drove from the scene. Brunner's story explained why the police had found only portions of Larisa's body. Brunner claimed that Anderson had also bragged about abducting Piper. He said that Anderson admitted to raping and strangling her before disposing of her body in Big Sioux River. Witnesses said that they saw Anderson on several occasions on the day of Piper's disappearance. Brunner explained that the reason for this was because Anderson had forgotten a couple of items and returned home to retrieve them. The police then went to the house of Anderson's grandmother, where they found the items in the exact spots as described by Anderson when talking to Brunner.

On 4 September 1997, Anderson was charged with murdering Larisa Dumansky. He was also charged with the rape and murder of Piper Streyle. His trial commenced in the first week of March and lasted one month. Brunner agreed to testify and was given a lighter sentence for the crimes he had committed.

On 6 April, the jury quickly returned its verdict. Anderson was found guilty on four counts including the rape and murder of Piper and the kidnapping and murder of Larisa. Three days later, the same jury sentenced Anderson to death by lethal injection. However, the state would be denied the chance to execute him. On 30 March 2002, while awaiting the outcome of his appeal, he was found dead in his cell, hanging by a sheet tied to a bar.

Glenn Walker was tried for his crimes in March 2000. He pleaded guilty to the attempted kidnapping of Amy Anderson, being an accessory to kidnapping and first-degree murder and conspiracy to kidnap Larisa Dumansky. He received a total of 30 years' imprisonment.

ALTON COLEMAN AND DEBRA BROWN

Alton Coleman (b. 1955) left middle school without completing his education. His mother was a prostitute who regularly used to have sex with her clients in front of him. He eventually went to live with his 73-year-old grandmother and, with no parental guidance, soon came to the notice of the police. Between 1973 and 1983, he was charged with sexual offences on no less than six occasions. Coleman was due to stand trial in Illinois accused of raping a 14-year-old girl when he fled and began his indiscriminate killing.

Debra Brown (b. 1963) was one of 11 children; she suffered a head injury when very young that left her mentally impaired. She met Coleman in 1983, and up until then, she had been of good character. During the summer of 1984, Coleman, then aged 28, and Brown, aged 21, embarked on a murderous killing spree throughout the American Midwest.

Their crimes began in May 1984 when Coleman befriended Juanita Wheat, who lived in Wisconsin and was the mother of nine-year-old Vernita. On 29 May 1984, Coleman abducted Vernita and murdered her. Her body was discovered on 19 June 1984 in an abandoned building. The body was badly decomposed and the cause of death was ligature strangulation.

On 18 June, two young girls, Tamika Turks and her nine-year-old sister Annie, disappeared on their way to the shops. They had been abducted by Brown and Coleman. Annie, the older girl, was forced to watch as Brown and Coleman killed Tamika. Brown held Tamika on the ground and covered her nose and mouth while Coleman continuously jumped up and down on her chest and face until her ribs fractured and punctured her vital organs. The older sister was then was forced to have sex with both Brown and Coleman before being beaten about the head and abandoned. Miraculously, she survived. A day later, Tamika's brutalised body was found in a wooded area.

The same day Tamika Turks's body was discovered, Donna Williams, 25, was reported missing by her parents. Her car had also gone missing. A week later, her car was found abandoned in Detroit with a forged identification card showing Brown's picture. Her disappearance was treated as a murder enquiry, and her body was found in an abandoned house on 11 July; she had been strangled.

The hunt was now on for Brown and Coleman. Police in four states were looking for them. In the meantime, two days after

Williams was reported missing, Brown and Coleman abducted a woman in Detroit. However, she managed to get away by crashing her car into oncoming traffic. Now on the run in Detroit, the pair committed two robberies to obtain money. On 28 June 1984, Coleman and Brown entered the home of Mr and Mrs Palmer Jones of Dearborn Heights, Michigan. Palmer was handcuffed by Coleman and then badly beaten. Mrs Jones was also attacked. Coleman ripped the Jones's phone from the wall and stole money and their car.

On 5 July 1984, Coleman and Brown arrived in Toledo, Ohio, where Coleman befriended Virginia Temple, the mother of several children. Her eldest child was Rachelle, aged nine. When neighbours were concerned about not having seen her for a time, the police were called. On entering the home, they found the very young children alone and frightened. Virginia's and Rachelle's bodies were discovered in a cupboard; both had been strangled. A bracelet was missing from the house, and this would later be found in Cincinnati under the body of Tonnie Storey, another victim of Brown and Coleman.

On 13 July, Brown and Coleman journeyed south, stopping off in Cincinnati. There they murdered Marlene Walters and left her husband Harry for dead. He survived and told the police that Coleman and Brown had enquired about a camper he had put up for sale. Walters sat on the couch as he and Coleman discussed the camper. Coleman picked up a wooden candlestick and, after admiring it, hit Harry Walters on the back of the head. The force of the blow broke the candlestick and drove a chunk of bone against Mr Walters's brain. From that point on, Mr Walters remembered little else. Sheri Walters, Harry and Marlene's daughter, came home from work at about 3.45pm. At the bottom of the basement steps, she found her father barely alive and her mother dead. Both had ligatures around their throats and electrical cords tied around their bare feet. Her mother's hands were bound behind her back and her father's hands were handcuffed behind his back. Her mother's head was covered with a bloody sheet.

Marlene Walters had been struck on the head approximately 20–25 times. Twelve lacerations, some of which were made with a pair of vice grips, covered her face and scalp. The back of her skull was smashed to pieces. Parts of her skull and brain were missing.

Coleman and Brown stole the Walters' car and headed to Kentucky, where they abandoned the vehicle in a cornfield in Williamsburg. They then kidnapped Oline Carmical and drove to Dayton, Ohio, leaving Carmical locked in the trunk of his abandoned car. Police managed to locate the car and the victim was rescued. Brown and Coleman then committed further robberies in Dayton, involving stealing cars and cash from elderly couples.

By now, the murderous pair had been on the run for 53 days. During this time, they had committed eight murders, seven rapes, three kidnappings and 14 armed robberies, but their luck was about to run out. They had been placed on the FBI's Ten Most Wanted list. By now, they had arrived in Illinois and while out walking they were seen by a friend of Coleman, who recognised them and told the police.

A major police operation began. Coleman and Brown were located watching baseball in a local park. Shortly before noon on 20 July 1984, police officers began to approach the unsuspecting couple. Coleman began walking away as plainclothes and uniformed officers approached. When challenged, he surrendered with no resistance. However, he told police they were mistaken in their identity, providing them with two aliases, with Brown identifying herself as Denise Johnson. Police searched both of them. Brown was in possession of a loaded revolver and Coleman had a long knife hidden in his boot, though neither went for their weapons.

Now in custody, their real identities were soon revealed but police forces across the US wanted to bring them to trial. In the end, Ohio was successful in convicting Coleman and Brown on two aggravated murder charges as well as other violent crimes.

They were both sentenced to death and then the lengthy appeals process began. In January 1991, the governor of Ohio commuted Brown's death sentence, saying she was retarded and 'dominated by' Coleman. She is now serving two life sentences in Ohio for her crimes. However, there are now legal issues taking place with regard to her being prosecuted in Indiana for murder.

Coleman's case went to numerous appeals over the following years. But after spending 6,000 days on death row, his last-ditch effort to avoid lethal injection was unsuccessful when, on 25 April 2002, the Ohio Supreme Court rejected his final appeal. On 26 April 2002, shortly before 10.00am, wearing a 'non-denominational' prayer shawl with crosses and Stars of David over his prison blues, Alton Coleman walked into the death chamber and quietly laid himself on the gurney. He remained still as the guards fastened restraints on him and attached the lines that would contain the three chemicals to a shunt already in place in his arm. He looked over at the witness room and appeared to say something, but it was impossible to hear him through the glass. A prison official asked if he had any final words, he shook his head and then the executioner pushed the button that would begin the execution process. Although just three chemicals are used to execute a prisoner – one to induce unconsciousness, another to stop breathing and a third to stop the heart – eight syringes, operated automatically once the button is pushed, are required. It often takes two or three very long minutes for all the syringes to empty. As the drugs began flowing, Alton Coleman began reciting Psalm 23. By the time he reached 'he leadeth me beside the still waters', the sodium pentothal began to take effect and Coleman lost consciousness. He was pronounced dead at 10.13am. He died without ever showing any remorse for his victims.

JERRY BRUDOS, AKA THE SHOE FETISH SLAYER

His mother, who had wanted a girl, rejected Jerry Brudos (b. 1939) at an early age; as a result, she often ignored and belittled him. His fetish for women's shoes manifested itself from the age of five, and he spent his teenage years in and out of mental hospitals. As a teenager he began stalking women, attacking them from behind. Knocking them down and then choking them and rendering them unconscious, he would then take their shoes and run off. At the age of 17, he dug a hole and kept young girls as sex slaves in it. Shortly after, he was found out and taken to a psychiatric hospital in Portland, Oregon, where he spent nine months. During this period, he was assessed and his fantasies were found to stem from the hatred he felt towards his mother in particular and women in general.

Brudos managed to curb his fantasies and married in 1961. It was at about this time, however, that he began complaining of bad headaches and blackouts, finding the only way to ease the pains was to prowl the streets after dark, stealing ladies' shoes and lacy underwear. From then on, he became more brazen, stalking women in and around Portland, Oregon.

On 26 January 1968, 19-year-old Linda Slawson disappeared while making her final house-call. She worked as a door-to-door saleswoman selling volumes of encyclopedias. On 21 April 1969, Sharon Wood, 24, left her secretarial job. She entered the basement level of a car park to look for her car. She sensed someone behind her and tried to return to an area where other people might be. But then someone tapped her shoulder and she turned around. A tall, podgy man confronted her, holding a pistol. He told her not to scream. She decided to fight him. She screamed and stepped away from him, but he grabbed her and held her in an arm-lock around the throat. He was twice her weight; she had barely a chance against him. She believed she was about to die. She kicked at him with her high-heeled shoes and screamed, grabbing the gun. Her attacker tried to silence her by putting his hand over her mouth; in an attempt to get him off she bit him, hard. She knew that she'd drawn blood. He tried to free himself but could not, so now he was struggling with her. He grabbed her hair and tried to force her to the floor, but she continued to resist with all her strength. He slammed her head on the concrete, dazing her. She then heard a car coming and her attacker picked up the gun he'd dropped and ran off. She then passed out. Miraculously, Sharon Wood survived. However, the next victim would not be as fortunate.

On 26 November 1968, another woman, Jan Whitney, 23, disappeared as she was on her way home. Her car was found locked in a lay-by. Four months later, on 27 March 1969, Karen Sprinker, 19, also went missing. She had failed to meet her mother for lunch. Her car was found in a car park near where she should have met her mother. Witnesses in the area described seeing a very tall and strange-looking man. One female witness said that when this person got close to her, she saw that he was in drag.

Four weeks later, Linda Salee, 22, disappeared from a shopping mall. She had gone to shop and was supposed to meet her boyfriend afterwards, but had failed to meet him that evening. Her car was later found abandoned. By now, the police saw a pattern emerging with the disappearances of all these young girls. Their worst fears were confirmed when the body of a woman was found by a fisherman in a nearby river. The body had been tied to an engine block in an attempt to weight it down. Closer examination showed that a nylon rope had been used to attach the body to the engine block. Copper wire had also been attached in a specific way, indicating that the killer may have been an electrician. It was believed that the cause of death was strangulation. They also found two small puncture wounds, each circled by a burn, on opposite sides of the rib cage, which appeared to have been caused by a needle. Dental records showed that the body was that of Linda Salee.

Police carried out a thorough search along the river and its immediate surroundings. They soon discovered the decomposing body of another female, also tied to an engine block. This victim had also been strangled, apparently with a strap used as a garrotte. The clothing, still on her body, matched what Karen

Sprinker's mother had described her daughter wearing. However, when the police lifted the body, they found that she was also clothed in a long-line black brassiere that appeared much too large to be hers. It had been padded with brown paper towels. In fact, her breasts had been removed and the padding appeared to have been placed there to absorb the blood and fluid. The body was later formally identified as that of Karen Sprinker.

Police now knew they were dealing with a serial killer and the investigation intensified. They went to the university where Karen had been a student and started to question other students. They were told that some female students had recently complained about getting strange phone calls from a man trying to lure them outside. There were also reports of a suspicious red-haired man seen loitering around campus. Detectives discovered one young woman who had actually ventured out on a brief date with a man claiming to be a lonely Vietnam veteran looking for company. This girl had no intention of seeing the man again, having found him to be very strange. He had apparently asked her why she wasn't afraid he might strangle her. The detectives asked her to contact them should he call again. To their surprise, he did, so she set a date and then she phoned the police.

The police went to the designated meeting place and saw a tall man enter the room. They approached him and learnt that his name was Jerry Brudos. While they believed he was a viable suspect, he seemed completely at ease, as if he had nothing to hide. That meant he was either innocent, or clever, arrogant and without remorse for what he was doing. The police had nothing with which to detain Brudos, but they kept him under surveillance. Having learnt where he lived, along with the rather significant fact that he'd worked as an electrician, they set out to research his background.

The pieces of the jigsaw were coming together. The police had now established that in January 1968 Brudos had lived in the same neighbourhood where the young encyclopedia salesgirl Linda Slawson had last been seen. Brudos indicated that he had moved to Salem in August or September 1968 and had gone to work in Lebanon, Oregon, close to the I-5 freeway where Jan Whitney had vanished in November. His current job in Halsey was only six miles from where the bodies had been found. When Karen Sprinker disappeared on 27 March, Brudos had lived within a short walking distance. The police hoped that searches of his house, garage and car might give them more direct evidence. In his garage, they found a lot of nylon rope. Some rope tied into a knot in his workshop appeared to be similar to the knots used on the bodies. He even let detectives take a sample. Police searched his vehicle and found that the interior had been thoroughly cleaned. That was suspicious, but not damning, and Brudos had a ready-made explanation. But he had no defence later on when an adolescent girl picked him out of a photo identification parade as being the man who had attempted to force her into a car. The police made the decision to arrest him. After his arrest and when searched, he was found to be wearing women's knickers. Brudos then elected to seek legal representation. On 30 May, he agreed to talk freely in an interview despite his attorney advising him not to do so. Brudos offered a confession.

He admitted that, between January 1968 and April 1969, he had killed and mutilated four women and thrown their bodies into a river after he cut parts from them. He also admitted attacking and attempting to kill several more. The detectives who interrogated him noted his complete absence of guilt or remorse, though he mourned his fate and felt badly for his wife and children. His first victim was Linda Slawson, who had naively followed him to the workshop behind his house in an attempt to sell him her encyclopedias. He had hit her with a lump of wood and knocked her out, then strangled her. Once alone with the dead girl, he quickly undressed her. He recalled every detail, at least of her underwear, and was especially pleased that she had been wearing a pair of red knickers. He then got some items of ladies' underwear from his own collection and re-dressed her in them. Realising that he could not keep her there, he removed her foot with a hacksaw, placed it in the freezer, and then took the body to the Willamette River. To make certain she would not be found he had tied her to a car engine before throwing her over the bridge. Then he went home and savoured the part of her that he'd kept – a reminder of his first kill and a trophy that he could play with. He had so many high-heeled shoes and he could try them on this severed foot and take pictures. He did that as long as he could, but when the foot deteriorated, he tied it to a weight and threw it into the river as well. Even as he had the dead girl on the floor of his workshop, he held a calm conversation with the rest of his family, urging them to go out and get some dinner at a fast-food restaurant.

The next murder he confessed to was of Jan Whitney, who had been missing for more than six months by that time. He told police that he had come across her after her car had broken down. She was with two men, he said, who looked to him like hippies, but he stopped anyway. For him, it was another unique opportunity that he could not pass up, and he played it out for maximum enjoyment. Jan apparently had given the men a ride and they weren't helping her to fix the car, so Brudos gave them all a ride, dropped the men off and then took Jan to his home. He told her to wait for him while he told his wife he was going to fix the car. Then he got into the back seat behind Jan, told her to close her eyes and began playing mind games. Foolishly, she complied. He put a strap over her head and around her neck to keep her from moving, and strangled her. Once she was dead, he had sex with the body in the car. Then he took her to his workshop, dressed her in some of his clothes and took pictures to remind him of his deeds. He also sexually violated the body several more times. After that, he tied her up and raised her into the air via a hook-and-pulley system he had fixed in the ceiling. Despite the danger that someone might discover her, he left her hanging there for several days.

Jan Whitney was only Brudos's second victim but already he

felt sure of himself. Before disposing of the body, he invited police to come and inspect some accidental damage to the garage. They failed to notice the stench of decomposition. Before disposing of her, he cut off her right breast, intending to make a plastic mould, but he did it all wrong. As with Slawson, he weighted Whitney's body down by tying it to a heavy engine part, and threw it into the Willamette River, but refused to give a specific location. Oddly, he was telling the police so much yet holding back key details as if he thought that keeping certain things back would hinder the prosecution, but they would still have sufficient evidence against him.

His third victim was Karen Sprinker, at the department store where she'd gone to meet her mother. He said he'd seen her and didn't like the shoes she was wearing. He produced a pistol and forced her to get her into his car, and they went right to his home, where he raped her and forced her to pose in the clothing of his choice. Then he killed her by hanging her by the neck from his hook. He then subjected the corpse to the same treatment as the others. He removed both breasts and dressed her in the long-line bra that was too large for her. He stuffed it to keep her from bleeding in his car and to make the bra look correctly fitted.

With Linda Salee, Brudos had used a fake police identity badge and threatened to arrest her for shoplifting to make her do what he wanted. After he abducted her, he took her back to his workshop and left her bound and gagged while he had dinner in the house. She then fought him when he tried to strangle her with the strap. He raped her as she died and then used wires stuck into her rib cage to try to 'make her dance' with an electrical current. It apparently did not work to his satisfaction.

On 2 June 1969, Brudos was charged with first-degree murder for the death of Karen Sprinker. He believed that he'd removed the evidence from his workshop by telling his wife to burn his stash of female clothing. Police went back to his house and found the garage and the pulley and chain just as he had described. They found nylon cord and a leather strap that might have been used for murder. From a shelf they removed a mould made from a female breast. They also discovered a hoard of women's shoes in various sizes and many items of ladies' underwear as well as a collection of photographs. Some were of Brudos in female underwear, but the most important ones contained horrifying images of the victims. They found one of a woman suspended from the hook and pulley with a black hood over her head. Another body had been dressed in several different garments and photographed. Brudos had cut the heads out of the pictures so he could enjoy the anonymous female form. The photograph that really caught their attention was one that would be crucial in the case against him. The photograph was of a girl's body, clothed in a black lace slip and knickers with suspenders, hung from the ceiling, the camera angled up to her crotch. Reflected in a mirror on the floor in the lower corner of the photo was the frozen image of a killer, caught unawares. It was Brudos, looking at the woman he had just murdered.

On 4 June 1969, Brudos stood trial. He initially pleaded not guilty on the basis that he was insane. However, when he realised that this was not going to work for him he changed his plea to guilty to the murders of Jan Whitney, Karen Sprinker and Linda Salee, all from Salem. He was sentenced to three consecutive terms of life imprisonment, with the chance for parole. He also admitted to a fourth murder, of Linda Slawson, but as her body was never found he was not prosecuted. He has made several appeals on legal issues, all of which have been turned down. The remains of Jan Whitney's body were recovered in summer 1970.

Jerome Brudos's three life sentences came to an end on 28 March 2006, when he died of natural causes at the age of 67. He was the longest-serving inmate (almost 37 years) at Oregon State Penitentiary when he died. Brudos's wife was arrested and tried as his accomplice. A neighbour claimed she had actually seen her help Brudos with a victim, but this testimony was discredited. Since there was no evidence that Brudos's wife knew about or participated in any of the crimes, as difficult as that might be to believe, she was acquitted. In 1970, she ended her eight-year marriage to Brudos, changed her name and moved with the children to an unknown location.

CAROL BUNDY AND DOUGLAS CLARK, AKA THE SUNSET STRIP KILLERS

The police investigation to catch the serial killers who came to be known as the Sunset Strip Killers started in earnest on 12 June 1980 along the Ventura Highway near Los Angeles. On that morning, a refuse collector came upon a grisly find close to rubbish he was collecting – the near-naked body of a teenage girl. The young brunette lay face down on a bush-covered embankment. She had been shot in the head with a small-calibre weapon. Nearby, a blonde girl around the same age was also found dead. She had been shot in the head and chest but her pink jumpsuit had not been removed. Nevertheless, it was slit up the leg as if whoever had killed her had a sexual motive either before or after death. There was also fresh blood on this girl's face.

The police suspected that the girls had been killed elsewhere, and that they might have been hitchhiking together. No ID was found on either of them. The police were aware that the bodies were found near the spot where another young female murder victim, Laura Collins, had been found in 1977. Her murder had not yet been solved. On Friday 13 June, the two young females were identified as Gina Marano, aged 15, and her step-sister Cynthia Chandler, aged 16.

As is the case with many murders, the police often receive calls from cranks wanting to 'confess' or from aggrieved people wanting to put forward suspects. On this occasion, one call they received was from an anonymous female who said her boyfriend had been involved in the killings. She knew details that had not been released to the press and stated that she and her boyfriend had recently washed the car, inside and out (this would be consistent with the way a killer would react when wanting to remove evidence). During the conversation, the phone cut off and she did not call back. If she had, some lives could have been saved and she herself might not have taken the path she did.

On 23 June, two more females were found, shot in a similar fashion. The first body found was that of prostitute Karen Jones, 24. She had been shot in the head with a small-calibre pistol. Her body was found behind a restaurant in Burbank. Not long after the first body was found, the headless body of a naked woman believed to be in her twenties was discovered beside a rubbish bin at the rear of another restaurant in Los Angeles. The body was soon identified as that of Exxie Wilson, aged 21, also a prostitute and a friend of Karen Jones. A thorough search of the area failed to find her missing head.

On the morning of 27 June, Jonathan Caravels went down the alley near his apartment at around 1am. He tried to park his car, encountered resistance and spotted a wooden box with an oversized lid. Hopeful that he had found something valuable, he went over to it. Part of the wood was shattered on the outside, as if someone had hit it or thrown it. Leaning over, he unlatched the metal clasp and lifted the lid. Inside was some coarse material, which smelt of something odd. Rummaging past the material, he got the surprise of his life. Wrapped in blue jeans and a T-shirt was a human head. He could see that this person was female and brunette, and that her mouth was slightly open, but he didn't pause for a closer look, immediately calling the police. An early crime scene examination revealed that the head was considerably colder than the outside air and may have been in a deep freeze and then washed. It didn't take long for them to realise that the head was that of Exxie Wilson. Inside the skull was a .25-calibre copper-jacketed bullet. Ballistics analysis determined that it was probably from an automatic known as a Raven and that the bullet that had killed Exxie was from the same gun that had killed the step-sisters and Karen Jones. They now knew they had a serial killer on their hands – one who had apparently committed two murders at the same time – but decided not to release all the details to the press.

THE EVIL WITHIN

Snake hunters searching the undergrowth discovered another body, this time in the San Fernando Valley. They came across an old mattress, beneath which were the mummified remains of another woman. The medical examiner believed she was about 17 years old. Her stomach appeared to have been slit open, and she had been shot three times with a small-calibre pistol. She had been dead at least three weeks, placing her first in line in the series of five; police feared that there could be more victims in wilderness areas. The body was later identified as that of Marnette Comer (aka Annette Ann Davis) from Sacramento. She had a history of running away from home and was a suspected prostitute. She had last been seen on 1 June. The bullets taken from her body had come from the weapon that had killed the other females.

On 9 August, the headless body of a man was found locked inside a van; it had started to decompose. The victim had been viciously stabbed nine separate times and also slashed across the buttocks, from which pieces had been removed. It was believed the man had been killed some five days previously. Police soon identified him as country singer John 'Jack' Robert Murray, 45, who sang part-time at Little Nashville, a bar located close to where he was found. The killer had removed Murray's head, but had left behind shell casings, which suggested that the victim had been shot. Aside from the beheading, it did not appear that this murder was connected with the string of killings that the police were investigating. Police recalled the anonymous phone call from the mystery woman who had claimed on the phone to be the killer's girlfriend and given police precise details about the murder. This woman would turn out to be 37-year-old Carol Bundy (b. 1942), who worked at a local medical centre.

On 11 August, Bundy had become upset at work and told other staff that she had been involved in some killings with a man called Douglas Clark (b. 1948). The police were notified and went to her home, where they arrested her. She handed them three pairs of knickers that she said had been taken from the victims, as well as a photo album of Clark in compromising positions with an 11-year-old girl. She also admitted that she had killed Jack Murray herself.

Another team of officers had gone to arrest Clark. They did not have any direct evidence at that time but managed to charge him with minor unconnected offences. They needed time to gather more evidence. Equally, they were concerned that he would destroy the evidence they needed for a murder conviction. Then the police had a lucky break. At Clark's workplace, a workman stumbled across the place in the boiler room where Clark had hidden two .25-calibre Raven automatics. They were given to the police and ballistics tests positively linked one of the guns to the five known victims. As a result, Clark was charged with those five murders. In the interim period, a pathologist tried to determine whether the same person had beheaded both Murray and Exxie Wilson, but he concluded that two different people had used two different knives.

Carol Bundy was arraigned on 13 August 1980 for the murder of Jack Murray and was held without bail until her preliminary hearing two weeks later. The prosecution case was that Murray had been killed because he was a witness to a crime whom Bundy wanted to prevent from giving evidence.

It often happens that when two killers are finally caught they try to blame each other. This turned out to be such a case. Carol Bundy stated that she had been having an affair with Jack Murray for some time, and then one night in December 1979 she met Douglas Clark, who started to pay her some attention. Eventually she moved in with Clark, but stated that she still continued to have sex with Murray. Clark dominated her, persuading her to buy two guns and register them in her name. He also had weird sexual fantasies. He wanted her to bring other women into their relationship for a threesome and he also got her to entice young girls into the apartment, specifically an 11-year-old neighbour. The girl was photographed naked and persuaded to get into the shower with the adults. Bundy did not seem to think this was wrong. Instead, she later admitted, she did not feel that this kid was 'competition', and believed that letting Clark have this experience was just a way to please him. It was a 'gift'. They even made a photo album of pictures of the girl with him, which Carol later turned over to the police.

Bundy told the police that by spring 1980, Clark had turned to murder. One day in April, he came home covered in blood. He lied about how the blood came to be on him but she discovered a bag of bloody women's clothing in the car. Clark then told her about Gina and Cynthia, the two step-sisters found murdered in June. He said he had picked them up at a bus stop. He made Cynthia perform oral sex on him and ordered Gina to look away. When she refused, he shot her in the head. Then he shot Cynthia. When it appeared that they were not dead, he shot them both again and took the bleeding corpses to a rented garage. There he played with them, posing them for his entertainment, and raped the bodies. In the early hours of the morning, he dumped the bodies. Clark also told Bundy about another murder he had committed – a male victim. His name was Vic Weiss and he had been found in the boot of a Rolls-Royce at the Sheraton Universal Hotel. The following morning, he took Bundy out to a ravine and pointed out an area where he had dumped a prostitute's body after shooting her (this was the mummified victim, the fifth one to be found), but he had kept her knickers, he bragged, as a souvenir. He described the entire incident in explicit detail, getting her as excited as he was about sexual murder. She had once been a partner in his violent fantasy life and she had seen that as a sign of real intimacy. She wanted to taste the feeling of murder and he was quite prepared to fulfil her desires.

On 20 June, Bundy went out cruising around with Clark. They found a young prostitute and lured her into the car on the pretext of giving Clark oral sex. Bundy climbed into the back armed with one of the guns; Clark had the other. They had planned this murder carefully. Bundy was supposed to signal whether or not she wanted to go ahead and shoot the girl herself, but things went wrong. Clark apparently became angry at something the prostitute was doing, so he reached for the gun and shot her in the head. He then covered the body, drove off and then dumped it a short time later, before taking Bundy home. Clark soon returned to the same location, where he picked up Exxie Wilson. He drove her to the Sizzlers restaurant on Ventura Boulevard at Studio City. She began to perform oral sex. While doing this, he shot her in the head. In an involuntary reaction, she bit his genitals, which angered him. He got a sharp knife from the boot of his car and cut off her head, placing it inside a rubbish sack. He drove off, leaving the body behind in the car park behind the restaurant.

He then came across Karen Jones. He had seen her earlier with Exxie Wilson. She agreed to get into the car with him, unaware that her friend's head was on the back seat. He shot her and pushed her out of the car near the Burbank studios. She was quickly found and Exxie's body was discovered on the same day a few hours later. He drove back to Bundy's place and put the head in the freezer. Over the next three days, they both used the severed head as a sex toy, on one occasion making it up to look like Barbie. Clark also used it to perform necrophilic oral sex and he even took it into the shower with him. He then placed it in a box and discarded it in an alley.

By now, police had amassed enough evidence to charge Clark with the murders of six women and one attempted murder. He went to trial in October 1987 and was found guilty on all counts on 28 January 1988, receiving the death penalty. He is still on death row in San Quentin prison, and still protests his innocence, stating that Carol Bundy was the main perpetrator of the murders. He has also suggested that Jack Murray was involved with her in most of the murders.

Carol Bundy came to trial on 2 May 1983 and pleaded guilty to the murder of Jack Murray. She was spared the death penalty for pleading guilty and making full confessions. She was sentenced to life imprisonment with a chance of parole in 2012. However, she died in prison of heart failure on 9 December 2003.

THEODORE ROBERT BUNDY

Ted Bundy (b. 1946) is looked on as one of – if not the most – notorious serial killers in the history of American crime. He spent his early years going through high school just like an ordinary child. But he became a compulsive thief, stealing from shops. He was arrested twice for shoplifting. He also had a fascination with images of sex. Through his college years, he was described as a handsome, articulate young man.

The first serious attack on a female Bundy was known to have committed took place on 4 January 1974. At around midnight, Bundy entered the basement bedroom of 18-year-old Joni Lenz, a dancer and student at the University of Washington. Bundy proceeded to hit her repeatedly with a metal rod from her bed frame while she slept, as well as sexually assaulting her with a speculum. Her room-mates found Lenz the following morning, barely alive and lying in a pool of her own blood. She survived the attack but had no memory of it and suffered permanent brain damage.

On 31 January 1974, Bundy struck again. His next victim was Lynda Ann Healy, another University of Washington student. He broke into her room, knocked her unconscious, dressed her in jeans and a shirt, wrapped her in a bed sheet and carried her away. A basement door leading directly outside was unlocked and was no doubt the point of entry. Healy may even have willingly let Bundy in. Because authorities mistakenly believed at first that foul play was not involved, a forensic examination was never carried out in her bedroom and an apparent semen stain on her bed was never tested. A year passed before her decapitated remains were found in the Cascade Mountains east of Seattle.

On 12 March, Bundy kidnapped and murdered a 19-year-old student, Donna Gail Manson, who was on her way to a jazz concert held on campus. She was never seen again, dead or alive.

On 17 April, Susan Rancourt, another student, disappeared from the college campus of Central Washington State College in Ellensburg. She was last seen at a meeting on the campus earlier that day. A man in a sling had been observed the same night attempting to obtain help getting a heavy load of books to his car.

On 6 May, another student, Kathy Parks, fell prey to Bundy. She was last seen on the campus of Oregon State University. She was not reported missing until the middle of the month. Her disappearance was followed by the disappearance of Brenda Ball, who was last seen leaving a tavern on 1 June. She was not reported missing for three weeks.

Bundy now had an insatiable urge to murder. His next victim was Georgeann Hawkins, a student at the University of Oregon. In the early hours of 11 June, she walked from her boyfriend's dormitory residence to her house, a distance of no more than 30yd. She was last seen by one of her boyfriend's fraternity approximately halfway down the alley that separated the two buildings. Bundy had been waiting in a car park behind Hawkins's house, using crutches and pretending to have trouble carrying his briefcase to his car. Hawkins agreed to assist him and he walked her to his waiting Volkswagen Beetle where he had laid a crowbar by the tyre. When they approached the vehicle, Bundy hit Hawkins over the head, knocking her unconscious. He then handcuffed her, pulled her into his vehicle and drove away. He raped and strangled her at a remote location, before disposing of her body.

Only six days after Hawkins's disappearance, Brenda Baker was found dead in a state park. The 15-year-old runaway had been missing since she left home on 25 May and was a known hitchhiker. Her cause of death could not be determined from her decomposed remains.

Bundy's Washington killing continued and on 14 July he abducted Janice Ott in broad daylight, at around 12.30pm at Lake Sammamish State Park. Ott was overheard talking to a man in a white outfit with a cast on his arm who said his name was

Ted and that he needed help with his sailing boat. Though she seemed annoyed at the request, she left with the man and was never seen alive again.

Denise Naslund disappeared at around 4.30pm the same afternoon. She left her boyfriend to use the toilet. She was seen at the toilet but never made it back to the beach where her boyfriend was waiting.

Bundy had now become careless and complacent. All his previous murders had been at night, but now he had been seen in broad daylight. Five different women told police they had seen a man wearing a white tennis outfit with his arm in a sling who called himself Ted. The witnesses said the man had approached girls on separate occasions asking for help unloading a sailing boat from his car. One went with Bundy as far as his Volkswagen, where there was no sailing boat, before refusing to accompany him further. Two more witnesses testified to seeing the same man approach Janice Ott with the same story, and to seeing Ott in his company, walking away from the beach with her bicycle. Her bicycle was found abandoned in the park the next day, but Ott herself had vanished.

The remains of Janice Ott and Denise Naslund were discovered on 7 September 1974 at Taylor Mountain. Also found at the same location were an extra femur bone and vertebra believed to belong to Georgeann Hawkins. The skulls – and only the skulls – of the other missing girls, Healy, Rancourt, Parks and Ball, were found in the same location on 2 March 1975. Although years later Bundy claimed that he had also dumped the body of Donna Manson there, no trace of her was ever found.

That autumn, Bundy moved to Utah to attend law school in Salt Lake City, where he resumed killing in October. Nancy Wilcox disappeared from Holladay, near Salt Lake City, Utah, on 2 October. Wilcox was last seen riding in a Volkswagen Beetle, a car that Bundy still owned.

On 18 October, Bundy murdered Melissa Smith, the 17-year-old daughter of a local police chief. After abducting her, Bundy raped, buggered and then strangled her with her own stockings. He stuffed dirt and twigs inside her vagina and touched up her make-up before disposing of her body, which was found nine days later.

On 31 October, Bundy claimed his next victim. She was Laura Aime, aged 17, who disappeared when she left a Hallowe'en party. Her remains were found nearly a month later by ramblers on the banks of a river in American Fork Canyon. She was naked, had been beaten beyond recognition, buggered and strangled with one of her own socks.

In Murray, Utah, on 8 November 1974, Carol DaRonch narrowly escaped with her life. Bundy approached her, claiming to be Officer Roseland of the Murray Police Department. He lured her into his car, hit her over the head and then attempted to place her in handcuffs. Fortunately, only one wrist was secured. She wrenched her door open with the other hand, rolled out of the car onto the highway and escaped with contusions to the head, still with one of her wrists in the handcuffs. Police were unable to obtain any fingerprints from the handcuffs, but they did find traces of blood on her coat – it might have been Bundy's, but there was not a sufficient quantity for any testing.

A few hours later, perhaps frustrated by the failed abduction of DaRonch, Bundy abducted Debby Kent, aged 17, who was attending a school play. She had left the play early to pick up her brother, but her car never left the car park. She disappeared, never to be seen again. Residents nearby reported hearing screams from the car park and a handcuff key that fitted the cuffs left on DaRonch's wrist was later found on the ground of the car park. Debby Kent was never found, dead or alive.

In 1975, while still attending law school at the University of Utah, Bundy shifted his crimes to Colorado. On 12 January, Caryn Campbell disappeared from the Wildwood Inn at Snowmass, Colorado, where she had been on holiday with her fiancé and his children. Her body was found on 17 February by the side of the road a few miles from the motel. She had severe head injuries and deep cuts on her body.

Four weeks later on 15 March, ski instructor Julie Cunningham from Vail, Colorado disappeared. Bundy later confessed that he used crutches to approach Cunningham, after asking her to help him carry some ski boots to his car. At the car, Bundy hit her with his crowbar and incapacitated her with handcuffs, later strangling her. Her body was another one never found.

On 6 April, Denise Oliverson disappeared after leaving her home for her parents' house in Grand Junction, Colorado. Her bike and sandals were found under a nearby viaduct. On 15 April, Melanie Cooley, 18, was last seen in Nederland, Colorado. She was found eight days later 20 miles away, dead from head injuries. Her hands had been bound and a pillowcase tied around her neck.

Still the murders continued. On 6 May, Lynette Culver, 13, went missing in Pocatello, Idaho, from the grounds of her junior high school. While on death row, Bundy later confessed that he had kidnapped Culver and had taken the girl to a room he had rented at a nearby hotel. He stated that after raping her, he had drowned her in the motel room bath and later dumped her body in a river.

Susan Curtis, 15, vanished on 28 June. She was abducted from the campus of Brigham Young University while attending a youth conference. She left her friends to walk back to a dormitory and was never seen again. Tragically, Curtis was from Bountiful, Utah, the same town from where another victim, Melissa Smith, had been abducted in November the previous year. The bodies of Cunningham, Culver, Curtis and Oliverson have never been recovered.

Bundy's luck was about to run out. Sometimes murderers find themselves initially arrested for lesser offences, and this was the case with Ted Bundy. On 16 August 1975, Bundy failed to stop for a police officer in Salt Lake City. A search of his car revealed a ski mask, a crowbar, handcuffs, rubbish bags and other items that were thought by the police to be burglary tools. Bundy remained cool during questioning, explaining that he needed the mask for skiing and had found the handcuffs in a skip. Detectives were suspicious, however, and obtained a search warrant for his apartment. The search uncovered a brochure from a hotel in Snowmass, Colorado. Bundy denied having been to Colorado, but the police decided to put him on an ID parade, believing that he was responsible for the Carol DaRonch kidnapping and assault. Carol DaRonch and two other witnesses all picked out Bundy.

Bundy's girlfriend, Liz Kendall, was interviewed by Utah detectives. She told them about his nocturnal sleeping habits, rough sexual practices and odd possessions, such as crutches, plaster of Paris and a fake moustache. It was becoming obvious to officers involved that Bundy could have something to do with the murders and disappearances in Utah, Washington and Colorado. Bundy soon made bail and, incredibly, moved in with Kendall at her Seattle apartment until his Utah trial for kidnapping.

Following a week-long trial, Bundy was convicted of DaRonch's kidnapping on 1 March 1976 and was sentenced to 15 years in Utah State Prison.

In the meantime, police knew that Bundy was the prime suspect for the murders of young girls in three states. There had been too many coincidences, but they needed hard evidence. They began speaking to Bundy's ex-girlfriends to try to obtain more information about him, in an effort to obtain evidence connecting him to the murders of Caryn Campbell and Melissa Smith. Detectives discovered in Bundy's Volkswagen car hairs that were examined by the FBI and found to match Campbell's and Smith's hair. Further examination of Caryn Campbell's remains showed that her skull bore impressions made by a blunt instrument and that those impressions matched the crowbar discovered in Bundy's car a year earlier. Colorado police decided to file charges against Bundy on 22 October 1976 for the murder of Caryn Campbell.

In April 1977, he was transferred to Garfield County Jail in Colorado to await trial for the murder of Caryn Campbell. He sacked his lawyer and elected to represent himself. His trial was set for 14 November 1977. Bundy was granted permission to leave the confines of the jail on occasion and utilise the courthouse library in Aspen to conduct research. What police didn't know was that he was planning an escape. On 7 June, during one of his trips to the library at the courthouse, Bundy jumped from an open window, injuring his ankle in the process, but still managing to escape. He was not wearing any leg irons or handcuffs, so he did not stand out among the ordinary citizens in the town of Aspen. It was an escape that Bundy had planned for a while. Aspen police were quick to set up roadblocks surrounding the town, yet Bundy knew to stay within the city limits for the time being and to lie low. Police launched a massive search, but he was able to evade capture. Bundy thought he had found a way to escape from the town – he discovered a car with the keys left in it. However, his luck did not last long. While trying to flee Aspen in the stolen vehicle, he was spotted and recaptured.

Almost seven months later, Bundy again attempted an escape, this time with more success. On 30 December 1977, he crawled up into the ceiling of the Garfield County Jail and made his way to another part of the building. He managed to find another opening in the ceiling that led down into the wardrobe of a warder's apartment. He sat and waited until he knew the apartment was empty, then casually walked out of the front door to his freedom. His escape went undiscovered until the following afternoon, more than 15 hours later. By the time police learnt of his escape, Bundy was well on his way to Chicago. Chicago was one of the few stops that Bundy would make along the route to his final destination, sunny Florida. By early January 1978, Ted Bundy, using his newly acquired name of Chris Hagen, had settled comfortably into a one-room apartment in Tallahassee, Florida. He stole on a regular basis to survive.

On the night of Saturday, 14 January, his urge to kill manifested itself again. At 3am, a student returning home found the front door open and heard screams coming from inside. She heard footsteps approaching the staircase near her so she hid in a doorway, out of view. She watched as a man with a blue knitted cap pulled over his eyes, holding a log with cloth around it, ran down the stairs and out the door. She immediately ran up the stairs to wake her room-mate and told her of the strange man she had seen leaving the building. Unsure of what to do, the girls made their way to the housemother's room. Yet, before they were able to make it to her room, they saw another room-mate, Karen, staggering down the hall. Her entire head was soaked with blood. They tried to help Karen and woke up the housemother and the two of them went to check on another room-mate nearby. They found their other room-mate, Kathy, in her room, alive but in a horrific state. She was covered in blood that was seeping from open wounds on her head. They phoned the police at once, who on attending found two other girls dead in their rooms lying in their beds. Someone had attacked them while they slept. Lisa Levy was the first girl who officers found dead. Pathologists who later performed the autopsy on her found that she had been beaten on the head with a log, raped and strangled. Upon further examination, they discovered bite marks on her buttocks and on one of her nipples. In fact, Lisa's nipple had been so severely bitten that it was almost severed from the rest of her breast. She had also had a can of hairspray inserted into her vagina. Post-mortem reports on Margaret Bowman, the other girl found dead, showed that she had suffered similar fatal injuries, although she had not been sexually assaulted and she showed no signs of bite marks. She had been strangled with a pair of tights found at the scene. She had also been beaten on the head, so severely that her skull was splintered and a portion of her brain was exposed.

Less than a mile from the scene of these horrific assaults, a young woman was awakened by loud banging noises coming from the apartment next to hers. She wondered what her friend in the adjoining apartment was doing to make so much noise at four in the morning. As the banging noises persisted, she became suspicious and woke her room-mate. As they listened, they heard Cheryl Thomas next door moaning. Frightened, they called to see if she was all right. When no one picked up the phone, they immediately called the police. They entered Cheryl's apartment and walked to her bedroom, where they found her sitting on the bed. Her face was just beginning to swell from the bludgeoning to her head. She was still somewhat conscious and half-naked, but lucky to be alive. Her skull had been fractured in five places, her jaw broken and her shoulder dislocated. She suffered permanent hearing loss and equilibrium problems. A mask made of tights similar to one found by detectives in Utah five months earlier was found wrapped up in Thomas's bed sheets, which were also stained with semen.

On 9 February 1978, Lake City police received a report of a missing 12-year-old girl, Kimberly Ann Leach, who had disappeared that day from her school. Police launched a massive search to find her. Her friend Priscilla saw Kimberly get into the car of a stranger the day she disappeared. Unfortunately, she was unable to accurately remember anything about the car or the driver. Police found Kimberly's body eight weeks later in a state park in Suwannee County, Florida. The young girl's body yielded little information due to advanced decomposition. However, police were to later find the evidence they needed in a van driven by Ted Bundy. Several days before Kimberly Leach disappeared, in another incident, a strange man in a white van approached a 14-year-old girl as she waited for her brother to pick her up. The man had claimed he was from the fire department and asked her if she attended the school nearby. She found it strange that an on-duty fireman was wearing check trousers and a navy jacket. She began to feel uncomfortable. She had been warned on many occasions by her father – the Chief of Detectives for the Jacksonville Police Department – not to talk with strangers. She was relieved when her brother drove up. Suspicious of the man, her brother ordered her into the car, followed the man and wrote down his number plate to give it to his father.

The police had the number plate checked; it belonged to a man named Randall Ragen, and the police decided to pay him a visit. Ragen informed the officers that his plates had been stolen and that he had already been issued new ones. Police later found out that the van the children had seen was also stolen and that they had an idea who it might have been. They took the children to the police station to show them photographs, Bundy's picture being among them. Both the children identified Bundy as being the man in the van.

By now, Bundy had made good his escape and abandoned the van. He set out towards Pensacola, Florida, in a new stolen car. This time he managed to find a vehicle he was more comfortable driving, a Volkswagen Beetle. A police officer was patrolling an area in West Pensacola when he saw an orange Volkswagen at 10pm on 15 February. He knew the area well, and most of the residents, yet he had never before seen that car. The officer decided to run a check on the number plates and soon found out that they were stolen. Immediately, he turned on his blue lights and began to follow the Volkswagen. Once again, as had happened in Utah several years earlier, Bundy started to flee, but then suddenly pulled over and stopped. The officer ordered him out of his car and told Bundy to lie down with his hands in front of him. As the officer began to handcuff Bundy, he rolled over and began to fight the officer, then managed to fight his way free and run. Just as soon as he did, the officer fired his weapon at him. Bundy dropped to the ground, pretending to have been shot. As the officer approached him lying on the ground, he was again attacked by Bundy. However, the officer was finally able to overpower Bundy and he was handcuffed and taken to the police station.

In the months following his arrest, police were able to obtain critical evidence to use against Bundy in the Kimberly Leach case. The white van that had been stolen by Bundy was found and they had three eye-witnesses who had seen him driving it the afternoon Kimberly had disappeared. Forensic tests conducted on the van yielded fibres of material that had come from Bundy's clothes. Tests also revealed Kimberly Leach's blood type on the van's carpet and semen and Bundy's blood type on her underwear. A further piece of evidence was Bundy's shoe impressions in the soil located next to the place Kimberly's body was found. Police felt confident with the information they had tying Bundy to the Leach murder and, on 31 July 1978, he was charged with the girl's murder. Soon after, he was also charged with the murders of the two students while he had been on the run. Facing the death penalty, Bundy would later plead in his own defence that he was not guilty of the murders.

Theodore Robert Bundy faced two murder trials within three years of each other. His first trial date was set for 25 June 1979, in Miami, Florida. The case related to the brutal attacks on the two students. The second trial was to take place in January 1980 in Orlando, Florida, where Bundy was to be tried for the murder of Kimberly Leach. However, it was to be the first murder trial that would seal his fate forever. Bundy defended himself in this trial. During the trial, a forensic dentist told the court that he had matched the bite marks found on the body of one of the victims to Bundy. On 23 July, Bundy was found guilty and sentenced to death in the electric chair.

After many delays, the Kimberly Leach trial began in Orlando, Florida, at the Orange County Courthouse on 7 January 1980. This time, Bundy decided not to represent himself, instead handing over the responsibility to defence attorneys Julius Africano and Lynn Thompson. Their strategy was to plead not guilty by reason of insanity, a plea that was risky but one of the few available options open to the defence. The tactics failed and, faced with strong evidence, Bundy was found guilty on 7

February. After less than seven hours of deliberation, again he was sentenced to death.

After numerous appeals were turned down, his execution finally took place on 24 January 1989 at approximately 7am. Outside the prison walls stood hundreds of onlookers and scores of news media representatives awaiting the news of Bundy's death. Following the prison spokesman's announcement that Bundy was officially dead, sounds of cheers came from the jubilant crowd and fireworks lit the sky. Shortly thereafter, a white hearse emerged from the prison gates with the remains of one of the country's most notorious serial killers. As the vehicle moved towards the crematorium, the surrounding crowd cheerfully applauded the end of a living nightmare.

RICHARD CHASE, AKA THE VAMPIRE OF SACRAMENTO

Having been abused by his mother from an early age, by the time Richard Chase (b. 1950) reached the age of 10, he was exhibiting the early signs that a serial killer might show: bedwetting, pyromania and zoo sadism (pleasure derived from cruelty to animals). In his adolescence, he took to drink and drugs. This led to him becoming impotent and he was unable to hold down a stable relationship. It was deemed that his erectile dysfunction was caused by 'psychological problems stemming from repressed anger'.

In his youth, Chase went to college and shared an apartment with other teenagers, but his irrational behaviour compelled them to move out, leaving him alone. This was the turning point in his life. Now alone in the apartment, he began to capture, kill and disembowel various animals, which he would then devour raw. He would put the entrails of the animals he had killed into a blender in order to make a drinkable paste of them. Chase reasoned that by drinking this he was preventing his heart from shrinking; he feared that if it shrank too much, it would disappear and then he would die.

In 1975, Chase was involuntarily committed to a mental

institution after being taken to hospital with blood poisoning, which he contracted after injecting rabbit blood into his veins. He escaped from the hospital and went home to his mother; he was apprehended and sent to an institution for the criminally insane, where he often shared fantasies about killing rabbits with the staff. He was once found with blood smeared around his mouth; hospital staff discovered that he had captured two birds through the bars on his bedroom windows, snapped their necks and sucked their blood out. Among themselves, the staff began referring to him as Dracula. After undergoing treatment, Chase was deemed no longer a danger to society and, in 1976, he was released into the recognisance of his parents. His mother, deciding that her son did not need to be on the anti-schizophrenic medication that he had been prescribed, foolishly weaned him off it. Now, roaming free and with no medication to help control his mind, he was a human time bomb – and it wasn't long before the fuse was lit.

On 29 December 1977, Chase killed his first victim in a drive-by shooting, in an apparent rehearsal for the crimes that followed. The victim was Ambrose Griffin, a 51-year-old engineer and father-of-two, who was helping his wife carry groceries into their home.

On 11 January 1978, Chase approached a female neighbour and asked for a cigarette, and then forcibly restrained her until she gave him the entire pack. Two weeks later, he attempted to enter the home of another woman but, finding that her doors were locked, went into her back yard and walked away. Chase later told detectives that he took locked doors as a sign that he was not welcome, but that unlocked doors were an invitation to come inside. While wandering around one day, he met a girl named Nancy Holden, with whom he had attended high school. He asked her for a lift but, frightened by his appearance, she refused. He walked down the street, where he broke into the home of a young married couple, stole some of their valuables, urinated into a drawer of their infant's clothing and defecated on their son's bed. The couple came home while Chase was still in the house. The husband attacked him, but Chase escaped.

Chase continued entering homes until he came across the home of David and Teresa Wallin. David was at work. Teresa was three months pregnant. She was in the middle of taking out the rubbish and had left her front door unlocked. Chase surprised her in her home and shot her three times, killing her – he used the same gun with which he'd killed Ambrose Griffin. He then dragged Teresa's body to her bedroom and raped it post-mortem while repeatedly stabbing it with a butcher's knife. When he had finished, he carved the corpse open and removed several of her internal organs, using a bucket to collect the blood and then taking it into the bathroom to bathe in it. He then sliced off her nipple and drank her blood, using an empty yoghurt container as a drinking glass. Before leaving, he went into the yard, found a pile of dog faeces and returned to stuff it into the corpse's mouth and throat.

On 23 January 1978, two days after killing Teresa Wallin, Chase purchased two puppies from a neighbour, then killed them and drank their blood, leaving the bodies on the neighbour's front lawn.

On 27 January, Chase committed his final murder. He entered the home of 38-year-old Evelyn Miroth, who was babysitting her 22-month-old nephew, David. Also present was Evelyn's six-year-old son Jason, and Dan Meredith, a neighbour who had come over to check on Evelyn. At the time, Evelyn was in the bath while Dan was looking after the children; he went into the front hallway when Chase entered the house. Dan Meredith was shot in the head at point-blank range with Chase's .22 handgun, killing him. Chase then turned the body over and stole the wallet and car keys. Jason ran to his mother's bedroom, where Chase shot him twice in the head at point-blank range; on the way to killing Jason, Chase also shot David in the head. Chase then entered the bathroom and fatally shot Evelyn once in the head. He dragged her corpse onto the bed, where he simultaneously committed buggery and drank her blood from a series of cuts to the back of the neck, which he had made. When he had finished, he inflicted on the body other mutilations with the knife, penetrating the anus and the uterus. This caused blood from her internal organs to flow into her abdomen, which he then cut open, draining the blood into a bucket; he then drank all of the blood. Chase then went to retrieve David's body. He took it to the bathroom, split the skull open in the bath and consumed some of the brain matter. Outside, a six-year-old girl with whom Jason Miroth had a play-date knocked on the door, startling Chase. He fled the residence, stealing Dan Meredith's car; the girl alerted a neighbour. The neighbour broke into the Miroth home where he discovered the bodies and contacted the police. A crime scene examination revealed handprints and footprints of the person whom the police believed to have been the killer.

Chase, meanwhile, took the baby's body home with him, where he chopped off the head and used the neck as a straw through which he sucked the blood out of the body. He then sliced the corpse open and consumed several internal organs and made his grotesque 'smoothies' out of others, finally disposing of the corpse at a nearby church.

Chase eventually came to the notice of the police as a viable suspect following the identification of his fingerprints at the house of Evelyn Miroth. They went to his apartment and knocked repeatedly, but Chase would not open the door. The police pretended they were going to leave and then waited. Chase emerged with a box in his arms and made his way towards his car. The police apprehended him, but not without a struggle. They noticed that he was wearing an orange parka that had dark stains on it and that his shoes appeared to be covered in blood. A .22 semi-automatic handgun was taken from him, which also had bloodstains on it. Then they found Dan Meredith's wallet in Chase's back pocket, along with a pair of latex gloves. The contents of the box he was carrying also proved interesting:

pieces of bloodstained paper and rags. They took him to the police station and interviewed him. He admitted to killing several dogs but stubbornly resisted talking about the murders. While he was in custody, police searched his apartment in the hope of finding a clue to the whereabouts of the missing baby.

What they found in the putrid-smelling place was disgusting. Nearly everything was bloodstained, including food and drinking glasses. In the kitchen, they found several small pieces of bone, and some dishes in the refrigerator with body parts. One container held human brain tissue. An electric blender was badly stained and smelt of rotting flesh. There were three pet collars but no animals to be found. Photographic overlays on human organs from a science book lay on a table, along with newspapers on which ads selling dogs were circled. A calendar showed the inscription 'Today' on the dates of the Wallin and Miroth murders and, chillingly, the same word was written on 44 more dates yet to come during that year.

Police officers continued the search for the missing baby, and finally the body was found. On 24 March, a church caretaker came upon a box containing the remains and called the police. When they arrived, they recognised the clothing of the missing boy from the Miroth home. The baby had been decapitated and the head lay underneath the torso, which was partially mummified. A hole in the centre of the head indicated that the child had been shot. There were several other stab wounds to the body and several ribs were broken. Beneath the body, too, was a ring of keys that fitted Dan Meredith's car. The police now had enough evidence to charge Chase.

In 1979, he stood trial on six counts of murder. In order to avoid the death penalty, his defence team tried to have Chase found guilty of second-degree murder only. Their case hinged on Chase's history of mental illness and the lack of planning of his crimes, evidence that they were not premeditated. But on 8 May, the jury found Chase guilty of six counts of first-degree murder. The defence asked for a clemency hearing, in which a judge determined that Chase was not legally insane. Chase was sentenced to die in the gas chamber.

While on death row, Chase became a feared presence in prison; the other inmates, aware of the graphic and bizarre nature of his crimes, feared him and, according to prison officials, they often tried to convince Chase to commit suicide, too fearful to get close enough to him to kill him themselves.

On 26 December 1980, a guard doing cell checks found Chase lying awkwardly on his bed and not breathing; he was pronounced dead. A post-mortem determined that he had committed suicide with an overdose of prescribed antidepressants that he had been saving up over the preceding weeks.

JOHN NORMAN COLLINS, AKA THE MICHIGAN MURDERER

In summer 1967, the first of a series of murders in and around the Michigan suburbs of Ypsilanti and Ann Arbor took place. Mary Fleszar, 19, was the victim. She had last been seen by a room-mate when she left their apartment near the university campus to go for a walk on 9 July. She was wearing a bright orange tent dress with large white polka dots, and a pair of sandals. She was 5ft tall, weighed about 110lb, wore glasses and had brown hair. She had not taken her handbag, but her car keys were gone and her car was parked across from where she normally left it, which her mother thought was odd. Half an hour after she left the apartment, a university police officer saw her walking alone. Later, a man sitting on his porch who knew her saw her walking towards her apartment. Then he saw a young man driving a blue-and-grey Chevrolet stop beside her, open his window and talk with her. She shook her head and walked on. He drove by again and pulled up in front of her. She again shook her head and walked around him. He backed out, accelerated with an angry screech and left. Concerned, the man on the porch watched her draw close to her building and then lost sight of her, but did not see the car return. He was the last person to see Fleszar alive. Her naked body was found on 7

August at an abandoned farm not far from where she lived. She had been stabbed 30 times in the chest with a knife or other sharp object. Her lower leg bones had been smashed just above the ankles. It also appeared that she had been brutally beaten. One of her hands was missing, along with the fingers of her other hand. Her clothing was found under a pile of rubbish.

The frozen naked body of Eileen Adams, 13, was found in a field on 19 December 1967. It had been wrapped in a rug and mattress cover, and tied with an electrical cord. She had been raped, strangled with the same electrical cord and stuffed into a sack. Her bra was tied around her neck. She had been cruelly beaten with a hammer, and a 3in nail was driven into her skull. Her stockings were arranged on her body, but her shoes were missing. There was evidence of sexual assault and her body was placed in plain sight. She had apparently been left alive but bound in such a way that her struggles to get free had tightened a telephone cord looped around her neck and tied to her ankles, which strangled her. Her shoes and coat were also missing. Police believed that her abductor had held her somewhere for up to two weeks before leaving her in the field.

It was almost seven months before another victim's body was found, on 6 July 1968. This was another college student, Joan Schell, aged 20, who had last been seen alive on 30 June, hitchhiking in front of the student union building, around 10.30pm. She had been sexually assaulted. Her throat was cut and she had been stabbed five times; her miniskirt was twisted around her neck. She'd been killed in a different place from where she was found.

On 21 March 1969, the body of another college student, Jane Mixer, 23, was found in a cemetery in Denton Township. She had been shot twice in the head with a .22-calibre gun. She too had been killed elsewhere. A stocking was twisted around her neck and her tights pulled down, but a sanitary napkin was still in place, which indicated no sexual attack.

On 26 March, the body of Maralynn Skelton, 16, was found.

She had last been seen the previous day hitchhiking in front of a shopping centre. Her skull was fractured; she had been whipped with a belt and sexually assaulted. She had also been killed elsewhere and dumped. A suspender belt was found wrapped around her neck.

The body count was now starting to rise and police searched for clues to the identity of the serial killer. On 15 April 1969, Dawn Basom, aged 13, was last seen leaving a house near the college campus. She was found dead the next day. She had been strangled with a black electrical wire and stabbed, and her breasts and buttocks were viciously slashed. A handkerchief and a piece of her blouse were stuffed in her mouth. She had been killed elsewhere, possibly in a deserted farmhouse where items of her clothing were later found.

Alice Kalom, 23, was the next victim. On 7 June 1969, she went to a party and was seen dancing with a young man with long hair. Her body was found near an abandoned barn. She had been raped and shot once in the head and stabbed twice in the chest. She had been killed elsewhere and her clothing was scattered around her body. Her shoes were missing.

Roxie Phillips, 17, disappeared on 30 June 1969. She had gone out to post a letter and meet a friend. A pair of boys looking for fossils found her body on 13 July in Pescadero Canyon just north of Carmel, California. She was badly decomposed and naked, except for a pair of sandals and a red-and-white cotton belt wrapped tightly around her neck. The body must have been carried to where it lay amid poison oak (Collins was treated in California that same week for poison oak). Some of Phillips's possessions were found strewn along Route 68. A friend of hers mentioned she had met a 'John' driving a silver Oldsmobile, who was going to college in Michigan and who rode motorcycles. She didn't think Roxie knew him, but she did admit that she had met him while he was cruising near Roxie's house.

Karen Sue Beineman, 18, was last seen on 23 July getting on the back of a motorcycle with a young man. She was later found, strangled, in a ravine. Her face was badly battered and she was naked. A piece of material was stuffed into her throat, her torn knickers were stuffed into her vagina and there were human hair clippings stuck to them. She had been killed elsewhere. Vital evidence found on her would ultimately lead police to her killer.

The witness told police that the young man with the motorcycle was John Norman Collins (b. 1947), who, at the time of the murder of Karen Beineman, was living at his uncle's house. His uncle just happened to be a police officer and on learning that his nephew was possibly a suspect looked around the house and garage. He acknowledged that something was amiss. He went into his basement and scraped up some of the paint, finding a stain that looked like blood. Immediately he called in forensic experts. The stain turned out to be varnish. However, they were soon to be rewarded in their search; one of them noticed hair clippings near the washing machine. The uncle explained that his wife had cut the children's hair. Aware of the odd clippings found on Beineman's knickers, the police gathered some from the basement floor to compare to those already at the lab. Then they noticed tiny droplets that looked like blood. When tested, they did indeed prove to be blood. After later tests revealed that the bloodstains were human and that the hairs might be consistent with those on the knickers, blood was found on Collins's car seat, even though his car had been thoroughly cleaned. A red-and-white piece of cotton fabric was also found. Forensic tests proved that the hair found in the garage was consistent with the hair found in Beineman's knickers. The blood from the car was found to match the blood of Alice Kalom. The police decided to arrest Collins. However, he denied any knowledge of any murders. He was, however, later charged with the murder of Karen Sue Beineman.

Collins's trial began on 30 June 1970 and, after deliberating for three days, the jury returned with a unanimous verdict that he was guilty of first-degree murder. He was subsequently sentenced to life imprisonment with a minimum of 20 years. He went through three appeals and even changed his name to Chapman to get a transfer to Canada, where he would have been eligible for parole in 1985. He also tried to escape by tunnelling out of the prison. The murders of the other six girls remain officially unsolved. To this day, Collins still protests his innocence. Since then, a police officer involved in the case made public that there was other evidence never made public, linking Collins to the other murders. In the case of Mary Fleszar, missing from her effects was an Expo 67 Canadian silver dollar that she wore around her neck. Such an item was apparently found on Collins's dresser, according to police, when his rooms were searched. He claimed that it was not his and denied that it had been in his room.

In the case of Joan Schell, she had last been seen getting into a car with three men. Collins's room-mate, Arnie Davis, said that he was in that car with Collins and another man whose name he claimed not to know. Collins had allegedly told the girl that he would take her to Ann Arbor in his own car. Davis says that they left the apartment together and Collins had come back two and a half hours later to say that he had failed to have the sexual encounter with her that he'd hoped for. He had her red handbag with him, which he said she had left in his car. He went through the wallet, says Davis, and called her a bitch. There was also speculation by the police that Davis was actually there when Collins and the other man together raped and killed Schell in a car park. Later, Collins apparently asked Davis to hide a hunting knife; the type of knife that could have made the wounds found on Schell. Collins told someone that he did not know Schell, although several witnesses claimed to have seen them both together that night. He told someone else that he'd had a date with her but had stood her up. No one checked out his alibi of being at his mother's that weekend, although someone said that he had overheard Collins on the phone to his mother, telling her that he was in some trouble. One person said that he talked obsessively about the wounds on Schell's body, claiming that he got the information from his uncle, a corporal on the state police force. However, Corporal Leik said he knew only what had been printed in the newspaper. He could not have told Collins the things he apparently knew.

The Dawn Basom murder was also mentioned. Young Dawn Basom lived across the street from an apartment complex where a girl whom Collins used to date lived. Dawn was strong and would not accept rides, even with men she knew. She was last seen near her home, walking along the road. A neighbour had seen two cars parked in front of a vacant house in their neighbourhood: a red Chevrolet and a blue Volkswagen. She had seen a young woman in the front seat of the red car sitting with a man with dark hair. Then both cars drove away. Many people believe that one man alone could not have forced Basom into a car, unless he had a gun. Glass particles on the soles of her shoes indicated that she was forced into the basement of an abandoned farmhouse, where it is thought she was killed. The link to Collins was his knowledge of the neighbourhood.

Collins was seen both on foot and on his motorcycle the day that Alice Kalom disappeared, not far from her apartment. Friends who stopped to talk with him claimed later to police that he had had a strange look on his face and seemed distant. He would not look them in the eye. Arnie Davis said that Collins had brought Kalom back to their apartment on 7 June. There was some commotion between them in Collins's room and Kalom broke away and fled. According to Davis, Collins chased her. He returned later alone. When she was found, there was a boot print on her skirt that was later matched to a boot that Collins owned. Blood found later in Collins's car and on his raincoat matched her type. The bullet found in her head could have come from a High Standard revolver, which Collins was said to have stolen a few months before in a burglary. The knife wounds were consistent with the hunting knife that Collins later told Davis to hide for him (as stated by Davis).

The body of Roxie Phillips had been dumped amid poison

oak; Collins had been treated for a case of poison oak. Also, 22 pubic hairs were found on one of his sweaters that were consistent with hers. If he had carried her over his shoulder in a state of rigor mortis, this would have accounted for the hairs being rubbed into his sweater. The one person who recalled the man that she and Roxie met gave the following information: his name was John, he was from Michigan, he was 5ft 11in tall with dark hair, he drove a silver-grey Oldsmobile, he was there with a friend in a camper, he was a college senior with the goal of being a teacher and he was in his twenties. That was a close match to Collins; too much to be coincidence.

On 25 November 2004, more than 35 years after these murders, there came a new development. DNA evidence came to light to connect a new suspect to one of the original murders. Gary Earl Leiterman, 62, was charged and convicted of the murder of Jane Mixer, the third victim in the series. Leiterman's DNA had been found on Mixer's knickers. There was now some serious doubt about whether Mixer had been one of Collins's victims. When found, she was fully dressed, unlike the other victims. In addition, she had been shot twice in the head and not mutilated in any manner or sexually assaulted. However, other victims had been dumped within a few miles of the cemetery, so it still seemed possible; Mixer also had a stocking tied around her neck. Other victims were strangled as well. Leiterman was convicted of murder and sentenced to life imprisonment. His lengthy appeal is still ongoing.

On 27 November 2006, it was announced that the same DNA technology had identified the killer of another girl, Eileen Adams, who had been linked to Collins. Semen found in the dead girl's knickers was matched to the DNA of a man named Robert Bowman, already wanted by police in two states. He remained at large until April 2011 when, at the age of 75, he was finally arrested and charged with the murder. He came to trial in August 2011 and pleaded not guilty. The jury could not reach a verdict and a retrial was ordered. That took place in

October 2011; the jury in this trial found him guilty and he was sentenced to life imprisonment.

JEFFREY DAHMER, AKA THE MILWAUKEE MONSTER

Jeffrey Dahmer's (b. 1960) first brush with the law was in August 1982. He was arrested for exposing himself in public. Four years later, he was charged again with public exposure after two boys accused him of masturbating in public. This time he was sentenced to a year in prison, of which he served 10 months. In 1988, he was arrested for fondling a 13-year-old boy in Milwaukee. He served 10 months of a one-year sentence in a work-release camp and was required to register as a sex offender. He convinced the judge that he needed therapy and he was released on five-year probation on good behaviour. Shortly thereafter, he committed a string of murders that would not end until his arrest in 1991.

However, it later came to light that Dahmer had committed his first murder back in 1978, when he was only 18. He picked up a hitchhiker named Steven Hicks when he was living with his parents in Ohio. They had sex and drank beer, but then Hicks wanted to leave. Dahmer couldn't stand the thought of Hicks leaving, so he struck him over the head with a barbell, killing him instantly. To get rid of the body he cut it up, packaged it up in plastic rubbish bags and buried the bags in the woods. Several years later, he returned to where he had buried the body, dug it up and crushed the remains with a sledgehammer before scattering them in the woods.

It was not until September 1987 that Dahmer's urge to kill manifested itself again. His victim was Steven Toumi. The two of them had been drinking heavily in one of the popular gay bars in Milwaukee, and went back to a hotel room. Dahmer apparently didn't know how he killed him, but when he awoke, Toumi was dead and blood was on Dahmer's mouth. Dahmer bought a large suitcase and stuffed the body inside. He then took the body to his grandmother's basement, where he had sex with it, masturbated on it, dismembered it and disposed of it in the rubbish.

Several months later, Dahmer selected his third victim, a 14-year-old Native American boy named Jamie Doxtator, who frequented the gay bars looking for sex. Dahmer's MO was now firmly established. He would meet and select his prey at gay bars or bath houses. He would offer to take them home, and offer money for posing for photographs or they would simply enjoy some beer and videos. He would then drug them, strangle them, masturbate over or have sex with the dead body. He would then dismember the body and dispose of it, sometimes keeping the skull or other body parts as souvenirs.

Dahmer's next victim, in late March 1988, was Richard Guerrero, a handsome young man of Mexican origin. Dahmer met him at a gay bar in Milwaukee. Guerrero met the same fate as the previous victims.

On 25 September 1988, Dahmer moved into an apartment on North 24th Street in Milwaukee. The very next day, he got into trouble. He offered a 13-year-old Laotian boy $50 to pose for some pictures. He drugged the boy and fondled him, but did not get violent or have intercourse with him. The boy's parents realised there was something wrong with him and took him to the hospital where it was confirmed that he had been drugged. The police arrested Dahmer for sexual exploitation of a child and second-degree sexual assault. On 30 January 1989, Dahmer pleaded guilty, claiming that he had thought the boy was much older than he was. He later received a sentence of probation with a one-year sentence in a correction house with day release, meaning he could leave the prison in the daytime and go back at night. After 10 months, the judge awarded him an early release.

While Dahmer awaited sentencing, he was again living at his grandmother's house. He met a black homosexual named Anthony Sears, 24, at a gay bar. As with the others, he offered Sears some money to pose for photos. When they reached Dahmer's grandmother's house, Sears was drugged and strangled.

Dahmer had sex with his corpse and then dismembered it. He kept the head and boiled it to remove the skin, later painting it grey, so that, in case of discovery, the skull would look like a plastic model used by medical students. Dahmer saved this trophy for two years, until it was recovered from his apartment on 23 July 1991. Later, he explained that he masturbated in front of the skulls for sexual gratification.

On 14 May 1990, Dahmer moved to another apartment at 924 North 25th Street, Milwaukee, and the killing continued in earnest; the murder rate escalated. Between May 1990 and July 1991, he was killing almost at a rate of one man a week. Most victims were either homosexual or bisexual. The youngest was 14 and the oldest was 31. In addition to his MO for luring and killing, Dahmer had a ritual that he would perform once he had murdered his victims. He would photograph the victims before cutting the bodies open so that he could remember each and every murder. He was fascinated by the colour of the viscera and sexually aroused by the heat that the freshly killed body would give off. Finally, he would dismember the body, photographing each stage of the process for future viewing pleasure. In order to dispose of the bodies he would experiment with various chemicals and acids that would reduce the flesh and bone to a black, evil-smelling sludge, which could be poured down a drain or toilet. Some parts of the bodies he chose to keep as trophies – frequently the genitals and head. The genitals he preserved in formaldehyde. The heads were boiled until the flesh came off. Once the skull was bare, he painted it with grey paint to look like plastic. From time to time, he ate the flesh of his victims in the belief that the people would come alive again in him. He tried various seasonings and meat tenderisers to make the human flesh tastier; eating it gave him an erection. His famous freezer contained strips of frozen human flesh. He even drank the blood. He also tried his own form of lobotomy on several of his victims. Once they were drugged, he drilled a hole in their skulls and injected hydrochloric acid into their brains. Needless to say, it caused death right away in a few victims, but one victim supposedly functioned minimally for a few days before dying.

Dahmer had a brush with the police on 27 May 1991. It has been suggested that if the two officers had been more alert the lives of 12 other men could have been saved. On that night, police received a call to say that a young man was running naked in the street near Dahmer's house. On arriving at the location, the police found 14-year-old Konerak Sinthasomphone in a distressed state and incoherent. Dahmer was also in attendance. Dahmer told police that they had had an argument while drinking and that Sinthasomphone was his 19-year-old lover. Despite the teenager's protests, police allowed Dahmer to take him home. Later that night Dahmer killed and dismembered Sinthasomphone, keeping his skull as a souvenir. What the police missed in the Dahmer apartment bedroom was the body of another victim, Tony Hughes, whose decomposing corpse had lain for three days on the bed.

Monday, 22 July 1991 was the day America would be stunned by Dahmer's arrest and the revelations that followed. At around midnight, two officers were parked up in their police car when they saw a black man, Tracy Edwards, with a pair of handcuffs dangling from one wrist. Edwards told them that he had gone with a man to his apartment and the man had tried to do things to him and handcuff him. Edwards directed them to the apartment and Jeffrey Dahmer opened the door. He was very calm and rational. He offered to get the key to the handcuffs in the bedroom. Edwards remembered that the knife that Dahmer had threatened him with was also in the bedroom. One of the officers decided to go into the bedroom himself and take a look. He noticed photographs lying around that shocked him: dismembered human bodies, skulls in the refrigerator. When he collected his wits, he told the other officer to handcuff Dahmer and place him under arrest. As the officer tried to handcuff Dahmer, he started to fight with the officer, who finally managed to subdue him. The other officer continued the search of Dahmer's apartment and came across a severed head in the refrigerator. A closer examination of the apartment revealed three more heads in the freezer. There was a cooking pot that contained decomposed hands and a penis. On the shelf above the kettle were two skulls. In a cupboard they found containers of ethyl alcohol, chloroform and formaldehyde, along with some glass jars holding male genitalia preserved in formaldehyde. There were many Polaroid photos taken by Dahmer at various stages of his victims' deaths. One showed a man's head, with the flesh still intact, lying in a sink. Another displayed a victim cut open from the neck to the groin, like a deer gutted after the kill, the cuts so clean the pelvic bone could clearly be seen.

Jeffrey Dahmer was interviewed, made a full confession and was charged with 17 murders, later reduced to 15. His trial began in July 1992. With the evidence overwhelmingly against him, Dahmer chose to plead not guilty by reason of insanity, arguing that his necrophilic urges were so strong that he could not control them. However, the jury found him to be sane and he was convicted of all charges.

He was sentenced to 15 life terms, totalling 937 years in prison. At his sentencing hearing, unusually for a serial killer, Dahmer expressed remorse for his actions, also saying that he wished for his own death. Dahmer served his sentence at the Columbia Correctional Institution in Wisconsin, where it is claimed that he became more and more religious over time and ultimately declared himself a born-again Christian. While in prison, Dahmer survived an attempt on his life. After attending a church service in the prison chapel, an inmate took a razor blade and tried to slash his throat. Dahmer escaped the incident with superficial wounds.

On 28 November 1994, he was not so lucky. Dahmer and another inmate were attacked and beaten to death by fellow inmate Christopher Scarver while on work detail in the prison gym. Much controversy surrounded the decision to allow Dahmer such a privilege as a work detail, as well as the pairing of Dahmer with Scarver, a man with a history of brutality who was incarcerated for murder. The fact that Scarver was black (and that most of Dahmer's victims were black) did not escape the notice of critics.

WAYNE ADAM FORD, AKA THE REMORSEFUL KILLER

On 26 October 1997, a duck hunter was canoeing near Eureka, California, when he noticed an object that resembled a mannequin on the muddy bank. When he approached the object, he realised that it was the butchered remains of a woman who was missing a head, arms and legs. When investigators arrived at the scene, they saw that the victim's body had been sliced down the middle and almost completely disembowelled. Moreover, the woman's breasts had been cut off and there were approximately 30 stab wounds on her body. Because there were no fingers to fingerprint, head, tattoos or unusual features on the torso, investigators were unable to identify the woman. The woman, whose remains were referred to as Jane Doe, was examined by the County Coroner. The coroner determined that she was probably between the ages of 18 and 25, and had a dark complexion. It was believed that the female had been dead at least three or four days before she was discovered. Almost three months later, the victim's arm and hand were found near a beach. However, the body parts had deteriorated so much that there was no way a fingerprint analysis could be conducted. Investigators believed that her identity might never be known.

In June 1998, another woman's body was found floating in the California Aqueduct near the town of Buttonwillow. The remains were taken to the Kern County Coroner's office for examination. During a post-mortem, it was discovered that the woman's death had probably been caused by strangulation. It was suggested that she had been raped and murdered several days prior to being found. Fingerprints later identified the victim as Tina Renee Gibbs, 26, who had been working as a street prostitute in Las Vegas in the months before her disappearance.

Four months later, on 25 September 1998, another naked body of a woman was found lying in a roadside ditch near Lodi, California. Several items were found lying nearby that were thought to be connected with the woman, including women's clothing, a bloodied tarpaulin, hair samples, a white plastic bag with the logo of a truck stop titled 'Flying J' and some pieces of jewellery. Police investigators hoped that the evidence would provide some clues as to the identity of the victim and how she died. A post-mortem determined that the woman had been dead for several days, due to the advanced state of decomposition. A puncture mark was found on one of the victim's breasts and there was evidence of suffocation. Police believed the woman was murdered in another location and thrown from a moving vehicle into the ditch. Fingerprints were taken of the victim and she was identified as Lanette White, 25, of Fontana, California. She had last been seen by her cousin on 20 September preparing to go to the shops to get milk for her baby. Friends and family became concerned when she never returned home. The last thing they ever expected was that she'd been murdered.

Patricia Anne Tamez, 21, was a prostitute and drug addict who used to roam the streets for a quick fix or to prostitute herself to support her drug habit. On 22 October 1998, she spent the early part of the afternoon soliciting sex from truckers in Victorville, California. After several hours she got her first customer; a man in a large, black truck pulled up and propositioned her. Following a brief conversation, Tamez got into the truck and drove off with the man towards the highway. The following evening, her naked and brutalised body was found floating in a nearby water treatment centre. When the authorities arrived, they recovered the woman's body from the water. To their surprise, they realised that one of her breasts had been cut off. It was obvious that she had been murdered. A post-mortem later revealed that the woman had taken a severe beating prior to her death. There was evidence that she had been bound, raped and hit on the head with a blunt object. Moreover, her attacker had broken her back and severed one of her breasts before he strangled her. During a search of the area, police found items that were possibly linked with the murder, including a bloodied towel, blouse, trousers and a .22-calibre air pistol. Police were not able to locate the victim's missing breast, nor did they have any clue as to the identity of the murderer. However, several weeks later, the detectives got their big break.

On 3 November 1998, long-haul trucker, Wayne Adam Ford (b. 1961), 36, walked into the Humboldt County Sheriff's Department in Eureka, accompanied by his brother Rod. Rod had spent the previous day trying to convince Wayne to turn himself in to police after he had made confessions of murder to him. Shortly after arriving at the department, Wayne amazed police officers when he tearfully broke down and confessed to murdering four women. His claims were further supported by the contents of a plastic bag found in his pocket during a search. Shockingly, the bag contained the severed breast of Patricia Tamez.

Ford made a full confession and told the police where he had disposed of the body parts of the victims. He confessed that he had picked up the unidentified woman who was hitchhiking near Eureka. He took her back to his trailer, had rough sex with her and then strangled her. It was a process he repeated on three other occasions. However, unlike with the other victims, he dismembered the unidentified woman in his bath with a saw and knives. He said that he dismembered her because it made it easier to dispose of her body. A search of Ford's trailer revealed even more critical evidence. In the kitchen police found a coffee can that was believed to have contained the unidentified female's breast. Moreover, a plastic bag with the 'Flying J' logo was also discovered, which matched the bag discovered earlier close to Lanette White's remains. In addition, the freezer in which Ford stored body parts was also found and confiscated.

On 6 November 1998, Ford appeared at Humboldt County's Superior Court. He was charged with only one count of first-degree murder, that of Jane Doe, the unidentified female. The other murders were not committed in the court's jurisdiction. Therefore, he could only be tried in the counties where the bodies were found. However, a new serial killer law was enacted approximately two months after his arrest, which allowed prosecutors the right to combine a series of murders in different jurisdictions into a single trial if they could prove that they were related. Thus, instead of him being tried for each murder separately in different counties, he would have just one trial for all four murders. Whether the law was constitutionally applicable to his case was the subject of another legal argument. Ford entered a not guilty plea on legal advice on the basis that he was allegedly prevented from having contact with a lawyer from the moment of his arrest to his court appearance. If it could be proven that he had been denied access to legal advice, then his confessions might be rendered inadmissible in a trial. This would turn out to be a difficult obstacle for the prosecution to overcome.

On 6 April 1999, a legal decision was made to have Ford arrested and charged in San Bernardino County for the murders of all four victims. The defence team lost their first battle and faced the prospect of their client receiving the death penalty. That August, Ford was transferred to West Valley Detention Centre in San Bernardino County to await his upcoming trial.

In November 2003, a hearing was held at San Bernardino County Superior Court to determine whether Wayne's confessions to police were admissible in court. First, his defence team argued that the confessions were the result of unreasonable police actions in the hours and days after Ford surrendered. However, the prosecution maintained that the confessions were legally obtained and that Ford had initially asked for an attorney but later changed his mind.

In January 2004 a judge ruled that most of Ford's confessions were admissible at trial. Yet those made after 5 November 1998, three days after he had turned himself in, could not be used by the prosecution because the police should have allowed him legal counsel by then. This meant that Ford's confessions regarding Lanette White, which were made on the third day of questioning, were jeopardised. Nevertheless, the prosecution decided that they would include the murder charge concerning White at trial because there was adequate evidence linking him to her death.

In June 2006, Ford was convicted on four counts of murder and sentenced to death. He is currently on death row awaiting execution.

JOHN WAYNE GACY, AKA THE KILLER CLOWN

John Wayne Gacy (b. 1942) seemed to have a very normal childhood. When Gacy was 11 years old, he was playing by a swing when he was hit in the head by one of the swings; the accident caused a blood clot in his brain. Between the ages of 11 and 16, Gacy had suffered a series of blackouts caused by the clot. However, the clot was not discovered until he was 16, when he was given medication to dissolve it. At the age of 17, Gacy was diagnosed with a heart ailment. He was hospitalised on several occasions for his problem throughout his life but doctors were not able to find an exact cause for the pain he was suffering. However, although he complained frequently about his heart (especially after his arrest), he never suffered any serious heart attack.

Gacy attended a business college and started a moderately successful career as a shoe salesman in Springfield, Illinois. He married in 1964 and moved to Iowa, where he managed a Kentucky Fried Chicken restaurant belonging to his wife's family. His wife gave birth to two children. However, his marriage fell apart after he was convicted and sentenced to 10 years in prison for child molestation in 1968. He was a model prisoner and was paroled in 1970 after serving less than two years. After he was released, he moved back to Chicago, managing to conceal his criminal record.

His mother had been impressed with how her son had readjusted to life outside the prison walls and she helped him obtain a house of his own outside Chicago's city limits. Gacy owned one half of his new house, located at 8213 West Summerdale Avenue in the Norwood Park Township, and his mother and sisters owned the remaining half. Gacy was very happy with his new two-bedroom 1950s ranch-style house located in a nice, clean, family-oriented neighbourhood. He was quick to make friends, in particular with his new neighbours, Edward and Lillie Grexa, who had lived in the neighbourhood since it had first been built.

After only seven months, Gacy became involved in another scandal involving young boys. He was arrested and charged with disorderly conduct. The charges stated that Gacy had forced a young boy, whom he had picked up at a bus terminal, to commit sexual acts on him. Gacy had been discharged from his parole for only a few months at this point. However, he slipped through the justice system when all charges against him were dropped, due to his young accuser failing to attend court.

On 1 June 1972, Gacy married Carole Hoff, a newly divorced mother of two daughters. Gacy had romanced the emotionally vulnerable woman, and she had immediately fallen for him. She was attracted to his charm and generosity and believed he would be a good provider for her and her children. She was aware of Gacy's previous convictions and she believed that he was reformed. How wrong could she be?

In 1974, Gacy started his owned painting and decorating company, and hired male youths, with the ulterior motive of seducing and having sex with them. This put a strain on his marriage and his wife divorced him in 1976. It was then that young boys started to go missing in and around the Chicago suburbs. One such young man was Robert Piest. The investigation into his disappearance would lead not only to the discovery of his body but the bodies of 32 other young men who had suffered similar fates – rocking the foundations of Chicago and shocking all of America.

Robert Piest was only 15 when he disappeared from just

outside the pharmacy where he had been working minutes earlier. His mother, who had come to pick him up from work, had been waiting inside the pharmacy for Robert, who had said he'd be right back after talking with a contractor who had offered him a job. Robert never returned. His mother began to worry as time passed. Eventually her worry turned to dread. She searched the pharmacy area outside and inside and still Robert was nowhere to be found. Three hours after Robert's disappearance, the Des Plaines Police Department was notified. Lieutenant Joseph Kozenczak led the investigation.

The police ascertained that the contractor who had offered the job to Piest was Gacy; an officer went to his house and asked about the missing boy. Gacy was asked to go with the officer to the police station for questioning; he went to the police station hours later and gave his statement to police. Gacy said he knew nothing about the boy's disappearance and left the station after further questioning. The officer ran a background check on Gacy the next day and was surprised to find that Gacy had served time for committing buggery on a teenager years earlier, so he obtained a search warrant for Gacy's house. It was there that he believed they would find Robert Piest.

On 13 December 1978, police entered Gacy's house on West Summerdale Avenue. Gacy was not at home during the investigation. Police seized a number of items, including some valium and marijuana, but no real evidence of value at that time. However, they were aware of a rancid smell about the house. Gacy was made aware of the search and was then put under 24-hour surveillance. Police then decided to arrest him on the marijuana charge.

Finally, after intense investigation and scientific work on items confiscated by police from Gacy's house, they came up with crucial evidence against Gacy. A ring found at Gacy's house belonged to another teenager who had disappeared a year earlier, named John Szyc. They also discovered that three former employees of Gacy had also mysteriously disappeared. Furthermore, the receipt for the roll of film that was found at Gacy's home had belonged to a co-worker of Robert Piest who had given it to Robert on the day of his disappearance. With this new information, the investigators began to realise the enormity of the case that was unfolding.

It was not long before police were back searching Gacy's house. Gacy had finally confessed to police that he did kill someone but said it had been in self-defence. He said that he had buried the body underneath his garage. Gacy told police where they could find the body and police marked the gravesite in the garage, though they did not immediately begin digging. They first wanted to search the crawl space under Gacy's house. It was not long before they discovered a suspicious mound of earth. Minutes after digging into the suspicious mound, investigators found the remains of a body. Believing that there may be more bodies buried, they conducted a slow but thorough search of the underneath of the house. On the first day that the police began their digging, they found two bodies. One of the bodies was that of John Butkovich, who was buried under the garage. The other body was the one found in the crawl space. As the days passed, the body count grew higher. Some of the victims were found with their underwear still lodged deep in their throats. Other victims were buried so close together that police believed they were probably killed or buried at the same time.

On Friday, 22 December 1978, Gacy finally confessed to police that he had killed at least 30 people and had buried most of the remains beneath the crawl space of his house. Gacy said that his first killing had taken place in January 1972 and the second in January 1974, about a year and a half after his marriage. He further confessed that he would lure his victims into being handcuffed and then sexually assault them. To muffle their screams, he would stuff a sock or underwear into their mouths and kill them by pulling a rope or board against their throats, as he raped them. Gacy admitted to sometimes keeping the dead bodies under his bed or in the attic for several hours before eventually burying them in the crawl space. He also confirmed to police that he had on several occasions killed more than one person in a day. However, the reason he gave for them being buried so close together was that he was running out of room and needed to conserve space.

By 28 December, police had removed a total of 27 bodies from Gacy's house. There was also another body found weeks earlier, but not in the crawl space. The naked corpse of Frank Wayne Landingin had been found in the Des Plaines River. At the time of the discovery, police were not yet aware of Gacy's crimes and the case was still under investigation. However, investigators found Landingin's driving licence in Gacy's home and connected him to the young man's murder. Landingin was not the only one of Gacy's victims to be found in the river. Also on 28 December, police removed from Des Plaines River the body of James Mazzara, who still had his underwear lodged in his throat. The coroner said that the underwear stuffed down the victim's throat had caused Mazzara to suffocate. Gacy told police that the reason he disposed of the bodies in the river was because he ran out of room in his crawl space and because he had been experiencing back problems from digging the graves. Mazzara was the 29th victim of Gacy's to be found; he would not be the last.

Under the concrete patio at Gacy's house, workmen found the body of a man still in good condition, preserved in the concrete. The man wore a pair of blue jeans, shorts and a wedding ring. Gacy's victims no longer included only young boys or suspected homosexuals, but now also married men. The following week, another body was discovered. The 31st body linked to Gacy was in the Illinois River. Police were able to discover the identity of the young man by a 'Tim Lee' tattoo on one of his arms. A friend of the victim's father had recognised the Tim Lee tattoo while reading a newspaper story about the discovery of a body in the river. The victim's name was Timothy O'Rourke. Still the body count rose. Yet another body was found on Gacy's property around the time O'Rourke was discovered. The body was located beneath the recreation room of Gacy's house. It was the last body to be found on Gacy's property. Soon after the discovery, the house was destroyed and reduced to rubble. Unfortunately, among the 32 bodies that were discovered, Robert Piest was still unaccounted for. Finally, in April 1979, Piest's remains were discovered in the Illinois River. His body had supposedly been lodged somewhere along the river making it difficult to find. However, strong winds must have dislodged the body and carried it to the locks at Dresden Dam where it was eventually discovered. A post-mortem report on Piest determined that he had suffocated from paper towels being lodged down his throat. Police investigators continued to match dental records and other clues to help identify the remaining victims who were found on Gacy's property. All but nine of the victims were finally identified. Although the search for the dead had finally come to an end, Gacy's trial was just beginning.

On Wednesday, 6 February 1980, John Wayne Gacy's murder trial began in the Cook County Criminal Courts Building in Chicago, Illinois. He pleaded not guilty by reason of insanity. His lawyer made the claim that Gacy had had moments of temporary insanity at the time of each individual murder, but before and afterwards, somehow regained his sanity to properly lure and dispose of victims. However, this plea was rejected outright.

While on trial, Gacy joked that the only thing he was guilty of was 'running a cemetery without a licence'. At one point in the trial, Gacy's defence also tried to claim that all 33 murders were accidental deaths as part of erotic asphyxia, but the Cook County Coroner immediately provided evidence that this was impossible. Also, Gacy had made an earlier confession to police and was unable to have this evidence suppressed. He was found guilty on 13 March 1980 and sentenced to death.

Gacy remained on death row in Stateville Penitentiary in Illinois until his execution date was set for 10 May 1994. After finishing his last meal, consisting of shrimp, fried chicken, fresh strawberries and French fries, he was taken to the execution chamber to be executed by lethal injection.

Gacy's execution proved problematic. As the execution began, the lethal chemicals unexpectedly solidified, clogging the IV tube that led into Gacy's arm and preventing any further passage. Blinds covering the window through which witnesses observed the execution were drawn, and the execution team replaced the clogged tube with a new one. Ten minutes later, the blinds were then reopened and the execution process resumed. It took 27 minutes for him to die. This apparently led to the state of Illinois adopting a different method of lethal injection. Gacy never expressed any remorse for his crimes or to the families of his victims.

After his execution, Gacy's brain was removed. It is currently in the possession of Dr Helen Morrison, who interviewed Gacy and other serial killers in an attempt to isolate common personality traits held by such people. However, an examination of Gacy's brain after his execution revealed no abnormalities. Dr Morrison said, 'Gacy did not fit into any psychological profile associated with serial killers, and the psychological reasons for his rampage will probably never be known.' During Gacy's trial, Dr Morrison herself appeared as a psychiatric witness and told the court that he had 'the emotional make-up of an infant'.

DONALD HENRY 'PEE WEE' GASKINS

Born in Prospect, South Carolina, Donald Gaskins (b. 1931) spent most of his youth in and out of reform school and later prison. Gaskins was small and of slight build (he was only 5ft 4in tall, hence his nickname). He was clever with his hands, and a natural around machines and motors. He left school at 11 to work on cars at a local garage, teaming up with two friends named Danny and Marsh in his spare time to form a marauding gang dubbed the Trouble Trio. Starting off with thefts of petrol from service stations after closing time, they soon graduated to residential burglaries, counselled along the way by Danny's ex-convict father. Buying an old car with the proceeds from their robberies, they ranged further afield, visiting prostitutes in Charleston and Columbia. Their sexual experiments also included younger boys, but the Trouble Trio made a critical mistake when they gang-raped Marsh's younger sister. Threats and promises of cash failed to secure her silence and parental wrath descended on the boys in full force. Danny's father defended him with a shotgun, but Gaskins and Marsh were strung up by their wrists in a barn and whipped bloody in relays by parents wielding a leather strap.

However, Gaskins still continued a life of crime, and one Saturday in 1946, he was prowling around a house when one of the tenants, a girl he knew, surprised him. She was armed with a hatchet, and slashed at Gaskins and chased him outside, where he disarmed her and struck back, gashing her arms and splitting her scalp. The girl survived to identify Gaskins, whereupon he was jailed for assault with a deadly weapon and intent to kill. The judge found him guilty as charged and consigned him to the South Carolina Industrial School for Boys until his 18th birthday.

Deemed sane and fit for normal custody, Gaskins was shipped back to the reformatory in 1950. Light duty soon gave way to threats of whipping in reprisal for his prior conduct, but he escaped and fled to Sumter, where he joined a travelling circus. He fell in love with a 13-year-old member of the crew and married her, the first of his six wives, on 22 January 1951. After one night together, for his bride's sake, Gaskins surrendered to the authorities and spent the last three months of his sentence in solitary confinement.

When finally released, he did take on various jobs but on one of these his employer's teenage daughter and a girlfriend cornered Gaskins in the barn, taunting him. Gaskins snapped, lashed out with a hammer and cracked the girl's skull. Jailed for arson, assault with a deadly weapon and attempted murder, the prosecutor promised Gaskins 18 months' confinement in return for a guilty plea, but Gaskins failed to get the deal in writing and Judge TB Greniker had other ideas. He pronounced a five-year sentence, and then added another year for contempt when Gaskins cursed him.

When Gaskins entered the South Carolina state prison in 1952, it struck him as 'the dreariest looking place on Earth'. There were new faces and new rules to memorise, but the reality of prison life remained unchanged. In place of dorms, the state penitentiary had cellblocks and 'Power Men' who took what they wanted by force. Gaskins went in expecting another round of gang rapes, but instead he was ignored until the afternoon when an inmate approached him on the yard and told him, 'You belong to Arthur.'

Over the next six months, while Gaskins was sharing his cell with a brutal rapist, he realised that the only way to save himself was to become a Power Man. To that end, knowing it meant murder: Gaskins started looking for the biggest, toughest inmate he could find. He chose Hazel Brazell, a convict so vicious that no one on either side of the bars dared call him by his despised first name. To ingratiate himself with Brazell, Gaskins used the same tactic he would employ with Rudolph Tyner almost 30 years later. He brought gifts of food from the kitchen, becoming a fixture around Brazell's cellblock, accepted as part of the crowd. On his fifth visit, Gaskins found Brazell on the toilet, with only one guard stationed outside his cell. Striking swiftly, he cut Brazell's throat with a stolen paring knife and warned the bodyguard to flee before the guards arrived. 'I surprised myself at how calm I was,' Gaskins later wrote in his autobiography, *Final Truth*. 'I didn't really feel nothing much at all.'

He admitted killing Brazell 'in a fight' and bargained a murder charge down to manslaughter, two-thirds of the nine-year sentence concurrent with his pre-existing term. 'I figured that was a damn fair deal,' Gaskins said, 'considering I wouldn't never again have to be afraid of anybody in prison no matter how long I was there.' He spent six months in solitary and emerged a Power Man in his own right, the 'Pee Wee' nickname now a label of respect.

Following his release he had many other brushes with the law, which resulted in further prison sentences, the last of which he was released from in 1968. Gaskins settled in Sumter, South Carolina, working in construction, stripping hot cars on weekends and cruising bars for sex. He raged and brooded over women who rejected him. He drove compulsively along the Carolina coast, later recalling, 'It was like I was looking for something special on them coastal highways, only I didn't know what.'

In September 1969, he found out. He came upon a young blonde female hitchhiker, bound for Charleston. Gaskins picked her up and propositioned her. When she laughed in his face, he beat her unconscious and drove to an old logging road. There, he raped and buggered his victim; he then tortured and mutilated her with a knife. She was still alive when he weighted her body and left her in a swamp to drown. Leaving the scene, Gaskins recalled, 'I felt truly the best I ever remembered feeling in my whole life.'

Gaskins later called that first impulsive homicide 'his miracle ... a beam of light, like a vision'. From that day on, he made a habit of patrolling the coastal highways on weekends, seeking victims and exploring future disposal sites. By Christmas 1969, he had committed two more 'coastal kills – ones where I didn't know the victims or their names or nothing about them'. It was recreational murder, refined over time until he could keep his victims alive and screaming for hours on end, sometimes for days.

By 1970, Gaskins was averaging one 'coastal kill' every six weeks, experimenting with different torture methods, disappointed when his victims died prematurely. 'I preferred for them to last as long as possible,' he wrote. The following year, he claimed 11 nameless victims, including his first kidnap-slaying of two girls at once. Ideas for tormenting his captives came to Gaskins as he browsed through hardware stores, eyeing the tools. 'I never gave no thought to stopping,' he admitted. 'They was a clock-kind of thing. When it was time, I went and killed.'

Up until now all of his victims had been young females. His first male victims were by accident, two long-haired boys whom Gaskins took for girls as he drove up behind them in March 1974. Gender would not save them, though. Gaskins drove them both to a hideout near Charleston, where he buggered and tortured both, cooking and cannibalising their severed genitals before he granted them the mercy of death.

Gaskins lost track of the victims he murdered for sport between September 1969 and December 1975. They were hard to recall, he explained, 'because they're mostly just a jumble of faces and bodies and memories of things I did to them'. In terms of numbers, he said, 'the closest figure I can come up with is 80 to 90'. Sadistic murder was addictive for Gaskins. 'I finally reached the point where I wanted the bothersomeness to start,' he wrote. 'I looked forward to it every month, because it felt so good relieving myself of it.'

The only coastal victim he recalled by name was 16-year-old Anne Colberson, picked up near Myrtle Beach in 1971. Gaskins was not hunting at the time, but he refused to miss a golden opportunity. Over four days of rape and torture, he became 'real fond of her'. Finally, 'because she had been so nice to me', Gaskins stunned her with a hammer and cut her throat before dropping her body into quicksand. The coastal kills were always recreational, though. However numerous the victims, however atrocious their sufferings, they meant nothing to Gaskins. The focus of his life lay inland, where murder and business mixed.

Before 1970, despite sporadic incidents of violence with family and friends, Gaskins maintained that he never gave 'any real serious thought whatsoever' to killing a personal acquaintance. 'The most important thing about 1970,' he wrote from prison, 'was that it was the year I started doing my "serious murders"' – defined as slayings of people he knew, whose deaths required more planning to avoid detection.

His first two 'serious' victims were a 15-year-old niece, Janice Kirby, and her 17-year-old friend, Patricia Alsobrook. Gaskins

Top left: Keith Hunter Jesperson, who signed letters to the press boasting of his kills with a smiling happy face.

Top right: The Freeway Killer, William Bonin, shown in court in LA in 1982. He spent 16 years on death row before being executed by lethal injection.

Bottom left: Ivan Milat in his Sydney home. Two of his backpacker victims were (*inset*) Gabor Neugebauer and (just seen) Anja Habschied.

Bottom right: Albert DeSalvo, known as the Boston Strangler, pictured with some jewellery he made and sold in jail, eight months before being stabbed to death in the prison hospital.

Top left: Forensic psychologists were permitted to examine the brain of John Wayne Gacy (*inset*) once the so-called Killer Clown had been executed.

Top right: Jeffrey Dahmer in Milwaukee County Circuit Court, where he pleaded not guilty by reason of insanity.

Bottom left: Ted Bundy, one of the most notorious serial killers in US criminal history.

Bottom right: Alton Coleman at his 1985 trial. He spent 6,000 days on death row before being executed.

Top left: Artwork by convicted serial killer Arthur Shawcross (*inset*), the Genesee River Killer.

Top right: Green River Killer Gary Ridgway.

Bottom left: The Railroad Killer, Ángel Reséndiz, in a Houston courtroom.

Bottom right: Wayne Adam Ford, the Remorseful Killer.

Top left: Andrew Kokoraleis, a member of the Ripper Crew who terrorised Chicago in the early 1980s.

Top right: Coral Eugene Watts, the Sunday Slasher, linked to murders in Texas and Michigan.

Bottom left: Edmund Kemper, whose co-ed victims were killed in Santa Cruz, California.

Bottom right: Riverside in California was where William Suff killed at least a dozen women.

Top: Andrei Chikatilo photographed in the courtroom cage especially constructed for his trial. Deemed sane and therefore eligible for the death penalty, he was found guilty of 52 murders in the Russian town Rostov-on-Don (*bottom left*).

Bottom right: Tsutomo Miyazaki attending an on-the-spot investigation his serial killing of girls in Tokyo.

Top: Photograph from the Düsseldorf official police criminal card of Pet[er] Kürten, convicted of nine murders and executed by guillotine in 1931.

Bottom left: Killer John Reginald Halliday Christie cuts a dashing figu[re] in this photo from c.1950. The Notting Hill murders attracted huge public interested, as demonstrated by the crowds who gathered outsid[e] Putney Police Station (*bottom right*) when the news of his discovery became known.

Top left: Acid Bath Murderer John Haigh after the 1949 hearing where he would be sentenced to death by hanging at Wandsworth Prison, an outcome eagerly awaited by large crowds (*top right*).

Bottom left: Yorkshire Ripper Peter Sutcliffe and his wife Sonia on their wedding day.

Bottom right: The secluded lane in Sheffield where Sutcliffe was arrested.

Top left: Fred West and wife Rose (*inset*) outside Gloucester Crown Court

Top right: 25 Cromwell Street, the House of Horrors where the Wests seduced and killed children and unsuspecting boarders.

Bottom left: 23 Cranley Gardens, Muswell Hill, where Dennis Nilsen (*bottom right*) killed and stored his victims.

had entertained thoughts of raping Kirby but saw no opportunity until one night in November 1970, when the girls were out drinking, in need of a ride home. Gaskins volunteered, taking them instead to an abandoned house where he ordered both to strip. The girls fought for their lives, clubbing Gaskins with a board before he drew a gun and overpowered them and beat them unconscious. After raping both, he drowned the girls and buried them in separate locations. Police questioned him about the double disappearance and, while he admitted talking to the girls on the last night they had been seen alive, he claimed they had left him and driven off in a car with several unknown boys. Lacking bodies or other evidence, the police investigation went cold.

A month later, Gaskins kidnapped, raped and murdered Peggy Cuttino, the 13-year-old daughter of a politically prominent family. This time, he left the body where it would be found. His alibi looked solid when police came calling, and they later focused on another suspect, William Pierce, already serving life in Georgia for a similar offence. Conviction of Cuttino's murder brought Pierce his second life sentence, a moot point since Georgia had no intention of releasing him. Years later, when Gaskins later confessed to the murder, embarrassed prosecutors rejected his statement, insisting Gaskins claimed the murder 'for publicity'.

Gaskins interrupted the murder spree to marry his pregnant girlfriend on 1 January 1971, but it was only a momentary distraction. His next 'serious' murder victim – and the first African-American he ever killed – was 20-year-old Martha Dicks, who frequented the garage where Gaskins worked part-time. For reasons best known to herself, Dicks seemed infatuated with Gaskins, boasting falsely to friends that they were lovers. Gaskins tolerated the jokes until Dicks claimed to be carrying his child. Inviting her to stay on one night after work, he fed Dicks a fatal overdose of pills and liquor, discarding her body in a roadside ditch. Rumours of sex and racism aside, Gaskins insisted, 'I didn't kill her for no reason besides her lying mouth.'

In late 1971, Gaskins moved to Charleston with his wife and child, committing his next two 'serious murders' there in 1972. The victims were Eddie Brown, a 20-year-old gunrunner, and his wife Bertie, described by Gaskins as 'the best-looking black girl I ever saw.' Gaskins sold guns to Brown, including stolen military weapons, but he grew nervous when Brown informed him that federal agents were making enquiries in and around Charleston, seeking illicit arms dealers. Fearing apprehension, Gaskins shot the Browns and left their bodies behind the barn where he had buried Janice Kirby in 1970.

Gaskins moved to Prospect, South Carolina, in July 1973, after his Charleston home burnt down. (He blamed arsonists for the fire, but never identified the culprits.) Before the year's end, he murdered three more victims, starting with 14-year-old runaway Jackie Freeman. Gaskins picked her up hitchhiking, in October, and held her captive for two days of rape, torture and cannibalism. 'I always thought of Jackie as special,' he recalled in his memoirs, 'not really a serious murder, but likewise not just another coastal kill.'

The weekend after Freeman's slaying, Gaskins bought a used hearse and put a sign in the window: 'WE HAUL ANYTHING, LIVING OR DEAD'. When asked about it over drinks, he explained that he wanted the vehicle 'because I kill so many people I need a hearse to haul them to my private cemetery'.

His first passengers were 23-year-old Doreen Dempsey and her two-year-old daughter, Robin Michelle. Gaskins knew Dempsey from his circus days. An unwed mother pregnant with her second child in December 1973, she planned on leaving town that month and accepted Gaskins's offer of a ride to the local bus station. Instead, he drove into the woods and there demanded sex. Doreen agreed and then balked when Gaskins started to undress her child. Gaskins killed Doreen with a hammer, then raped and buggered the child before strangling her to death and burying both of them together. Years later, he would recall his brutal assault on Robin Michelle as the best sex of his life.

Gaskins's 'serious murders' continued in 1974, beginning with 30-year-old car thief Johnny Sellars. Sellars owed Gaskins $1,000 for car parts, but he was slow to pay. Finally, tired of excuses, Gaskins lured Sellars to the woods and shot him with a rifle. Later the same night, hoping to forestall investigation into his disappearance, Gaskins called on Sellars's girlfriend, 22-year-old Jessie Ruth Judy, and stabbed her to death, taking her body to the forest for burial beside her lover.

Horace Jones, another car thief, made the fatal mistake of trying to romance Gaskins's current wife in 1974. 'That pissed me off,' Gaskins recalled, 'but the way he went about doing it. I mean if he had come straight to me like a man and asked to make a deal with me for my wife, I would probably have given her to him, for a night or a week, or to keep, if the offer was good enough.' As it was, he shot Jones in the woods and took $200 from the body before leaving it in a shallow grave.

By December 1974, Gaskins was a grandfather, settled into a routine that suited him and satisfied his needs. That Christmas season, he recalled, was 'the happiest and peacefullest I can remember'. He didn't know it yet, but he was running out of time. 1975 was his busiest killing year. He started January with a threesome, a man and two women, describing them as 'hippie types'. Their van had broken down near Georgetown. Gaskins offered them a lift to the nearest garage, then detoured to a nearby swamp and handcuffed his captives at gunpoint. Before he drowned the trio, Gaskins said, 'It was hard to say which one suffered most. I tried to make it equal.'

Gaskins made a critical mistake when he recruited ex-convict Walter Neely to help him dispose of the van. Neely drove the vehicle to Gaskins's garage, where Gaskins customised and repainted it for sale out of state. The drive made Neely an accessory after the fact and Gaskins trusted his simple-minded helper to keep a secret. Before the year's end, he would regret that choice.

Gaskins's first 'serious murder' of the year involved a contract to kill Silas Yates, a wealthy Florence County farmer. He accepted $1,500 for the job, on behalf of 27-year-old Suzanne Kipper, furious at Yates for taking back a car, two horses and other gifts he had given her while they were romantically involved. Two go-betweens on the contract, John Powell and John Owens, handled negotiations between Gaskins and Kipper. Gaskins recruited Diane Neely, his friend Walter's ex-wife, to lure Yates from home on the night of 12 February 1975, by claiming that her car had broken down near his house. Gaskins waited in the darkness to abduct Yates at gunpoint and drive him to the woods, where Powell and Owens watched him knife Yates to death; they then helped Gaskins bury the body. Kipper subsequently married Owens, while Gaskins used his knowledge of the murder to blackmail her for sex.

This contract killing came back to haunt Gaskins when Diane Neely moved in with Avery Howard, a 35-year-old ex-convict whom Gaskins knew from state prison. She told Howard about the murder and together they approached Gaskins with a demand for $5,000 to remain silent. Gaskins agreed to meet them in the woods outside Prospect and bring the cash. The blackmailers arrived to find an open grave and Gaskins with a pistol in his hand. Both were shot and then buried.

Still Gaskins continued his relentless killing. Kim Ghelkins was the next to die; she was a 13-year-old friend of Gaskins who angered him by rejecting his sexual overtures. He reacted in typical style by raping, torturing and strangling her, disposing of her body in the woods. Diane Neely's brother, 25-year-old Dennis Bellamy, teamed up with 15-year-old half-brother Johnny Knight to burgle Gaskins's garage that summer, thus earning themselves a death sentence. Gaskins took Walter Neely along to help bury the pair in his 'private cemetery', taking the time to point out the surrounding graves of Johnny Sellars, Jessie Judy,

Avery Howard and Walter's ex-wife. Again, for reasons never clear, he trusted Neely and allowed him to survive.

By October 1975, Kim Ghelkins's parents knew enough of her movements to suspect Gaskins of murder. A Sumter deputy sheriff searched Gaskins's home and found some of Kim's clothes in his wardrobe, afterwards securing statements that she was often seen in his company. The evidence would not support a murder charge, but Gaskins was indicted for contributing to the delinquency of a minor. He returned from Georgia on 14 November 1975 to find police waiting for him at his house. Gaskins made his way to the local bus station, planning a return to Georgia, but officers detained him before he could leave.

Gaskins remained in custody for three weeks before the death knell sounded on him. Under intense interrogation, Walter Neely had finally told all to police on advice from a neighbourhood minister. He led authorities to Gaskins's graveyard, where Bellamy and Knight were unearthed on 4 December. A day later, diggers found the bodies of Sellars, Judy, Howard and Neely. On 10 December, Walter led them to the graves of Doreen Dempsey and her child. Gaskins struck a pose of injured innocence, but all in vain. Looking back on that chaotic month, he would recall, 'the coroner had the bodies, Jesus had Walter, and the law had me'.

On 27 April 1976, Gaskins and Walter Neely were each charged with eight counts of first-degree murder. Police also detained James Judy, husband of the murdered Jessie, on one count of murder and an accessory charge. Prosecutor T Kenneth Summerford arranged for Gaskins to be tried alone in the Bellamy case, because bullets from the victim's body matched a pistol Gaskins had been carrying at his arrest in December 1975.

At his trial, on 24 May 1976, Gaskins feigned innocence, blaming Bellamy's murder on Walter Neely. Bellamy and Johnny Knight were both alive the last time he saw them, Gaskins testified, leaving his garage with Neely. For all he knew, Walter had stolen his pistol to murder the men and then replaced it without his knowledge. Jurors dismissed his explanation and convicted him on 28 May, whereupon he was sentenced to die.

Gaskins's attorney urged him to make a deal with prosecutors to avoid another death sentence on his seven pending murder charges. Gaskins agreed, confessing to the crimes and adding details under the influence of 'truth serum', but he could have saved the effort. In November 1976, the US Supreme Court invalidated South Carolina's death penalty statute and his capital sentence was commuted to life, with seven more consecutive life terms added for good measure.

That was not to be the end; the law came after him next for Silas Yates's murder, indicting him with John Owens, John Powell and Suzanne Kipper (now married to Owens). At trial, in April 1977, Gaskins claimed he was the decoy who lured Yates from his home in 1975, while Powell and Owens did the killing, but all four defendants were sentenced to life. (Powell and Owens were paroled in the late 1980s, prompting Gaskins to remark, 'some life sentences don't last as long as others'. Kipper escaped in October 1990 and remained at large until February 1993, when she was recaptured in Michigan.)

In 1978, South Carolina passed a new death penalty statute and new charges were filed against Gaskins for Johnny Knight's murder. The state was now seeking the death penalty. However, Gaskins was not made aware that such retroactive prosecutions are forbidden. Bargaining for life imprisonment, he confessed to still more murders, giving police the whereabouts of a hitchhiker's body in place of Janice Kirby's since he feared discovery of other victims buried near her grave site, yet unnamed. This last round of confessions made Gaskins South Carolina's most prolific serial killer to date.

With his reputation and his mechanical skills, it was easy to become a maintenance trusty, an inmate with the freedom to move around the confines of the prison. However, despite being incarcerated he had one further opportunity to kill. Another convicted killer, Rudolph Tyner, was awaiting execution but the appeals process was never-ending and there was also a suggestion that he may even earn a reprieve. Tyner's worst problem on death row was the need continually to feed his insatiable drugs addiction.

Outside the prison walls, Tony Cimo, the son of the victims murdered by Tyner, was hatching a plan to accelerate Tyner's execution. Through prison contacts, he negotiated for a contract to be put out on Tyner. The word finally got to Gaskins, who agreed to kill Tyner for the right price.

In his work in the prison, Gaskins had free access to condemned inmates, mending broken pipes, toilets, light fixtures; anything at all. Unknown to Cimo, Gaskins also had a tape recorder, capturing their conversations for posterity; a blackmail tool as good as money in the bank if he should ever manage to escape from custody.

Gaskins decided poison was the way to go. Befriending Tyner on his visits to death row, Gaskins began to slip Tyner junk food, marijuana, pills and heroin. Tyner received the gifts, unquestioning, and begged for more. Cimo supplied a box of candy laced with poison 'strong enough to kill a horse', but Tyner merely suffered stomach pains. Over the following 12 months, Gaskins repeated the experiment five times, spiking his target's food and drugs with ever-larger toxic doses, all in vain. Tyner lived on, oblivious to the 'coincidences' linking the gifts and with stomach-churning trips to the hospital.

Gaskins gave up on poison and decided to construct a bomb. Cimo supplied the wiring, hardware and C-4 plastic explosive (smuggled past distracted guards in the hollowed-out heels of cowboy boots). Tyner agreed to let Gaskins connect a homemade intercom between their cells. Gaskins strung wire through prison heating ducts, constructed a 'receiver' for his target from a plastic cup and packed it with C-4. The two men synchronised their watches for a test run on the evening of 12 September 1982. At the appointed hour, Tyner pressed the loaded plastic cup against his ear and spoke to Gaskins, on the far side of the wall between their cells. 'The last thing he heard through that speaker cup before it blew his head off,' Gaskins later said, 'was me laughing.'

Press reports initially described Tyner's death as suicide, but there are no real secrets in prison. Prisoners started talking, and Tony Cimo was arrested and soon confessed his role in the plot. A grand jury was empanelled, indicting Gaskins and Cimo with two inmate accessories for murder and conspiracy. The state of South Carolina had failed to execute Donald Gaskins for his previous murders. Now, it was prepared to try again.

Tony Cimo received a 25-year prison sentence with parole eligibility after 30 months. He served the minimum and returned to the seaside town of Murrell's Inlet, where he died from a prescription drug overdose on 10 June 2001.

Gaskins, meanwhile, spent the first three years of his new sentence not on death row, but in a rat-infested isolation unit. His attorneys appealed the confinement in 1985, but the authorities cited 'reliable information' that Gaskins planned to have accomplices kidnap the prosecutor's child and bargain for his release. Only after his petition for release from solitary was rejected did police 'determine the report was an empty threat'. A year later, freed from solitary after the isolation unit was condemned as not fit for human habitation, Gaskins found death row 'a lot nicer' than his previous quarters. In 1990, Gaskins and the state's electric chair were moved again, this time to the Broad River Correctional Institute outside Columbia.

Gaskins filled his last months with an art scam, tracing cartoon characters for sale to collectors of death row memorabilia, and dictating his memoirs on tape for author Wilton Earl to publish in 1993. As death approached, Gaskins became philosophical. 'I truly don't mind dying,' he wrote. 'I've lived a damned full and good life.' In fact, he decided, it was even better than that. 'I have walked the same path as God,' Gaskins raved. 'By taking lives and making others afraid, I became God's equal. Through killing others, I became my own master. Through my own power I come to my own redemption.' He was even optimistic about his date with the chair, saying, 'When they put me to death, I'll die remembering the freedom and pleasure of my life. I'll die knowing that there are others coming along to take my place, and that most of them won't never get caught.'

There was no escape this time for Gaskins. The US Supreme Court rejected his final appeal in June 1991, clearing the way for Gaskins to be executed in September. Hours before his date with 'Old Sparky', Gaskins slashed his arms from wrists to elbows with a razor blade he had swallowed days earlier then regurgitated, in a futile effort to postpone death. Prison medics stitched his wounds in time for Gaskins to be executed at 1.05am on 6 September 1991.

The exact number of victims murdered by Gaskins was never known. Police believed that the number may have been as high as 200. Gaskins went on record as suggesting that the total may be around 90.

ED GEIN

Ed Gein (b. 1906) lived with his parents, who ran a small family shop in Wisconsin. They eventually purchased a farm on the outskirts of another small town, also in Wisconsin. Gein's mother was very religious and drummed into her boys the innate immorality of the world, the evils of drink and the belief that all women (herself excluded) were whores. According to his mother, the only acceptable form of sex was for biological reproduction. She reserved time every afternoon to read to them from the Bible, usually selecting graphic verses from the Old Testament dealing with death, murder and divine retribution.

When Gein reached puberty, his mother became increasingly strict, once dousing him in scalding water after she caught him masturbating in the bath, grabbing his genitals and calling them the 'curse of man'. With a slight growth over one eye and an effeminate demeanour, the young Gein became a target for bullies. Despite this, he did reasonably well at school. His father died in 1940 and by then he had begun to reject his mother's views on life. His brother died mysteriously in a fire at the farm, also in 1940. In 1945 his mother died, leaving him all alone at the farmhouse.

During the late 1940s and 1950s, police began to notice an increase in missing person cases. There were four cases in particular they took an interest in. The first was that of an eight-year-old girl named Georgia Weckler, who had disappeared while coming home from school on 1 May 1947. Hundreds of residents and police searched an area of 10 square miles around her home address, hoping to find the young girl. Unfortunately, Georgia was never seen or heard of again.

Another girl disappeared six years later in La Crosse, Wisconsin. Fifteen-year-old Evelyn Hartley was babysitting at the time she disappeared. The girl's father immediately drove to where she had been, but nobody answered the door. When he peered through a window, he could see one of his daughter's shoes and her glasses on the floor. He tried to enter the house, but all the doors and windows were locked, except for one, the back basement window. It was at that window where he discovered bloodstains. Petrified, he entered the house and discovered signs of a struggle.

Immediately he contacted the police. When they arrived at the house, they found more evidence of a struggle, including bloodstains on the grass leading away from the house, a bloody handprint on a neighbouring house, footprints and the girl's other shoe on the basement floor. A larger area was searched but Evelyn was nowhere to be found. A few days later, police discovered some bloodied articles of clothing that belonged to Evelyn near a highway outside La Crosse. The worst was suspected.

In November 1952, two men stopped for a drink at a bar in Plainfield, Wisconsin, before heading out to hunt deer. Victor Travis and Ray Burgess spent several hours at the bar before leaving. The two men and their car were never seen again. A massive search was conducted but there was no trace of them. They had simply vanished.

In winter 1954, a Plainfield tavern-keeper by the name of Mary Hogan mysteriously disappeared. Police suspected foul play when they discovered blood on the tavern floor that trailed into the car park.

In mid-November 1957, a robbery took place at a local shop where the female owner, Bernice Worden, was abducted. The police had reason to believe Gein was involved and went to his farmhouse to talk to him. When they arrived at the farmhouse, there was no sign of Gein. They went inside the dimly lit room and noticed the stench that immediately hit them. The smell of filth and decomposition was overwhelming. One of the officers went into the kitchen. It was dark and he felt something brush against his jacket. He flashed his torch to see what it was and saw a dangling carcass hanging upside down from the beams. The carcass had been decapitated, slit open and gutted. He initially thought it was a deer carcass. However, after a few moments the officer realised that it wasn't a deer at all; it was the headless body of the missing woman, Bernice Worden. She had been shot and killed before being butchered.

The officers started a search and soon uncovered more grisly secrets. There were severed heads acting as bedposts in the bedroom. Human skin had been used to upholster the chair seats. Several human skulls had been made into soup bowls. A single human heart was in a saucepan on the stove. A facemask made out of facial skin was found in a paper bag. There was a necklace made out of human lips. In the wardrobe they found a waistcoat made up of vaginas and breasts sewn together. In addition there was a belt made solely from nipples. In another wardrobe was an entire wardrobe made from human skin consisting of leggings, a gutted torso (including breasts) and an array of tanned, dead-skin masks.

Gein was later arrested and interviewed and initially remained silent. However, the following day he confessed in detail how he had murdered Bernice Worden and how he had acquired all the body parts found at the farm, which he stated he had dug up from the graves of recently buried middle-aged women he thought resembled his mother. He would take the bodies home, where he skinned them, subjecting the skin to a tanning process, then using it to make his macabre possessions. Gein denied having sex with the bodies he exhumed, saying that they smelt too bad. During interrogation, Gein also admitted to the shooting of Mary Hogan, the local tavern-owner missing since 1954.

Gein told police that shortly after his mother's death he had decided he wanted a sex change, hence the female 'attire' manufactured from body parts – he could wear it and pretend to be his mother, rather than change his sex. Gein showed no signs of remorse and he appeared to have no concept of the enormity of his crimes. The police continued to search the land around his farm. They discovered within Gein's farmhouse the remains of 10 women. Although Gein swore that the remaining body parts of eight women were taken from local graveyards, the police had their doubts. They believed that it was highly possible that the remains came from other women he had murdered. The only way to ascertain whether the remains came from women's corpses was to examine the graves that Gein claimed he had robbed. Following much controversy over the morality of exhuming the bodies, police were finally permitted to dig up the graves of the women he claimed to have desecrated. All of the coffins showed clear signs of having been tampered with. In most cases, the bodies or parts of the bodies were missing.

A further discovery on the farm would again raise the issue of whether Gein did, in fact, murder others. On 29 November, police unearthed more skeletal human remains, suspected to be Victor Travis, who had disappeared years earlier. The remains were immediately taken to a crime lab and examined. Tests showed that the body was not that of a male but of a large, middle-aged woman, another victim of Gein's grave-robbing.

THE USA

Police tried desperately to implicate Gein in the disappearance of Victor Travis and the three other people who had vanished years earlier in the Plainfield area. The only murders Gein could be held accountable for were Bernice Worden and Mary Hogan.

Gein was deemed not competent to stand trial and was confined to a mental hospital. However, after spending 10 years in the mental institution, the courts finally decided he was competent to stand trial for the murder of Bernice Worden. The proceedings began on 22 January 1968, to determine whether he was guilty of the murder of Bernice Worden. The actual trial began on 7 November 1968. However, Gein was found not guilty by reason of insanity and was sentenced to spend the rest of his life in a mental institution, where he came to be regarded as a model patient. On 26 July 1984, he died after a long battle with cancer. He was buried in Plainfield cemetery next to his mother, not far from the graves that he had robbed years earlier. His gravestone in the Plainfield cemetery was frequently vandalised; souvenir seekers would chip off pieces of his gravestone before the bulk of it was stolen in 2000. The gravestone was recovered in June 2001 near Seattle and is presently displayed in a museum in Wautoma, Wisconsin.

ROBERT HANSEN

Born at Pocahontas, Iowa, in 1940, in his youth, Robert Hansen (b. 1940) was skinny and painfully shy, afflicted with a stammer and a severe case of acne that left him permanently scarred. Shunned by the attractive girls in school, he grew up hating them and nursing fantasies of cruel revenge. Hansen spent much of his early life as a loner and was a victim of bullying by his peers and his strict, domineering father.

Hansen married in 1960. On 7 December that year, he was arrested for burning down a local school bus garage, a crime for which he served 20 months in prison. His wife divorced him while he was incarcerated. Over the next few years, he was jailed several more times for petty theft and drifted through a series of menial jobs. In 1967, he moved to Anchorage, Alaska, seeking a fresh start with his second wife, whom he had married in 1963. While he was well liked by his neighbours and was famed as a local hunting champion, his life eventually fell into disarray.

In 1972, Hansen was arrested and charged with the abduction and attempted rape of a housewife and the rape of a prostitute. Serving less than six months on a reduced charge, he was again arrested for shoplifting a chainsaw. In 1976, he was convicted of theft and was sentenced to five years in prison, but the verdict was overturned on appeal, the Alaska Supreme Court regarding his sentence as 'too harsh'. In 1977, he was imprisoned for theft and diagnosed with bipolar affective disorder.

In 1980, construction workers digging near Eklutna Road discovered the partial remains of a woman buried in a shallow grave. Animals had taken off with the majority of the remains and there was very little evidence at the scene. The victim was never identified and was dubbed 'Eklutna Annie' by police. Later that same year, another body was found in a nearby gravel pit. The victim was later identified as Joanne Messina, a local topless dancer. Unfortunately, her body was badly decomposed and, as with Eklutna Annie, the police were unable to obtain any evidence from the crime scene.

On 12 September 1982, a third body was found. On that day, two off-duty police officers were out in the wilderness hunting. As darkness began to fall they decided to call it a day. The trek back to their camp was not easy, but both men were familiar with the area and cut across a wide sandbar. However, as they progressed up the river, they noticed a boot sticking out of the sand. Upon closer inspection, the two men were taken aback. Sticking out of the sand was a partially decomposed bone joint. Once they registered what they were looking at, both men retreated from the crime scene. The last thing they wanted to do was to disturb or contaminate any evidence. After making a note of the location, the men made their way back to their camp.

Forensics experts conducted a thorough examination of the

crime scene and began sifting through the sand around the body. It took several hours for them to finish sifting, but in the end it paid dividends. They found a single shell casing from a .223-calibre bullet, used in high-powered rifles such as M-16s, Mini-14s or AR-15s.

Back in Anchorage, a preliminary post-mortem revealed that the victim was female, of undetermined age and had been dead for approximately six months. The cause of death was three gunshot wounds from .223-calibre bullets. Ace bandages were found mingled in with the remains, causing investigators to suspect that the victim had been blindfolded at the time of death. It took a little over two weeks to finally identify the body as that of 24-year-old Sherry Morrow, a dancer from the Wild Cherry Bar in downtown Anchorage. She had last been seen on 17 November 1981. According to friends, she was going to see a man who had offered her $300 to pose for some pictures. The police then reopened the files on other missing prostitutes.

On the night of 13 June 1983, the police got a lucky break. That evening, a lorry driver was passing through town when he noticed a frantic young female waving her arms and calling out to him. The girl had a pair of handcuffs dangling from one of her wrists and her clothing was dishevelled. She told the driver that a man was after her and asked him to take her to the Big Timber Motel. Once inside, she had the front desk clerk make a telephone call for her to her pimp. As she waited outside for her pimp, the lorry driver drove straight to the Anchorage Police Department and reported the incident.

When a police officer arrived at the Big Timber Motel, he found the girl alone and still in handcuffs. Once he removed her cuffs, she began telling him her story. She had been approached on the street by a male aged about 40; he had distinctive red hair, and had offered her $200 for oral sex. She agreed, but midway through the act the man locked handcuffs around her wrist and pulled out a gun. He told her if she cooperated he would not kill her. He then drove to his house. Once inside, the man brutally raped her, bit her nipples, and at one point shoved a hammer into her vagina. After a brief rest, the man said that he was going to fly her to his cabin in the mountains and told her he would let her go if she cooperated. Upon their arrival at the airport, he pushed her inside a small plane and began loading supplies. At that point she knew she was in serious trouble. She waited until his back was turned, pushed opened the plane door and ran for her life. The man chased after her at first, but then stopped when he saw her wave down the lorry.

After she had made a formal statement, police officers drove the young prostitute to Merrill Field, the airport where she said she had been taken. They were hoping she could identify her abductor's plane. As they drove through the small airport, she spotted a blue-and-white Piper Super Cub, tail number N3089Z, and identified the plane. A check with the flight tower revealed that the plane belonged to Robert Hansen, who lived on Old Harbour Road. Officers then went to Hansen's house. Hansen became outraged when confronted with the young woman's charges. He claimed to have never met the girl, and said 'You can't rape a prostitute, can you?' He said that he had spent the entire evening with two friends. His alibi checked out and no formal charges were filed.

On 2 September 1983, another body was found along the Knik River. The remains were partially decomposed and buried in a shallow grave. The victim was later identified as 17-year-old Paula Golding, a topless dancer and prostitute from Anchorage. She had gone missing some five months earlier. The post-mortem revealed that she had been shot with a .223-calibre bullet. Police were now convinced that they had a serial killer within the community, and turned their attentions back to Hansen, attempting to disprove the original alibi he had put forward regarding the abduction of the young prostitute. Police decided to bring in for questioning the two males who had given Hansen his alibi. Both men confessed and said that they had not been with Robert Hansen on the night the young prostitute was abducted and brought to the airport. Police also learnt from Hansen's friends that he was committing insurance fraud. He had reported several burglaries of his house to the police, but these reports were false; the burglaries never occurred. Hansen was hiding the items he alleged were stolen in his basement. The police took out search warrants on his house and his plane.

On 27 October 1983, the police made the decision to move in on Hansen. They followed him to work and asked him to come with them to the police station for questioning. Hansen never bothered to ask why they wanted to talk to him and agreed to go along. Simultaneously, officers executed the search warrants on his house and plane. At the house, they found weapons but at first nothing to implicate Hansen in any of the murders. However, just as they were about to leave, one of the officers discovered a hidden space tucked away in the attic rafters. Within it, they discovered a Remington 552 rifle, a Thompson contender 7mm single-shot pistol, an aviation map with specific locations marked off, various pieces of jewellery, newspaper clippings, a Winchester 12-gauge shotgun, a driving licence and various ID cards, some of which belonged to the dead women. As incriminating as all these items were, the most important piece of evidence was a .223-calibre Mini-14 rifle.

Hansen was then formally arrested and interviewed. He denied all knowledge of the murders. He was charged with assault, kidnapping, firearms offences, theft and insurance fraud. On 3 November 1983, an Anchorage grand jury returned indictments against Hansen. These were first-degree assault and kidnapping, five counts of misconduct in the possession of a handgun, theft in the second degree and theft by deception in insurance fraud. Police were still awaiting the ballistic test results on Hansen's rifle, so it was decided to not charge him with murder at this stage. Hansen pleaded not guilty to all charges. Bail was set at half a million dollars.

The ballistic test results finally came through on 20 November, showing that Hansen's rifle and the shell casings found at the murder sites matched. The firing pin and the extractor markings were identical. When confronted with the mass of evidence now against him, he asked his attorney to make a deal with the authorities.

In exchange for a full confession, the District Attorney guaranteed him that he would only be charged with the four cases that they knew of and he would be able to serve his time in a federal facility, rather than a maximum-security institution. Hansen reluctantly agreed to the conditions. During the confession that followed, he told of how he would abduct his victims, then take them on his plane to his remote cabin in the wilderness when, after raping and torturing them, he would let them go. After giving them a head start, he would track them down, killing them with either his hunting knife or his high-powered rifle. Hansen referred to the killings as his 'summertime project'. He stated that he had hoped to forcefully teach his victims a lesson for their whoring and stripping ways.

Hansen was provided with a large aerial map of the region. He identified 15 gravesites, 12 of which were unknown to the investigators. Since it would have been nearly impossible to locate any of the graves going by Hansen's checkmarks on the map, investigators decided to fly him to each location. The following day, Hansen accompanied the men to Anchorage International Airport, where they boarded a large military helicopter. Hansen led investigators to the various sites, at that time heavily covered in snow. The police marked the trees with orange paint, so that when the snow melted they could return and search for the bodies. By the end of the day, Hansen had revealed the gravesites of 12 unknown women.

On 18 February 1984, Robert Hansen pleaded guilty to four charges of first-degree murder in the cases of Paula Golding, Joanna Messina, Sherry Morrow and 'Eklutna Annie'. One week later, on 27 February, Hansen was sentenced to 461 years plus life, without chance of parole. By May 1984, police had found only seven bodies at the gravesites Robert Hansen had pointed out to them. No other bodies were ever recovered.

DENNIS RADER, AKA THE BTK KILLER

On 15 January 1974, 15-year-old Charlie Otero arrived home from school in Wichita, Kansas. As he opened the front door and walked into the living room, nothing seemed out of the ordinary. But he called out and there was no response. Not even a bark from his dog. Charlie walked toward his parents' bedroom. He saw his father Joseph lying face down on the floor at the foot of his bed; his wrists and ankles had been bound. His mother Julie was lying on the bed bound in a similar fashion; she had been gagged. For a few seconds, Charlie could not move. Moments later, he came to his senses and ran out in desperation to get help for his parents, not realising that he had experienced only a portion of the horror that the house would soon reveal.

When the police arrived, they were shocked to find nine-year-old Joseph Otero in his bedroom laying face down on the floor at the foot of his bed. His wrists and ankles were also bound and a hood had been placed over his head. Downstairs in the basement, Charlie's 11-year-old sister, Josephine, was found hanging by her neck from a pipe; she was partially naked and dressed only in a sweatshirt and socks. She had also been gagged. All four of the victims had been strangled with lengths of cord cut from a Venetian blind. The police found no similar cords in the house so it was presumed the killer had come armed with the cords, hoods, tape and wire-cutters and may have been in possession of a gun. Semen was found throughout the house, and it appeared that the killer had masturbated on some of the victims, although none had been sexually assaulted. There was no evidence of forced entry, robbery or signs of a struggle.

The times of death were estimated at around 8.00am. The police theorised that while Joseph Otero was driving the older three children to school, the murderer gained entry to the house where Julie and her two younger children were by themselves.

Once the killer had subdued and bound the three of them, he waited for Joseph to come home to take the younger two children to school and caught him by surprise. After murdering the family, the killer took the Otero family car and parked it at a nearby shop. The neighbours told police they had seen a man with a dark complexion leaving the Oteros' home in their car. The way the victims had been tied, gagged and then slain suggested to the police that they had a fetish killer on their hands, but the enquiry was eventually wound down with no suspects emerging.

On 4 April 1974, Kathryn Bright was murdered in her home. Her brother, also present, managed to escape. Both had returned home to find the killer lying in wait. He had obviously selected Kathryn as a victim but had not expected her to return home with her brother.

In early 1977, Shirley Vian Relford was the next victim. She was strangled in her own home with her children in the house. The killer was forced to make a quick exit when the children said that a neighbour would soon be coming round, leaving the children unharmed.

On 8 December 1977, police received an emergency call. They were told to go to a specific address where they would find the occupier, Nancy Jo Fox, murdered. The call was traced to a public telephone box where witnesses recalled a blond man, approximately 6ft tall, using the phone booth moments earlier. Unfortunately, the quality of the recording was too poor for investigators to use for any type of voice analysis in the future.

Police went to the address and noticed that a window had been broken, allowing entry to the home. Upon entering the house, officers discovered 25-year-old Nancy Jo Fox dead in her bedroom, a nylon stocking twisted around her neck. Unlike previous victims, she was fully clothed. Fox's driving licence was missing from the scene. Police theorised that the killer had taken the licence as a memento of the crime. The murder had occurred at night; semen was also found at the scene, but Fox had not been sexually assaulted. Again, the police were unable to obtain any evidence to link to a suspect. In early 1978, police received letters from a person purporting to be the killer. He called himself BTK (for Bound, Tortured, Killed). Letters were also sent to the press. In one letter, he claimed to have killed seven victims.

On 28 April 1979, the killer waited inside a house for the 63-year-old female resident to come home. When she did not show up, he left in an angry mood and later sent the woman a note along with one of her scarves. 'Be glad you weren't here,' he wrote, 'because I was.' Nothing more was heard from the killer and the murders appeared to stop.

In 1983, a team of detectives set out to re-investigate the murders. They went on a cross-country trip, collecting saliva and blood samples from over 200 people who had been flagged by their computer as suspects in the case. The samples collected were all voluntary; only five of the men refused. The blood tests ultimately eliminated all but 12 of the names on the list (including the five who refused the tests). The re-investigation continued into 1984. By this time there had been major advances in DNA technology; as a result, all of the evidence previously gathered was reassessed. But in spite of all the new technology and extensive police work, no further clues to the killer's identity were uncovered. Then the killings started again.

On 27 April 1985, Marine Hedge, 53, was abducted from her home. Her body was found eight days later on a rural dirt road near the edge of Park City. She had been strangled with a pair of tights.

On 16 September 1986, the killer struck again; mother-of-two Vicki Wegerle was found strangled in her own home. There was no sign of a forced entry.

There was then a five-year gap until the next murder on 19 January 1991. The next victim was Dolores Davis, 62. Her killer had cut the phone line at her home and then thrown a brick through a glass door to gain access. She was then abducted. Her body was found 13 days later under a bridge. Her hands and feet had been bound with her tights, which had been used to strangle her. After disposing of her body, the killer drove her car to another location and abandoned it.

From March 2004, a local newspaper received in total a series of 11 letters, in which the writer claimed that he had murdered Vicki Wegerle on 16 September 1986, and enclosed photographs of the body and a photocopy of her driving licence, which had been stolen at the time of the murder. In May 2004, a word puzzle was received, and in June a package was found taped to a stop sign in Wichita containing graphic descriptions of the Otero murders. In July, a package was left at a public library. This contained more bizarre material, including the claim that the writer was responsible for the death of 19-year-old Jake Allen in Kansas earlier that same month. This claim was found to be false, as the death had been by suicide. In October 2004, a Manila envelope was dropped into a post box. It contained a series of cards with images of terror and child bondage pasted onto them.

In December 2004, the Wichita police received another package from the killer. This time, the package was found in Wichita's Murdock Park. It contained the driving licence of Nancy Fox, which had been noted as stolen at the scene of the crime, as well as a doll that was symbolically bound at the hands and feet with a plastic bag tied over its head. In early February, there were postcards and another cereal box left at a rural location containing another bound doll that symbolised the murder of 11-year-old Josephine Otero. The killer asked in the letter whether, if he put his writings onto a floppy disk, the disk could be traced or not. He received his answer in a newspaper, saying it would be okay. On 16 February 2005, a floppy disk was sent to the Fox TV station in Wichita. Forensic analysis quickly determined that the disk had been used by the Christ Lutheran Church in Wichita and also included the name Dennis as a user. An Internet search determined that Rader was president of the church council. As a result, Dennis Rader was arrested on 25 February 2005.

Following Rader's arrest, the police went to his daughter who provided a DNA sample that enabled police to link Rader's DNA to eight murders.

On 1 March 2005, Rader was officially indicted on 10 murder charges. On 5 May 2005, Rader finally came to trial. He pleaded not guilty by reason of insanity and the case was adjourned. He came back to court on 27 June, when he changed his plea to guilty and withdrew his insanity plea. He described his murders in graphic detail, starting with the Otero family back in 1974. He stated he had gone to the house between 7 and 7.30am. He claimed that he did not know them, but that he had selected Julie Otero and her daughter Josephine to be participants in his sexual fantasy. He had planned the timing, expecting that only Julie Otero and the two youngest children would be in the house. He never expected Joseph Otero to be there and it caused him to panic and lose control. That morning, he cut the phone lines and waited at the back door. He claimed he was having second thoughts about the whole plan when Joseph Otero Junior opened the back door to let the dog out, but then Rader went in through the back door and threatened the family with a pistol. The dog didn't take kindly to him and so he insisted that the dog be put outside. He then realised that he didn't have a mask on and that he could be identified at a later date, so he made a decision to go ahead and 'put 'em down', or strangle them. The words 'put 'em down' referenced euthanising animals; that's all they were to him.

He then put a bag over Joseph Otero's head and tightened it with cords, which he had brought along with him for this purpose, but Otero did not die right away. Then he was going to strangle Julie Otero. He stated that he had never strangled anyone before, so he really didn't know how much pressure to apply or how long it would take. Joseph Otero began to put up a fight and tore a hole in the plastic bag, so he put another couple of bags and some clothing over his head and tightened the cords. After that, he strangled Julie Otero. He said she passed out and he thought she was dead. He then strangled Josephine and she passed out. He thought she was dead, and then he went over and put a bag on Joseph Junior's head, and then Julie Otero came round. He went back and strangled her again, finally killing her. Before she died, she pleaded with him to save her son. Rader stated that he had actually taken the bag off. He was really upset at that point in time. He then went and put another bag over Otero Junior's head and took him into the other bedroom, putting another bag over his head as well as a cloth, so he couldn't tear a hole in it. Young Joseph subsequently died. Rader went back upstairs to find that Josephine had woken up. He then took her to the basement and hanged her. He had sexual fantasies and masturbated on her body. He then said he went through the house, cleaning up the scene, before leaving and taking the car.

Rader then went on to describe the murder of Kathryn Bright on 4 April 1974. He said that he used to cruise the area selecting targets; Kathryn Bright was one. He was driving by one day and saw her go into the house with somebody. He later broke into her house and waited for her to come home, not expecting her to have her brother with her. He pulled a handgun on them. He made Kathryn's brother tie her up and then he tied Kevin's feet to the bedpost. He then moved Kathryn to another bedroom and went back to strangle Kevin but Kevin had loosened some of his bonds and started to struggle with him. He shot him and assumed he was dead. He then went back to strangle Kathryn, but she had not been tied up well and she struggled with him. Just as he thought he had Kathryn subdued, he heard Kevin in the other bedroom. When he tried to re-strangle Kevin, the struggle started again. Kevin tried to get one of the two handguns he had with him and almost succeeded, but Rader took the other handgun and shot Kevin again. Believing that Kevin was finally dead, he went back to finish off Kathryn. She continued to struggle, so he stabbed her several times underneath the ribs. At the same time, he heard Kevin escaping through the front door of the house. Rader watched him running off down the road. He quickly cleaned up as much as he could and left, but still he ran into trouble. He had what he thought were Kathryn's car keys and jumped in the car only to find he had the wrong keys. He then panicked and ran off down the road.

Rader said that the killing of Shirley Vian Relford on 17 March 1977 had not been planned. On the pretext of looking for someone, he knocked on her door and one of her children answered. He claimed to be a private detective, then produced a pistol and forced his way through the door. Inside, he found Shirley with her other children. He told Relford that he had a problem with sexual fantasies and was going to tie her and her kids up. They started crying and became upset so he moved them to the bathroom and tied the door shut so they couldn't open it. He then tied Relford up but she threw up. He got her a glass of water, comforted her and then put a bag over her head and strangled her. The children had mentioned that a neighbour was going to look in on them, so he quickly put his killing tools, tape, cords and other items back in his briefcase and left.

Describing the murder of Nancy Fox on 8 December 1977, Rader said that he had been watching her for some time and knew all about her before committing the crime. For example, he knew what time she normally came home from work, so on the day in question, after he had ascertained that no one was in her apartment, he cut the phone lines and broke in and waited for her in the kitchen. When she came home, he confronted her, telling her he had a sexual problem and that he would have to tie her up and have sex with her. She became upset and told him to hurry up and get it over with. She asked to go to the bathroom. He told her she could but that she must come out undressed. She went to the bathroom and when she came out he made her lie on the bed, where he handcuffed her and tied her feet. He partially undressed and got on top of her. He then took his belt and proceeded to strangle her. He took the belt from around her throat and replaced it with her tights, which he tied tight. He then masturbated before removing some personal items, cleaned up the scene and left.

Rader said his next victim was Marine Hedge, who lived down the street from him, so once he had selected her as a potential victim, it was easy for him to keep watch on her. They knew each other in a very casual way – she was a keen gardener and he would acknowledge her when he passed by her working in the grounds around her house. On the appointed day, Rader broke into Hedge's house and waited for her to return. When Hedge came home, she had a man with her who stayed about an hour. When the guest left, Rader silently went into her bedroom, and she screamed. He jumped on the bed and strangled her manually. He then stripped her, put her in a blanket, took her body to the boot of her car and drove the car to a local church where he took some pictures of her body to show different forms of bondage. He then put her body back into her car and drove around, disposing of it a short time later in a ditch and covering it with brush.

When discussing the murder of Vicki Wegerle on 16 September 1986, Rader explained that he had targeted her, having planned to go to her house posing as a repair man. He knocked on the door and she let him in. He went over to the telephone, pretending to check it. When she had her back turned, he pulled out his pistol and told her to go back to the bedroom, where he used some fabric to tie her hands, but they came loose and she tried to fight him off. He grabbed one of her stockings and strangled her with it until she stopped moving. When he thought she was dead, he rearranged her clothes and took several photos of her but he had to make a hasty retreat. She had mentioned something about her husband coming home, so he got out quickly. Vicki Wegerle was fatally injured from the strangling but was not yet dead when he left her home. Sadly, she died soon afterwards.

His next victim was Dolores Davis. Rader entered her house

by throwing a lump of concrete through a plate-glass window. She came out of the bedroom and thought a car had hit her house. He told her that he was a fugitive on the run and needed food and a car; then he handcuffed and tortured her. He placed a thin painted plastic mask on her face to make her look more feminine. The mask had been painted a flesh colour with red lips and darkened eyebrows to make it look quite lifelike in appearance. Rader was so wrapped up in his fantasy when he was torturing her that he was oblivious to her pleas when she begged him to spare her life. Finally, he strangled her. As with most of the other murders, he took some personal items from her bedroom. He wrapped her in a blanket and dragged her to the boot of her car and took her away, leaving her body under a bridge. However, he had carelessly left one of his guns in her house, so he drove back to the house, collected his gun and walked back to his own car. After killing Davis, Rader wore some of her clothes that he had stolen, along with a mask and a wig. He would often dress up as a woman, posing in various bondage positions and taking pictures of himself with a remotely operated camera. In the pictures, he appeared markedly distressed, as if he were the victim. He told the judge that all of the murders he had committed were based on sexual fantasies.

The prosecution had amassed other evidence, which included photographs of Rader wearing tights and a bra and practising bondage on himself, as well as a knife and a gag used on Julie Otero. There were dolls taken from his home, which were bound with rope and handcuffed. There were many pictures, which he used specifically to fuel his perverted fantasies, that he kept hidden in his house and office. These included binders with cut-out pictures of models and starlets such as Meg Ryan, index cards with child swimsuit models on them and sexual fantasies written on the reverse, jewellery and clothing from his victims and newspaper clippings. Other photographs included pictures Rader took of himself wearing a mask and lying partially covered in a grave that he'd intended for Davis. Davis was never buried there because Rader simply didn't have the time to do it; instead, he just dumped her body and the mask under the bridge and decided to go back the following day. When he did, he claimed that he freaked out at the sight of her body because animals had ravaged her remains. The prosecution was intent on portraying Rader as a sadistic and evil man, with no regard for human life.

During Rader's sentencing hearing on 18 August 2005, family members of the victims courageously stood before the man who had murdered their loved ones and for the first time told him what they thought of him and his horrendous actions. Rader was repeatedly called a monster and a coward, and the family members asked the judge for the harshest sentence possible. Some were so overcome with emotion that they were unable to say what they felt. Rader's evil was beyond comprehension or words. During the statements, Rader showed signs of emotion, wiping his eyes periodically as if he were overcome with grief for what he had done.

Finally, the long-anticipated sentencing of Rader commenced. The judge sentenced him to a total of 175 years, to be served consecutively. Specifically, he sentenced him to nine life terms and gave him 40 years in prison with no chance of parole for the Dolores Davis murder; the judge also ordered that Rader pay restitution to the families of his victims as well as court costs. It was the severest sentence that he could give Rader under Kansas state law. He has an earliest possible release date of 26 February 2180.

RICARDO 'RICHARD' MUÑOZ RAMIREZ, AKA THE NIGHT STALKER

Between 1984 and 1985, the residents of Los Angeles County lived in fear of the anonymous Night Stalker, as he was called, because he always carried out his attacks at night. The killer would creep silently into his victims' bedrooms. Any males in the house were killed swiftly with a bullet to the head. Females were kept alive to be raped and degraded.

THE USA

On 28 June 1984, the Night Stalker claimed his first known victim in Los Angeles. He entered the home of Jennie Vincow, aged 79, through an insecure window. After making a cursory search and finding nothing of value to steal, he stabbed the sleeping woman and then cut her throat. The act of killing aroused him and he had sex with the body before leaving.

On 17 March 1985, at 11.30pm, 20-year-old Angela Barrios was just returning home from a long day at work. She shared a condominium with a room-mate in Rosemead, a middle-class town northeast of LA. She pulled her car into the driveway and opened the garage door with a remote control. All she wanted to do was get inside and unwind; she was tired and hadn't had dinner yet. But as she got out of her car, she heard something behind her. A dark figure suddenly rushed up to her. He was tall and dressed entirely in black. A navy blue baseball cap was pulled down low over his brow. He was holding a gun.

He pointed the gun in her face, holding it just inches from her nose. Angela pleaded with him not to kill her. She tried not to look at his face, hoping that he might spare her, but she couldn't help but glance at him. His eyes were cold and hard. She continued to beg for mercy, but he ignored her – perhaps her pleading angered him – and he pulled the trigger. The sound of the gunshot was like an explosion in the enclosed garage. Angela collapsed on the concrete floor. She was alive but too afraid to move. The gunman stepped over her and went to the door that led to her apartment, kicking her body out of the way so he could open it.

Angela lay perfectly still, playing dead. After a while – she didn't know how long – she realised that her hand was bleeding and she was still holding her keys. She'd raised her hands instinctively when the man had menaced her with the gun and the bullet had miraculously hit the keys and ricocheted away. Angela collected herself and got to her feet. She had started to run out of the garage when she heard another gunshot behind her. She kept running, just hoping to escape, but she ran into the man in black as he was coming out the front door of her condo.

She tried to get away from him, but her legs were shaky. She stumbled back towards her car in the garage, convinced that he was going to finish her off. But instead of pursuing her, the man shoved the gun into his belt and fled. Her room-mate, Dayle Okazaki, aged 34, had not been so lucky. Angela found her face down on the kitchen floor in a pool of her own blood. There was blood everywhere: on the walls, furniture and appliances. Angela ran to her side to check for signs of life, but Okazaki had been shot through the forehead. Angela grabbed the phone and called the police. Later, when the police searched the crime scene, they found the killer's baseball cap in the garage.

Within an hour of killing Okazaki, the killer struck again. He attacked 30-year-old Tsai-Lian Yu, dragging her out of her car onto the road. He shot her several times and fled. A policeman found Yu still breathing, but she died before the ambulance arrived. The two attacks occurring on the same day bolstered media attention and, in turn, caused panic and fear among the public. The news media dubbed the attacker, who was described as having long curly hair, bulging eyes and wide-spaced rotting teeth, the Walk-in Killer and the Valley Intruder.

On 20 March, three days after his previous murder, an eight-year-old girl was abducted from her home, sexually assaulted and murdered. On 27 March, Vincent Zazzara, aged 64, and his wife Maxine, aged 44, were attacked. Both were shot and Maxine Zazzara's body was mutilated with several stab wounds and a T-shaped carving on her left breast. Her eyes had been gouged out. The post-mortem determined that the mutilations were made after death. Police found footprints, which they believed were the killer's, in the flowerbeds. This evidence and the bullets found at the scene, which were matched to those found at previous attacks, made the police realise that a serial killer was on the loose.

Six weeks after killing the Zazzaras, the killer struck again.

His next victim was Harold Wu, aged 66, who was shot in the head, and his wife, Jean Wu, aged 63, who was punched, bound and then violently raped. For unknown reasons, the killer decided to let her live. The killer's attacks were now gaining momentum. He was now leaving behind more clues to his identity and he was renamed the Night Stalker by the media. Survivors of his attacks provided the police with a description: Hispanic male, long dark hair and foul smelling.

On 29 May 1985, the killer struck again. Malvia Keller, 83, and her invalid sister, Blanche Wolfe, 80, were both beaten with a hammer. An attempt was made to rape Keller, but this failed. Using lipstick, the killer drew pentagrams on Keller's thigh and on the wall in the bedroom. Blanche survived the attack. The following day Ruth Wilson, 41, was bound, raped and buggered by her attacker, while her 12-year-old son was locked in a cupboard. Her attacker slashed her once, and then bound her and her son together and left.

One month later, on 27 June, the Night Stalker raped a six-year-old girl in Arcadia. A day later, the body of 32-year-old Patty Elaine Higgins was found in her Arcadia home; her throat had been cut. A few days later, on 2 July, the body of 75-year-old Mary Louise Cannon was found in her Arcadia home. Like Patty Higgins, she had been beaten and her throat had been cut. The house had been ransacked.

On 5 July, the killer returned to Arcadia and attacked 16-year-old Deirdre Palmer savagely with a tyre lever. She survived. Two days later, on 7 July, the body of Joyce Lucille Nelson was found in her home in Monterey Park. The 61-year-old had been beaten to death with a blunt object. Later that same night in Monterey Park, Linda Fortuna, a 63-year-old registered nurse, was awakened at around 3.30am by a 'tall, bony man dressed in black'. The man, who fitted the description of the Night Stalker, was pointing a gun at her. He ordered her out of bed and into the bathroom, warning her to be quiet. After ransacking the house, he returned to her, forcing her back onto her bed. He attempted to rape and bugger her but could not maintain an erection. He was frustrated and humiliated and she was sure he would kill her. He screamed at her furiously, but then gathered up the valuables he wanted and left. She was astounded that he had spared her life.

Less than two weeks later, on 20 July, the Night Stalker chose a new location in the Los Angeles area of Glendale. Maxson Kneiling and his wife Lela, both 66, were found in their bed, both shot in the head and horribly slashed with a knife. Maxson had been butchered so brutally his head was barely attached to his body. Police experts had difficulty re-creating the attack based on the evidence. It's possible that the Stalker killed them both quickly with his gun and then mutilated them post-mortem, but, given his developing *modus operandi*, it's also possible that he kept Lela Kneiling alive to play out his perverse fantasies. However, he may also have failed to perform sexually with Lela Kneiling, just as he had with Linda Fortuna. And so he turned 20 July into a double event, striking again, this time in Sun Valley. Chitat Assawahem, 32, was shot in his sleep. His wife Sakima, 29, was raped, forced to perform oral sex on the intruder and then beaten mercilessly. He then buggered the couple's eight-year-old son. The attacker tied Sakima Assawahem up in her bedroom and left, but not before taking $30,000 in cash and jewellery.

On 6 August, the killer targeted another couple, Christopher and Virginia Petersen, aged 38 and 27. Following his pattern, he broke into the Petersens' Northridge bedroom and shot them both in the head. But they didn't die. In fact, Christopher Petersen, a powerfully built truck driver, got out of bed and chased the intruder away despite having a bullet lodged in his brain. Miraculously, the Petersens survived their wounds.

Two nights after the attack on the Petersens, the Stalker struck again, this time in Diamond Bar, California. Ahmed Zia, 35, was shot in the head and killed while he slept. The Stalker then raped and buggered Suu Kyi Zia, 28, forcing her to perform oral sex on him.

THE USA

Los Angeles County was terrified. The Night Stalker's crimes were becoming more frequent. The cooling-off periods were shortening and his rage was escalating. There was little doubt that he would strike again. The only questions were where and when?

It wasn't long before they were answered. On 18 August 1985, Peter and Barbara Pan were found in their blood-soaked bed in Lake Merced, a suburb of San Francisco. Both had been shot in the head. Peter Pan, a 66-year-old accountant, was pronounced dead at the scene. Barbara Pan, 64, survived but would be an invalid for the rest of her life. Scrawled on the wall in lipstick were an inverted pentagram and the words 'Jack the Knife', which is from a song called 'The Ripper' by heavy metal band Judas Priest. Local police determined that the killer had come in through an open window. Fearing that LA's Night Stalker had moved to their city, murder squad detectives sent a bullet removed from Peter Pan to a forensic team in Los Angeles. The bullet matched others recovered from two of the Night Stalker's Los Angeles crime scenes.

Police in San Francisco searched their unsolved murder files and came up with two incidents that fitted the Stalker's MO. On 20 February 1985, sisters Mary and Christina Caldwell, aged 70 and 50, had been stabbed to death in their Telegraph Hill apartment. If this was indeed the work of the Night Stalker, he had committed this crime about a month before the night he killed Dayle Okazaki and Tsai-Lian Yu and wounded Angela Barrios.

The police also discovered that on 2 June, the day after the murders of the elderly sisters Blanche Wolfe and Malvia Keller, Theodore Wildings, 25, was shot in the head while he slept in his apartment in the Cow Hollow section of San Francisco. His girlfriend, Nancy Brien, 25, was then brutally raped by the killer.

Could the Night Stalker have been active in San Francisco as well as Los Angeles throughout 1985 without the San Francisco police realising it?

THE EVIL WITHIN

Police traced the manager of a lodging house who claimed that a young man who fitted the Stalker's description had stayed at his establishment from time to time over the past year and a half. The manager remembered that the man had rotten teeth and smelt bad. The police checked the room he had last stayed in. On the bathroom door they found a drawing of a pentagram. The man had checked out during the day on 17 August. The Pans had been attacked that night. Police then located a man from the El Sobrante district who said he had purchased some jewellery – a diamond ring and a pair of cufflinks – from a young man who fitted the Stalker's description. Further investigation revealed that these items had belonged to Peter Pan.

The police got their first big break in the case following another attack that took place on 24 August 1985, 50 miles south of Los Angeles in Mission Viejo. The Night Stalker broke into the Mediterranean Village apartment of Bill Carns, 29, and his fiancée, Inez Erickson, 27. Bill Carns was shot in the head and Inez Erickson raped. The attacker demanded that she swear her love for Satan and afterwards forced her to perform oral sex on him. He then tied her up and left. She struggled to the window and saw the car the attacker was driving. She was able to give a description both of her attacker and his stolen orange Toyota estate car. A teenager later identified the car from news reports and wrote down half of its registration number. The stolen car was located on 28 August. It had been stolen from LA's Chinatown district while the owner was dining at a restaurant. The police kept the car under surveillance for nearly 24 hours in the hope that the Night Stalker would return for it, but he didn't.

Police were able to obtain a fingerprint from one of the vehicle's mirrors, which matched a print taken from a windowsill at the Pans' house near San Francisco. The prints belonged to Ricardo 'Richard' Muñoz Ramirez (b. 1960). At long last the police knew who their suspect was. Now they had to find him before he struck again.

Police published his photograph in the major Californian

newspapers, and the next day, in the Latin Quarter of LA, Ramirez was identified as he was trying to steal a car. He was chased, surrounded and severely beaten by an angry mob. Police had to break up the mob to prevent them from killing Ramirez.

Following his arrest and subsequent interviews, Ramirez was charged with 14 murders and 31 other felonies related to his murder, rape and robbery spree. A fifteenth murder in San Francisco was held in abeyance with the potential for a trial in Orange County for rape and attempted murder.

The trial did not begin until 30 January 1989, following almost three years of legal arguments. Ramirez had pleaded not guilty. However, on 20 September, almost two months after they had begun deliberating, the jury announced that they had reached a unanimous decision. Ramirez elected not to attend the verdict. On each of the counts he faced, the jury had found him guilty and had affirmed 19 'special circumstances' that made him eligible for the death penalty.

His defence team asked him to assist with the mitigation against the death penalty being imposed, because without mitigating factors, he surely would be condemned to death. 'Dying doesn't scare me,' he responded. 'I'll be in hell. With Satan.' He told his lawyers that he would not beg. So, to everyone's surprise, they offered no witnesses and did not call him to plead for his life. On 3 October 1989, after four days of deliberations, the jury voted for the death penalty for Richard Ramirez. Ramirez, who was present for this, was led from the courtroom smiling. 'Big deal,' he said. 'Death always went with the territory.' Later, as he was led in shackles back to the county jail, he added for reporters, 'I'll see you in Disneyland.'

On 9 November, he was officially sentenced to death 19 times. Ramirez chatted with his attorneys throughout. Afterwards, he added to his dark image with his rather incomprehensible speech to the court: 'You do not understand me. I do not expect you to. You are not capable of it. I am beyond your experience. I am beyond good and evil. Legions of the night, night breed, repeat not the errors of night prowler and show no mercy. I will be avenged. Lucifer dwells within us all.'

He denounced the court officials as liars, haters and parasitic worms. He said that he'd been misunderstood. He was led away eventually to join the 262 inmates already on death row in San Quentin. He remains there to this day, awaiting execution.

Of all the serial killers who have plagued the modern world, the Night Stalker was perhaps the most sensational in the way he committed his crimes. He was a living nightmare, a bogeyman who invaded bedrooms and tore innocent people from their dreams.

ÁNGEL MATURINO RESÉNDIZ, AKA THE RAILROAD KILLER

Ángel Reséndiz (b. 1959) first came to the attention of the police in 1979. He was arrested for car theft and assault in Florida and was sentenced to a 20-year prison term. He was paroled within six years and deported back to Mexico. But, undeterred, he continued crossing the border back to the USA and continued to commit crimes and receive prison sentences, being deported after each sentence.

In 1997, Reséndiz embarked on a murderous killing spree that would terrorise the residents of towns in the states of Texas. His MO was unique. He would illegally ride the railway that criss-crossed the state, jumping off whenever he felt the need to kill and rob. He would enter the homes of unsuspecting people near the rail tracks. If there was a man in the house, Reséndiz would bludgeon him with a heavy instrument. He would then attack the female, raping and killing her before stealing property, then leaving and jumping back on a passing train to make his getaway.

The dates of Reséndiz's known murders and his victims are set out below.

- 28 August 1997, in Lexington, Kentucky. Christopher Maier was a 21-year-old University of Kentucky student. He was walking along the rail tracks with his girlfriend when they were attacked by Reséndiz, who bludgeoned Maier to death. Reséndiz raped and severely beat Maier's girlfriend before leaving her for dead, but miraculously she survived.

- 4 October 1998, in Hughes Springs, Texas. Leafie Mason, an 81-year-old female, was beaten to death by Reséndiz, who entered her house through a window. He beat her savagely with a tyre lever. Fifty yards outside her door was the Kansas City Southern Rail line.

- 17 December 1998, at West University Place, Texas. Claudia Benton, 39, was raped, stabbed and bludgeoned repeatedly after Reséndiz entered her home, which was near the West University train tracks. He then made his getaway in her Jeep Cherokee, which police found in San Antonio, Texas. They found Reséndiz's fingerprints on the steering column. Strangely enough, the police only issued a warrant for his arrest for burglary, but not for murder.

- 2 May 1999, in Weimar, Texas. Norman J Sirnic, 46, and his wife Karen Sirnic, 47, were both bludgeoned to death by a sledgehammer in a parsonage of the United Church of Christ, where Norman Sirnic was a pastor. The building was located adjacent to a railway. Reséndiz stole their red Mazda, which was also found in San Antonio, Texas, three weeks later. Reséndiz's fingerprints were found within the vehicle, which gave the police a positive link to the previous murder of Claudia Benton.

- 4 June 1999, in Houston, Texas. Noemi Dominguez, a 26-year-old schoolteacher at Benjamin Franklin Elementary School, was also bludgeoned to death in her apartment near the rail tracks. Reséndiz then stole her white Honda Civic, which was found seven days later by police on the International Bridge in Del Rio, Texas. On the same date in Fayette County, Texas, Josephine Konvicka, 73, was murdered with a blow to the head from a pointed garden tool while she lay sleeping. Reséndiz attempted to steal the car but was unable to take it away as he could not find the car keys.

- 15 June 1999, in Gorham, Illinois. George Morber Senior, 80, and Carolyn Frederick, 52, were also brutally murdered by Reséndiz. He shot George Morber in the head with a shotgun and then clubbed Carolyn Frederick to death. Their house was located only 100yd from a railway line. A witness saw a man matching Reséndiz's description driving Carolyn Frederick's red pick-up truck in Cairo, Illinois, 60 miles south of Gorham.

By now, the police search to trace and arrest Reséndiz had gained momentum. In June 1999, the FBI placed the Railroad Killer on its Ten Most Wanted list. The FBI's initial reward of $50,000 for information leading to Reséndiz's capture escalated within days to $125,000. In the meantime, police in Jackson County, Illinois, officially linked Reséndiz with the murder of the Gorham killings after his fingerprints were matched. The police in Louisville, Kentucky, were able to do this as well. On 1 July, police in Fayette County, Texas, identified DNA from Noemi Dominguez in Josephine Konvicka's home, indicating that after Reséndiz had killed the younger woman, he drove her car to the other woman's home and committed a second murder.

Police missed the opportunity of making an arrest when, on 2 June, the Border Patrol apprehended Reséndiz near El Paso as he was attempting to cross the US–Mexico border illegally. While he was in custody, the United States Immigration and Naturalization Service performed a computer search on him, checking his fingerprints and photo against a list of possible fugitives. Because the system failed to identify him as a wanted man, he was deported back to Mexico.

The slip-up proved to be much more than an embarrassment. It was an error of immense proportions. After his release, Reséndiz immediately found his way back into the US where, within 48 hours, as a result of a computer error, he went on to kill four more innocent people.

On 7 July 1999, the FBI enlisted the help of Reséndiz's

common-law wife, Julietta Reyes. Surprisingly, Julietta handed over to the FBI 93 items of jewellery that she had been sent by Reséndiz. She believed they belonged to his victims, and this turned out to be correct. Relatives of Noemi Dominguez quickly identified 13 of the items. George Benton, husband of the murdered Claudia Benton, also identified several items of her property.

The Texas Rangers decided to try another plan to arrest him. They had traced Reséndiz to Mexico, where he had absconded after the double murder in Illinois. At that point he was believed to be hiding near the town of Ciudad Juarez. They contacted his sister Manuela, who was very close to him. They wanted her to try to persuade him to give himself up in an effort to prevent him killing again, or being killed by police should he be located within the US. If he surrendered himself, they said he would be assured of three things. First, his personal safety would be guaranteed while in jail. Second, he would have regular visiting rights so that his wife, sister and others could visit him. Third, he would have a psychological evaluation while he was in custody. The District Attorney endorsed these proposals in writing. Reséndiz, surprisingly, agreed to give himself up and, on 13 July, crossed the border back into the US where he was met and arrested by a single Texas Ranger in company with his sister.

The police were puzzled as to why Reséndiz surrendered so freely in a state that has executed more people than any other. He must have known that, if convicted of any of the murders in Texas, which seemed very likely, he would face the death penalty. The surrender agreement was very concise in detail. In no way was it set out to mislead or confuse Reséndiz into believing he would be spared due punishment. One possible speculation for Reséndiz's easy surrender was that he feared bounty hunters who, it was known, had gathered in Mexico to collect the reward. Another theory is that the Mexican authorities were currently investigating similar crimes, which he may have been responsible for.

Reséndiz was formally charged with seven murders but only convicted of one of those killings, that of Claudia Benton. In addition, he admitted to two earlier killings on 23 March 1997, in Ocala, Florida. Jesse Howell, 19, was bludgeoned to death with an air-hose coupling and left beside the railway tracks. His girlfriend, Wendy Von Huben, 16, was raped, strangled, suffocated and buried in a shallow grave.

On Wednesday, 12 April 2006, the San Antonio Police Department announced that it had cleared the unsolved murder of Michael White, who was found shot to death in July 1991 in the front yard of a vacant house in downtown San Antonio. According to police, Reséndiz gave them precise details about the murder and was named the prime suspect.

Prior to his case coming to trial, his defence team tried to raise a defence of insanity. However, he was deemed fit to stand trial. He was found guilty and sentenced to death by lethal injection. On 21 June 2006, a Houston judge ruled that Reséndiz was mentally competent to be executed. Upon hearing the judge's ruling, Reséndiz said, 'I don't believe in death. I know the body is going to go to waste. But me, as a person, I'm eternal. I'm going to be alive forever.'

He was executed on 27 June 2006, in Huntsville, Texas. When asked if he had any last words he made a statement directed at the husband of Claudia Benton, who was there to watch his execution. He said: 'Yes sir. I want to ask if it is in your heart to forgive me. You don't have to. I know I allowed the devil to rule my life. I just ask you to forgive me and ask the Lord to forgive me for allowing the devil to deceive me. I thank God for having patience with me. I don't deserve to cause you pain. You did not deserve this. I deserve what I am getting.'

GARY RIDGWAY, AKA THE GREEN RIVER KILLER

On 15 August 1982, Robert Ainsworth was sailing a raft down the Green River towards the edge of Seattle's city limits. As he drifted slowly downstream, he noticed a middle-aged balding man standing by the riverbank and a second, younger man sitting in a nearby pick-up truck. Ainsworth thought that the men were out for a day's fishing. As he passed them by, he acknowledged them; little did he know that moments later he would stumble across a river of death.

As Ainsworth peered into the clear waters, staring eyes met his gaze. He thought he saw the face of a black woman floating just beneath the surface of the water. His immediate thought was that it was a mannequin and, being curious, he tried to dislodge it. As he did so, he overturned his raft and fell into the river. To his horror, he realised that the figure was not a mannequin, but a dead woman. Seconds later, he saw another floating corpse of a half-naked black woman, partially submerged in the water. He managed to scramble out of the river in terror and contacted the police.

Soon after they arrived at the scene, detectives sealed off the area and began a search for evidence. During the search, a detective made another macabre discovery. He found a third body, that of a young girl who was partially clothed. Unlike the other two girls, this one was found in a grassy area less than 10yd from where the other victims lay in the water. It was obvious that she had died from asphyxiation. The girl had a pair of blue trousers knotted around her neck. She also showed signs of a struggle, because she had bruises on her arms and legs. She was later identified as Opal Mills, 16. It was believed that she had been murdered within 24 hours prior to her discovery.

Following an examination of the bodies at the scene, Chief Medical Examiner Donald Reay determined that all three females had died of strangulation. The two females found in the water were later identified as Marcia Chapman, 31, and Cynthia Hinds, 17, and both were found to have pyramid-shaped rocks lodged in their vaginal cavities. They had both been weighted down in the water by rocks. Reay further determined that Chapman, a mother of two who had gone missing two weeks earlier, had been dead for over a week. She showed advanced signs of decomposition. However, Hinds was believed to have been in the river for a period of only several days. The three bodies were not the only ones to be found in and around Washington State's Green River. Several days earlier, the body of a woman named Deborah Bonner had been discovered. Her naked body had been found slumped over a log in the Green River. She too had been strangled to death.

Just a month earlier, another young girl, identified as Wendy Lee Coffield, had been found strangled and floating in the Green River. Moreover, six months prior to Coffield's discovery, the body of her friend, Leanne Wilcox, was found several miles from the river in an area of wasteland. Within the space of six months, six bodies had been discovered in or near the river. The detectives at the scene quickly realised that there was a serial killer on the loose. The massive police investigation that followed was initially deluged with an influx of information, so much so that the police at that time did not have the means to process the ever-increasing amount of data and evidence and much of it was lost, misplaced or overlooked entirely. In fact, the situation got so bad that at one point they called for volunteers to assist in the ongoing investigation.

During their investigation, the police ascertained that many of the murdered women knew each other and shared a similar history of prostitution. They decided to commence their search for the killer in the area the girls were known to frequent. They conducted hundreds of interviews with many prostitutes who worked the main strip in Seattle. Investigators tried to obtain information on any suspicious people the women might have encountered. However, many of the prostitutes were reluctant to talk because of their blatant mistrust of the police.

The police reviewed reports of assaults made by prostitutes, which they thought might be related to the Green River murders. Two of these reports, made by two separate prostitutes, claimed that a man in a blue-and-white truck had abducted them and attempted to kill them. According to one account given by Susan

Widmark, 21, a middle-aged man in a blue-and-white truck had solicited her. Once Widmark was in his truck, he pointed a pistol to her head and sped off towards the highway. He took her to a desolate road, turned off the engine and proceeded to rape her violently. Following the rape, he allowed her to dress while he began to drive away from the scene with her still in the car. While driving, he made reference to the recent river murders, while continuing to hold a gun to her head. Fearing for her life, she managed to escape from the vehicle while at a red light. Widmark was able to make out part of the registration number of the truck before the man sped away.

A similar incident involved Debra Estes, 15, who made a report to police in late August 1982, concerning a rape. Estes told police that she was walking down the highway when a man in a blue-and-white pick-up truck approached her and offered her a ride. She accepted and climbed into the vehicle. To her amazement, the man pulled out a pistol and pointed it at her head. He forced her to give him oral sex before releasing her into the woods, handcuffed, and driving off. She immediately fled the scene looking for help.

Seeing a pattern emerging that might be related to the Green River murders, the taskforce decided to follow the lead and search for this truck and driver. They hoped that new information concerning the man would give them a break in the case. That September, a butcher named Charles Clinton Clark was stopped by police in his blue-and-white truck while driving along Seattle's main strip. After a background check was conducted, it was discovered that Clark owned two handguns. Investigators believed that Clark might be the man they were looking for. They obtained his driving licence photo and showed it to both Widmark and Estes. Both women positively identified Clark as their attacker.

Clark was arrested and his house and vehicle were searched. The police found the two handguns that were allegedly used in the assaults. After interrogation by police, Clark admitted to attacking the women. However, there was speculation as to whether he was the Green River Killer because he was known to release his victims following an attack. Moreover, Clark had solid alibis for the times when many of the Green River victims disappeared.

While Clark was being interviewed for the rapes of Widmark and Estes, 19-year-old Mary Bridgett Meehan disappeared during a walk. Meehan was more than eight months pregnant and went missing near the Western Six Motel. The motel was located on the strip and was a frequent hangout and workplace for many of the prostitutes who fell victim to the Green River Killer.

On 26 September 1982, the decomposing remains of a 17-year-old prostitute named Gisele A Lovvorn were discovered. She had gone missing more than two months before. A biker found her naked body near abandoned houses south of Seattle–Tacoma International Airport. She had been strangled to death with a pair of men's black socks. Intriguingly, at the time of her disappearance, she was blonde. Yet, when her body was discovered her hair was dyed black. Although her body was not found in the direct vicinity of the now-infamous river, police believed that she was a victim of the Green River Killer.

Between September 1982 and April 1983, approximately 14 women disappeared. Those missing included Mary Meehan, Debra Estes, Denise Bush, Shawnda Summers, Shirley Sherrill, Rebecca Marrero, Colleen Brockman, Alma Smith, Delores Williams, Gail Matthews, Andrea Childers, Sandra Gabbert, Kimi-Kai Pitsor and Marie Malvar. The ages of the women ranged between 15 and 23 years old. All were known prostitutes who solicited in the same area of Seattle. On 8 May 1983, another body was discovered that was later identified as Carol Ann Christensen, 21. Her remains were found by a family hunting for mushrooms in a wooded area near Maple Valley; her head was covered by a brown paper bag. When it was removed, it was found that she had a fish carefully placed on top of her neck and another fish placed on her left breast and a bottle between her legs. Her hands were crossed over her stomach and freshly ground beef was placed on top of her left hand. Further examination revealed that she was strangled with a cord. Intriguingly, she also showed signs of having been in water at some point, even though the river was miles away. The police speculated that she was yet another victim of the Green River Killer.

During the spring and summer of 1983, nine more young women, many of whom were prostitutes, disappeared. Those missing included Martina Authorlee and Cheryl Lee Wims, 18, Yvonne Antosh, 19, Carrie Rois, 15, Constance Naon, 21, Tammie Liles, 16, Keli McGuiness, 18, Tina Thompson, 22 and April Buttram, 17. The majority of the girls were placed on the ever-growing list of possible Green River Killer murders. However, there were some that police chose to disregard because they were found outside the area where the Green River Killer was known to dispose of bodies.

During the summer, several more bodies were discovered. In June, unidentified remains, believed to be of a 17–19-year-old white woman, were found on Southwest Tualatin Road. On 11 August, the body of missing Shawnda Summers was discovered near Seattle–Tacoma International Airport. One day later, the remains of another body, which remained unidentified, were found at the Sea-Tac International Airport North site. The autumn and winter of 1983 would also yield as many disappearances and even more bodies. Between September and December 1983, nine more women went missing and seven bodies were discovered, all of whom were believed to have been abducted and murdered by the Green River Killer. The missing women, who were mostly prostitutes, included Debbie Abernathy, 26, Tracy Ann Winston, 19, Patricia Osborn (believed to be aged 19), Maureen Feeney, 19, Mary Sue Bello, 25, Pammy Avent, 16, Delise Plager, 22, Kim Nelson, 26, and Lisa Lorraine Yates, 19.

Police then found the body of Delores Williams, who had gone missing on 8 March 1983. Her remains were discovered on 18 September at Star Lake. That same day, the remains of

Gail Matthews, 23, were also discovered at the same location. Over the next few months, the bodies of five more women were discovered.

On 15 October, the skeletal remains of Yvonne Antosh, last seen on 31 May, were found near Soos Creek on Auburn Black Diamond Road. She was one of the few victims to have had a missing person's report filed on her. Twelve days later, the partially buried skeleton of Constance Naon was found in an area south of Sea-Tac International Airport.

Investigators believed that there were probably more bodies to be found in that area, so they decided to conduct a search with the assistance of a team of teenage explorer boy scouts. On 29 October, during a sweep of the empty land surrounding the airport, one of the scouts found a skeleton covered with rubbish beneath some bushes. The remains were later identified as Kelly Ware, 22. The killer claimed two more victims, whose bodies were discovered before the New Year. On 13 November, following an extensive search of land surrounding an area south of Sea-Tac, the badly decomposed remains of Mary Meehan and her unborn baby were found. Several inexplicable items were found on or near the body, including two small pieces of plastic, a large clump of hair near the pubic region of the body, a patch of skin attached to the skull with fibres on it, three small bones, two halved yellow pencils and some clear plastic tubing.

One month later, on 15 December, the skull of Kimi-Kai Pitsor was found in Auburn, Washington, near Mountain View Cemetery. It seemed as if the killer had found a new burial site to place his victims. It would be the fifth known 'dumping ground' used for the disposal of the bodies. By now, the police had called in more investigators. It was feared many more murders would occur in the coming months, and this prediction proved to be correct. On 14 February 1984, the skeletal remains of a woman, who was later identified as Denise Louise Plager, were discovered 40 miles from the city close to I-90. She was the first victim to be found that year, but not the last. Over the next two months, approximately nine more bodies were found. Some of those found included Cheryl Wims, 18, Lisa Yates, 26, Debbie Abernathy, 26, Terry Milligan, 16, Sandra Gabbert, 17, and Alma Smith, 22. The other victims remained unidentified. All of the girls had one thing in common: a history of prostitution.

In mid-April, a volunteer taskforce worker and psychic, Barbara Kubik-Pattern, had a vision that another woman's body would be found close to I-90. Kubik-Pattern immediately contacted the police and told them about her vision, but became increasingly frustrated when they failed to act on the new information. Taking matters into her own hands, she and her daughter set out to find the woman. Following the leads revealed by her vision, Kubik-Pattern and her daughter eventually came across another body. Immediately after the discovery, the two women drove to a nearby search area that was patrolled by the police. When Kubik-Pattern informed one of the officers of her discovery, she was rebuffed and even threatened with arrest for obstruction of the guarded perimeter. Angered, she then informed reporters of her discovery. Finally, police officers approached her as she talked with the reporters and asked her to show them the body. Shortly thereafter the police were confronted with the gruesome discovery.

The decomposing remains were those of Amina Agisheff, 36. She had last been seen on 7 July 1982, walking home from her work at a restaurant in downtown Seattle. Agisheff did not fit the description of many of the other victims. She was older and a waitress, not a prostitute. Agisheff was also in a stable relationship at the time of her disappearance and was a mother of two. Although there were obvious differences between Agisheff's lifestyle and those of the other victims and the location where her body was disposed of, investigators believed that she was also a victim of the Green River Killer.

On 26 May, two children playing on Jovita Road in Pierce County were shocked when they discovered a skeleton. The police were immediately alerted to the new finding. Following a medical examination, it was discovered that the remains were of 15-year-old runaway Colleen Brockman. Investigators still had no new leads to the identity of the killer, apart from the location of the bodies and the shoe print. After almost three years, the murderous killing spree continued.

Although the murders seemed to have slowed down, they did not cease altogether. Between October and December 1984, two more bodies, identified as Mary Sue Bello, 25, and Martina Authorlee, 18, were discovered. Both bodies were found off Highway 410. The total body count had climbed to 31, although only 28 of the victims were actually looked on as being victims of the Green River Killer.

On 10 March 1985, another partially buried body was found near Star Lake Road. The victim was eventually identified as Carrie Rois, 15. She had disappeared during the summer of 1983. In mid-June, a man bulldozing a patch of land in Tigard, Oregon, discovered the skeletal remains of two more women. The remains were later identified as Denise Bush, 23, and Shirley Sherrill, 19. Both girls were known prostitutes in Seattle. The discovery of the two women confirmed the fact that the Green River Killer's territory had extended out of the state. It seemed that a new dumping ground had been revealed.

It was not until the winter that the skeletal remains of three more victims were found. The first remains were identified as belonging to Mary West, and were uncovered in a wooded area in Seward Park in Seattle. The other two remains were of Kimi-Kai Pitsor and another unidentified white female between 14 and 19 years old. The unusual aspect of this more recent discovery was that Pitsor's remains had been found in two different locations. In December 1983, her skull had been discovered in Mountain View Cemetery and two years later the remainder of her body was found a short distance away in a ravine. It was possible that an animal dragged the skull from the body sometime after death; however, there was no evidence that this had occurred. The police believed it was the work of the killer.

Police were uncertain about the killer's motive for dividing the body between two different locations. They speculated that it was intended to taunt them or confuse the investigation.

During this time, the public became increasingly aware of the lack of results from the police – anger and fear reached a boiling point. The media publicly ridiculed the police for not apprehending the killer after this length of time. To make matters worse, that summer the skeletal remains of three more women were discovered east of Seattle: Maureen Feeney, 19, Kim Nelson, 26, and another unidentifiable young woman. Feeney was the only one of the three whom investigators were able to link to a career in prostitution. The number of victims was quickly climbing towards a staggering 40.

In December 1986, two more bodies were discovered, this time much further away in an area north of Vancouver, British Columbia. Yet again, the killer seemed to be taunting investigators. Even more intriguing was that the partial remains of several other women had been scattered alongside the bodies of the two women. Even though the bodies were located a great distance from the others, there was no doubt in the investigators' minds that the work was that of the Green River Killer.

In 1987, investigators came upon a suspect by the name of Gary Ridgway (b. 1949) who had previously been under scrutiny. He had been arrested in May 1984 after attempting to solicit an undercover police officer posing as a prostitute. However, Ridgway was released without charge after he successfully passed a lie detector test. Police now looked deeper into Ridgway's past; they discovered that he had been arrested for choking a prostitute in 1980 near Sea-Tac International Airport. He had pleaded self-defence, claiming the woman bit him, and he was soon after released from police custody with no charge.

The police now had cause to be highly suspicious of Ridgway and decided to delve even further into his past. They discovered that police had stopped and questioned the man back in 1982 while he was in his truck with a prostitute. The prostitute he had been with was one of the women on the Green River murder list, Keli McGuiness.

It also transpired that police had questioned Ridgway back in 1983 in connection with the kidnapping of murder victim Marie Malvar. A witness, Malvar's boyfriend, had followed the truck to the suspect's house after recognising it as the one that he'd last seen his girlfriend in.

The police decided to trace Ridgway's ex-wife in an effort to obtain more information. They learnt from her that he often frequented the sites where bodies had been discovered. Looking back on previous statements, they discovered that several prostitutes claimed to have seen a man matching the suspect's description regularly cruising the strip between 1982 and 1983. It turned out that Ridgway passed the strip almost daily on his way to work as a truck painter. When they went to his workplace and examined his work records they ascertained that he had been absent or off-duty on every occasion a victim disappeared.

Finally, on 8 April 1987, the police obtained a warrant and searched Ridgway's house. They obtained samples from him for DNA comparisons. However, at that time there was insufficient evidence to arrest him and he was released from police custody.

In June 1987, three boys stumbled across the partially buried skeletal remains of a young woman while searching for aluminium cans. The girl, who was identified as Cindy Ann Smith, 17, was found in a ravine behind the Green River Community College. She had been missing for approximately three years before her discovery. More bodies of missing young women were discovered in the year that followed, some of which included missing runaway Debbie Gonzales, 14, and Debra Estes, 15, who had disappeared six years earlier. Their deaths were attributed to the Green River Killer.

In October 1989, two more skeletal remains of young women were found. One of the victims, identified as Andrea Childers, was found on wasteland near Star Lake. Like many of the young women found before her, the cause of death remained unclear due to the state of decomposition. In early February 1990, the skull of Denise Bush was found in a wooded area in Southgate Park in Tukwila, Washington. The remainder of Bush's body had been located in Oregon five years earlier. Once again, it seemed as if the killer was purposely moving the bones around in an effort to confuse police, who by now were beginning to believe that the killer had defeated them. Morale among the officers was at an all-time low.

In July 1991, the investigation was reduced to just one investigator. After nine years, 49 victims and $15 million, the police still had not caught the Green River Killer. The investigation at that time became known as the country's largest unsolved murder case. The case remained dormant for 10 years.

In April 2001, almost 20 years after the first known Green River murder, the police renewed investigations into the murders. This time, the taskforce had technology on its side. All the evidence from the case was re-examined and some of the forensic samples were sent to laboratories. The first to be sent were found with three victims murdered between 1982 and 1983 – Opal Mills, Marcia Chapman and Carol Christensen. The samples consisted of semen, supposedly from the killer, found on some of the bodies. The semen samples underwent a newly developed DNA-testing method and were compared with samples taken from Ridgway in April 1987.

On 10 September 2001, a match was made between the semen samples taken from the victims and Ridgway. On 30 November, Ridgway was stopped by investigators on his way home from work and arrested on four counts of aggravated murder. The charges included those of the three girls and also Cynthia Hinds, in which circumstantial evidence was also found connecting him with her death. The elusive killer whom investigators had sought for 20 years was finally in police custody.

Ridgway, at the time of his arrest, worked for a computer company. At the time of the murders, he had been employed as a truck painter for 30 years at the Kentworth truck factory in Renton, Washington. Ridgway owned many trucks during that time. He allegedly had an unusual sexual appetite. His three ex-wives and several ex-girlfriends stated that he was sexually insatiable, demanding sex several times a day. Often, he would want to have sex in a public area or in the woods, even in the areas where some of the bodies had been discovered. Ridgway was also known to have been obsessed with prostitutes, a fixation that bordered on a love–hate relationship. Neighbours knew him to constantly complain about prostitutes conducting business in his neighbourhood, but at the same time he frequently took advantage of them. It was possible that he was torn by his uncontrollable lusts and his staunch religious beliefs. He became a religious fanatic, often crying following sermons and reading the Bible.

Ridgway confessed to more confirmed murders than any other American serial killer. Over a period of five months of police and prosecutor interviews, he confessed to 48 murders, 42 of the 48 murders on the police's list of probable Green River Killer victims and six more murders, including one as late as 2000.

On 5 November 2003, Ridgway entered a guilty plea to 48 charges of first-degree murder as part of a plea-bargain agreed to in the preceding June, which would spare him execution in exchange for his cooperation in locating the remains of his victims and providing other details. In his statement accompanying his guilty plea, Ridgway explained that all of his victims had been killed inside King County, Washington, and that he had transported and dumped the remains of the two women near Portland to confuse the police.

Public opinion remains divided on whether a confessed murderer of 48 people should be spared execution in a state that has the death penalty and imposes it on people who have killed far fewer victims. Deputy prosecutor Jeffrey Baird noted in court that the deal contained the names of 48 victims who would not be the subject of 'State v. Ridgway if it were not for the plea agreement'. King County Prosecuting Attorney, Norm Maleng, explained his decision to make the deal: 'We could have gone forward with seven counts, but that is all we could have ever hoped to solve. At the end of that trial, whatever the outcome, there would have been lingering doubts about the rest of these crimes. This agreement was the avenue to the truth. And in the end, the search for the truth is still why we have a criminal justice system ... Gary Ridgway does not deserve our mercy. He does not deserve to live. The mercy provided by today's resolution is directed not at Ridgway, but toward the families who have suffered so much ...'

On 18 December 2003, King County Superior Court Judge Richard Jones sentenced Ridgway to 48 life sentences with no possibility of parole and one life sentence, to be served consecutively. He is currently serving his sentence at Washington State Penitentiary in Walla Walla, Washington.

Ridgway led prosecutors to three more bodies in 2003. On 16 August of that year, remains of a 16-year-old female were found near Enumclaw, Washington, and identified as belonging to Pammy Annette Avent, who was believed to have been a victim of the Green River Killer. The remains of Marie Malvar and April Buttram were found the following month.

On 23 November 2005, a hiker found the skull of one of the 48 women Ridgway had admitted murdering in his 2003 plea-bargain with King County prosecutors. A man hiking in a wooded area, southeast of Seattle, found the skull of Tracy Winston, who was 19 when she had disappeared on 12 September 1983.

In another twist to the case, in February 2011 teenagers found a skull of another missing person, Rebecca Marreos, who had disappeared 28 years before. Ridgway had previously confessed to her abduction and murder, but due to the body not being found her murder was not included in the main indictment relating to the original 48 murders.

As a result Ridgway was formally charged with Marreos's

murder. He pleaded guilty and was sentenced to a further life imprisonment sentence, which will run concurrently to his current life sentences.

JOEL RIFKIN

It is a known fact that many serial killers have been apprehended not because they were found committing a crime, nor thanks to forensic technology, but simply because they took a risk, become careless or were simply stopped by police on a routine check, after committing an unrelated crime – a road traffic offence, for instance. The arrest of Joel Rifkin (b. 1959) falls into this latter category.

The beginning of the end for Joel Rifkin was 3.15am on 28 June 1993, when two New York state troopers saw a Mazda pick-up truck with no rear number plate. They attempted to stop the vehicle but it sped away. A chase then ensued involving other police vehicles, ending with the Mazda pick-up crashing into a telegraph pole. The driver was detained and offered no resistance. He was identified as 34-year-old Joel David Rifkin, residing on Garden Street in East Meadow, Long Island. He was scruffy in appearance and a thick layer of Noxzema was smeared across his moustache. When told his truck had no rear number plate, Rifkin assured the officers it had been present when he left his home, some 40 minutes earlier. He could offer no explanation as to why he had sped away from the officers, but the reason was revealed moments later.

Police could smell a foul odour coming from the back of Rifkin's truck and, on pulling back a tarpaulin, discovered a woman's naked, decomposing body. She appeared to have been dead for several days. That explained Rifkin's use of Noxzema. This was a trick for handling dead bodies, to mitigate the stench of decomposition; film makers had depicted this technique two years earlier in the Oscar-winning film, *The Silence of the Lambs*.

When asked about the body, Rifkin said, 'She was a prostitute.

I picked her up on Allen Street in Manhattan. I had sex with her, then things went bad and I strangled her. Do you think I need a lawyer?' Rifkin was arrested. The body found in the back of his truck was soon identified as Tiffany Bresciani, a 22-year-old native of Louisiana and a drug addict. She had been working as a prostitute in Manhattan for the past two years in order to feed her drug habit.

At the time of Rifkin's arrest, other officers carried out a search of his home, where he lived with his 71-year-old mother. The search lasted six hours. When they left, they had seized many items that would later link Rifkin to other murders. A bedroom upstairs yielded 75 pieces of women's jewellery, photographs, various items of feminine clothing, make-up cases, a woman's curling iron, purses and wallets, plus a mixed bag of ID cards. One driving licence belonged to Mary DeLuca, who had been found dead in Cornwall, New York, in October 1991. Another belonged to Jenny Soto, whose body was found floating in the Harlem River in November 1992. Rifkin's bedroom reading material included a book on the unidentified Green River Killer and news clippings about the case of New York serial killer Arthur Shawcross.

In Rifkin's garage, detectives examined a wheelbarrow, from which they extracted 85g of human blood. A pair of women's knickers lay on the floor, near a stockpile of rope and tarpaulin. A chainsaw found in the garage was stained with blood and pieces of human flesh.

Detectives began interrogating Rifkin at 8.25am on 28 June 1993. They questioned him for eight hours, but for some reason never recorded the interviews. Rifkin later claimed that he asked for a lawyer at least 20 times and this was always refused. The written transcript of his interview, presumably reconstructed from memory, suggests that Rifkin had been offered a lawyer and declined.

He described 17 murders, writing out the names he remembered and sketching maps to help police find those victims still missing. Rifkin was dispassionate, referring to the murders as 'events' or 'incidents', and listing his victims by number.

He said that his first murder was in March 1989 while driving around Manhattan's East Village looking for prostitutes. At about 10pm, he selected a young woman he remembered only as 'Susie'. She was a hardcore drug addict, demanding several stops to purchase crack before they drove back to Long Island. After listless sex, Susie again asked Rifkin to take her out in search of drugs. Instead, he picked up a souvenir howitzer shell and beat her furiously. 'I just lost control,' he said later. 'I stopped when I got tired.' Susie was still alive and she fought back when he tried to move her, biting one of Rifkin's fingers deeply before he strangled her to death. After placing her body in a plastic rubbish bag, Rifkin cleaned up the blood and signs of combat in his living room, then lay down and slept for several hours as if nothing had happened. Upon waking, he dragged Susie down to the basement of his house, draped her body across the washer and dryer, and then used that makeshift operating table to dismember her corpse with a knife. In his mind, the grim task was 'reduced to biology class'. To foil identification, Rifkin severed Susie's fingertips and pulled her teeth with pliers, then jammed her severed head into an old paint can. The other parts went into rubbish bags and then into his mother's car.

Rifkin drove the body parts across the state line to New Jersey, dropping the head and legs in the woods near Hopewell. Doubling back from there, he returned to Manhattan, throwing the arms and torso into the East River. Rifkin believed that his victim would never be found, but he had been careless. On 5 March 1989, a member of the Hopewell Valley Golf Club sliced his ball into the woods along the seventh green and found the can containing Susie's head. Rifkin suffered 'a major anxiety attack' after learning that Susie was HIV positive, following the case as police prepared artists' renderings of the victim in life and checked them against a list of 700 missing women. Susie has never been identified. Her case remained unsolved until Rifkin confessed.

He waited more than a year to claim his second victim, prostitute Julie Blackbird. Rifkin drove her home to East Meadow when his mother was again out of town, and they spent the night together. At about nine the next morning, Rifkin recalled 'completely bugging out', beating Blackbird with a heavy table leg before he strangled her. When she was dead, he considered raping her body in conscious emulation of serial killer Ted Bundy, but the prospect repulsed him.

Determined not to bungle the disposal this time, Rifkin went out to purchase cement and a large mortar pan. He dismembered the corpse as before, placing the head, arms and legs in buckets weighted with concrete; the torso filled a milk crate by itself. Driving into Manhattan, he disposed of Blackbird's head and torso in the East River and then dropped her weighted arms and legs into a Brooklyn barge canal. The remains were never found. Knowledge of Blackbird's fate came only from Rifkin's confession and from her diary found in his bedroom.

Barbara Jacobs was the next to die, a 31-year-old drug addict and prostitute. Rifkin picked her up on 13 July 1991 and took her home to East Meadow for sex. When she fell asleep, he clubbed her with the same table leg he had used on Julie Blackbird, and then manually strangled her. Rifkin wrapped Jacobs in plastic, folded her into a cardboard box, and placed her in the back of his mother's Toyota pick-up. He drove to the Hudson River, dropping her into the water near a cement plant. She was found hours later by firefighters on a training exercise. This time, though, Rifkin was unfazed by the discovery of the body.

Mary Ellen DeLuca, a 22-year-old Long Island resident, was the next victim. She was last seen alive at 11pm on 1 September 1991. Rifkin found her on Jamaica Avenue in Queens and drove her around New York until sunrise, buying drugs for her at various stops. Rifkin asked DeLuca if she wanted to die and she allegedly said yes. As he strangled her, Rifkin recalled, 'She did nothing, just accepted it.' He remembered her murder as 'one of the weird ones'.

It also left Rifkin with a new problem. He was scared to drag the body out in broad daylight. He drew inspiration from Hitchcock's *Frenzy* and went out to purchase a trunk, squeezing DeLuca inside it. From the motel, he drove upstate to Orange County and left DeLuca's body in a lay-by. She was found on 1 October, naked except for a brassiere, without ID. Decomposition made it impossible to determine a cause of death and she was buried nameless.

Rifkin's selection process was erratic – the prostitutes he patronised on a near-nightly basis were usually spared, with others chosen apparently on a whim. One early September night he picked up 30-year-old Yun Lee, a Korean native he had been with before; she was his second prostitute in an hour. That may explain his failure to perform as Lee went to work. He struck her on impulse, strangling her while she 'mouthed something about making a big mistake'. It was Rifkin's first murder of someone he had known beforehand and he experienced fleeting remorse. 'Actually,' he later said, 'I thought I liked her.' Rifkin placed Lee into the same trunk he'd used for Mary DeLuca and dropped her in the East River. She was found on 23 September, eight days before DeLuca. Lee's ex-husband identified the body, sparing her from an unmarked grave.

Rifkin could not recall the name of 'number six', murdered a few days prior to Christmas 1991. He picked her up in Manhattan and strangled her in his car during oral sex, describing the event as 'very quick'. Afterwards, he drove back to Long Island with the body slumped beside him, concealing her under a tarpaulin at his rented workplace. Next, he drove to a recycling plant, where he had once worked part-time, and helped himself to a 200-litre oil drum. There was ample room for the body in the barrel, safely hidden for their ride to the South Bronx, where Rifkin rolled her into the East River. As he was about to leave he was confronted by police officers who accused him of illegal dumping, but Rifkin persuaded them he was collecting junk instead. They let him go with just a warning.

The method of disposing of his victims using an oil drum worked so well for Rifkin that he purchased several more for use as makeshift coffins. He used the next one on Lorraine Orvieto, a 28-year-old prostitute and crack addict. Rifkin found Orvieto on 26 December 1991 in Long Island. He parked near a schoolyard fence and strangled her while she performed oral sex, discovering her HIV-positive status when he found a bottle of AZT in her handbag. He kept the pills, along with Orvieto's jewellery and ID, as souvenirs of the kill. Rifkin stuffed her lifeless body into an oil drum, drove to Brooklyn and dropped it into Coney Island Creek. A fisherman found her on 11 July 1992.

One week after he killed Lorraine Orvieto, on 2 January 1992, Rifkin killed again. At 39, Mary Ann Holloman was his oldest victim, again a prostitute and crack addict. After picking her up, Rifkin drove her to the same car park where he had taken Yun Lee and strangled her while she was giving him oral sex. Later, he recalled the act as 'very automatic. Not much with that one.' He followed the same disposal procedure as with Orvieto, disposing of her body in an oil drum in Coney Island Creek. Her floating remains were found one week later, two days before Orvieto's body was found. Unlike Orvieto, Holloman was identified from dental records and returned to her family for burial. Two floating bodies in as many days suggested a serial killer at large, but New York police had their hands full with 2,000 murders a year in those days and junkie prostitutes were never high-priority.

Rifkin's ninth victim surfaced before numbers seven and eight. He was vague on the details in later confessions, unable to recall the woman's name, if he had ever known it. He remembered her tattoos, the fact that he had picked her up in Manhattan and the way she fought for life when he began to strangle her. He dropped her into Brooklyn's Newtown Creek, where she was spotted floating with the current; a foot was seen protruding from the rusty barrel on 13 May 1992. The cocaine in her system suggested to detectives that she might have been a drug 'mule', killed accidentally by the rupture of drug-filled condoms in her stomach. Police learnt of their mistake a year later, when Rifkin confessed to her slaying, but 'number nine' remains anonymous, the last Jane Doe.

His next victim was Iris Sanchez, a 25-year-old crack addict. He picked Sanchez up in broad daylight, driving her to a Manhattan housing project. After strangling Sanchez during sex, he drove her body across Brooklyn Bridge, seeking a drop-off point. The site he chose was an illegal dump, within sight of JFK International Airport. Rifkin wedged the body underneath a rotting mattress, first relieving Sanchez of her watch and other jewellery. She would not be found until June 1993, when Rifkin drew detectives a map.

On 25 May 1992, Rifkin picked up Anna Lopez, aged 33. He took her to a backstreet for sex before strangling her. Rifkin drove through the night to Brewster, in Putnam County, and dumped her body in a lay-by. A motorist stopping to relieve himself found Lopez the following day. She was missing one earring, later found in Rifkin's bedroom.

Violet O'Neill was his next victim; the first he had taken home to East Meadow in nearly a year. He picked her up in the city, strangled her after sex at his mother's house and dismembered her body in the bath. Rifkin consigned her remains to the waters surrounding Manhattan. Her body surfaced in the Hudson River, wrapped in black plastic; her arms and legs were later found in a discarded suitcase.

Mary Catherine Williams, another prostitute and drug addict, was Rifkin's next victim. Prior to murdering her, Rifkin had dated her several times. On 2 October 1992, he picked her up and bought her drugs. He then tried to strangle her when she dozed off in his mother's car. She woke up fighting for her life, kicking the gearstick hard enough to snap it off before Rifkin smothered her. Rifkin drove the body to a Westchester suburb, where she was found on 21 December 1992. He kept her credit cards and a wicker handbag filled with costume jewellery, so much, in fact, that the amount would briefly cause detectives to inflate the number of victims. Williams was buried as others had been before, in a nameless pauper's grave, until Rifkin confessed to her murder six months after her body was found.

Jenny Soto was the last victim of 1992. She was a 23-year-old drug addict whom Rifkin picked up at about 11pm on 16 November, near the Williamsburg Bridge in lower Manhattan. He strangled her in his car after sex but he admitted that she was the 'the toughest one to kill'; she broke all ten fingernails as she clawed Rifkin's face and neck. Wounded from the battle, Rifkin claimed her bra and knickers, earrings, ID cards and drug syringe as trophies for his cache. He rolled Soto into the Harlem River, near the spot where Yun Lee had been found 14 months earlier. Her body was discovered the following day, and she was identified from fingerprint records of her last arrest. Soto's fight for life capped Rifkin's own frenzied 'acceleration period' and also left him with embarrassing wounds to explain. He did not kill again for 15 weeks and, when he did, he intended to be more careful.

Rifkin's first victim of 1993 was Leah Evens, 28; like all the others she was a prostitute and drug addict. Rifkin found her soliciting on 27 February 1993. He picked her up and they had sex in an abandoned car park. Evens started to undress, and then stopped, demanding greater privacy. Rifkin refused, strangling her when she started to cry. Afterwards, he drove her body to the far eastern end of Long Island and buried her in the woods. She was the only one of his victims buried in a shallow grave. Hikers found her on 9 May, after they discovered a withered hand protruding from the ground. A forensic anthropologist started to reconstruct the victim's face, but Rifkin confessed before the model was finished. Police found Evens' driving licence at his home.

Lauren Marquez was a 28-year-old addict and prostitute, and Rifkin's next victim. Rifkin picked her up on 2 April 1993 and drove to a point near the Manhattan Bridge, clutching at her throat without the usual preliminaries. Briefly distracted by a man who passed the car walking a dog, he almost let Marquez escape. She fought him, resisting strangulation until he snapped her neck. Rifkin dumped her body in the Suffolk County Pine Barrens, where she lay undiscovered until his arrest. Besides a broken neck, Marquez had fractured ribs, though Rifkin claimed he could not remember hitting her. She was identified through DNA testing on 20 August 1993.

Rifkin's last victim, Tiffany Bresciani, was from Metairie, Louisiana, and had been drawn to New York by dreams of acting or dancing. Instead, she wound up hooked on heroin, performing for strangers in strip clubs and bars. By the time Rifkin found her, in the pre-dawn hours of 24 June 1993, she was his second hooker of the night, and his fourth within two days. Rifkin picked her up on Allen Street and drove her to the car park of the *New York Post*, where he strangled her at 5.30am. From there, he drove back to East Meadow, stopping at stores along the way for rope and tarpaulin, while Bresciani's body lay sprawled across the back seat of his mother's car. By the time he got home, he had wrapped the body in a tarpaulin, which he concealed in the boot. Rifkin had just arrived home when his mother demanded her car keys and embarked on a 30-minute shopping trip, with the body still in the boot. Rifkin had no time to move the body, but his mother never knew. Relieved of his 'little anxiety attack', Rifkin moved Bresciani into the cluttered garage, leaving her body on a wheelbarrow. Then, as if in a fugue state, he spent the next three days working on his pick-up, ignoring the summer heat and pervasive reek of decomposing flesh. He was on his way to dump the corpse near Melville's Republic Airport, some 15 miles north of his house, when he was stopped by the police, who found Bresciani's body in his boot. The killing game was over, but the quest for justice had only just begun.

Following his arrest and before finally coming to trial, there were a number of legal arguments raised by his defence, which revolved around Rifkin's confession and the suggestion that he had asked for legal advice and that this had been refused. However, these were negated. The full trial began on 20 April 1994. The jury was made up of seven men and five women. Rifkin pleaded not guilty by reason of insanity. However, the jury did not accept this and on 9 May found him guilty. He was sentenced to 25 years to life for murder.

In 2002, New York's Supreme Court rejected Rifkin's appeal against his convictions for the murder of nine women. His lawyer argued that his statements to the police at the time of his arrest should be suppressed because he had not been informed of his rights. Joel Rifkin is now serving 203 years to life in the Clinton Correctional Facility, New York. He will be eligible for parole in 2197.

ARTHUR SHAWCROSS, AKA THE GENESEE RIVER KILLER

Arthur Shawcross (b. 1945) was unique as far as serial killers were concerned, having been arrested and imprisoned for a series of killings and then released back into society with the opportunity to kill again, which he grasped with both hands.

It was in May 1972 that Shawcross committed his first murder. His first victim was 10-year-old Jack Blake, in Watertown, New York. He had disappeared near the apartments where Shawcross lived. Jack's mother had an instinct about Shawcross, then 27, who had taken Jack and his older brother fishing a few days before. When she confronted Shawcross, he offered several conflicting stories. That seemed suspicious, but with no body and no evidence, the police could do nothing. Searches for the boy turned up nothing. Shawcross said to his interrogators that the boy had pestered him, so he'd hit him and had accidentally killed him. This story would eventually change.

Four months later, eight-year-old Karen Ann Hill was visiting Watertown with her mother when she disappeared. Her body was found under a bridge that crossed the Black River. She'd been raped and murdered. Mud, leaves and other debris had been forced down her throat and inside her clothing. Shawcross, who often fished under the bridge, was a suspect. Detective Charles Kubinski of the Watertown Police Department knew him. With persistence and skill, he eventually got Shawcross to confess to the crime. He also gathered enough information about Jack Blake that the police were finally able to locate the boy's body. Due to its advanced state of decomposition, it was unclear whether Jack had been sexually assaulted, but, like Karen Ann Hill, he'd been asphyxiated. Shawcross had admitted to having sex with the girl and forcing himself on her while she screamed.

Shawcross confessed to both murders but was later able to obtain a plea-bargain with the prosecutors. He would plead guilty to killing only Karen Ann Hill on a charge of manslaughter instead of first-degree murder. In return, the charge of killing Jake Blake would be dropped. With little evidence to go on, prosecutors went along with this and the self-confessed double child-killer was given a 25-year sentence.

Shawcross served 15 years before being released on parole in March 1987. He had difficulty settling down as he was constantly hounded where he lived and worked as soon as neighbours and employers found out about his criminal record. Eventually, he settled in Rochester, New York, and moved in with a woman named Rosie Whalley with whom he had formed a stable relationship. But deep within, the monster was awakening and the urge to kill subsequently engulfed him. The results of his cruel and evil deeds would surface on 24 March 1988, in the Genesee River Gorge, Rochester, New York.

A group of fishermen discovered what they thought was a mannequin in the chilly waters, but soon discovered it to be the body of a woman, clad in jeans and a sweatshirt. Detectives could see from the serious bruises that this woman had been beaten, but they allowed the medical examiner, Dr Forbes, to complete a full examination and autopsy before making a final judgment. He noted that she had been strangled. Vaginal trauma, surrounded by teeth marks, was also evident, although this might as easily have occurred after death as before. She appeared to have been viciously kicked in the groin. Although she'd been in water, she had not drowned. There was no water in her lungs, so her killer had disposed of her body there after she had died. Dr Forbes determined that her wounds had been made by a blunt object, but could not identify just what had made the patterned indentation, about 2in wide, across her chest. It had left a mark but had not broken the skin.

It wasn't long before she was identified as Dorothy 'Dotsie' Blackburn, 27, a local prostitute and mother of three. Her sister had filed a missing persons report on 18 March and it was she who identified the body. Prostitute murders were not unusual and this woman had been a cocaine addict with a debt. Prostitution was a high-risk occupation with a low risk of discovery for whoever decided to target such women for murder. The Rochester police examined the shooting and knifing murders of two other prostitutes in the area, but at the time were unable to link them.

The case went cold. However, the police did investigate the killings of several more prostitutes during the summer of 1989, although none of the cases seemed clearly linked to one another and none seemed unusual. One woman had been dumped along the roadway on an exit ramp, another shot and a third one killed by a car in a way that looked suspicious.

On 9 September 1988, a man looking for empty bottles to sell came across another set of remains. He spotted a bone sticking up and believed it was from a dead deer, but on closer inspection saw a pile of clothing. He immediately contacted the police who found it to be the decomposing body of a woman. This woman had apparently floated upriver and debris had snagged her body. No one had seen her there and she had decomposed considerably, making it difficult for the medical examiner to offer a cause of death, although he listed it as probable asphyxia. There were no knife or gunshot wounds evident in the bones. Who was she?

The police found 138 possible matches for identity purposes

from reports of missing women, but all were eventually eliminated. Unable to identify her or to find someone like her reported missing from the area, the police enlisted the help of a forensic anthropologist to reconstruct what her face had looked like from the skull. It was a long, involved process, but he produced a clay bust and added a wig and fake eyeballs, and the police photographed the final product and published it in the local papers. The victim's distraught father identified her as Anna Steffen and dental records confirmed this. The police believed a drug dealer or pimp had killed her. Her body had been discovered far away from where Blackburn's had been found, so while their manner of death and disposal may have been similar, the police were not linking them and no one was talking about a serial killer.

On Saturday, 21 October, six weeks later, three fishermen went into the gorge and came across the remains of a decomposing headless corpse, mostly bones, hidden in tall grass along the riverbank. The body was that of a female; her neck was broken and the cause of her death was difficult to determine, but she seemed to have been killed by blunt impact with something. An employee of the county jail read about the discovery and reported that a homeless woman named Dorothy Keeler, aged 60, had not been seen in some time. The remains were again given to the forensic anthropologist and an identification was made.

Six days later, a boy retrieving a ball saw a foot sticking out from beneath a pile of debris and cardboard near a YMCA hostel not far from the gorge. He summoned the police, who uncovered a decomposing, maggot-infested body dressed in black trousers and a sweater. The dead woman was identified as Patty Ives.

The number of victims was rising; four apparently dead by asphyxia, with three in quick succession. The pressure was now on to stop the killer. It was suggested that the strangler killed quickly and that he was probably quite strong; he appeared to strangle the women without much effort and little sign of a struggle on their part. As the victims were prostitutes, the police tried to enlist the help of the other working girls. On average, around 35 women worked the area at any given time, though many came and went. The police sat in unmarked cars, watching them and allowing them to ply their trade. They were told about a transvestite who seemed to get the most action, but there was nothing overtly suspicious about him. The women were tentative about this unusual arrangement, not altogether trustful that the police watching them wouldn't just arrest them. Neither side was used to working with the other. Yet the prostitutes also felt safer. Despite all of this, other prostitutes soon went missing. One such person was blonde Maria Welch, who resembled Patty Ives in build. Then the body of a petite blonde was discovered dumped in the gorge, down a steep slope, wearing only a pair of boots. Her cause of death was asphyxia and bruises on the body indicated that she'd been beaten. Everyone assumed this victim was Maria, but they were wrong. Her name was Frances Brown. Enquiries revealed that she had met a man named 'Mike' prior to her death.

The police thought they had a series of six to eight women who had been killed by the same man. Checking files of sexual predators who'd been paroled from upper New York prisons, they found nothing to indicate that they had one living in their area.

On 15 November, Kimberly Logan, a black prostitute, was discovered dead beneath a pile of leaves in the back yard of a house. She'd been battered and kicked in the abdomen. The medical examiner found leaves stuffed down her throat. She had not been found near the gorge. Eight days later, a man out walking his dog went into a marshy area near an industrial estate. He came to a clearing where he spotted a piece of stiff carpeting, iced over. Walking closer, he saw a bare foot beneath it. The police's worst fears had come true. It was the body of another victim of the mysterious killer.

The woman, who had been preserved somewhat by the cold weather and the covering, lay face down. Spots on her skin suggested decomposition, so she had been killed as much as two or three weeks earlier. A considerable amount of blood had settled into her back, which meant that she had been lying on her back after death for a period of time, and now here she was on her face. Someone had come and turned her over. Her position suggested that she'd been anally penetrated after death. She'd also been strangled, but that wasn't all. When they turned her over, they saw that some time after she had died, she'd been cut from the top of the chest between her breasts all the way into the vaginal area, like a gutted deer. Upon close inspection, it looked as if the vaginal lips had been removed. This killer had returned for some perverted pleasure. Yet the analysis at the morgue indicated that there was no semen in or on the body. In the weeds, the police found a knife and a bloody towel, but there were no fingerprints and very little physical evidence.

The victim was soon identified as the missing June Stott. As far as anyone knew, she was not a prostitute and had never taken drugs. This made investigators wonder whether this murder was part of the series or something new. She had also been found seven miles downriver from where other bodies had been left. Did they have several killers on their hands, or was just one killer disposing of bodies all over the place? This victim had been covered, like some of the others, and asphyxiated.

Local police decided to enlist the help of the FBI. There were now 11 unsolved cases of prostitute murders in and around Rochester in a 12-month period. The average number of murders per year was three or four. Yet before the FBI even arrived, a hunter found the body of Elizabeth Gibson, a prostitute, on 27 November in a swamp in a neighbouring county. She had been strangled. What linked her to the others was a witness. Jo Ann Van Nostrand, a prostitute, had happened to see a regular client whom she knew as 'Mitch' the day before with a prostitute whom she recognised as Elizabeth Gibson. A newsflash that day on television told her a woman had been found murdered. Jo Ann went directly to the police to tell them about Mitch. They took her to the station, but Jo Ann did not know Mitch's real name or where he worked. However, police believed that she had given them a solid lead. At the very least, they knew how the man operated and what kind of car he drove. What they did not know was that the killer would change cars and still remain in the shadows.

Towards the end of December, several more women were reported missing and one of them was someone everyone had felt certain would never fall victim to a killer. June Cicero was one of the most streetwise prostitutes in Rochester, and another prostitute, Darlene Trippi, had teamed up with Jo Ann Van Nostrand for safety. Just before she disappeared, June Cicero had boasted to the police about how she wasn't afraid of the man. It was he who ought to be afraid of her. They had believed her. Also missing at this time was a black prostitute named Felicia Stephens and the long-missing Maria Welch.

On 31 December, a state trooper on road patrol in a rural area outside Rochester spotted a pair of black jeans discarded and frozen along the roadside. He stopped to investigate and went through the pockets. He found an identification card in the name of Felicia Stephens. With this discovery, everyone assumed that she was dead. It was also clear, since the jeans had been found not far from Salmon Creek, that the killer was returning to former dumping grounds. Then Stephens's boots were found in separate areas. She could not get along in the freezing temperatures without those. A thorough search was almost impossible at that time of year, even with search dogs. Everything was under snow or frozen over, and trying to walk out on the water proved treacherous. Four missing women and no one had found a body; it was frustrating for the police. They decided to fly over the areas where bodies had been found in an attempt to locate more. They flew low over Salmon Creek, scanning back and forth, alert to anything unusual. Suddenly they saw something near a bridge. They flew closer and saw what appeared to be a human figure lying splayed out and face down on the surface of the ice. She was wearing a white top, as Felicia

Stephens had been when last seen, but nothing else. They hovered for a closer look and made out a female with darkish skin, but not black. It could not be Felicia Stephens, but they had three other missing women, so it could be one of them. Then they noticed a Chevrolet Celebrity on the bridge, so they radioed to patrol units on the ground to check it out. A large, overweight man was there and he appeared to be urinating. Then he got into his car and drove away.

When officers arrived at the location, they found the body was that of the streetwise prostitute, June Cicero. She had been asphyxiated by strangulation and then mutilated post-mortem. Her genital area had been sawed clean through, probably while she was frozen. Now the investigators had to learn who this man was who had been on the bridge and find out what he had to say for himself. Perhaps he'd seen something that would help.

Patrol units were hot on the trail of the man in the vehicle and the helicopter team followed. They watched as the car pulled into a car park across the street from the Wedgewood Nursing Home in Spencerport. The driver went into the nursing home, and a check on the registration number revealed that the car belonged to a woman named Clara Neal. The troopers took over while the helicopter team returned to protect the crime scene. They saw that there were fresh footprints in the snow. Those would be good evidence. They preserved the scene and called for more support.

Police went to the nursing home and asked the man in the Celebrity for ID, which he produced. His name was Arthur John Shawcross, aged 44 (although with his greying hair he looked much older), and he said he thought that they'd followed him because he'd urinated out in the woods. That was his story, anyway, and he agreed to cooperate with the police. When asked for his driving licence, he admitted he did not have one and then revealed that he had been in jail for manslaughter.

That revelation struck everyone at once. This was no ordinary citizen who'd happened to get close to a crime scene. This was a one-time killer. The profilers had told them that this offender was returning to his victims, and that could very well be what they'd caught him doing. By a sheer stroke of luck, they had flown over the scene at the very time he'd decided to have another look at his brutal handiwork.

Despite what they now knew, the police weren't sure that they had the killer. They had to be careful. Interrogators often make mistakes by showing their eagerness and trying to rush someone into a confession. They had spent too many hours on this case to go in blind. Shawcross was persuaded to accompany the police to the State Police Barracks for further questioning. He was happy to oblige and even signed forms that gave the police permission to search the car and his home. The police then took both him and Clara Neal (in a different car) to Brockport.

Shawcross openly admitted that he'd been arrested 16 years earlier in Watertown because 'two kids died'. He would not elaborate on these crimes. He insisted it was just a coincidence that he was parked over the body on Salmon Creek, that he was just driving around and had stopped to urinate when the helicopter flew over. He hadn't seen anything. Though excited by what they heard and by the feeling they finally had the killer right in front of them, the investigators continued to build a rapport rather than press for details. They wanted Shawcross to feel comfortable talking with them, because they intended to question him again and they wanted it to be voluntary. They had him in the interrogation room for about five hours, and took Clara home before they released him. He did finally tell them more details about how he had killed the children, raping the little girl anally before he'd strangled her. Everyone was disgusted but they tried not to show their feelings. Shawcross also told them how he'd had sexual relations with his younger sister, and he thought that had something to do with why he had assaulted a child, as well as why he had killed so many people in Vietnam. He liked to talk about his 'accomplishments' there. He'd been quite the soldier. The police decided to release Shawcross in order to make further enquiries. Before they released him, they asked to take his photograph, which Shawcross allowed.

Police then showed it to several of the prostitutes working Lyell Avenue. One was Jo Ann Van Nostrand, who had told the police about 'Mitch'. She immediately identified Shawcross. Several other prostitutes identified him as well. They all knew him as a regular customer who'd never been a problem.

The police quickly built up a profile on Shawcross and his background before talking with him again. They also wanted to know how a sex offender who'd been imprisoned for manslaughter and paedophilia had been released into their area without anyone finding the records. This last part was on everyone's minds, since they had done a thorough search several times. They were stunned when they discovered the truth.

It would appear that, following his release and the constant hounding he was receiving everywhere he went, the parole board decided to cover up his trail and made his file inaccessible (even to other police departments), settling him in Rochester with his wife. During the flurry of publicity surrounding this decision in the weeks that followed, the board defended its decisions by saying that Shawcross would have been released the following year anyway. A year was insignificant. Yet it was a year that had resulted in many deaths.

When officers asked Clara to show them where she and Shawcross had been for their lovers' rendezvous, each place was significant: they were all areas where bodies had been dumped.

Following Shawcross's release, the police kept him under surveillance, and then there was a new development in the enquiry. At a spot not far from where June Cicero's body had been found, a deer hunter stumbled across the frozen body of Felicia Stephens, whose ID and clothing had been found previously on the roadside. She was lying face down, with her buttocks slightly elevated, the way many of the other victims had been found.

The police again went to see Shawcross and asked if he would mind going with them again to clear some things up. In the amiable manner he had adopted with them, he agreed to go and they drove him to places where bodies had been found. They talked with him about Jo Ann Van Nostrand, letting him know what they knew: Shawcross seemed unfazed, even when they said they knew what he'd done. When they told him that he'd been spotted with one of the victims on the last day she was seen alive, he shrugged it off as coincidence. The police reminded him of his legal rights, but he said he didn't have any problem talking to them. As they pressed a little more with evidence they had, Shawcross reacted in anger, but then settled down again. They feared the interview might reach an impasse, yet when Shawcross mentioned how concerned he was about Clara Neal the police knew they had his attention. They suggested that since the car belonged to Clara, she might be involved. Shawcross became agitated by this. He was asked again if Clara was involved. His reply stunned the police momentarily. 'No,' he admitted, hanging his head, 'Clara's not involved.'

The police now knew they were on the brink of Shawcross confessing. Within 28 minutes of starting the interview, he'd come close to admitting what he'd done. In another minute, he was talking about killing Elizabeth Gibson and, as they suspected, he offered reasons of provocation. She'd tried to steal his wallet, so he'd slapped her again and again. (Later he would say that the police had provided this excuse so he had used it.) At one point, he said, she had looked just like his rejecting mother, so he'd continued to hit her. She'd kicked at him and broke the gearstick of his car, which further angered him. He put his wrist against her throat and held it there until she went still. When he let go and checked, she was dead, so he'd driven around with her for a while, looking for a place to dispose of her. When he found one, he'd removed her clothes and placed her face down in the woods. Then he drove home, throwing her clothing out of the car window as he drove along.

Then the police got another vital break in the investigation. A search of Clara's car had revealed an earring that matched one they had found on June Cicero. Shawcross then went on the defensive. He did not believe the police actually had evidence. They brought in his wife and Clara for questioning and then pressured him to spare these two the anguish of a long-drawn-out investigation. He considered this and then asked for a map and the photographs of the victims that they had shown him before. They laid out 16 open cases and he eliminated those that were not associated with him.

For each murder, Shawcross had a reason. Some victims had ridiculed him, some had tried to steal, one would not shut up, several had threatened to turn him in as the killer, and one, the homeless woman, had said she'd tell his wife about their affair. The first victim, Dorothy Blackburn, supposedly had bitten his penis during oral sex. 'There was blood everywhere,' he said. 'I thought I was gonna die.' So, in retaliation, he had grabbed her by the throat and bit into her genital area and then later had strangled her to death. 'I choked her for a good ten minutes.' Some of them he smothered with something over their faces and with others he'd pressed his arm across their throats. As for the mutilation of June Stott, a woman he had known and had welcomed to his home for meals, it was to 'aid in decomposition', because he had 'cared' about her. His explanations were hollow, but at least he was offering details and solving the mysteries.

As Shawcross continued his confession, it became clear what the strange marks were that had been found across Dorothy Blackburn's chest. He said he liked to sit his victims in the front passenger seat of his car before disposing of them, so he used to use a bungee cord to tie them in place. The detectives showed him photographs of the two missing women, Maria Welch and Darlene Trippi. He admitted that he had killed them both and marked on a map where he had left the bodies. Later that evening, he led police to the exact places where he had dumped their bodies. One had been left sitting up in some bushes near the river and the other was dumped in water near some houses. The pool had iced over, making the victim look like some ethereal underwater fairy out of Arthurian mythology. Both women had been strangled.

As police drove Shawcross back from these places, they took him by the area where they had found Felicia Stephens and noticed that he seemed to recognise it, though he initially denied it, saying, 'I don't do black women.' Yet they used what they'd observed of his behaviour as leverage to get him to confess to her murder too. According to Shawcross, Stephens had run up to his car to solicit his business and her head had become caught in his automatic car window, nearly killing her, so he'd pulled her into the car to finish strangling her. He was adamant that there had been nothing intimate; he did not like black prostitutes. (He later told someone he had killed a black prostitute to throw the police off his trail.)

In November 1990, Shawcross was indicted on 10 first-degree murder charges and pleaded not guilty by reason of insanity. After five weeks of dramatic testimony and courtroom demonstrations, the jury was not sufficiently impressed with the defence interpretation of Shawcross's behaviour. They took half a day to find him both sane and guilty of murder in the second degree (not premeditated) on 10 counts. Shawcross was sentenced to 25 years to life on each of the 10 counts, meaning that he would have to serve 250 years in prison before being eligible for a parole hearing.

A second trial for Elizabeth Gibson's murder in Wayne County had been scheduled, but there seemed little reason to proceed. Shawcross's attorney advised him to plead guilty on that charge, which he did, and he was given a further life sentence.

Shawcross died of a heart attack in November 2008.

LEMUEL WARREN SMITH

Lemuel Warren Smith was born in New York in 1941. By the time he was 17, Lemuel stood a massive 6ft 4in tall and played basketball for Amsterdam High. He was considered a local hero for the team and there was talk of a promising future in sports. But, in 1958, the family decided to move to Maryland. Shortly before the move, Smith was arrested for beating to death a woman, Dorothy Waterstreet, with a lead pipe in an Amsterdam dry-cleaner's. It was the first of the many serious crimes committed by Lemuel Smith. However, due to legal technicalities, he never stood trial for this offence.

During the following summer, while under continuing pressure from Amsterdam police, Smith was relocated to Baltimore, Maryland, where he abducted a 25-year-old female and almost beat her to death. A witness interrupted Smith and he ran away from the victim, who survived the savage attack. Smith was quickly arrested and, on 12 April 1959, was sentenced to 20 years in prison for assault.

After nearly 10 years in custody, Smith was paroled in May 1968, and he quickly reasserted his violent nature. On 20 May 1969, he kidnapped and sexually assaulted a woman, but she managed to escape. Later that same day, he kidnapped and raped a 46-year-old friend of his mother's. When the woman convinced Smith to let her go, he was arrested again and eventually sentenced to 4–15 years in a New York prison. Freed on 5 October 1976, it was less than one month before he killed again.

In November, Robert Hedderman, 48, and Hedderman's secretary, Margaret Byron, 59, were found brutally murdered in the back of Hedderman's shop in Albany, New York. Both had been stabbed and their throats had been cut. Human faeces were found at the crime scene, which would later prove valuable. Lemuel Smith worked nearby and hair and blood evidence made him a prime suspect.

On 23 December 1976, while police were investigating the double murder, Joan Richburg, 24, was raped, murdered and mutilated in her car in a car park at the Colonie Shopping Centre, New York. The pattern of brutality and more hair evidence made Smith the prime suspect in that murder as well, but police did not have enough evidence at that time to arrest and question him.

On 10 January 1977, a large black man tried to lure a 22-year-old woman out of a gift shop in Albany. When she resisted, he took her 60-year-old grandmother hostage and threatened to kill her. When members of the public came to her assistance, he threw the woman down, knocking her unconscious, and deliberately stepped on her hand, breaking it. Several years later, the grandmother saw a picture of Smith in the newspaper and identified him as her attacker.

In July 1977, Marilee Wilson, 30, was abducted from downtown Schenectady. She was taken to a wooded area, where she was raped and her body brutalised before being left to die. Her attacker rammed sticks into her mouth and other parts of her body, causing massive internal injuries. She was burnt with a cigarette and bitten on her nose, face and nipples. The bites on Wilson's body left definitive impressions, which would later be of evidential value. Smith was known to frequent the area and witnesses recalled Wilson being accosted by a large black man. Schenectady police made Smith the prime suspect in her murder.

On 19 August 1977, Marianne Maggio, 18, who worked in the same area as Marilee Wilson, was kidnapped and raped. Following the rape, her attacker forced her to drive towards Albany, where police stopped the car and arrested Lemuel Smith without incident.

Now that Smith was in custody, the police had to try to gather as much evidence as was possible to link him to the murders they suspected him of. An officer looking at photographs of Marilee Wilson noticed that a mark on her nose might be a bite mark. She was exhumed and the bite mark was positively matched to an imprint of Lemuel Smith's bite pattern. The police also tried an ingenious experiment, which would turn out to be a major turning point in the investigation of the murders.

In October 1977, Smith was taken to a sports stadium in Albany. He and four other men were randomly placed behind five screens at one end of the stadium. At the other end of the stadium, a police dog was given the scent of the faeces and stained clothing from the Hedderman store murders 11 months earlier. The dog crossed the entire stadium directly to Lemuel Smith. Out of sight of the dog, the five men were randomly rearranged and the experiment was repeated with the same result. It was successful a third time as well.

On 5 March 1978, with the pressure from the dog experiment and the bite mark match, Smith confessed to five murders, including the murder of Dorothy Waterstreet nearly 20 years earlier.

Along with his confessions, Smith revealed disturbing secrets about lifelong mental problems including a claim that he suffered from multiple personality disorder. He said that the spirit of his deceased brother, John Junior, who had died as an infant before Lemuel was born, was controlling him. One counsellor described that other personalities besides John Junior might exist inside Smith. They also determined that he had suffered multiple head injuries as a child and teenager and that he had suffered further mental abuse as a result of overzealous religious convictions, especially from his father.

Smith's lawyers and doctors feared he might not be fit to stand trial by reason of insanity. However, it was decided to go ahead with the rape and kidnapping trials. Two doctors testified to his delusions but stopped short of saying that he was criminally insane. Smith was found guilty of rape in Saratoga County, New York, on 9 March 1978 and was sentenced to 10–20 years in prison.

On 21 July 1978, a four-day trial in Schenectady ended with Smith being found guilty of kidnapping and he was sentenced to another 25 years to life. Soon after this, Lemuel Smith unsuccessfully attempted suicide. In Albany, Smith was indicted for the Hedderman double murder. He was found guilty on 2 February 1979 and sentenced to another 50 years to life. Despite the weight of evidence against him for the murders of Marilee

Wilson and Joan Richburg, it was decided not to proceed with a trial as there was no death penalty, and with the sentences already given to him there was no likelihood of him ever being released. However, despite being incarcerated he would have one last opportunity to kill again; this time, the murder would cause outrage around the country.

In 1981, Lemuel Smith was serving his sentence in the maximum-security Green Haven Correctional Facility. On 15 May 1981, Green Haven corrections officer Donna Payant mysteriously disappeared while on duty. Hundreds of corrections officers combed the entire prison grounds throughout the night and into the following morning. Rubbish bins were periodically emptied into a truck, which two senior correction officers escorted to a rubbish tip 20 miles away. When the rubbish was spread out at the tip, officers found Payant's mutilated body. Her hands were tied around her back. Her uniform was ripped and there was a dark-coloured cord wrapped tightly around her neck. She had severe cutting injuries on her nose, lips and eyelids. Her nipples appeared to have been either cut or bitten off and there were some strange bruises on her cheek and neck. It was the first time in the United States that a female corrections officer had ever been killed inside a prison. New York governor, Hugh Carey, officially vowed 'a swift response'.

The same medical examiner who had discovered the bite marks on Marilee Wilson was called to examine bite marks found on Payant's body. He quickly identified the bite marks, and Lemuel Smith was charged with Payant's murder on 6 June 1981. The charge carried a mandatory death sentence.

The trial of Lemuel Smith opened in Duchess County Court in Poughkeepsie on 20 January 1983. The prosecution case relied solely on the identification of the bite marks, which had been identified as those of Smith from a previous murder that he had confessed to. Despite his defence team trying to rule out the evidence from the previous trial as being inadmissible, it was allowed. On 21 April, the jury found him guilty of the murder of

Donna Payant. Despite being sentenced to death in the electric chair, Smith successfully lodged an appeal based on a breach of the American constitution. The Appeal Court ruled in his favour and his sentence was commuted to life. As punishment for the Payant murder, and due to the threat he posed even while in prison, Lemuel Smith spent the next 20 years of his life in near-isolation, the longest such span by a prisoner at that time. He will spend the rest of his natural life behind bars.

GERALD STANO

The young Gerald Stano (b. 1951) acquired several minor criminal convictions, and in 1967 the Stano family moved to Norristown, Pennsylvania. His parents hoped that the change in environment might help curb his odd behaviour. However, nothing changed and if anything he became worse. He began missing school on a regular basis and continued to steal money from his family and classmates. On one occasion, he stole a large sum of money from his father's wallet and paid members of the school track team to run behind him so he would finish a race first. Despite all of his failings, Stano finally received his high-school diploma at the age of 21. But it did not take long for him to revert to his old ways. Just weeks after being hired, he was sacked for stealing money from employees' purses. From then on he moved from job to job, unable to hold a job down for any length of time. In the early 1970s, Stano moved to Florida where he again moved from one job to another. In 1975, he tried to get his life back on track. He stopped his previous abuse of alcohol and drugs and began dating a local hairstylist. Stano fell in love with the pretty 22-year-old woman and, on 21 June 1975, they married. Within months of his wedding, he started drinking heavily again and began to physically abuse his wife. Six months later, the marriage was over; his wife filed for divorce and he moved back in with his parents.

On Sunday, 17 February 1980, Detective Sergeant Paul Crow was called to a desolate area behind the Daytona Beach Airport, where two college students had stumbled on the decomposed remains of a young woman. As Detective Crow examined the crime scene, he noted the condition and location of the body. It was covered with branches and obviously posed. The victim was lying on her back, with her arms positioned at her side and her head turned upward. The body was completely clothed and there was no visual indication of sexual molestation. Crow surmised that she had been dead for at least two weeks and, because of the advanced state of decomposition, it was not immediately clear what had caused her death. When he turned the young woman over, Crow discovered several puncture wounds to the back, suggesting that her killer had become enraged and had stabbed her repeatedly. The young woman was later identified as 20-year-old Mary Carol Maher, a local college student. An autopsy revealed that she had suffered multiple stab wounds to the back, chest and legs.

On the morning of 25 March 1980, a local prostitute walked into the Daytona Beach police station and asked to speak with an officer. Detective Jim Gadberry escorted the young woman into his office and took her statement. She said that she had been walking along Atlantic Avenue when a man in a red Gremlin with tinted windows pulled up beside her. The two quickly agreed on a price and she directed him to her motel room. Once there, the man refused to pay up front and the two began to argue. The man produced a knife and sliced her right thigh open. Afterwards, he berated her for prostituting herself and fled the scene. The wound was deep and the young woman needed 27 stitches. She was extremely angry about the attack and made it clear that she wanted the man arrested for assault. She was adamant that she would recognise him if she saw him again and described him as being of average height and slightly overweight. He wore glasses and had a moustache. She was also certain that she had just seen the man's car parked at a local apartment building.

After taking the woman's statement, Gadberry drove to the apartment complex the woman had mentioned in her statement.

He was unable to spot the man's car, but less than a mile away he spotted a red 1977 Gremlin that appeared to match her description. He wrote down the car's registration number. On his arrival back at police headquarters, Gadberry did a computer check on the Gremlin's registration number and discovered that the vehicle was registered to Gerald Eugene Stano, a 28-year-old man from Ormond Beach. As the detective looked over the suspect's records, he noticed that the man had a long list of arrests, but had never been convicted of anything. He had also been a prime suspect in several other assaults on local prostitutes. Gadberry took a picture of Stano to the victim, and she positively identified the suspect as the man who had assaulted her. She signed an affidavit charging him with aggravated assault and battery.

On 1 April 1980, Gadberry and Detective Crow brought Stano in for questioning. Before the interrogation began, Crow gave Gadberry certain questions to ask Stano to which he already knew the answers. He wanted to see how Stano reacted when telling the truth and when lying. Crow soon discovered that whenever Stano was telling the truth he would lean forward in his chair and when he was lying he would lean back.

After an hour of relentless questioning, Stano finally confessed to the assault on the prostitute. Then Crow took over. Sitting directly across from Stano, he said: 'Gerald, I'm Detective Sergeant Paul Crow. I've got a problem that I think you might be able to help me with. I've got a missing girl [...] I just wondered if you had seen her.' Crow then produced a photo of Mary Carol Maher and placed it on the table. Stano studied the photo for a few minutes. 'Yeah, I've seen her before,' he said. He then went on to describe seeing her at a local hotel the previous month. When Crow asked him if he had approached the girl, Stano leaned back and said he gave her a ride to Atlantic Avenue and had not seen her since then.

Crow knew Stano was lying and decided to change the subject. 'Gerald, what are you upset about?' he asked. Stano leaned forward and looked directly into Crow's eyes. 'Today's "the day you got me day",' he said. 'Today's the day my parents adopted me.' According to police reports, Stano began to talk about his childhood and his relationship with his parents. After a while, Crow brought the subject back to Mary Carol Maher. Stano changed his earlier statement about dropping her off on Atlantic Avenue and said that he drove her around a while and eventually stopped at a local supermarket to purchase beer. After more questioning, Stano finally confessed to her murder. He told the officer: 'I stabbed her several times in the chest. She opened the door and tried to get out, but I cut her on the leg and pulled her back in. I shut the door, she fell forward and hit her head against the dashboard and started gurgling. I stabbed her a couple more times in the back, because she was messing up my car. She just went limp. So I took her.'

They then drove to the location where Stano said he had disposed of the body. When they arrived at the location, Stano showed Crow and Gadberry where he left the body and described how he had posed it. When they drove back to the police station, Stano signed a written confession to Mary Carol's murder.

Later that evening, Stano was asked about another missing female, Toni Van Haddocks, a 26-year-old prostitute, who had been reported missing on 15 February. Crow took a photo of the girl into the interrogation room and placed it in front of Stano. As soon as he looked at the photo, Stano leant back and said he had never met her. Crow knew he was lying, but he did not yet have enough information about the case to question him and decided to wait. In the meantime, Stano was charged with the first-degree murder of Mary Carol Maher and remanded in custody.

On 15 April 1980, a resident of Holly Hill, near Daytona Beach, discovered a human skull in his garden. Police scoured the area and eventually found more bones and some torn clothing. Apparently wild animals had discovered the corpse and scattered the remains. A post-mortem later identified the victim as Toni Van Haddocks. Her death was attributed to multiple stab wounds to the head.

Once Crow learnt of the victim's identity, he brought Stano back to the interrogation room and began questioning him. Stano initially denied killing the young woman, but with each hour that passed he began to crumble. In the end, he confessed and signed a written confession to the murder of Toni Van Haddocks. Crow began to wonder how many more women Stano might have murdered and started to search through all the unsolved cases dating back to 1975. The list soon began to grow.

Sixteen-year-old Linda Hamilton was found dead on 22 July 1975, near an old Native American burial ground. She had last been seen walking down Atlantic Avenue. In January 1976, the body of 24-year-old Nancy Heard was found near Bulow Creek Road, just north of Ormond Beach. Her body was posed and covered with tree branches. She had last been seen hitchhiking, also on Atlantic Avenue. Ramona Neal was another possible victim. She was an 18-year-old girl from Georgia, who was found in Tomoka State Park in May 1976. Her body had also been concealed with branches.

It is a known fact that some serial killers will roam hundreds of miles to find a victim and Crow began to wonder just how many counties Stano might have travelled through in search of his prey. After going through all of the local files, he started to look into nearby counties. In Bradford, 100 miles west of Daytona, the body of a young woman was discovered in a swampy area. She had last been seen in Daytona Beach, near Atlantic Avenue. The crime scene was similar to the others, including the now all-too-familiar branches used to conceal the body. In the small town of Titusville, 50 miles south of Brevard County, another young woman was discovered. She had last been seen hitchhiking along Atlantic Avenue, in Daytona Beach. She was found posed and covered in brush.

While looking through Stano's past, Crow learnt that Stano

had lived in various parts of Florida since the early 1970s and briefly in New Jersey. Crow contacted the police department in Stuart, Florida, and learnt that they had several unsolved murders of young women in that area during the mid-1970s. Crow then contacted officials in New Jersey and learnt of at least two similar murders that took place in the early 1970s. All of the victims were young women, posed and covered with tree branches. Detective Crow knew it was not going to be easy getting Stano to admit to another murder, though, let alone a dozen or so more.

Finally, with the weight of evidence amassing against him, Stano decided that he would have to arrange a plea-bargain in order to save his own life. Prosecutors had the confessions, but they did not want to risk a long court battle and agreed that if Stano pleaded guilty to the murders of Mary Carol Maher, Toni Van Haddocks and Nancy Heard, and that his confessions in the other cases would be read into the court record, he would receive three consecutive life sentences, each carrying a mandatory minimum of 25 years behind bars. Stano agreed and, on 2 September 1981, the court accepted the plea-bargain and imposed the three life sentences.

While serving his sentence, Stano enjoyed bragging about his crimes and revelled in all the publicity he received while in the county jail. However, when he was moved to a state prison, no one seemed to care about him. Stano decided to contact Crow and admit to further murders, even if it meant he could face the death penalty.

During the interviews with Crow that followed, Stano confessed to the murders of 17-year-old Cathy Lee Scharf, of Port Orange, Florida, whose decomposed remains were discovered on 19 January 1974, in a ditch near Titusville, Florida; 24-year-old Susan Bickrest, of Daytona Beach, Florida, whose body was found floating in Spruce Spring Creek in December 1975; and 23-year-old Mary Muldoon, of Ormond Beach, Florida, whose body was discovered in a ditch in November 1977. As Stano recalled each murder, Crow was awestruck at the sheer magnitude of the crimes. How could such a young man have committed so many murders in such a short period of time?

Stano went on to confess to the murders of 19-year-old Janine Ligotino and 17-year-old Ann Arceneaux, whose bodies were discovered in 1973 near Gainesville, Florida; 17-year-old Barbara Ann Baur, whose body was found in 1974 near Starke, Florida, and an as-yet-unidentified woman, who was found in Altamonte Springs, Florida, in 1974. In addition there were 34-year-old Bonnie Hughes, 18-year-old Diana Valleck, 21-year-old Emily Branch, 17-year-old Christina Goodson, 23-year-old Phoebe Winston, 18-year-old Joan Foster and 12-year-old Susan Basile.

As their meeting was about to end, Stano remembered two others: 35-year-old Sandra DuBose, whose body was discovered on a deserted road near Daytona Beach in 1978, and 17-year-old Dorothy Williams, whose body was discovered in a drainage ditch near Atlantic Avenue in 1979. Stano assured Crow that he had now confessed to every murder he had ever committed.

On 8 June 1983, Stano entered guilty pleas in the murders of Susan Bickrest and Mary Muldoon. He waived his right to a hearing and Judge Foxman sentenced him to death. Stano showed no emotion as the sentence was read and was quickly escorted back to Florida State Prison. In September 1983, Stano was convicted of Cathy Lee Scharf's murder. The state allowed Stano's taped confession as evidence, in which he admitted to picking up Scharf while she was hitchhiking and then murdering her. The jury convicted Stano of first-degree murder and recommended death. The trial court found four aggravating factors: he had a previous conviction for a violent felony; the murder was committed during a kidnapping; the murder was heinous, atrocious, or cruel; and the murder was cold, calculated and premeditated. The trial court sentenced Stano to death, and two years later his conviction and sentence were affirmed on appeal.

During the next three years, Stano went on to confess to more murders. It is unknown how many he actually committed and some began to wonder if he was confessing to some he had only heard about through the grapevine. Police continued to collect names, but no further charges were ever brought.

On 22 May 1986, the governor of Florida signed Stano's first death warrant. After many stays of execution and appeals, Stano was finally executed in the electric chair on 23 March 1998. Gerald Stano said nothing to the guards as they escorted him down the path to the death chamber. As the guards strapped him into the chair, Raymond Neal waited anxiously behind the witness-viewing window, approximately 3ft away from the man who had murdered his sister. Neal later told reporters. 'The power slammed into him and he jerked as much as he could and that was it. I saw the life going out of his hands. I felt like a ton of bricks had been lifted off my back. Afterward, me and my brothers smoked cigars to celebrate. I can't express the feeling. I felt so much better. I'm so glad Florida has the guts to keep the electric chair. At least there was a split-second of pain. With lethal injection, you just go to sleep.' In the end, Gerald Stano had confessed to the murders of 41 women. Several of the victims have yet to be identified. Most police officials now consider the cases closed.

WILLIAM SUFF, AKA THE RIVERSIDE PROSTITUTE KILLER

Very little is known about William Suff's early life. According to classmates at school, Suff (b. 1950) was a friendly person. However, the image of the friendly personality was brought crashing down in 1974 when Suff, then 24, and his former wife were arrested and later convicted of beating their two-year-old daughter to death. Suff was sentenced to 70 years in prison, but earnt his parole in March 1984, after serving only 10 years. His wife served a mere 20 months before having her conviction overturned.

When paroled, Suff appeared to revert to his old self. Friends described him as a mild-mannered man, who kept to himself and spent his free time writing stories and cookery books. On at least one occasion, his chilli recipes won him first prize at a local cooking competition. However, this mild-mannered man had a dark secret, which was soon to surface.

On 30 October 1986, a local man was wending his way through the streets of an industrial estate a short distance from Riverside, California, near Agua Mansa Road and Market Street, when he noticed the body of a young woman wedged in a drainage ditch. The woman was lying on her back, her blouse and shorts ripped to shreds. She was covered in blood and it looked as though her genital area had been mutilated. The young woman was later identified as 23-year-old Michelle Yvette Gutierrez, a former resident of Corpus Christi, Texas. A post-mortem revealed she had suffered severe trauma to the anal and vaginal areas and multiple stab wounds were discovered on her face, chest and buttocks. Ligature marks on her neck suggested that she had been strangled as the gruesome mutilations took place. Police had a brutal murder on their hands and few clues to follow.

On 11 December, police were called to the scene of another murder. The victim was 24-year-old Charlotte Jean Palmer, a transient from Anna, Illinois. Her body was discovered near Highway 74 in Romoland, approximately 25 miles away from the Gutierrez murder site, and it was not immediately apparent whether the two deaths were related. To make matters worse, Palmer's body was so badly decomposed the coroner was unable to determine the cause of death.

In January 1987, the naked and mutilated body of 37-year-old Linda Ann Ortega was found along a dirt road in Lake Elsinore. She had been dead for at least three days and high levels of alcohol and cocaine were found in her blood. Ortega, a part-time fast-food worker, had convictions for drugs and prostitution.

Police now had three similar murders and were beginning to wonder if they had a serial killer on their hands. Their worst fears were confirmed on 2 May 1987, when the body of 27-year-old Martha Bess Young was discovered in a ravine not far from the Ortega murder site. She was discovered naked and in a spread eagled position. As with Ortega, she had convictions for prostitution and high levels of drugs were found in her body. The County Coroner later determined that she had been dead for approximately three weeks and had died from a combination of being strangled coupled with a lethal dose of amphetamines that had been administered to her.

It was almost two years before the killer's evil deeds surfaced again. This might have been due to the fact that the killer had found a new location or locations for disposing of the bodies or perhaps another reason forced him to stop temporarily.

Regardless, by 1989, two years since his last known murder, the killer had struck again. On 27 January 1989, the body of 37-year-old Linda Mae Ruiz, a known prostitute, was discovered on the beach of Lake Elsinore. The victim's head was buried in the sand and the post-mortem revealed large quantities of alcohol in the blood. Sand was found in the victim's throat and the cause of death was listed as acute asphyxiation. Five months later, on 28 June 1989, the body of 28-year-old Kimberly Lyttle was discovered in Cottonwood Canyon. Again, she was a known prostitute and drug user. Her bruised and battered body was taken to the County Coroner's office, where a post-mortem revealed the presence of alcohol and drugs. The official cause of death was listed as asphyxiation. A forensic examination revealed several pubic hairs and fibres, unrelated to the victim herself, on her body. This evidence alone told them very little about the killer, but if a suspect were to emerge, the samples could play a major role in identifying him. On 11 November 1989, the bludgeoned and mutilated body of 36-year-old Judy Lynn Angel was found near Temescal Canyon Road, just northwest of Lake Elsinore. She had arrests for prostitution and possession of drugs. During the post-mortem, the coroner discovered several deep gashes on the victim's hands. The injuries appeared to be defence wounds, which meant she had tried to fend off her attacker. The victim had also suffered several blows to the face, which ultimately crushed her skull.

On 13 December 1989, a month after the discovery of Judy Lynn Angel's remains, the body of 23-year-old Christina Leal was found in Quail Valley. Unlike previous victims, she was fully clothed and did not appear to have suffered serious abuse or mutilation prior to death. Like the other victims, though, she had previous arrests for drugs and prostitution. A crime scene examination revealed tyre tracks and the police made several impressions that could later be used to compare with a suspect's vehicle. The victim's hands were encased in paper bags to preserve anything that might be under the nails.

Later that day, during the victim's autopsy, the County Coroner discovered that the victim had been stabbed directly in the heart. Due to the victim's clothing, the wound was not immediately noticeable, which suggested the killer had dressed her after the murder. The knife wound, while potentially fatal, was not the immediate cause of death. The victim had died as a result of asphyxiation by strangulation. Several pubic hairs and fibres were also removed from the body, which would later be matched to the ones discovered on Kimberly Lyttle. Then, as the coroner inspected the victim's genital area, he made a startling discovery. The killer had pushed a light bulb up into the victim's womb, something no investigator had ever seen done before. The killer's crimes were escalating. The murders were becoming more perverse and the time between the killings was getting shorter. There was no doubt that he would strike again, but without a single suspect to pursue it was impossible to know where to focus the investigation.

On the morning of 18 January 1990, in Lake Elsinore, a jogger had stumbled upon the half-naked body of a female, whom police soon identified as a 24-year-old prostitute named Darla Jane Ferguson. She had died as a result of strangulation, which was so severe that she had nearly bitten off her own tongue. As with the previous crime scene, police found tyre tracks and made several impressions. These were later matched to those taken from other crime scenes.

Less than a month later, on 8 February 1990, farmers working at an orchard in High Grove discovered the naked body of 35-year-old Carol Lynn Miller. Another known prostitute and drug addict, Carol had gone missing one month earlier. The cause of death was listed as multiple stab wounds to the chest and asphyxiation. The coroner also made note of a wound near Carol's right nipple. Pubic hairs were discovered on the victim, which were later matched to the ones on file from the previous murders.

On the afternoon of 6 November 1990, a man working at an industrial plant on Palmyrita Avenue in northeast Riverside, not far from the location where Miller was found, discovered the naked and mutilated corpse of a female hidden under some tree branches. This was by far the killer's most brutal crime yet. The victim, 33-year-old Cheryl Coker, a prostitute and drug user, had suffered severe mutilations to her body and, most shocking of all, the killer had removed her right breast and placed it next to her. Police found shoe prints at the scene and took several photographs and impressions before transporting the body to the mortuary. It was later determined that the victim had died as a result of strangulation.

On 21 December 1990, a handyman was emptying dustbins at a factory complex on Iowa Avenue when he discovered the naked and carefully posed body of a young woman. Police identified the victim as 27-year-old Susan Tenfold, a local prostitute and drug addict. There was no evidence of mutilation and the County Coroner later determined that she died of strangulation.

Forty-two-year-old Kathleen Leslie Milne was discovered on 19 January 1991. A passing motorist spotted her body alongside the road northwest of Lake Elsinore. According to the post-mortem report, she had been rendered unconscious by several blows to the head and then strangled. She had been dead less than 24 hours. As the killer's body count continued to rise, so did the demands for justice. There was public outrage about the faceless killer. People were claiming that the police were not putting much effort into the investigation due to the victims being prostitutes. In an effort to find the killer, all available law enforcement personnel began combing the area. At one point, the manhunt grew to include more than 20 law-enforcement agencies. Regardless of the spotlight on him, the killer was undaunted and continued to elude identification and capture.

On the morning of 27 April 1991, a tramp stumbled on the body of 24-year-old Cherie Michelle Payseur, a part-time maid and prostitute. Her lifeless body had been left in a flowerbed in a bowling alley car park. She had been raped and strangled and was found with a toilet plunger protruding from her vagina. On 4 July 1991, picnickers near Railroad Canyon Road discovered the remains of 37-year-old Sherry Ann Latham, a known prostitute and drug user. Her hand was wrapped around some nearby branches, suggesting that she was still alive when the killer left. She had made one last feeble attempt to crawl away before succumbing to her injuries. The post-mortem revealed that she had been strangled. Feline hairs were discovered on her corpse. According to her friends, she did not own a cat, leading police to wonder if her killer did.

Just when it seemed the police were never going to get a break, they had some luck. On 15 August 1991, a man driving a grey van picked up a prostitute near the University of California. The woman later told police that everything was going fine at first, but then the man suddenly became angry and began assaulting her for no reason. Luckily, the girl managed to jump out of the vehicle and run down the street. The man quickly sped off, but stopped at a nearby corner and picked up the girl's friend, a 23-year-old prostitute named Kelly Marie Hammond. Later that same night, investigators found Hammond's naked body near the intersection of Sampson Avenue and Delilah Street. The victim had been strangled and her body was still warm. Police had just missed the killer they so desperately sought. The woman who escaped the killer's clutches was able to help investigators create a composite sketch of the suspect and his vehicle. Police quickly released details of the van and the driver to the newspapers and television.

On 13 September 1991, a construction worker found the body of 30-year-old Catherine McDonald, a known drug user and prostitute, near a building site in Tiscany Hills. Police first thought the murder might be unrelated to the others. The victim was African-American, whereas all the previous victims had been Caucasian. However, on closer inspection they noticed that the victim's right breast had been removed. But, unlike Cheryl Coker's mutilation, it was not lying next to the victim's corpse. Apparently the killer had taken it with him. Investigators surmised that the killer had heard the recent broadcasts stating that the killer was probably a white male who preyed exclusively on white women. The murder of a black woman was to show the media he had no fear.

The following month, on 30 October 1991, a man was driving along Summerhill Drive when he spotted something he thought was a mannequin by the roadside; a closer inspection showed it to be the body of a woman. The victim was 35-year-old Delilah Zamora Wallace, a prostitute, drug addict and mother of five. The coroner listed the cause of death as asphyxiation. The death toll was now at 18 and investigators still didn't have one viable suspect. The killer was striking at least once a month now. Investigators knew it was only a matter of time before he killed again and with each new killing he was becoming more brazen.

Two days before Christmas 1991, Eleanor Ojeda Casares' naked body was found near Victoria Avenue, close to the Riverside police station. The 39-year-old drug addict and prostitute had been strangled and her right breast was missing. The proximity of the body to the police station angered police, who were convinced that the killer purposely placed her there in order to embarrass them.

On the night of 9 January 1992, Officer Frank Orta was

patrolling University Avenue, an area known for prostitution and drugs, when he suddenly noticed a van, matching the description of the suspect's van, making an illegal U-turn. When Orta flashed his lights and siren, the 1989 Mitsubishi pulled off to the side and stopped. The driver was a man by the name of William Suff. He was polite, but on running his name through the computer, Orta discovered that Suff's driving licence was suspended and his vehicle registration had expired. The suspect was then transported to the Riverside police station for questioning.

Back at Riverside police headquarters, the police arrested Suff on suspicion of multiple murders. They began questioning him. The interrogation lasted for hours and Suff repeatedly denied any involvement in the prostitution murders. The police knew they were going to need evidence to gain a conviction and without a confession their job became even harder. The police obtained blood and hair samples from Suff, though, which, when analysed, would be crucial to the prosecution case.

Microscopic samples of hair found at two murder scenes matched Suff's own hairs, and fibres from a pillow, blanket and sleeping bag found inside Suff's van were similar to those discovered near the bodies of Kim Lyttle and Christina Leal. In addition, a towel that had covered Lyttle's naked body contained two fibres similar to the carpeting in Suff's vehicle. Other fibres, which were found on Suff's car seat, matched those of a T-shirt and sock found on Leal's body.

On 28 February 1992, Suff was arraigned before Judge Becky Dugan in Division 22 of the Riverside Municipal Courthouse on two charges of murder relating to Kim Lyttle and Christina Leal. Suff entered a plea of not guilty. After hearing arguments from both sides, the judge ruled that there was enough evidence to send the case for trial, which began on 25 March 1995 before Judge W Charles Morgan in the Riverside Hall of Justice. A jury consisting of seven men and five women was sworn in to hear the case. After 54 days of testimony and four days of deliberations, the jury found Suff guilty on 12 of the 13 counts of first-degree murder and one count of attempted murder. The jury also found Suff guilty of multiple murder, use of a deadly weapon and lying in wait. The following day, 17 August 1995, Suff was given the death sentence. Although convicted of 12 murders, police believe he may have been responsible for as many as 22.

William Suff is still on death row at San Quentin Prison, where he is awaiting execution. He continues to maintain his innocence and claims that police used him as a scapegoat. It has been rumoured that Suff used two of his victims' breasts in chillis he prepared for the Riverside County employees' annual picnic, but that information has never been confirmed.

EDMUND EMIL KEMPER, AKA THE CO-ED KILLER

Edmund Kemper was born in Burbank, California, in 1948. Kemper began displaying strange behaviour at an early age. He mutilated two of the family cats and was caught playing games with his sister that involved portraying death rituals. Following these incidents, he was sent to live with his father but later ran away back to his mother, who again sent him away, this time to live with his grandparents on a farm in California. The farm life, away from his family, was not good for him. He soon became bored, agitated, lonely and homesick.

However, the event that took place on 27 August 1964 when Kemper was still only 15 would change the rest of his life. On that day, he was with his grandparents on their farm. There was an argument with his 66-year-old grandmother. Kemper became so angry he picked up a rifle and went to shoot birds. When his grandmother told him off again, he turned and shot her instead. He shot her in the head and then shot her twice in the back. Still enraged, he also stabbed her repeatedly with a kitchen knife in the back. But then he had to do something to hide his crime from his grandfather. He dragged her body into the bedroom. Then his 72-year-old grandfather drove up; Kemper heard his car outside. Kemper went to the window and made the decision to shoot his grandfather as well. As his grandfather got out of the car, Kemper raised the rifle and shot him, then hid the body in the garage. Not knowing what to do next, he phoned his mother in Montana, who alerted the police. Kemper was then arrested and charged with his grandparents' murders.

Not surprisingly, following the motiveless double murder Kemper was diagnosed with what was called 'personality trait disturbance, passive aggressive type'. He was committed to the Atascadero State Hospital for the Criminally Insane, where he remained until 1969. He was released against the objections of psychiatrists and placed into his mother's custody in Santa Cruz. By this time, Kemper was 20 years of age and a giant of a man measuring 6ft 7in tall and weighing around 300lb. He also managed to have his juvenile records sealed, making it difficult for checks to be carried out on him in the future.

For the next two years, Kemper held down odd jobs and enjoyed cruising around. He also made a habit of picking up young female hitchhikers. Santa Cruz seemed to be just the place at that time for beautiful Californian students. Kemper, after missing out on his teens while in the mental hospital, took an interest in these young women and their willingness to accept rides. Working for the Highways Department allowed him freedom to cruise the highways. But more and more his thoughts turned to what he could do to the female students – he prepared to embark on his killing spree, placing plastic bags, knives, a blanket and handcuffs in the boot of his car.

On 7 May 1972, Kemper picked up two girls from Fresno State College, Mary Ann Pesce and Anita Luchessa, who were hitchhiking. He took them to a secluded area where he stabbed them both to death and then took the bodies home to his mother's house, where he dismembered them, playing with various organs and taking Polaroid pictures. He then packed their remains in plastic bags and buried the bodies in the Santa Cruz Mountains, throwing the heads into a deep ravine beside the road. When the girls failed to arrive at their destination, their families contacted the police. But runaways were all too frequent in those days and the girls had left behind no clues as to where they had gone, so there was little the authorities could do. Then, on 15 August, the remains of a female head were recovered from an area in the mountains and identified as belonging to Pisce. No other remains were found, but it was assumed that both girls were dead.

On 14 September, Kemper picked up a 15-year-old high-school girl named Aiko Koo. He suffocated her and then raped her lifeless body. He took her body back home, just like the others, and dismembered her. The next morning, he was visited by a state psychiatrist who had come to monitor his mental health. All the time the meeting took place, Koo's head lay in the boot of Kemper's car outside. Once his meeting was finished, he then drove back to the mountains and buried the body.

Kemper then waited until 9 January 1973, when he picked up a student from Santa Cruz named Cindy Schall. He forced her into his boot and shot her before bringing her back to his mother's again, having sex with her body, dismembering it, then placing the remains in a bag and throwing them off a cliff into the ocean at Carmel. He had thought of burying her head in his mother's garden, facing up to her bedroom. He said that his mother liked people looking up to her, so he thought that might have been fitting.

Less than two days later, dismembered arms and legs were found on a cliff overlooking the Pacific Ocean. Then an upper torso washed ashore, which was identified via lung X-rays as Schall's. Eventually, a lower torso came in. A surfer also found Schall's left hand, which offered fingerprints, but her head and right hand remained missing.

By now, the town of Santa Cruz was gripped with fear. The young students from the campus were warned not to accept lifts from people outside the safety of the campus. This did nothing to stop Kemper, who drove his mother's car with her university campus ID sticker on the windscreen.

Less than a month after murdering Cindy Schall, Kemper picked two more women up, Rosalind Thorpe and Alice Lui. He picked up Rosalind first and her presence in the car apparently reassured Alice, who willingly got in. Lui sat in the back, right behind Thorpe. As they drove along, Kemper was moving his pistol from down below his leg into his lap. He picked it up and pulled the trigger. Thorpe fell against the window. Lui panicked, and he had to fire through her hands. She was moving around and he missed twice. He hit her in the temple, aimed again and fired, but she was still alive as he approached the university gate; she was breathing loudly and moaning. Two young men were on duty at the security gate, but when they saw Kemper's university sticker, they waved him through. As before, he took the bodies home, where he dismembered them both. He disposed of the remains in Eden Canyon, near San Francisco.

On 4 March, hikers came across a human skull and jawbone not far from Highway 1 in San Mateo County. They were not from the same person. The police searched the area and found another skull that went with the jawbone, so they knew they had two victims who had been killed close together. They had reports of several missing female hitchhikers, so they compared what they had to the descriptions, and identified the remains of Rosalind Thorpe and Alice Lui. Lui had been shot twice in the head, Thorpe once. It was not long thereafter that the university decided to institute a bus system that would assist off-campus students to get safely to their classes.

By now, Kemper was controlled by his need to kill. That Easter, he realised what he had been wanting all along. That weekend, as his mother lay asleep in her bed, he attacked her, repeatedly beating her with a claw hammer until she was dead. He followed this by decapitating her and raping the headless corpse. He finished by removing her larynx and trying to feed it through the waste disposal unit. He then called a friend of his mother's, Sally Hallett, inviting her to a surprise dinner for his mother. Once she arrived, he clubbed and strangled her, cutting off her head and leaving the body in his own bed while he slept in his mother's.

THE USA

On 23 April 1973, the Santa Cruz police received a call that they could not quite believe. It was from a phone booth in Pueblo, Colorado, from Edmund Kemper. He told them that he had committed murder, in fact a double murder, four days previously. He also said that he had killed his mother on Good Friday and her friend a short time later. He told police both bodies were still in the house. He also confessed over the phone to six more murders and asked police to come and arrest him. But the officer who took the first call believed it was a hoax call and ignored it, suggesting that he call again later. Kemper did so, but once again had a difficult time convincing the person at the other end of the line to take him seriously. He continued to place calls until he was able to persuade an officer to check out his mother's house. He said that an officer, Sergeant Aluffi, had been there not long before to confiscate the .44-calibre revolver he had purchased; Aluffi would know.

Sergeant Aluffi did indeed know, and went to the home himself. As he entered, he smelt the revolting odour of decomposition. When he opened a cupboard and saw blood and hair, he secured the scene and called in the coroner and detectives. To their amazement, they found the two bodies, just as Kemper had described. Both had been decapitated, and Kemper's mother's body had been battered and apparently used for darts practice. Her tongue and larynx, Kemper had said, were chopped up, having been placed in the waste disposal unit, which had spat them back out. Police now knew they had captured the Co-Ed Killer.

When Kemper was questioned, the story that unfolded was as bizarre as any the police had yet heard. He went on for hours, confessing everything that he had done to the six students, his mother and her friend. Adding these to the murders of his grandparents years earlier, he had committed 10 murders in all. To prove his story, he took detectives to areas where he had buried or thrown away parts of his victims that had not yet been found. He described having sex with the heads of his victims and said that he'd loved the feeling of totally possessing them and their property.

Edmund Kemper was indicted on eight counts of first-degree murder on 7 May 1973. The Chief Public Defender of Santa Cruz County, attorney Jim Jackson, took on Kemper's defence, which he offered as an insanity plea. While awaiting trial, Kemper twice tried to commit suicide by slashing his wrists, but failed. The trial began on 23 October 1973; three prosecution psychiatrists deemed him sane. It lasted less than three weeks. How many of his outrageous admissions were actually true is anyone's guess. While Kemper had admitted to cannibalism during a psychiatric analysis, he recanted this later, claiming it was meant as part of an insanity defence.

On 8 November, the jury deliberated for five hours, before finding Kemper sane and guilty of eight counts of first-degree murder. Although Kemper hoped to receive the death penalty, he was convicted during a time when the Supreme Court had placed a moratorium on capital punishment and all death sentences were commuted to life imprisonment. The death penalty became applicable only to crimes committed after 1 January 1974. Before passing sentence, the judge asked him what he thought his punishment should be. It wasn't difficult for him to come up with something, as he'd been thinking about this moment since childhood. He told the judge that he believed he ought to be tortured to death. Sadly, that was not an option for the judge to consider. Instead, Kemper was sentenced to life imprisonment.

At the time of writing, Kemper is held in a maximum-security prison at Folsom in California. He has been eligible to be considered for parole periodically, but so far has declined, stating that he did not feel ready to be freed.

CORAL EUGENE WATTS, AKA THE SUNDAY SLASHER

Coral Watts (b. 1953) was originally named Carl but developed an affection for the state of Texas and changed his name to Coral, which is a southern pronunciation of Carl. In his early teens, he began having violent dreams that disturbed his sleeping patterns. He was restless when he slept because he would spend the night trying to fight off what he called 'the evil spirits of women'.

At 15, he felt the urge to act out his dreams. One day he knocked on the apartment door of Joan Gave, 26, while on his paper round. When she answered the door, Watts punched and kicked her. He then continued delivering papers as if nothing happened. The police arrested Watts at his home. He was ordered to undergo psychiatric treatment at the Lafayette Clinic in Detroit. On his sixteenth birthday, Watts was released from the clinic.

Watts returned to high school, graduating at 19. In 1974, after one year of working as a mechanic for a Detroit wheel company, Watts enrolled at Western Michigan University in Kalamazoo. Soon after he enrolled, a series of attacks took place around the campus. Initially they were minor but later they became more serious.

On 25 October 1974, Lenore Knizacky, 23, heard a knock at her door. When she answered it, she was confronted by a young black man who was asking after someone called Charles. Without warning, the man attacked her and started to strangle her. She fought him off and he fled the apartment.

On 30 October, Gloria Steele, 19, also received a knock at her apartment door. Again, it was a black man looking for someone called Charles. As she opened the door, she was also attacked by the man, who this time was armed with a knife. She was stabbed 33 times and died at the scene.

On 12 November, there was a similar incident where the same man tried to attack another woman at her apartment. She managed to fight him off. As the man sped off in a car, the woman was able to catch a glimpse of his number plate. She informed the police, who traced the car to Coral Eugene Watts.

Watts was arrested for assault and battery after the two surviving women identified him in a police line-up. During questioning, Watts confessed to attacking at least a dozen more women, yet he never admitted to the murder of Gloria Steele. He was ordered to undergo psychiatric evaluation at Kalamazoo State Hospital before his court hearing. Psychiatrists found that Watts lacked remorse for his actions and was impulsive, reckless and emotionally detached. However, they did not think he suffered from any kind of psychosis and believed that he was able to distinguish right from wrong. They eventually diagnosed him with antisocial personality disorder. During his stay at the mental hospital, he slipped into temporary depression. He attempted suicide by hanging himself with a cord.

In the summer of 1975, Watts was officially evaluated again. Psychiatrists found that he suffered from depression and posed a danger to himself and others. However, despite his behavioural problems, he was found fit enough to stand trial for the assaults. He was sentenced to one year in jail. Unfortunately, he never stood trial for Steele's murder because prosecutors lacked strong enough evidence to convict him. He was released in the summer of 1976. After his release, he began dating a woman named Valeria, whom he married in 1979.

Over the course of the next 12 months, many more women were attacked and murdered. One of them was Jeanne Clyne, 44, who was attacked on Hallowe'en in 1979, as she walked home from a doctor's appointment. She was accosted in broad daylight along a busy suburban road near her home in Grosse Point Farms. She died from 11 stab wounds. The police were unable to find any evidence leading them to a suspect. Initially, detectives suspected Jeanne's husband, but he was later cleared.

On 20 April 1980 in Ann Arbor, Michigan, high school student Shirley Small, 17, was stabbed to death outside her home. A similar attack took place against Glenda Richmond, also outside her Ann Arbor home, during that summer. The 26-year-old manager of a diner was found dead with 28 stab wounds to her chest. The police found no evidence to point to a viable suspect.

On 14 September, University of Michigan graduate student Rebecca Huff, 20, was found murdered outside her home. She had been stabbed approximately 50 times. Her case was significant because it was one of the first murders that would point to Watts being involved and thus prompted one of Ann Arbor's largest murder investigations. However, it would be two months before the link between Watts and Rebecca Huff was made.

On 15 November, police had a lucky break. Two policemen were patrolling the area around the main street of Ann Arbor around 5am. They noticed a suspicious man in a car slowly following a woman walking home. The woman realised she was being followed and tried to hide in a doorway, hoping the man would move on. The police officers pulled over Watts's car and arrested him for driving with expired number plates and a suspended licence. They also searched his car and found several screwdrivers and a box with wood-filing tools. Yet their most significant find was a dictionary with the etched words, 'Rebecca is a lover', which belonged to Rebecca Huff. It turned out to be their biggest clue yet linking Watts to the murder, yet it still was not enough evidence to convict him.

The police began 24-hour surveillance of Watts. His movements were monitored with the help of a tracking device that was hidden under his car. Officers hoped to catch him in the act so they could arrest and convict him. They were certain that he was the murderer they desperately sought.

However, Watts knew that he was being watched and he suppressed his urge to kill or assault for two months. With no evidence to go on, the police ended their surveillance and decided to bring him in for questioning. He was interviewed for approximately nine hours, but by the end police were still no further forward. Eventually, he was released from police custody due to lack of evidence.

At the time, police suspected Watts of at least two attempted murders and believed him to have possibly committed five in and around the Detroit area. In the spring of 1981, Watts moved to

Columbus, Texas, where he found work at an oil company. He spent the weekend nights driving more than 70 miles to the Houston area, which became his new hunting ground.

On Sunday, 23 May 1982, Michele Maday, 20, heard a knock at her Houston apartment door. When she opened it, a suspicious-looking man stood before her. Suddenly, the stranger attacked; he beat her and choked her into unconsciousness. While she lay on the floor, the man went to her bathroom, filled her bath with water, and then drowned her before running away.

Later that day, Lori Lister, 21, left her boyfriend's home and drove back to her Houston apartment. She parked her car and walked towards the front door of her apartment building. She was not aware that she was being followed. As she got out her key and approached the stairs to her apartment, a man with a red hooded sweatshirt suddenly came up behind her and strangled her into semi-unconsciousness. She was certain she was going to die, but managed to let out a small scream. The neighbours overheard the muffled cry and immediately called the police. In the meantime, the man dragged Lori up the stairs to her apartment where he confronted her room-mate Melinda Aguilar, 18. The attacker threatened to slash Melinda's throat if she screamed. He then choked her until her body went limp. The man had no idea that she was just pretending to be unconscious. He took some hangers and wrapped Melinda's hands behind her back and placed her on the bed. Then he wrapped Lori's hands and feet with hangers. While Melinda was in the bedroom, the intruder went to the bathroom and filled the bath with water. Melinda waited for an opportune moment and then jumped off the bedroom's first-floor balcony. She screamed for help, hoping that it wasn't too late to save her friend.

Moments later, the police arrived. The intruder, who heard the sirens, tried to escape but police apprehended him in the apartment complex courtyard. The neighbour who had initially alerted the police ran to Lori's apartment and found her head submerged in the bath. Luckily, she just managed to escape death. Police identified her attacker as Carl 'Coral' Eugene Watts, 29, a Houston mechanic. When they asked him why he tried to kill the women, he told them that they had 'evil eyes' and he wanted to 'release their spirits'.

However, it was difficult building a full case against Watts because of the different methods he had used to kill. He never sexually assaulted his victims and chose strangers to attack. He rarely left evidence behind at the scene because he killed within minutes of encountering his victims.

Following the attacks on Lori Lister and Melinda Aguilar in May 1982, Harris County Assistant District Attorney Ira Jones came up with an idea that would prompt Watts to make a specific and detailed confession to the crimes of which he was suspected. Jones offered Watts a deal. In exchange for information and murder confessions, he would receive immunity to murder charges. Watts agreed and several days later he took police to the burial sites of three of his victims. Watts eventually admitted attacking 19 women, 13 of whom he said he murdered.

Watts told police that he was responsible for the 1979 Detroit murder of Jeanne Clyne, although he did not admit to killing Glenda Richard, Shirley Small or Rebecca Huff, despite Huff's dictionary being found in his car. He was more forthcoming about his Houston victims. He confessed to drowning University of Texas student Linda Tilley, 22, in her apartment complex swimming pool in September 1981. He also admitted to stabbing to death Elizabeth Montgomery, 25, one week later.

Watts confessed to killing another woman just a few miles away on the same day Elizabeth Montgomery was murdered. Susan Wolf, 21, was returning home from a shopping trip for ice cream when she was stabbed to death several feet from her apartment. Watts admitted to another murder that occurred in January 1982, that of Phyllis Tamm, 27, whom he attacked as she was out jogging. Watts claimed that he choked her with his hands and then hung her from a tree branch with an elastic strap.

Two days later, he murdered architecture student Margaret

Fossi, 25; who apparently died from a blow to the throat. Her body was found in the boot of her car at Rice University. Watts said that he took her shoes, the blueprints she was carrying and her handbag and burnt them. Interestingly, Watts often stole items from his victims and burnt them, hoping to 'kill the spirit'. He claimed that the reason he committed the murders was because the women had 'evil eyes'.

Watts also told police that he slashed the throat of a woman trying to change a flat tyre on the side of the freeway. That same month, he claimed to have attacked two other Houston women, one whose throat was also slashed and the other who was stabbed with an ice pick. Amazingly, all three women had managed to survive the fearsome attacks.

Watts also confessed to the murders of Elena Semander, 20; Emily LaQua, 14; Anna Ledet, 34; Yolanda Gracia, 21; Carrie Jefferson, 32; Suzanne Searles, 25 and Michele Maday, 20. He also admitted to attacking three other women. Despite his confession, he was never charged with any of the murders because of the immunity bargain he had struck.

Watts is alleged to have admitted to at least 80 more murders in Michigan and Canada. However, he didn't give investigators the details of any of those crimes because he was not granted immunity for them. In the end, his strategy to receive the lightest possible penalty for his crimes worked. In court, he pleaded guilty to one count of burglary with intent to kill, just as he bargained for. He eventually received 60 years in a penitentiary, and made a chilling statement. He told the police, 'If they ever let me out, I'll kill again.' They had no doubt that he would keep his promise, for he had long since lost control over his violent impulses and needed to kill to be happy.

Several months into his sentence, Watts attempted an escape. He greased himself with hair gel and tried to squeeze out of his cell window. However, his attempt failed when he got stuck. From that moment on, he adopted a more legal method for getting out of prison – he began appealing against his sentence.

In 1989, the Texas Court of Criminal Appeals reviewed his case. The Appeal Court judge stated that Watts, when initially arrested, had failed to be informed that the bath water he attempted to drown Lori Lister in was construed as a lethal weapon. Consequently, the court ruled that he was not required to serve his entire sentence. With remission for good behaviour, his sentence would be halved, giving him a final release date of 9 May 2006. With this, he would be considered one of the first self-confessed serial killers to be legally released in US history. During the interim period, he was eligible for parole. However, he would not be granted it. The Texas Board of Pardons and Paroles refused him parole on six occasions between 1990 and 2004.

In view of Watts's impending release, police in Michigan and Texas were working hard to find old cases in which evidence might have been overlooked. State police forensic scientists were also hoping to use DNA tests, unavailable in the 1980s, to link Watts to some of the crimes. It was clear to the authorities that should Watts be released he would pose a threat to society and undoubtedly kill again.

At last, 22 years after Watts's initial sentencing, new evidence came to light that linked him to a historic murder. In 2004, Joseph Foy came forward claiming that he had witnessed Watts murder a woman in December 1979. Foy had recently seen a television programme where an appeal had gone out to viewers to come forward with any new information on Coral Watts or his crimes. He immediately contacted the police and told them what he had witnessed approximately 25 years earlier.

Foy claimed he had seen murder victim Helen Mae Dutcher, 36, struggling in an alleyway with a man who repeatedly stabbed her in the neck and back. Dutcher died moments later from 12 stab wounds. Foy went to the police station to report the crime and a composite picture of the attacker was drawn up. However, after an investigation the police were unable to identify the attacker.

The police, now in possession of Foy's statement, charged

Watts with Dutcher's murder and he was extradited back to Michigan to stand trial. If he were found guilty, he would have to serve a mandatory life sentence without parole.

In November 2004, Watts's trial began and he entered a plea of not guilty. There then followed various legal arguments about the admissibility of his original murder confessions. In the end, the trial judge agreed for them to be used as they showed evidence of similar fact and a definite pattern of behaviour.

The main prosecution witness was Joseph Foy. The defence suggested that he could not have been close enough to make a positive identification. Foy was 25yd away from the suspect and it was dark on the night in question. On 18 November, the jury returned a verdict. Watts was found guilty of the first-degree murder of Helen Dutcher. Watts reacted to the verdict by rolling his eyes and shaking his head, whereas the victims' families rejoiced after hearing the verdict and 'embraced each other and Joseph Foy'. On 7 December, Watts was sentenced to life imprisonment with no parole.

Following on from this trial, authorities in Michigan started making moves to try him for the murder of Western Michigan University student Gloria Steele, who was stabbed to death in 1974. On 25 July 2007, Watts's trial for the Steele murder began in Kalamazoo, Michigan. He was found guilty and sentenced to a further term of life imprisonment.

Watts was at that time incarcerated at a maximum-security prison in Ionia, Michigan. He died there of prostate cancer on 21 September 2007.

ANDREW KOKORALEIS, TOMMY KOKORALEIS, ROBIN GECHT AND EDWARD SPREITZER, AKA THE RIPPER CREW

It was almost a case of history repeating itself. Over 100 years had passed since the infamous murders of Jack the Ripper in Victorian London in 1888. But in 1981 in Chicago a series of grisly murders rekindled the memory of those horrifying murders.

THE USA

A serial killer, dubbed a modern-day Jack the Ripper by the media, was stalking young women in Chicago, killing them and mutilating their bodies. Like the detectives of Victorian London, police had no clues as to the identity of the killer.

The series of killings began on 23 May 1981, when 28-year-old Linda Sutton was abducted from a Chicago suburb. Ten days later, her mutilated body minus the left breast was recovered from a field nearby. She had been bound with handcuffs, had a cloth gag in her mouth and still wore a sweater and knickers; both had been pulled down to her thighs. Stuffed in her socks was a small bundle of dollar bills, so robbery had not been a motive.

On 12 February 1982, a 35-year-old cocktail waitress was abducted from her car. She had possibly sought help at the time of abduction. Her handbag was on the front seat and the keys were still in the ignition. A search turned up her naked body on an embankment near the road. She had been raped, tortured and mutilated; one of her breasts had been cut off.

A few days later, the body of a Hispanic woman wearing an engagement ring was discovered. She had also been raped and strangled. While her breasts were not removed, they had been badly bitten. Her killer had also masturbated over her body. A psychiatric assessment of this crime pegged the attacker as a local man who probably loved animals and had a family. He also had a dark side that no one knew about, turning into a cruel psychopathic murderer at night.

The next acknowledged victim in the series disappeared. On 15 May 1982, 21-year-old Lorraine Borowski was due to open up the office where she worked. When the other employees turned up for work, they found the office locked. Borowski's shoes and scattered contents from her handbag were strewn outside the door. Police were called at once, but it would be five more months before her body was found, on 10 October, in a nearby cemetery. Advanced decomposition left the cause of death a mystery.

Two weeks later, on 29 May, Shui Mak was reported missing from Hanover Park, in Cook County. Her mutilated body was found at Barrington on 30 September.

On 13 June, prostitute Angel York was picked up in a van. She told police she had been picked up by two men in a red van who initially handcuffed her. They then raped her and tortured her, forcing her at one point to use a large knife to cut her own breast. This, she stated, drove one man into a frenzy. He cut her more and then masturbated into the wound before closing it with duct tape. They then threw her out of the van. She gave police details of her attackers but they were unable to trace them.

The murders then became more frequent. On 28 August, teenage prostitute Sandra Delaware was found stabbed and strangled to death on the bank of the Chicago River, her left breast neatly amputated and her bra knotted around her throat.

Rose Davis, aged 30, was found in an identical condition in a Chicago alley, on 8 September – stabbed, raped and strangled. A black sock was tied around her neck and her clothing was in disarray. Her face was crushed and she was lying in a pool of blood. She had been beaten with a hatchet. Deep cuts were evident on her breasts and her abdomen was full of small puncture wounds.

Three days later, 42-year-old Carole Pappas, wife of the Chicago Cubs' pitcher, vanished without a trace from a department store in nearby Wheaton, Illinois.

On 6 October, police got their first break in the case. That morning, prostitute Beverly Washington, aged 20, was found naked and severely wounded beside a Chicago railway track. Her left breast had been severed, the right deeply slashed, but she was breathing and emergency treatment saved her life. Hours later, in a seemingly unrelated incident, drug dealer Rafael Torado was killed and a male companion wounded, when the occupants of a cruising van peppered the phone booth they were in with rifle fire.

The details of the van and occupants as given by the two

surviving victims proved to be helpful in making an arrest. Within three weeks, on 20 October 1982, the police pulled over a red van and questioned the driver. He had red hair and did not resemble the victim's description, but the van was a perfect match. The driver told them his name was Eddie Spreitzer, and that the van belonged to his boss, Robin Gecht (b. 1953). The officers directed Spreitzer (b. 1958) to Gecht's house and had him beckon Gecht outside. They hoped that he would be their man and, when he came out, he did indeed fit the description, down to his shirt and boots. Yet he acted as if he had no worries at all and was quite willing to help. Either he was innocent of these crimes or utterly arrogant, confident that he was untouchable.

Gecht was an unemployed carpenter, aged 28. He was identified by one of the victims and police charged him with the assault on Beverly Washington. They also suspected him of being responsible for wounding prostitute Cynthia Smith before she escaped from his van. Gecht was an odd character, once accused of molesting his own younger sister. Authorities immediately linked him with the Ripper slayings, but they had no proof and he was released on bail.

At first, Spreitzer and Gecht did not yield much useful information, but eventually Spreitzer appeared as if he would break down. He seemed to be genuinely afraid of Gecht. Police questioned Spreitzer yet again and he succumbed, feeling guilty about what he had done. Spreitzer's interrogation produced a 78-page statement.

Spreitzer first admitted to driving the van as Gecht committed a drive-by shooting in which a man died and another was left paralysed. Police quickly identified the incident. Then Gecht directed him to slow down to pick up a black prostitute. Gecht had sex with her, then took her into an alley and used a knife to remove her left breast. He placed it in the van, on the floor. Spreitzer was quite upset as he spilled out these gory details, claiming he did not like all the blood. He added that during such incidents, Gecht sometimes had sex with the breast on the spot.

He also described how Gecht had shot a black woman in the head, chained her up and used bowling balls to weight her down in water. He believed that she had never been found. He also told how he had watched Gecht batter a woman with a hammer; the sight of this had made him vomit. But on another woman, he removed the breasts himself, cutting off both. He thought she was dead when he did this, but did not try to find out for certain. He said that Gecht had forced him to have sexual contact with the woman's gaping wounds. By the time Spreitzer was finished, he had given details of seven murders and one aggravated battery.

Meanwhile, detectives had learnt that Gecht was one of four men who rented adjoining rooms at Villa Park's Rip Van Winkle Motel, several months before Linda Sutton was murdered nearby. The manager remembered them as party animals, frequently bringing women to their rooms, and he surprised investigators with one further piece of information: he believed that the men were 'some kind of cultists', perhaps devil worshippers. Two of the Rip Van Winkle tenants, brothers Thomas and Andrew Kokoraleis (b. 1958 and 1961), had been kind enough to leave a forwarding address, for any post they might receive. Police found 23-year-old Thomas Kokoraleis at home when they called. Following questioning, he agreed to go with them to the police station where he was given a lie-detector test, which he failed. When questioned in greater depth, he told police about a 'satanic chapel' that had been set up in Gecht's upstairs bedroom, where captive women were tortured with knives and ice picks, gang-raped and finally sacrificed to Satan by members of a tiny cult including Gecht, Thomas's brother Andrew and 23-year-old Edward Spreitzer.

Thomas went on to describe the cultic rituals, which included severing one or both breasts with a thin wire garrotte, each celebrant 'taking communion' by eating a piece before the relic was consigned to Gecht's trophy box. At one point, Kokoraleis told detectives, he had counted 15 breasts inside the box. Some other victims had been murdered at the Rip Van Winkle Motel, out in Villa Park. Thomas identified a picture of Lorraine Borowski as a woman he had picked up, with his brother, and had taken to the motel, where she met her death. Thomas told the police that they would all kneel together around the altar and Gecht would produce the freshly removed breasts. He would read passages from the Bible as each man masturbated into the body part. When everyone was finished, Gecht would cut it up and hand around the pieces for them to eat. Thomas said that he had witnessed two murders himself and had participated in nearly a dozen such rituals. When the detectives asked him why he had done such macabre and illegal activities, he told them in all seriousness that Gecht had the power to make them do whatever he wanted. 'You just have to do it,' he said with conviction. Apparently he was convinced that Gecht had some supernatural connection, and he had been afraid of what Gecht might do to him if he did not do as he was told.

On 5 November, police arrested 20-year-old Andrew Kokoraleis. A search of Gecht's apartment had revealed the satanic chapel described by Thomas Kokoraleis. Police found a rifle, which they were able to connect to the Torado shootings. Satanic literature was also retrieved from the apartment occupied by Andrew Kokoraleis. With their suspects in custody, police speculated that the gang might have murdered 18 women in as many months. Thomas Kokoraleis was charged with the murder of Lorraine Borowski on 12 November and formally indicted by a grand jury four days later. Brother Andrew and Edward Spreitzer were charged on 14 November with the rape and murder of victim Rose Davis.

Robin Gecht was found mentally competent despite trying to raise an insanity plea and his trial opened on 20 September. Gecht took the witness stand the next day, confessing to the attack on Beverly Washington. Convicted on all charges, he received a sentence of 120 years in prison. Although Gecht's associates and other witnesses implicated him in some of the deaths, police never had enough evidence to charge him with murder. Although he initially confessed to murder, Thomas Kokoraleis changed his plea to not guilty, with his attorneys seeking to stop the reading of his statements in forthcoming trials, but on 4 December 1983, the confessions were admitted in evidence.

On 2 April 1984, Edward Spreitzer pleaded guilty to four counts of murder, including victims Davis, Delaware, Mak and Torado. Sentenced to life on each count, he received additional time on conviction for charges of rape, deviant sexual assault and attempted murder.

On 18 May 1984, Thomas Kokoraleis was convicted of Lorraine Borowski's murder. He was sentenced to life imprisonment, with a scheduled release date of September 30, 2017. While awaiting sentencing, he led police to a field where Carole Pappas was allegedly buried, but searchers could find no remains. On 7 September 1984, he was given a further life sentence for the murder of Pappas, whose body was later found in 1987 in a shallow pond only four blocks from the Pappas home, with the cause of death being accidental drowning.

Andrew Kokoraleis was tried in two separate counties. The first trial was for the murder of Rose Beck Davis. In his confession, he had admitted that he had abducted Davis with the other men, forced her into the van and had beaten her with a hatchet until she was dead. The jury deliberated for just over three hours before finding him guilty of rape and murder. They sentenced him to life in prison.

At his second trial, Andrew Kokoraleis decided to recant everything he had confessed to and denied that he had killed or raped anyone. He claimed that the police had coerced each of his confessions, had made false promises and had even beaten him into admitting what they wanted him to say. Andrew insisted that they had told him exactly what to say. He also indicated that one police officer had told him the details of the crime scene, giving him all that he needed to confess. Yet when Detective Warren Wilkes took the stand to describe his interrogation, he said that when he had shown Kokoraleis a line of photos, he had picked out Lorraine Borowski and said, 'That's the girl Eddie Spreitzer and I killed in the cemetery.'

The jury deliberated for just three hours. They found Andrew Kokoraleis guilty of the murder of Lorraine Borowski and sentenced him to death. At his sentencing hearing, he once again denied the charges and his attorneys argued later that, despite the verdict, the act did not merit the death penalty. In addition, a prison chaplain and a counsellor testified that Kokoraleis was non-threatening and could be rehabilitated. In addition, Kokoraleis argued that he had received ineffectual counsel at sentencing and that, in the case of the murder of Rose Beck Davis (from the earlier trial), that offence had not warranted the death penalty but life in prison. He insisted that the court had not proven his intent to kill or any degree of premeditation. Nevertheless, the court saw otherwise, as the panel of judges dismissed the appeals and upheld the sentence in 1989. He was executed by lethal injection on 16 March 1999.

Spreitzer pleaded guilty on 2 April 1984 to murdering Rose Davis, Sandra Delaware, Shui Mak and drug dealer Rafael Torado. He received life sentences for each murder, as well as time for a multitude of charges, from rape to deviant sexual assault. Yet he still had to go to trial for the Linda Sutton murder. He appeared in a bench trial in front of Judge Edward Kowal on 25 February 1986, but retained his right to have a jury decide his sentence. He admitted that he and his comrades had abducted Linda Sutton as she was walking near Wrigley Field and took her to a wooded field near a hotel where he was staying. He then handcuffed her, raped her and removed her breasts. Then she was raped again and left to die.

Spreitzer's bid for mercy failed. He was convicted on 4 March of aggravated kidnapping and murder. Two weeks later on 20 March, a jury deliberated for an hour before giving him the death penalty for this crime. He exhausted all of his appeals, despite claims by his attorney Gary Prichard that he had been denied due process and that an examination after the trial indicated that he had brain damage. Prichard argued that the jury had not been correctly instructed. Yet, despite the appearance that this case was now at an end, there was one more unexpected development.

In October 2002, when Spreitzer was 41, he was among 140 of 159 Illinois death row inmates having their cases heard, influenced by the moratorium on capital punishment. Clemency was not granted to Spreitzer, but as Governor Ryan was leaving office in January 2003, he pardoned four of the 164 death row inmates and offered blanket clemency to the rest, including Edward Spreitzer. The families of the victims were outraged and vowed to fight for justice. Spreitzer may have at last won reprieve, but he faces life in prison with no parole.

CHAPTER 9

UNITED KINGDOM

JOHN REGINALD HALLIDAY CHRISTIE

John Christie was born in Halifax in Yorkshire in 1898 and as a child was abused by his father and dominated by his mother and sisters. His one happy childhood memory, at the age of eight, was seeing his grandfather's body as it lay at rest in the family home; he felt powerful in front of the lifeless, helpless body of a man he had once feared. Christie attended Halifax Secondary School when he was 11, and was a very bright pupil. He was skilled at detailed work, and it was later found that he had an IQ of 128. He sang in the choir and became a boy scout but was unpopular among his peers. Upon leaving school in 1913, Christie became an assistant cinema projector. The cinema and photography were two interests that he would retain for the rest of his life.

By the time Christie reached puberty, he already associated sex with death, dominance and violent aggression, and this made him impotent unless he was in complete control. His first attempts at sex were failures, leaving him branded 'Reggie-No-Dick' and 'Can't-Do-It-Christie' throughout adolescence. He was a hypochondriac and suffered from a personality disorder; he would often exaggerate or feign illness to get attention.

Christie later joined the army and after his discharge met 22-

year-old Ethel Simpson. They were married on 10 May 1920. It was a dysfunctional marriage, with Christie sighting his impotence as a reason to visit prostitutes. Friends and neighbours said that his wife stayed with him out of fear. They separated after four years, when Christie moved to London.

Over the next decade, Christie was convicted for many petty criminal offences and served several terms of imprisonment. Christie and his wife reconciled after his release from one such sentence in November 1933, but he did not change his ways. He continued to seek out prostitutes to relieve his increasingly violent sexual urges, which now included necrophilia.

Christie and his wife lived in the ground-floor flat of 10 Rillington Place, in London's Notting Hill, from December 1938. When war was declared in 1939, he applied to join the police force and was accepted, despite his criminal record. Assigned to Harrow Road police station, he enjoyed the respect that came with his position. Christie was both hard-working and efficient. He began an intimate relationship with a woman who worked at the police station whose husband was a serving soldier. The relationship lasted until December 1943, when Christie resigned from the police. The husband had caught Christie with his wife and beat him up. Following this incident, Christie started to invite women to his house while his wife was away visiting relatives.

One such woman was an Austrian girl named Ruth Fuerst, a tall, spirited 21-year-old with brown eyes and hair. Having taken a job in a munitions factory, she lived in a single room not far from Rillington Place. There is some evidence that she may also have earnt money from time to time as a prostitute. One day when they were in bed, Christie strangled her while they were having sex. He wrapped her in her leopardskin coat and put her under the floorboards in the front room, with the rest of her clothes. As soon as he was able, Christie removed the body from the house and placed it in the wash-house out the back. He started to dig in the garden, on the right-hand side, but was interrupted by the return of Ethel, so they had a cup of tea together. He waited until she went to bed that night and then returned to his gruesome task. He placed the dead woman, with her clothes, into the hole, covered it with earth and went to bed. The next day, he straightened the garden and raked it over. He pulled up some of Ruth's clothing and burnt it in an old dustbin. Months later, Christie accidentally unearthed her skull. He put it into the dustbin to be burnt with the other rubbish. Fuerst's disappearance was reported to the police on 1 September, but her whereabouts remained a mystery.

In the company canteen of a radio firm where Christie was now employed, he met his second victim, Muriel Eady, 32, who worked in the assembly department. She lived with her aunt and had a steady boyfriend. She was short and heavily built, with dark brown hair. Christie often invited Muriel and her friend for tea, served by Ethel. Once, the foursome went to the movies together. Christie decided to lure her into his home so he could repeat what he had done to Ruth Fuerst. 'I planned it all out very carefully,' he later wrote.

In October 1944, Ethel went to Sheffield to visit relatives, giving Christie his opportunity. Christie had told Muriel that, due to his first-aid background from his time with the War Reserve, he had a remedy for the catarrh that she suffered from. She came over alone. This time, he would avoid a struggle. He had prepared himself. Christie told Muriel that he had a special kind of inhaler that would work quite well. Into a jar he had put some inhalant, disguised with the odour of Friar's Balsam. He had made two holes in the top of the jar, one of which he used for a small hose that he ran to the gas supply. That tube ran into the liquid and another tube came out the other hole and did not touch the liquid, but was meant to keep the stuff from smelling like gas. According to his own account, after first giving her a cup of tea, he had Muriel sit on a kitchen chair with a scarf over her head to inhale his concoction. As Muriel breathed in, she inhaled carbon monoxide. In less than a minute, it weakened her, which gave

Christie the opportunity to strangle her with a stocking, having sex with her as he was strangling her. Christie once again experienced the peaceful thrill over the body of his victim. He then placed her in the communal wash-house while he dug a hole for her in the garden. He buried her, fully clothed, not far from the first grave. Later, digging around in the garden, he came across a broken femur bone, which he used to prop up the trellis.

It was later suggested that Christie was a necrophile, but others claim that any sexual activity always took place before his victims' deaths. Necrophilia is defined as having sex with the unconscious or dead, and keeping them close – and Christie certainly kept the bodies of Ruth and Muriel nearby. There are three types of necrophile: violent, fantasy and romantic.

The violent types have an overpowering urge to be near a body, so they kill in order to achieve this. They may then keep the body around to sexually assault it again, or to visit it where they left it.

Fantasy necrophiles make death a central part of their erotic imagery. They may ask a lover to 'play dead' during a sexual act or take photos of that person looking dead, over which they can later masturbate. Christie apparently needed his victims to be unconscious, in a deathlike pose, if not actually dead.

The romantic types feel such a strong bond with their victims that they keep them around after death. They may not touch them again, but derive comfort from their proximity. It does not matter, in this case, whether Christie had sex with a dying woman or a corpse. He kept each one close by.

Some have argued that Christie killed his victims because he feared the consequences of his wife finding out, but such a motive would apply only to the first two cases, as his wife was to be his third victim. With the first one, he said that he strangled her while having intercourse and that as he pulled away from her, excrement and urine came out of her, which would indicate that she was dead before he was finished. So we can surmise that the dying women excited him. Perhaps the origin of this was a desire to punish the girl who ridiculed him after a failed adolescent encounter. In any event, killing women made Christie feel peaceful and powerful.

In 1948, 10 Rillington Place was to be the subject of more drama and intrigue. The Christies had decided to take in lodgers and, as a result, Timothy Evans and his wife took up residence. Several months later, Beryl Evans gave birth to a daughter. She soon fell pregnant for a second time and tried many ways to abort the baby, allegedly seeking the help of Christie. What he actually did has never been made clear; in any event, Mrs Evans was dead when her husband returned home. Christie told Timothy Evans that the abortion techniques and blood poisoning had killed his wife. However, it was later suggested that Christie had strangled her. Christie said that they should not report the death to the police as they would both get into trouble and that he should leave the baby with friends and go back to Wales for a short time. But before he did so, they needed to hide the body – Christie told Evans he would hide it down a drain at the house.

While in Wales, Evans's aunt confronted him about where his wife and daughter were. Having few mental resources to cope with all of this, it was not long before Evans arrived at the Merthyr Tydfil police station, telling police he had disposed of his wife by putting her down the drain. Police were not sure what to make of this. He had not actually confessed to killing anyone, but what he did say needed to be checked out.

Evans went on to explain that his wife was dead but that he had not killed her. Afraid that mentioning Christie, a former police officer, would only end up incriminating him, Evans claimed that a stranger had given him something to help his wife abort a baby. He had met a man, he said, who had given him some medication intended for spontaneous abortion. He allowed his wife to take the bottle from him, but he warned her not to use it. That day, however, when he returned from work, he found her dead. He attended to the baby and wondered what he should do. He was afraid that the police would think he had killed her.

The next morning, he said, he had put his wife's body head first down the drain outside the front door. He then stayed home from work but later went in to give notice. He also made arrangements to have someone look after his child. He wanted someone to please find his wife and get this situation resolved.

While Evans waited in Wales, the police in London were notified. They went to the house to investigate. It became immediately apparent that something was amiss when it took three men to move the manhole cover. Evans could not have done this by himself, as he claimed. Once they had it raised, they could see that there was no body. Back in Merthyr, Evans was told of this discovery. He was amazed, but immediately changed his statement. He would now tell the truth.

He said that there was no stranger who had given him abortion pills. Rather, it had been his landlord, Christie, who had put Beryl Evans down the drain. Evans had claimed to have done it only to protect himself from Christie. He said that Christie had offered to help his wife abort the child, but warned that the concoction he used was dangerous and could kill her. She wanted to try it, so when Evans left for work on 8 November, his wife had gone to see Christie. The stuff she took had killed her. When Evans returned home, he found her bleeding from every orifice.

He had attended to the baby while Christie moved the body. Christie returned with the story that he had left her in a nieghbour's flat for the time being. He would wait until dark to put the body down one of the drains. He then told Evans that he knew of some people who would take the baby. Evans was to give Christie all of the baby's things. When Evans came home on Thursday, his child was gone. Christie had said he had taken care of everything. He told Evans to sell his furniture and leave, which he did.

As the investigation intensified, Evans added to his story. He admitted that he had helped Christie to carry his wife down to the other flat, but only because Christie could not do it on his own. He also said he had visited Christie several weeks later to enquire after his daughter but was told it was too soon to see her. He wanted to find out the address of the couple who had taken his child. He wanted to know how she was.

The police investigated the house and garden at 10 Rillington Place, but their search was superficial. They failed to notice the human thighbone from one of Christie's previous victims in the garden that propped up a fence, let alone do any digging, which may have revealed the bodies. What they did find in Evans's mostly empty apartment was puzzling. Among a pile of papers by a window, there were clippings from the newspaper of a sensational torso murder, known as the Stanley Setty case. This was odd, since Evans did not read, but the apparent plant by someone else failed to register with anyone. It just looked incriminating. They also found a stolen briefcase.

Evans was arrested for the theft of the briefcase and brought back to London for further questioning. Christie was also summoned for an interview that lasted six hours. He knew exactly what to say and the police accepted him as one of their own. Another officer questioned Ethel Christie, who had been coached by her husband. Christie dismissed Evans's accusations as ridiculous. The man was a known liar. He then went on to recount how violent the Evans's marriage had been.

When Mrs Evans and the baby could not be located, the police searched the house again. They then went into the back yard and tried to get into the wash-house, but the door was stuck. Ethel Christie brought them a piece of metal to loosen it. Inside, it was dark. They noticed some wood standing against the sink. One of the officers reached behind it and felt something. They moved the wood and saw what appeared to be a package wrapped in a green tablecloth and tied up with cord. Ethel claimed she had never seen it before and did not know what it was. They pulled the package out further and untied the cord. A pair of feet slipped out, revealing the decaying corpse of Beryl Evans. Further searching produced the body of the baby, lying under some wood behind the door. Both had been strangled. A man's tie was still around the baby's neck.

Dr Donald Teare, the Home Office pathologist, arrived to examine the bodies. He then took them to Kensington Mortuary. A post-mortem indicated that both had been dead about three weeks. Beryl had been bruised over the lip and right eye, as if she had been hit. She had been strangled with a cord of some kind, like a rope. There was no evidence that she had taken anything to induce an abortion but there was bruising inside her vagina. Unaccountably, the doctor neglected to take a vaginal swab to check for semen. Christie was asked to identify the clothing taken from the two corpses. He knew Beryl's skirt and blouse, but claimed he did not know the tie that had been around the baby's neck. He thought he might have seen it on Evans.

When Evans was brought back to London from Wales, all he was told on the way was that he was going to be questioned about a briefcase found in his apartment that belonged to someone else. When he arrived in London, however, there was no doubt in his mind that he was being arrested for murder. He was shown the pile of clothing taken from the bodies, with the tie on top, and was told that his wife and daughter had been found. Tears came to his eyes and he bent down and picked up the tie.

That night, police took two more confessions from Evans. He first admitted that he was responsible for the deaths of his wife and child and added that it was a relief to get it off his chest. He said he had killed his wife because she was running up debts. They had quarrelled and he had hit her. Then he had strangled her with a piece of rope. He wrapped Beryl's body in the tablecloth in which she had been found and took it to the apartment below. After that, he put it in the wash-house at midnight on 8 November. The next day, he fed the baby and left her alone all day. He repeated this again the day after. Then he quit his job and came home and killed his child by strangling her with his tie. He put her into the wash-house as well.

Later that night, Evans offered a longer confession, which took about 75 minutes to record and read back to him. Evans apparently claimed that, in fact, he was up all night talking with the police, until 5am. Painstakingly, Evans went through as much detail as he could recall about the days leading up to the murder, including hitting Beryl in the face. After that, in a fit of temper, he strangled her. He included putting her in the wash-house and using wood to hide the body. However, he twice made the statement that he had locked the wash-house door and this was untrue, since the carpenters had been in and out of it all week without having to get someone to unlock it. Also, the wood used to hide the bodies had come from the flooring that was pulled up on 11 November, which the carpenter recalled Christie asking for. At any rate, it was not available on the 8th and 10th. Moreover, Evans failed to provide an explanation as to why he killed his baby daughter. He also said he left the rope around Beryl's neck, although no rope was ever found. Beryl weighed a little less than Evans. It would have been easy for him to have silently dragged her body past where the Christies' bedroom overlooked the back yard. He also said that he left his baby unattended for two long days, but no one had reported her crying.

It is quite apparent that the police edited the statements and possibly even guided Evans's confession. People who feel coerced or who seek relief have been known to confess to crimes they did not commit. This is not altogether unlikely in this case, especially in light of Evans's limited intelligence. He later retracted the whole confession when speaking to his mother, but for some reason continued with his confessions to the police, and at no time did he ever protest his innocence to anyone other than his mother.

On 11 January 1950, Evans was tried at the Old Bailey for the murder of his daughter. His wife's murder was also included in the prosecution case, and this contained major flaws that were not highlighted by Evans's defence lawyers. This failure on their part would sadly lead to the conviction of Evans for the murder of his baby. On 9 March 1950, Timothy Evans was hanged.

THE EVIL WITHIN

Once the publicity and media attention Christie had been receiving in relation to the Evans trial was over, he and his wife settled back down in Rillington Place. However, Ethel Christie felt that it was time to move to a new place, especially since the third floor flat was now occupied by some recently-arrived Jamaicans. She thought they were low-class and frightening, and was extremely uncomfortable sharing an outhouse with them. In addition, Christie continually complained about various physical problems. Shortly after the trial, he had gone into a deep depression, losing about 28lbs. He also lost his job at the post office, due to certain disclosures during the trial about past crimes. Finally, he consented to a three-week observation period. A psychiatrist wanted to hospitalise him for analysis, but he refused to leave his wife alone. Nevertheless, he continued to visit his own doctor, going 33 times in eight months for stress-related symptoms. Christie became angry with his wife, whose presence stopped him from accomplishing certain schemes. She had also been taunting him about his impotence, which angered him.

On Thursday, 11 December, five days after Christie had lost his job, his wife went to watch television with a friend, Rosie. The next day, she took the washing to Maxwell Laundries and appeared, to those who saw her, well and cheerful. She said nothing to anyone about taking a trip. However, after that, no one saw her again. Christie then began to tell neighbours that his wife had gone off to Sheffield, saying that he had a new job there and would follow her shortly. Some of them were surprised that she had not said goodbye, nor mentioned any such plans. To relatives, he said that she was not feeling well enough to write to them or send Christmas greetings. He sent a few gifts 'from Ethel and Reg'. Oddly, he began to sprinkle his house and garden with a strong disinfectant, which people soon began to notice. In January, Christie sold all his furniture to a dealer. He also sold his wife's wedding ring and watch. Without a bed, he slept on an old mattress on the floor. All he had left were three chairs, one of which was of particular value to him, and a kitchen table. To get money, he forged his wife's signature on an account she had and emptied it. With that, he stayed in his unfurnished flat into March, no longer even bothering to answer the letters from relatives enquiring after his wife.

One day he noticed a woman, Mrs Reilly, looking for a place to rent and invited her to look at his flat. She brought her husband, which Christie had not anticipated. They decided to take the flat, paying three months' rent in advance. Christie borrowed a suitcase from them and moved out on 20 March. He had his dog destroyed but left his cat with the tenants. He took their money and left. The Reillys had not been in the flat even one day when they learnt from the real landlord that Christie had no right to rent the flat, and they were asked to leave. They and the landlord argued about the rent money, but since the place smelt so bad, they were happy to vacate it. Christie himself was on the move. He did not wish to be around when certain discoveries were made.

The landlord now had an empty flat, so he allowed the upstairs tenant, Beresford Brown, to use the kitchen. Brown noticed a bad smell, so he began to clean things up. It then occurred to him that he might install a new shelf on the wall for his wireless radio. He began to knock on the walls and discovered one that sounded hollow. He assumed there was a cupboard behind. Brown pulled away some of the wallpaper, revealing a door, though it was closed fast. He shone a light through the crack and then stepped back, uncertain of what he had seen. It looked to him as if a naked woman were inside that wall. He called the police without hesitation.

When they arrived and opened the door fully, they saw the body of a woman sitting amid some rubble. She was leaning forward, her back to them. Behind her was a similarly sized object, wrapped in a blanket. The blanket was knotted to the victim's bra, which was pulled up high, towards her neck. Otherwise, she wore only a garter belt and stockings. Her black sweater and white jacket were pulled up around her neck. She was removed and taken to the front room for a photograph and examination. It was soon clear that she had been strangled with a ligature. Her wrists were tied in front of her with a handkerchief that had been tied in a reef knot. The body was fairly well preserved. Next, the police focused on the other object in the cupboard. As they photographed it, they noticed another tall, wrapped object just beyond it. They pulled out the first one and soon discovered that it was another body. It had been stood on its head in the cupboard and propped upside down against the wall. The blanket had been fastened with a sock into a reef knot around the ankles, and the head was wrapped in a pillowcase, also tied into a reef knot with a stocking. The third object was yet another body. This one was also upside down, with the head beneath the second body. The ankles were tied with an electrical cord, using a reef knot. A cloth covered the head and was similarly knotted. The investigators noticed some floorboards loose in the parlour, so they pulled these up and found more loose rubble. They started to dig and quickly found yet another female body. They left the property with a police guard for the night and determined to return the next day to make a thorough examination.

At the mortuary, four post-mortems were performed. The results were as follows:

- First body: a female brunette, aged around 20 (later determined to be 26); she had been dead around four weeks. She had died from strangulation and carbon monoxide poisoning. It was surmised that she had been under the effects of the poisoning when she was strangled with a smooth-surface type of cord. She had been sexually assaulted at the time of death, or shortly after. Scratch marks on her back indicated that she had been dragged across the floor after death.
- Second body: a female aged about 25-years-old with light brown hair, poorly manicured hands and feet; healthy. She

was pinkish in colour, a sign of gas poisoning, and had been asphyxiated by strangulation. She had also had sexual intercourse near the time of death, and had been drinking heavily that day. She wore a cotton cardigan and vest, and another white vest had been placed between her legs in a nappy-like fashion. She had died 8–12 weeks earlier.

- Third body: a blonde female aged about 25, poorly manicured. She wore a dress, petticoat, bra, cardigan and two vests, with a piece of material placed between her legs. She was pinkish in colour and had been gassed and asphyxiated. She had been drinking shortly before death, which had taken place 8–12 weeks earlier. She was six months pregnant.

- Fourth body: this body, brought to the mortuary the following day, was of a woman in her fifties, plump and with several teeth missing. She had been rolled up in a flannel blanket, and her head covered with a pillowcase. A silk nightgown and a flowered dress were wrapped around her, under the blanket. She wore stockings, pulled up. She had been dead for 12–15 weeks. Unlike the others, there were no signs of coal gas poisoning or sexual intercourse. She had been strangled, probably by ligature.

The police's next task was to identify the bodies. It was not hard to discover that the older woman under the floorboards was Ethel Christie. The others were all prostitutes whom Christie had brought home to his near-empty flat: Hectorina McLennan, 26; Kathleen Maloney, 26; and Rita Nelson, 25.

Police went through the entire flat. They found a man's suit under the floor of the common hall area, which had been open during the time of the Evans murders. In the kitchen cupboard was a man's tie, fashioned into a reef knot. They also found potassium cyanide in another area of the apartment and a tobacco tin that contained four clumps of pubic hair, none of which came from the bodies found in the kitchen. The presence of the pubic hair collection indicated another type of perversion, but Christie had to be caught before anyone could make sense of it.

Police had also searched the garden. They found the human femur this time, in plain view supporting the trellis. More bones were found in flowerbeds and some blackened skull bones with teeth and pieces of a dress turned up in a dustbin. Bones were also found beneath an orange blossom bush. Nearby was a newspaper fragment dated 19 July 1943. A quantity of hair was discovered, along with some teeth. The police determined that, although only one skull was found, there were two female bodies in the garden. That made a total of six at the house.

The skeletons were reconstructed for identification purposes. It was soon determined from a tooth crown that one of the victims, both of whom were female, was from Germany or Austria. She was young, around 21, and around 5ft 6in tall. The other was between 32 and 35, and only about 5ft 1in tall. They had both been in the garden at least three years and may have been there as long as 10 years.

It was soon discovered that Ruth Margaret Fuerst had arrived in England from Austria in 1939 and had been missing since 24 August 1943. She was then 21 and measured about 5ft 6in tall. When she disappeared, she had been staying in Notting Hill. The other victim seemed likely to be Muriel Amelia Eady, 32, who had worked at a factory with Christie. She was 5ft 1in tall and had dark hair. The hair in Christie's garden matched hair from one of Eady's dresses, still kept at her former home. She had been wearing a black wool dress when last seen, like the remains of one found in the garden.

The search was now on to find and arrest Christie. On 20 March 1953, he booked a room at the King's Cross Rowton House, giving his real name and address. He asked for seven nights, but only stayed four. It could be that he heard about the full-scale police search for him and decided it would be better to find another place to stay – at this point his name was on the front page of every newspaper. While he was at large, he was considered a danger to unwary females. As he ran out of money, he walked around wherever he could and took naps on benches and in cinemas. Eventually he wandered to the banks of the Thames.

On the last day of March, a police officer spotted him on the Putney Embankment. By that time, Christie had been wandering for ten days. The constable asked him who he was and he gave a false name and address. Then he was asked to take off his hat, exposing the high, balding forehead said to be characteristic of Christie, and he was arrested. On his person were his identity card, a ration book, his Union card, an ambulance badge and, oddly, an old newspaper clipping about the remand of Timothy Evans, with details about those killings. At Putney police station, Christie willingly gave his statement about the murders, but only talked about four. He hinted that there was something else that he could not quite remember, possibly hedging to see if the police had yet discovered the skeletons in the garden.

With regard to the death of his wife, he said that her moving around in bed awakened him. Her face was blue and she was choking. It seemed to him too late to call for assistance; he tried but failed to restore her breathing. Unable to bear her suffering, he got a stocking and strangled her. He then found a bottle that had contained phenobarbitone tablets, which was now nearly empty. They were for his insomnia and he realised that she had taken them to kill herself. She had been deeply depressed over the new tenants, whom she thought were persecuting her (according to Christie). He left her there in the bed for two or three days and then, when he recalled that there were some loose boards in the front room and a depression in the ground beneath, he wrapped her in a blanket and placed her there to keep her near him. 'I thought that was the best way to lay her to rest.' He claimed he did not know what else to do, as if he did not already have two corpses out in the garden. The other three women, too, were 'not his fault'. Since they were women of disrepute, he claimed they were the aggressors, with him, a man of virtue who had no choice but do what he did. In his statement, Christie reversed the order of when he met the first two, but given their relative positions in the cupboard, the true sequence of events was fairly obvious. Medical tests also confirmed that Rita Nelson was the first to die. Nelson, 25, had allegedly demanded money from Christie in the street. (Christie says this was Kathleen Maloney, but it was Rita Nelson whom he killed first, so he seems to have mixed up the names.) According to Christie's account, Nelson (or Maloney) told him she would scream and accuse him of assault if he didn't give her 30 shillings. He walked away and she followed, forcing her way into his house. She picked up a frying pan to hit him. They struggled and she fell back onto a chair that happened to have a rope hanging from it. Christie blacked out and woke up to find her strangled. He left her there, had some tea and went to bed. When he discovered her still there in the morning, he wrapped her up, placed the 'nappy' on her and shoved her into the cupboard. 'I pulled away a small cupboard in the corner,' he recalled, 'and gained access to a small alcove.'

Around the same time, Christie encountered Kathleen Maloney, 26, although he recalled that it was February. Christie had met her three weeks before. He had gone with her and another prostitute to a room where he had taken photographs of the other girl in the nude. On this night, he went into a Notting Hill café and sat at a table where Kathleen and another girl were discussing their search for flats. Kathleen was an orphan who had given birth thus far to five illegitimate children. That night, she went home with Christie and was never seen again. He later claimed that she had made advances as a way to get him to use his influence with the landlord and then threatened violence. He said he only recalled that she was on the floor and that he put her into the cupboard right away. He did not recall killing her, though he had, in fact, since devised a new gas contraption. Christie placed her in the chair, an easy matter since she was quite drunk, and used the gas. Then he strangled her with a rope. He had intercourse with her and placed a 'nappy' between her legs. He then went to bed. (He did not confess the sexual contact or the gassing of these women until later.) The next morning, he made tea, with the body still sitting in the chair. He wrapped her body in a blanket, put a pillowcase over her head and placed her inside the alcove. Her body lay on the floor with her legs vertical against the back wall. He covered her with dirt and ashes and then closed up the cupboard.

Christie's statement about Hectorina McLennan, 26, indicated that she and her boyfriend were hard up for a place to stay, so he had invited them to share with him. They stayed together in a barely furnished flat for several uncomfortable days. In one version of the story, Christie had asked the two people to leave. The girl returned alone the next night to wait for her boyfriend and when Christie tried to get her out, they struggled. Some of her clothing got torn. She fell limp and sank to the floor and Christie thought that some of her clothing got wrapped around her neck. He pulled her into the kitchen and sat her on a chair. She seemed to be dead, so he hid her body in the cupboard as well.

He also confessed another version. While Hectorina and her boyfriend were at the Labour Exchange, Christie showed up and invited Hectorina to come to his house that morning alone. He poured her a drink and then unfastened a clasp that released the gas. She tried to leave, but he stopped her in the hallway. 'I seized hold of her by the neck and applied just sufficient pressure to make her limp. I took her back to the kitchen and I decided that it was essential to use the gas again. I made love to her, and then put her back in the chair. I killed her.' He shoved her into the alcove in a sitting position, keeping her upright by hooking her brassiere to the blanket around Maloney's legs. When Hectorina's boyfriend came looking for her, Christie denied having seen her. He invited the man in to have a look around and made him some tea, whereupon he noticed a nasty odour. However, he left without further exploration.

In Brixton prison, several psychiatrists examined Christie,

who provided many details, of varying reliability. The doctors were unanimous in their dislike of the man. He was 'nauseating' and 'snivelling'. He seemed always to whisper when asked a question that he did not like, similar behaviour to the Evans trial. He also dissociated when describing his foul deeds, talking about himself in the third person as if he were a spectator. His confessions were peppered with evasions and lies.

Christie also boasted about his nefarious deeds to other inmates, comparing himself to the infamous John George Haigh, the acid-bath killer who had also murdered six women. Christie claimed that his goal had been 12. Once confronted with evidence, he quickly admitted to killing his first two victims, but resisted the idea that he had killed the Evans mother and child. Then he changed his confession to an admission of killing Beryl Evans, but not her child. Beryl's was a mercy killing, similar to his wife's. She had tried to kill herself with gas and when Christie rescued her (according to him), she begged him to help her do it. The next day, he gassed and then strangled her. (He could not have done this, since holding the gas close to her would have affected him as well. None of his details about rescuing her and then assisting her were supported by medical fact.) Christie claimed that Beryl offered him sex in exchange for his assistance and he tried but failed to perform. He later said to a chaplain that he did not think he had murdered Beryl Evans, but had had the impression from his lawyer that for an insanity defence it would be better for him to admit to as many murders as possible. When asked about the pubic hair collection, he said that one clump was Beryl's. Her body was exhumed for comparison, but it was evident that no hair had been cut from her. To whom this hair belonged remained a mystery, as Christie could not or would not tell.

He stood trial at the Old Bailey on 22 June 1953 on the charge of murdering his wife. Christie pleaded not guilty by reason of insanity. The trial lasted only four days and the jury deliberated only an hour and 20 minutes, returning a guilty verdict. He was sentenced to death. Christie did not appeal and there appeared to be no medical grounds for reprieve. He was hanged at Pentonville Prison on 15 July 1953.

Christie's conviction, and his confession to Beryl Evans's murder, raised questions about the execution of Timothy Evans three years earlier, but a brief enquiry at the time found no reason to doubt Evans's guilt in the murder of his daughter. Several years later, journalist Ludovic Kennedy and barrister Michael Eddowes fought to clear Evans's name. Evans was granted a posthumous pardon in 1966. The outcry over the Evans case contributed to the abolition of the death penalty in the United Kingdom.

On 16 November 2004, Timothy Evans's half-sister, Mary Westlake, started a case to overturn a decision by the Criminal Cases Review Commission not to refer Evans's case to the Court of Appeal to have his conviction quashed. She argued that although the previous enquiries concluded that Evans probably did not kill his daughter, they did not declare him innocent, since a pardon is a forgiveness of crimes committed. The request to refer the case was dismissed on 19 November 2004, with the judges saying that the cost and resources of quashing the conviction could not be justified, although they did accept that Evans did not murder his wife or baby.

JOHN GEORGE HAIGH, AKA THE ACID BATH MURDERER

John Haigh was born in Wakefield, Yorkshire, in 1909 and grew up in the nearby village of Outwood. His parents, John and Emily, were members of the Plymouth Brethren. He was confined to living within a 10ft fence that his father put up around their garden to lock out the outside world. Haigh won a scholarship to Queen Elizabeth Grammar School, Wakefield. He then won another scholarship, his parents having switched their belief from the non-conformist Brethren to the high church of Wakefield Cathedral, where he became a choirboy.

Haigh, however, developed a passion for cars and dishonesty. After leaving school, he was apprenticed to a firm of motor engineers, which at least satisfied one of his hobbies. After a year, he left the garage business and took a job in insurance and advertising. However, he was later sacked after being suspected of stealing from the petty cash box.

On 6 July 1934, Haigh married Betty Hammer, 21, a lively woman described in some accounts as a good-time girl. The marriage soon floundered. The same year, Haigh was jailed for fraud. Betty gave birth while he was in prison, but she gave the baby up for adoption and left Haigh.

It wasn't long before Haigh's dishonesty caught up with him again. He was arrested for car fraud for which he was sentenced to 15 months' imprisonment. Upon his release, he attempted to reform by becoming a partner in a dry-cleaning business. Sadly, this also failed when his business partner was killed in a motorcycle accident.

He then moved to London and became chauffeur to William McSwann, wealthy owner of an amusement park. Haigh and McSwann became friends but Haigh still wanted to set himself up in business. He did, but as a bogus solicitor, earning himself four years in jail for fraud. Haigh was released just after the start of World War II, and then jailed again for theft. While in prison, he dreamt up what he considered the perfect murder: disposing of the body by dissolving it in acid. He experimented with mice and found it took only 30 minutes for the body to disappear.

He was freed in 1944 and became an accountant with an engineering firm. Soon after, by chance, he bumped into McSwann again in London. McSwann introduced Haigh to his parents, Donald and Amy, who mentioned that they had invested in property. On 6 September 1944, McSwann disappeared. Haigh had lured him to a basement at 79 Gloucester Road, London, where he hit him over the head and killed him. He then put McSwann's body into a 33-gallon drum and tipped sulphuric acid onto it. Two days later, he returned to find the body had become sludge, which he poured down a manhole.

He told McSwann's parents their son had fled to Scotland to

avoid being called up for military service. When McSwann's parents became curious about why their son had not returned after the war was coming to an end, Haigh murdered them too. On 2 July 1945, he lured them to the same Gloucester Road address where he had murdered their son and disposed of them in the same way.

Haigh stole Donald McSwann's pension cheques, sold his parents' properties, making about £8,000 (worth approximately £80,000 today), and moved into the Onslow Court Hotel, Kensington. By the summer of 1947, Haigh, a gambler, was running short of money so he needed to find another couple to kill and rob.

Dr Archibald Henderson and his wife Rose were the unfortunate victims. Haigh met them after purporting to show an interest in a house they were selling. On 12 February 1948, he drove Dr Henderson to Crawley, on the pretext of showing him an invention. When they arrived, he shot him in the head with a revolver he had earlier stolen from the doctor's house. He then lured Rose Henderson to the workshop, claiming that her husband had fallen ill, and shot her. By now, he had rented a small workshop in Leopold Road, Crawley, West Sussex, and moved acid and drums there from Gloucester Road. After disposing of the bodies in acid, he forged a letter from the Hendersons and sold all their possessions for £8,000, except their dog, which he kept.

Haigh's next and final victim was Olive Durand-Deacon, 69, a widow and fellow resident at the Onslow Court. Fancying herself something of an engineer, she mentioned to Haigh an idea she had had for artificial fingernails. He invited her down to the Crawley workshop on 18 February 1949 and, once inside, he shot her in the back of the head, stripped her of her valuables, including a Persian lamb coat, and put her into the acid bath. Two days later, Durand-Deacon's friend, Constance Lane, reported her missing.

Detectives soon discovered Haigh's record of theft and fraud and searched the workshop. Police not only found Haigh's attaché case containing a dry cleaner's receipt for Mrs Durand-Deacon's coat, but also papers referring to the Hendersons and McSwanns, as well as a .32-calibre pistol that had recently been fired.

As a result, he was arrested, and when questioned by Detective Inspector Albert Webb, Haigh asked him: 'Tell me, frankly, what are the chances of anybody being released from Broadmoor Hospital?' The inspector said he could not discuss that sort of thing, so Haigh replied: 'Well, if I told you the truth, you would not believe me. It sounds too fantastic to believe.' Apparently thinking that he would be sent to Broadmoor, he waved away Webb's cautioning words and said, 'I will tell you about it. Mrs Durand-Deacon no longer exists. She has disappeared completely and no trace of her can ever be found again. I have destroyed her with acid. You will find the sludge, which remains at Leopold Road. Every trace has gone.' He then showed his naive arrogance with, 'How can you prove murder without a body?' This admission seemed rather inexplicable at first, but as Haigh's history was uncovered, it became clear what his intentions had been.

While in prison years before, Haigh had discussed this point of law with fellow prisoners. He had convinced himself that if there is no corpse (which is what he understood the term *corpus delicti* to mean; it is in fact Latin for 'the body of the crime'), there could be no conviction. In fact, he had talked about this legal issue so often, he had acquired the nickname 'Ol' Corpus Delicti'. He was convinced that the police had to have a physical body to actually prosecute someone for murder, and there were ways to make sure that did not happen. He had also mentioned that to get real money, one had to prey on older, wealthy women.

However, Haigh had not taken into account the weight of circumstantial evidence, even without a body, that can be used to prove the overwhelming probability of guilt. He had already offered a confession, which in itself went a long way towards helping the police prove their case. They only needed some corroborating evidence. They had Mrs Durand-Deacon's coat and jewellery. It was time to find out if they could recover any evidence from the 'sludge'. Further investigation of the sludge at the workshop by the forensic pathologist Keith Simpson revealed three human gallstones. Haigh was once again cautioned not to speak, but he went on to offer a full description of what he had done to Mrs Durand-Deacon. He dictated a statement that took two and a half hours to write down.

Haigh was still arrogant and sure that there would not be enough evidence to convict him of murder. He then confessed that he had not only killed Durand-Deacon, the McSwanns and the Hendersons, but also three other people, a young man called Max, a girl from Eastbourne and a woman from Hammersmith. The three others might have been part of Haigh's attempt to convince the police of insanity. He went on to describe the murders in intricate detail.

In Haigh's diary, found later by police, there is a cross etched in red crayon under the entry for 9 September; this may have been the day he either killed or disposed of McSwann. Haigh claimed that he had a sudden need for blood so he had hit McSwann over the head with a blunt instrument, possibly a table leg or a pipe. Then he slit his throat. 'I got a mug and took some blood, from his neck, in the mug, and drank it.' He left the body there overnight to die and had to decide what he was now to do with it. That was the night when Haigh dreamt of a forest of blood.

In the meantime, a massive forensic examination was being conducted at his home. In the yard outside the storehouse, the police found the acid sludge that Haigh had described. They also noted a lot of zig-zagging marks from where someone had rolled and dragged something heavy over towards that area. The ground was covered in debris and the sludge was mixed up with dirt and rubbish. Its depth was some 3–4in covering an area of 4–5ft. The doctor's professional eye detected something unusual, about the size of a cherry, which to anyone else might look like a stone lying around. However, it was a significant find: a gall-bladder stone. The acid had not dissolved it. Also embedded in the greasy, undissolved fat were some good specimens of human bone. One of these appeared to be from a left foot. (Haigh would later say that he believed this was from Henderson, whom he had not fully dissolved, rather than Durand-Deacon.)

The forensic team gathered 474lb of grease and earth to cart back to a lab for closer examination. They also brought in a 33-gallon green drum that had the same greasy substance inside. At the bottom of this drum, a hairpin was stuck in the grease. Inside the building, a fine spatter of bloodstains was noted on the wall and carefully photographed. The wall was then scraped for analysis. The inspector thought the spray was consistent with someone getting shot while bent over the bench, possibly looking at paper, as Haigh had described killing Mrs Durand-Deacon. Tests indicated that the blood was human, but its group could not be identified.

For three days, the sludge was carefully sifted – the technicians had to wear rubber gloves and cover their arms in Vaseline to protect themselves from the acid. However, the painstaking search paid off. They found 28lb of human body fat; three faceted gallstones; part of a left foot, not quite eroded; 18 fragments of human bone; intact upper and lower dentures; the handle of a red plastic bag; and a lipstick container.

A further test on one of the gallstones proved that it was human. The bone fragments were identified as a left ankle pivot bone, centre of the right foot, right heel, right angle pivot bone, femur, pelvic bone, spinal column, and others too eroded for precise identification. They had been dissolved in sulphuric acid, just as Haigh had described. The investigators' great stroke of luck was the fact that sulphuric acid did not work on plastic as it did on human tissue. It would take at least three weeks for the acid to finally eliminate it. Thus, if Haigh had been arrested later or had chosen to wait with his confession, the forensic team would have had much less success in finding identifiable evidence.

The dentures were an important find. The team could now go to Mrs Durand-Deacon's dentist to see if they had a match. Mrs Durand-Deacon's gum shrinkage problems had sent her to her dentist, Helen Mayo, on many occasions. Mayo kept a cast of her patients' upper and lower jaws. She knew that she had supplied Mrs Durand-Deacon with the dentures found at Crawley.

Simpson took the bones to his laboratory and discovered evidence of osteoarthritis in the joints. He soon determined that Mrs Durand-Deacon had suffered from this bone ailment. The police made a plaster cast of the left foot and it proved to fit perfectly into one of her shoes. Bloodstains were also found on the Persian coat, which was traced back to Durand-Deacon from repairs made to it, and blood was found on the cuff of one of Haigh's shirtsleeves. The handbag strap was identified as having belonged to a bag owned by Durand-Deacon, the one she had carried when she drove to Crawley with Haigh. Later, the rest of the bag was found in the yard, apparently thrown there casually by Haigh, and matched to the strap.

Dr Turfitt, the police scientist on the forensic team, decided to experiment with sulphuric acid to test Haigh's theories. He used an amputated human foot, a sheep's leg and other organic materials, finding that the acid worked at varying speeds, depending on how much water was present. Fat proved highly resistant, and it had been Mrs Durand-Deacon's weight that had preserved those items found in the sludge.

Haigh's trial opened on 18 July 1949 and he pleaded not guilty. His defence team was hoping for him to be found insane. However, after hearing all the evidence against him it took only 15 minutes for the jury to find him guilty of murder.

The judge asked if he had anything to say for himself. He cocked his head and said, 'Nothing at all.' The judge donned a black cap and sentenced Haigh to be hanged.

After Haigh's trial, two more medical officials observed him in

Wandsworth Prison and they found no sign of insanity. To their mind, he was shamming. The Home Secretary, under the Criminal Lunatics Act of 1884, ordered a special medical inquiry, just to be sure. Three eminent psychiatrists examined Haigh's case thoroughly. All believed that Haigh was malingering. He was not insane and did not suffer from a mental disease or defect that would free him of moral responsibility for his actions. There was no reason to interfere with the course of the law. Haigh insisted that he was not afraid to be hanged. Madame Tussaud's requested a fitting for a death mask, which Haigh was more than happy to provide.

On 6 August 1949, at Wandsworth Prison, Haigh was executed. He bequeathed his clothing to Madame Tussaud's Chamber of Horrors, where a wax figure of him was erected. He sent instructions that it must always be kept in perfect condition, the trousers creased, the hair parted, his shirt cuffs showing. Among other murderers cast in wax, Haigh received his place in history.

PETER SUTCLIFFE, AKA THE YORKSHIRE RIPPER

Peter Sutcliffe was born in Bingley, West Yorkshire, in 1946, the son of a mill worker. He was described as being a loner throughout his school years. On leaving school at the age of 15, he moved from job to job over the next few years before meeting his wife Sonia Szurma in 1966. They married in 1974. Shortly after his marriage, he was made redundant from Anderton International, a spring manufacturer where he was working night shifts. He used the pay-off to buy a goods vehicle and obtained his HGV licence in June 1975. Shortly after this, his wife Sonia suffered a number of miscarriages, and eventually they were told that she would not be able to have children. After this, Sonia returned to a teacher-training course. When she completed the course in 1977 and began teaching, they started to save the extra money to buy their first house.

Sutcliffe's first known attack was in September 1969. Sutcliffe and his friend Trevor Birdsall were sitting in Trevor's minivan in St Paul's Road, near Manningham Park, Bradford. Sutcliffe had been looking for a prostitute he had a grievance with, but had not found her. He suddenly left the vehicle and began to walk up St Paul's Road and out of sight. He came back about 10 minutes later, and was out of breath, as if he had been running. He told Trevor to drive off quickly. As they began heading towards Bingley, Sutcliffe claimed that he followed an 'old cow' to a house somewhere and said he had hit her on the back of the head with a stone in a sock. He removed a sock from his pocket and dumped its contents out of the window.

The next day, two police officers visited Peter Sutcliffe at his home at 57 Cornwall Road, Bingley. The woman whom Sutcliffe had attacked had noted the number of Trevor's minivan. Sutcliffe readily admitted to the police that he had struck the woman, but claimed it was only with his hand. He was given a stern lecture by the police, but also was told that he was 'very lucky' as the woman, for her own reasons, did not want to press charges for assault. Besides being a known prostitute, her common-law husband was serving a sentence for assault. Apparently, she wanted nothing more to do with the incident.

The events that it was later suggested turned Sutcliffe against prostitutes went back to when he had first started dating Sonia Szurma. She had been his regular Saturday-night date and a serious girlfriend. However, Sutcliffe's brother Mick had spotted her with an Italian boy who was a local ice-cream salesman. Sutcliffe, feeling betrayed and utterly devastated, decided to confront her, but Sonia refused to answer any of his questions about the situation, or comment on whether their relationship was over or not.

That night, Sutcliffe decided to take his revenge by going with a prostitute. Driving up Manningham Lane, he went past the Royal Standard pub and at a petrol station he saw a prostitute waiting for customers. Having confirmed that she was 'doing business', they agreed on a price of £5. He'd given her a £10 note and she told him she would give his change later. They got to her house and went inside. She started going upstairs and he realised he just didn't want to go through with it. He felt disgusted with her and himself. He went upstairs behind her and into the bedroom, and even unzipped her dress, but told her straight out that he didn't want to do anything with her. She could keep the money, but he asked for his change. She told him they would have to go back to the garage where he'd picked her up, to get some change, so he drove her there. He felt worse than ever about Sonia. They went back to the garage by car and she went inside; there were two men in there. She didn't come back out. One of the men came banging on his car roof when he refused to go away, then produced a wrench and threatened him. Then he saw the girl come out with another heavily built man. They walked off together laughing; the men were obviously her minders. Sutcliffe felt stupid. He drove home angrier than ever. He felt outraged, humiliated and embarrassed.

Three weeks later, Sutcliffe saw the same prostitute in the Lumb Lane pub, and approached her. He told her that he hadn't forgotten about the incident and that she should put things right so there would be no hard feelings. He was giving her the opportunity to give back the money owed to him. She thought this was a huge joke and, as she knew everybody else in the pub, went round telling them all. Soon everyone was laughing at Sutcliffe. He left, but was now determined to seek out the woman again.

On 29 September 1969, Sutcliffe again went out looking for a prostitute to attack. This time he took a hammer and a long-bladed knife. He was arrested in the garden of a house in the Manningham area of Bradford after a policeman on patrol had spotted his car with its lights on and the engine running. The policeman discovered Sutcliffe hiding behind a hedge with a hammer. He claimed that a hubcap had flown off his front wheel and that he had been looking for it – the hammer was to help secure the hubcap again. Sutcliffe was charged and fined £25 for 'going equipped for theft', but his real reason for being out – to attack a prostitute – remained secret. Sutcliffe managed to slip the long-bladed knife down a gap between the side of the police vehicle and the mudguard cover inside the police van that came to collect him.

On 4 July 1975, in Keighley, 36-year-old Anna Patricia Rogulski decided to walk across town to her boyfrend's house, after having an argument and parting with him earlier that night. As she fruitlessly banged on his front door, Sutcliffe stood in the shadows nearby, watching. Finally, in frustration, Rogulski removed one of her shoes and broke the glass of a downstairs window. As she knelt to put her shoe back on, Sutcliffe quickly emerged from the shadows and struck a savage blow to her head with a hammer. Rogulski had not seen or heard anything and was unconscious as he dealt her another two hammer blows. He paused momentarily to catch his breath as the blood from Rogulski's wounds seeped across the cobblestones. He lifted her skirt and pulled down her knickers. As he returned the hammer to his pocket and took out a knife, his anger, under control until now, found expression with each slashing cut across her stomach. A neighbour who had heard the noises came out. As the neighbour stood peering out into the alley, trying to focus in the poor light, Sutcliffe pulled himself together and spoke calmly as he reassured the man that all was well and to go back inside. In a moment, Sutcliffe was gone as quickly as he had come. Miraculously, Rogulski survived, but her life would never be the same again. After her discharge from hospital she returned to her home, where she would live alone, barricaded behind a network of wires and alarms. She was terrified of strangers and rarely went out. When she did, she walked in the middle of the street, as she was afraid of the shadows and terrified of people approaching her from behind. There was no boyfriend now, and no prospects of marriage. The £15,000 she received from the Criminal Compensation Board could not buy back her life. She died on 17 April 2008 of natural causes.

Olive Smelt, a 46-year-old housewife, was to be Sutcliffe's next victim. On Friday, 15 August 1975, Peter drove his friend Trevor Birdsall to Halifax where they drank in a number of pubs. It was in one of these pubs that Peter had first seen Smelt. She had followed her usual Friday-night pattern of meeting her girlfriends for a drink. Sutcliffe and Birdsall were known to her and her friends and gave them all a lift home. Smelt was dropped off in Boothtown Road, a short walk from her home, at about 11.45pm.

At the same time, Sutcliffe got out and left Trevor alone in his car. As Smelt took a short cut through an alleyway, Sutcliffe walked up behind her and overtook her, inflicting a heavy blow on the back of her head with a hammer. He hit her again as she fell to the ground then slashed at her back with his knife just above her buttocks. However, he was again prevented from completing his task. He saw a car approaching, so he left Smelt and returned to the car where Trevor was waiting and they drove off. All of this occurred in the space of 10 minutes. Like Sutcliffe's first victim, Smelt also survived the horrifying attack.

The attack left a lasting impression on Smelt. She suffered from severe depression and memory loss. For months, she wished that she were dead. She took no interest in her life and lived in fear, especially of men, sometimes even of her husband. Their relationship was permanently altered and she rarely felt like having sex. Her past enjoyment of homemaking and cooking was lost and she now completed these tasks in a robotic fashion. Her oldest daughter suffered a nervous breakdown, which doctors were sure was a direct result of the attack, and, for many years, her son would continue to lock the door whenever he left his mother alone in the house. Despite the similarities between the two apparently motiveless attacks on Anna Rogulski and Olive Smelt, it would be three years before police would link them and be able to prove that they had both been committed by Sutcliffe. A similar attack was also committed by Sutcliffe that August: Tracy Browne, aged 14. She was struck from behind and hit on the head five times while walking in a country lane. She, like the other two women, survived.

Sutcliffe committed his first murder in October 1975. His victim was Wilomena McCann, known as Wilma. She was 28 years old and a mother of four. Her body was found on the morning of 30 October 1975, lying face up on a sloping grass embankment of the Prince Philip playing fields, off Scott Hall Road, just 100yd from her council home in nearby Scott Hall Avenue. McCann had been struck twice on the back of the head and then stabbed in the neck, chest and abdomen 15 times. There were traces of semen found on the back of her trousers and knickers.

On the night of McCann's death, she had left her three younger children in the care of her eldest daughter, nine-year-old Sonja, to go out drinking. She was drinking heavily until closing time at 10.30pm and then she made her way home. Along the way, a lorry driver stopped when Wilma flagged him down, but continued on his way when he was greeted with a mixture of incoherent instructions and abuse, leaving her by the side of the road. A West Indian man saw her being picked up at about 1.30am; he was the second last person to see her alive. Soon after 5am, a neighbour found Wilma's two eldest daughters huddled together at the bus stop. They were cold, confused and frightened, and waiting for their mother, who hadn't come home.

A team of 150 police officers was set up. They interviewed 7,000 householders and 6,000 lorry drivers. They painstakingly took hundreds of statements from anyone with even the remotest connection to Wilma, but still they never came close to finding her killer.

Sutcliffe did not kill again until Tuesday 20 January 1976. His victim on that night was Emily Monica Jackson, 42, who was working as a prostitute to get extra money for her husband and family. Emily and her husband Sydney would drive their blue Commer van into Leeds where Sydney would wait for his wife in one of the bars while she used the van to work. On the night of

Tuesday, 20 January 1976, they parked their van in the car park of the Gaiety pub and went inside. They had a drink together then Emily went outside to look for business. Sydney was to wait inside until she returned at closing time. When she wasn't there to meet him, he took a taxi home, expecting her to follow in the van shortly after – but she never returned home.

Emily's mutilated body was found just after 8am the following morning, only 800yd from the Gaiety. After murdering her, Sutcliffe had left her lying on her back with her legs apart. She was still wearing her tights and knickers, but her bra was pulled up, exposing her breasts. Peter had struck Emily on the head twice with his hammer and then stabbed her lower neck, upper chest and lower abdomen 51 times with a sharpened Phillips screwdriver. Sutcliffe's need to vent his anger on the already-dead Emily caused him to make a slip, though; he stomped on Emily's right thigh, leaving the impression of a heavy ribbed Wellington boot. The boot was further identified as a Dunlop Warwick, probably size seven, definitely no larger than an eight. Another print was found in the sand nearby.

Sutcliffe lost his job as a lorry driver, curtailing his travelling. However, his need to kill was becoming unbearable, as Marcella Claxton, a 20-year-old prostitute, would soon discover. At around 4am on 9 May, she was walking home from a drinking party held by friends in Chapeltown, an area of Leeds. A large white car pulled up alongside her. She wasn't working that night but she asked the driver for a lift. That driver was Sutcliffe. Instead of driving her home, he drove her to Soldier's Field just off Roundhay Road. He offered Marcella £5 to get out of the car and undress for sex on the grass, but she refused the offer. As they both got out of the car, Marcella heard a thud as Sutcliffe dropped something and it hit the ground. He told her it was his wallet. Marcella then went behind a tree to urinate. Sutcliffe walked towards her and the next thing she felt was the blow of Sutcliffe's hammer as he brought it down on the back of her head, and then she felt the second blow. She lay back on the grass, looking at the blood on her hand from where she had touched her head. Sutcliffe stood nearby. She remembered vividly that his hair and beard were black and crinkly and that he was masturbating as he watched her bleeding on the ground. He went back to the white car with the red upholstery to get some tissues to clean himself up. When he finished, he threw the tissues on the ground and placed a £5 note in Marcella's hand, warning her not to call the police as he got back into his car.

Marcella, her clothes now covered in blood, managed to half-walk, half-crawl to a nearby telephone box where she called for an ambulance. As she sat on the floor and waited for help, she saw Sutcliffe drive past many times looking for her, probably to finish the job and rid himself of a vital witness. The gaping wound in the back of her head required 52 stitches and a seven-day stay in hospital. For months after the attack, she would hate men, barely able to be in the same room with them. Years after the attack, she was still plagued by depression and dizzy spells and was unable to hold down a job. The birth of her son Adrian coincided with Sutcliffe's subsequent arrest in 1981.

The senseless attacks were, by now, the main topic of conversation among prostitutes and the patrons of the many pubs in the Leeds area, and they were compared to the notorious crimes of Jack the Ripper in the previous century. Prostitutes, in an attempt to protect themselves, were seen working in groups, making it very clear to their clients that the details of their cars and registration numbers were being recorded. Increased police activity in the area put further pressure on the already strained relationship between the prostitutes and officers of the law, creating a formidable barrier to the police enquiry.

On Saturday, 5 February, 28-year-old Irene Richardson left her lodgings in Cowper Street, Chapeltown, at 11.30pm to go to Tiffany's Club. En route she met Sutcliffe, who drove her to Soldier's Field, the scene of a previous attack. After attacking her savagely, he left her lying face down, placing her coat over her inert and bloodied body. He had fractured her skull with the three blows he inflicted with his hammer. One of the blows had been so severe that a circular piece of her skull had actually penetrated her brain. He had stabbed her in the neck and throat, and three more times in the stomach, savage downward strokes that had caused her intestines to spill out. When her coat was removed, police found that while her bra was still in place, her skirt had been lifted up and her tights pulled off the right leg and down. One of the two pairs of knickers she had been wearing had been removed and stuffed down her tights, while the other pair was still in place. Her calf-length brown boots had been removed and placed neatly over her thighs. A vaginal swab showed the presence of semen but it was considered to have been from sexual activity prior to the attack.

A further examination of the crime scene revealed tyre tracks from which casts were taken. The tracks indicated that the killer had used a medium-sized car or van. Checks with tyre manufacturers established that the vehicle had been fitted with two 'India Autoway' tyres and a 'Penman' brand on the rear offside, all of them cross-ply. With the assistance of tyre manufacturers, a list of 26 possible car models was drawn up. It seemed that a genuine break had finally been made in the investigation. Police officers, without the benefits of computerisation, had moved into local vehicle taxation offices each night to hand-check all the vehicles in West Yorkshire compatible with the list. The final list contained 100,000 cars – an overwhelming investigative task for the police.

On Saturday, 23 April, Patricia Atkinson became Sutcliffe's next victim. By the time he came across her, she was drunk. Together, they walked to his car and then drove back to her flat. As they entered through her front door, Sutcliffe struck the back of Atkinson's head with the same hammer he had used on all of his previous victims. Before her unconscious body hit the floor, he struck her three more times. As the blood poured from her wounds, he began to remove her overcoat. He then lifted her, carried her to the bedroom and threw her down on the bed.

There, he ripped open her black leather jacket and blue shirt. Pulling up her bra to reveal her breasts, he then pulled her jeans down to her ankles. With a chisel he had removed from his pocket, he began to stab at her now-exposed stomach. He turned her over and stabbed her in the back but did not penetrate the skin. Then he quickly turned her back over to stab her stomach again, leaving a total of six stab wounds. Before he left her, he pulled her jeans back up and, without realising it, he left a size seven Dunlop Warwick wellington boot print on the bottom bed sheet.

His next victim was the youngest, 16-year-old Jayne McDonald, who met her untimely death at the hands of Sutcliffe on 25 June 1977. She was going out dancing and was in a happy mood. She kissed her father goodbye before she left their home in Reginald Terrace, Chapeltown, for the last time. After the dance, Jayne had gone with friends to buy chips in the city centre, but missed the last bus home.

At 11.50pm, she began walking home with Mark Jones, a young man she had met earlier that night. He was to organise a lift home for her with his sister, but the sister wasn't home when they got there. Jayne and Mark continued walking together, stopping for a brief kiss and cuddle, as far as the Florence Nightingale public house. It was 1.30am when they went their separate ways. At a kiosk near the Dock Green pub, near the corner of Beckett Street, Jayne stopped at 1.45am to call a taxi, but there was no answer. As she approached the playground, she did not see Sutcliffe lurking in the shadows waiting to pounce on her as she passed by.

Two children found her body at 9.45am on Sunday, 26 June, near a wall inside the playground where Sutcliffe had dragged her. She was lying face down, her skirt was in disarray and her white halterneck top was pulled up to expose her breasts. He had struck her three times on the back of the head with his hammer and then stabbed her repeatedly in the chest and once in the back.

Following McDonald's murder – an 'innocent young woman'

rather than a prostitute – the police were inundated with information from the public. People who might before have been interested only in hearing the gory details of the attacks now felt personally affronted and threatened by the man they dubbed the Yorkshire Ripper. Where previously witnesses had been reluctant to admit to any connection with the murdered prostitutes, people from the surrounding area were now readily volunteering information to help the police in their attempts to catch Jayne's killer. Despite extensive enquiries, Sutcliffe evaded detection and was undeterred.

On Saturday, 9 July 1977 Sutcliffe headed off to the red-light district in Bradford. As he trawled the streets at 2am, he saw Maureen Long waiting in a long queue at a taxi rank. He was driving his white Ford Corsair. He pulled alongside her and offered her a lift. Long foolishly accepted and got in. Sutcliffe drove her to Bowling Back Lane, where he struck a massive blow to the back of her head. As she lay on the ground, he stabbed her in the abdomen and back. The barking of a dog nearby interrupted his frenzied attack and he left Maureen for dead and fled the scene. His car was seen leaving the area by a night watchman who was working nearby, at 3.27am. He described the car as a Ford Cortina Mark II, white with a black roof. The next morning, two women living in a nearby caravan heard cries for help, went to investigate and found Long lying seriously injured on the ground. The injuries she sustained would have killed most people, but somehow she survived. She described her attacker as being white, with a large build, about 35, with light brown, shoulder-length hair. He was about 6ft tall, with puffy cheeks and big hands. She wasn't sure about the colour of the car; it might have been white or yellow, or blue.

Sutcliffe carried on with his life as normal; it was really beginning to improve. On Monday, 26 September, he and his wife moved into their new home and he bought himself another second-hand Ford Corsair, a red one to replace the white Corsair he had sold on 31 August.

UNITED KINGDOM

The following Saturday, 1 October 1977, after spending the day working on his new car, Sutcliffe decided to take it out for a test drive and finished up in Manchester. By 9.30pm, he had selected his next victim, Jean Bernadette Jordan, aged 20. She got into his car near her home in Moss Side. She took Sutcliffe to a quiet area of vacant land between some allotments and the Southern Cemetery, where she had sexual intercourse with him for £5. Before getting out of the car, she put the £5 note in a hidden compartment of her handbag. Once out of the car, Sutcliffe used his hammer to hit her over the head a total of 13 times. He then hid her body in undergrowth near the fence between the cemetery and the allotments.

Sutcliffe then returned home but began to worry about the £5 note he had given Jean Jordan. It was a brand-new note and it might be possible to trace it back to him. By Sunday, 9 October, there still had been no word of the discovery of Jean's body in the papers. Sutcliffe drove back to the body and found it exactly as he had left it, but her handbag was missing. As he searched the area, he became frantic at the prospect of the police finding the £5 note. When his frustration and fury were at their peak, he dragged the lifeless and already rotting body away from its hiding place. He tore Jean's clothes from her body, and then stabbed her over and over again. Eighteen times he stabbed at her breasts, chest, stomach and vagina. They were fierce slashing swipes, some 8in deep. One extended from her left shoulder down to her right knee. When the rage subsided, Sutcliffe thought again of the £5 note, and attempted to cut off Jean's head. His intention was to divert police attention by disposing of her head somewhere else.

When he realised that it was an impossible task with only a small hacksaw and a broken pane of glass, he gave up and went home. The unrecognisable body of Jean Jordan was found on 10 October. She was later identified from her fingerprints.

On Saturday 15 October, Jean Jordan's handbag was found only 100yd from where her body had lain the week before. The £5 note Sutcliffe had given her that he so desperately wanted to retrieve was found in the hidden pocket where she had placed it. The note, with the serial number AW51 121565, was brand new, issued only a couple of days before she was killed. The Bank of England established that the note was part of a consignment sent to the Shipley and Bingley branches of the Midland Bank, right in the heart of the Yorkshire Ripper area.

It was quickly established that the note in question had been part of a bundle of £500 and had been the fifth-last note in a sequence of 69. The note had been part of a batch of £17,500 that had been distributed to a number of firms in the Bradford and Shipley area which employed almost 8,000 men in total.

A team of officers concentrated on tracing the note for a total of three months. They interviewed 5,000 of those 8,000 men. One of the firms they concentrated on was T & WH Clark (Holdings Ltd) in Canal Road, Shipley. They interviewed the men who worked there, including Peter William Sutcliffe of Garden Lane, Heaton. There had been nothing about Peter, or the other 5,000 men, that had seemed suspicious. They had even spoken to his wife, Sonia, who had not contradicted Sutcliffe's movements in any way on the nights in question.

Despite the high police presence and activity in the areas where the murders had taken place, Sutcliffe could not resist the urge to seek out another victim. However, this victim was later able to provide a strong identification of him and his car. On 14 December, a prostitute named Marilyn Moore, aged 25, left a friend's home in Gathorne Terrace, near the Gaiety pub, at 8pm. As she walked along, she noticed a dark-coloured car drive slowly towards her, and was sure that the driver was a potential client. She was proved correct and saw the car parked near a junction known as Frankland Place. The driver was leaning against his door. He was about 30, with a stocky build, around 5ft 6in tall with dark, wavy hair and a beard. He was wearing a yellow shirt, a navy blue or black zip-up anorak and blue jeans, and appeared to be waving to someone in a nearby house. This was none other than Peter Sutcliffe.

Sutcliffe asked Moore if she was 'doing business' and they agreed a price before she got into the car with him. As they drove off to a secluded location about a mile and a half away, he told her that his name was Dave and that the person he had been waving to was his girlfriend. When they arrived at their destination, Sutcliffe suggested that they have sex in the back seat, but when Moore got out of the car she found that the back door was locked. As Sutcliffe came behind her to open the door, Moore felt a sickening blow to the top of her head. She screamed loudly and attempted to protect her head with her hands. She fell to the ground, frantically grabbing her attacker's trousers as she fell, then felt further blows before losing consciousness. A dog barked at the sound of her screams and Sutcliffe left before he could finish. Moore remembered hearing him walk back to his car and slam the door, and then she heard the back wheels skid as he hurriedly drove away. Slowly, Moore managed to get herself to her feet and stumble towards a telephone. Before she reached it, a man and woman, noticing the blood running from her head, stopped to help and called an ambulance. She was rushed to Leeds General Infirmary and underwent an emergency operation. Moore stayed in hospital until just before New Year's Eve, but it was a long time before she could face returning to Leeds, with a hole in the back of her head and scars all over her scalp.

The police now knew that Marilyn had been another of the Yorkshire Ripper's victims. This was confirmed when the tyre tracks left by his car were matched to those found at the site of Irene Richardson's death. Despite this new evidence, the hunt for the Ripper continued without success. The senior police officer leading the investigation decided to pull his officers out of Bradford, accepting that they had probably met the killer and failed to recognise him.

By the end of January 1978, police were beginning to wonder whether the Ripper had been scared off by his unsuccessful attack on Marilyn Moore. What they did not know at the time was that Sutcliffe had, in fact, killed again on the night of 21 January. However, his victim, Yvonne Pearson, would not be found until the end of March, when her severely mutilated body was discovered under an old sofa on waste ground off Arthington Street, Bradford. She had been bludgeoned with a large blunt instrument, presumed to have been a rock. This caused police to wonder. This was not the Ripper's usual method, but many of the other characteristics of this murder were similar to the earlier deaths.

Yvonne Pearson had left her two girls, aged two years and five months, in the care of a babysitter on the night of 21 January 1978 to see if she could earn some money. Her first stop that night had been the Flying Dutchman pub, which she was seen leaving at 9.30pm. Soon after that, Sutcliffe invited her to get into his car to do 'some business'. When they parked, he hit her repeatedly on the head with a lump hammer. When she was dead, he hid her body under the sofa and jumped on her chest until her ribs had broken. Fear of discovery by people in the area had cut short his time with Yvonne and he had not stabbed her. A newspaper, dated one month after her death, was placed under her body, leading police to believe that the killer had later returned to the scene of the crime.

Any hopes police may have had that the killer had stopped were soon shattered. On Tuesday, 31 January 1978, in the red-light district of Huddersfield, Sutcliffe was again trawling the streets. He came across Helen Rytka, who was soliciting. She had previously been working in company with her sister and both had been careful to take the registration numbers of each other's clients. However, there was a short time gap during which they became separated and when Helen got into Sutcliffe's car her sister was not around to take down the details. Sutcliffe drove to a timber yard near the railway, a common haunt of prostitutes and their clients. He convinced her to get into the back seat and, as she did so, he struck her with the hammer. He missed and hit the car door instead, alerting Helen to the danger she was in, but before she had a chance to scream he had hit her again. She immediately crumpled to the ground. It was then that Sutcliffe realised they were in full view of two taxi drivers, who stood talking nearby. Taking Helen by the hair, he dragged her to the back of the wood yard. Still alive, she vainly attempted to protect herself from the hammer as Sutcliffe crashed it down onto her head again. Scared that the taxi drivers would notice them, Sutcliffe lay on top of Helen and covered her mouth with his hand, then had sex with her as she lay bleeding. Finally, the taxi drivers left and Peter got up to find his hammer, which he had dropped. While he searched, Helen attempted to escape. As she ran from him, Peter hit her several more times on the back of the head. Still alive, she was dragged to the front of the car, where Sutcliffe stabbed her through the heart and lungs with a kitchen knife he had hidden in his car.

Helen's sister arrived at their meeting point only five minutes after Helen had left with Sutcliffe. After waiting for some time in the freezing cold, she gave up and went home, assuming that Helen would be waiting for her there. Fear of the police prevented her from reporting Helen's disappearance until Thursday. On Friday, 3 February, a police dog located Helen's body where Sutcliffe had left it on the previous Tuesday.

It was another two months before Sutcliffe killed again. His next victim was 41-year-old Vera Millward. She left her home on Tuesday, 16 May, to buy some cigarettes and pick up some painkillers from the nearby hospital. Sometime after purchasing her cigarettes, she met Sutcliffe. In the grounds of the Manchester Royal Infirmary, in a well-lit area, Sutcliffe struck Vera on the head three times, then, undressing her in his usual manner, he slashed her so viciously across her stomach that her intestines spilled out. He also stabbed her repeatedly in the one wound on her back, just below the lower left ribs, and punctured her right eyelid, bruising her eye. Her screams for help were heard and ignored by a man and his son entering the hospital at the time of her attack. People in this area were well accustomed to such cries in the night. When he had finished with her, Sutcliffe dragged her body 4yd away and dumped her by a chain-link fence, on a rubbish pile in a corner of the car park. She was found at 8.10am the following morning, lying on her right side, face down with her arms folded beneath her and her legs straight. He had placed her shoes neatly on her body. Tyre tracks were found nearby. They matched those left at the murder site of Irene Richardson and at the site where Marilyn Moore had been attacked. But still the police were no nearer catching the killer.

It was then a further 11 months before Sutcliffe killed again. During that period, his mother died, at the age of 59. He had always been close to her and he was grief-stricken. In this time, he had replaced the red Corsair with a metallic-grey Sunbeam Rapier. At work, he was a conscientious driver who kept immaculate logs and repair records. His workmates saw him as a bit of a loner who kept very much to himself and never showed any signs of violence – nor did he swear or speak crudely about sex or women. When police interviewed him again because his registration number had been noted in red-light areas, he was not noticeably concerned. He explained that driving to and from work regularly took him through those areas.

During the time of the murders, police had received a number of letters from people claiming to be the Yorkshire Ripper. Two of these had originated from Sunderland in the northeast of England, and the police had looked at them in great detail but doubted their authenticity. However, on 23 March 1979 they received a third letter, also from Sunderland, which contained a reference to the Vera Millward murder. This made them wonder. Saliva samples from the envelope were tested and this time they got a result; they indicated the rare blood group B, the same as that of Joan Harrison's killer. Forensic tests now confirmed that all three of the letters were from the same source. The writer predicted that the next victim would be 'an old slut' in Bradford or Liverpool.

This prediction was to prove incorrect when on Wednesday, 4

April 1979, the killer struck again. Josephine Whitaker, aged 19 and a building-society clerk, had walked the short mile to her grandparents' home in Halifax to show them the new watch she had bought. Her grandmother had been out when she arrived, so she watched television with her grandfather to await her grandmother's return at 11pm. Tom and Mary Priestley always enjoyed their granddaughter's weekly Sunday visits, and had been pleasantly surprised by this extra midweek visit. When Jo, as they called her, decided to go home, her grandparents tried to talk her into staying the night. It was only a 10-minute walk home, which she had done many times before.

It was almost midnight by the time Whitaker reached Saville Park, an area of open grassland surrounded by well-lit roads. As she walked across the damp grass in the park, she met Peter Sutcliffe, who stopped her to ask the time. She looked towards the town clock in the distance and Peter took the hammer from his jacket, crashing it down on her head. As she lay on the grass, he hit her again, and then dragged her 10yd back into the darkness, away from the road. He pulled her clothing back and stabbed her 25 times, in her breasts, stomach and thighs; even in her vagina. He left her lying like a bundle of rags. One of her tan shoes still lay at the roadside where his attack had begun. She had been almost in sight of her home when she was murdered. The next morning, at 6.30am, a woman waiting at a bus stop found the body and called the police.

The pathologist's report revealed that there had been traces of a mineral oil used in engineering shops in Josephine Whitaker's wounds. It was soon confirmed that the particles were similar to those found on one of the envelopes of the mysterious letters from Sunderland. The letters were seen as credible evidence that could lead to the capture of the elusive Yorkshire Ripper.

The police then dispatched a team of detectives to carry out enquiries in Sunderland. Two months later, they received a cassette tape from the writer of the letters, which sent them on a wild goose chase as they then searched for a killer with a Geordie accent. While police officials debated whether or not to go public with the tape, news of its arrival and contents were leaked to the press. The decision was made and a press conference, at which the tape was played, was called on Tuesday, 26 June 1979. Despite public appeals and extensive enquiries, the man whose voice was on the tape and who is believed to have written the three letters was not traced. In the end, police had serious doubts about whether the tape and the letters were actually genuine.

Then Peter Sutcliffe struck again, throwing the police enquiry wide open once more. On the night of 1 September 1979, Barbara Janine Leach went to the Manville Arms in Bradford with five of her closest friends. Barbara was a student at Bradford University and lived with a group of students in a house in Grove Terrace, just across Great Horton Road from the university. Also at the Manville Arms that night was Peter Sutcliffe. He had seen Barbara from across the other side of the room and had watched her continuously. At closing time, 11pm, he left and waited in his car outside. Barbara, along with her five friends, had stayed behind to help clean up and have a drink with the landlord. When they finally left at 12.45am, Sutcliffe was watching nearby as the group walked towards Great Horton Road. As they were about to turn left into Grove Terrace, Barbara decided to go for a walk and invited her friend, Paul Smith, to join her. When he declined the offer, she asked him to wait for her, as she didn't have a key. He agreed and they parted company.

As he watched Barbara walk down Great Horton Road alone, Sutcliffe started the car and drove down to Back Ash Grove, where he parked. Armed with the hammer and knife, he got out of the car and walked quickly along the alleyway, knowing that Barbara would soon be walking past at the other end. He waited for her in the shadows of Back Ash Grove, listening to the echo of her boots on the pavement as she walked towards him. As she passed, he sprang, smashing the hammer into her head. With just one blow she was dead.

Sutcliffe then dragged the lifeless body back into the shadows of the side entrance towards Back Ash Grove. In the yard behind number 13, he dropped her body and tore at her clothing, exposing her breasts, abdomen and knickers. He stabbed her eight times, then dragged her body close to some rubbish bins and covered her with a piece of old carpet lying nearby. When Leach was reported missing the following day a search began, and her body was found that afternoon. Professor Gee, the pathologist who had worked on all of the Yorkshire Ripper cases, believed that the knife used to stab Leach was the same one used on Josephine Whitaker. With the deaths of two victims who were not prostitutes in non-red light areas in a six-month period, the West Yorkshire public now began venting its anger on the police. All this time, Peter Sutcliffe was living only five minutes away from the police headquarters in Bradford.

By 1979, police were able to use their new national database. By entering the makes and registration numbers of vehicles sighted in the areas of the attacks, the computer could chart precise flow patterns of individual vehicles. It was hoped that witness information about a particular type of car in the area of an attack could be matched with vehicle registration numbers recorded in the area and then cross-checked against other records. Through this process, the police were able to eliminate 200,000 vehicles – including the one driven by Sutcliffe.

While the use of the computer saved thousands of man-hours in some way, it also created an avalanche of new information that had to be checked. By the beginning of 1980, the police were faced with millions of facts – five million in the case of car registration numbers alone – and they were now swamped, barely able to keep up.

Since January 1979, when police had searched for the owner of the £5 note found in Jean Jordan's handbag, they had returned many times to interview employees of firms such as the haulier Clark's, where Peter Sutcliffe worked. Sutcliffe had been interviewed on a number of occasions and his workmates had taken to calling him the Ripper because of the apparent police interest in him. Even as late as 1980, Sutcliffe was never considered to be a strong suspect, despite the fact that he had a gap in his front teeth, his car had been spotted in red-light districts a number of times, his blood type was of the B group but he was not a secretor, he had the right boot size and his name was on the now dramatically shortened list of 300 possible recipients of the £5 note.

Another vital error the police made was that none of the men interviewed at this time were given blood tests, nor were any placed under surveillance or their boot sizes checked. The overwhelming reason for Sutcliffe not being considered a viable suspect, even after a total of nine interviews with police, was that he had provided alibis verified by Sonia, and because he did not have a Geordie accent – a frightening indication of how assumptions can prejudice an investigation to the point where vital clues are missed.

In April 1979, during his travels, Sutcliffe met and had an affair with a woman from Glasgow, Theresa Douglas, whom he visited on many occasions. Sutcliffe was also stopped by police for drink-driving around this time, an offence for which he was likely to lose his licence. But he was nervous for a far more important reason than this. What if the arresting police were to find that he had been interviewed many times in the Yorkshire Ripper investigations? Would he be revealed as the killer, wanted in what had become known as the crime investigation of the century? However, luck was on his side yet again; there were no cross-checks done and he was soon free to go home.

As he waited for his impending court appearance, due in January 1981, Sutcliffe attacked four women, killing two of them. The first attack occurred in the respectable suburb of Farsley, Leeds. His 47-year-old victim, Marguerite Walls, was a civil servant who worked at the Department of Education and Science at Farsley. She worked late on the night of 20 August 1980, as she had wanted to clear her desk before she started her holiday the following day. She left her office building at 10.30pm to begin the short walk home, taking the longest but safest route along well-lit streets. In New Street, as she walked past the entrance to a local magistrate's house, Peter Sutcliffe jumped out from behind the fence where he had waited for her and hit her on the head with his hammer. Marguerite did not fall to the ground as he expected her to. Instead, she began to scream, and a second blow to the head still did not stop her screaming as she held her now-bleeding head. To stop her screaming, he grabbed her by the neck and strangled her. As he did so, he dragged her into the driveway and through the overgrown bushes of a property called Claremont. By this time, Marguerite was dead. Sutcliffe ripped at her clothes, tearing them from her and scattering them around the garden. His anger and frustration at his failure to bring his knife rose; he rained blows on her body with his hammer. Before leaving her, he covered her body with leaves. As he left the garden, he checked that the street was quiet before stepping out from the darkness. Fifteen minutes later, he was safely home. When Marguerite was found the following morning, only 400yd from her home, it was soon determined that, although she had been bludgeoned with a hammer, her strangulation ruled her out as a victim of the Ripper.

Sutcliffe's next attack was also in Leeds, in Headingley. It was 24 September when Dr Upadhya Bandara was walking home after visiting friends in Headingley. As she walked past the Kentucky Fried Chicken shop, she noticed a man inside staring at her. She walked on past North Lane, and then turned right into St Michael's Lane. As she turned into Chapel Lane, an alley that cut through to Cardigan Road, she was hurled to the ground. Sutcliffe slammed his hammer into her head, rendering her unconscious. He held her around the neck with a ligature to prevent her escape. Bandara lay bleeding on the ground as Sutcliffe picked up her shoes and handbag and took them several yards away. Before he could resume his attack, he heard footsteps and fled. The footsteps belonged to Valerie Nicholas, whose house backed onto the lane. She had heard noises at 10.30pm and had gone out to investigate. Her actions saved the life of Bandara, who later recovered from the attack. The police in Headingley, for whatever reason, did not believe that the Yorkshire Ripper had attacked Dr Upadhya Bandara, despite the fact that she described her attacker as having black hair and a full beard and moustache.

Sutcliffe's next attack, on 5 November 1980, was in Huddersfield, but at the time this was not looked on as the work of the Ripper. Theresa Sykes, a 16-year-old who lived with her boyfriend and their three-month-old son, was followed by Sutcliffe from the Minstrel pub. She was walking across grassland not far from her home when he attacked her with his hammer, hitting her three times about the head. One of the blows was so severe that it penetrated her skull. Theresa screamed as Peter struck her. Her boyfriend watched in horror from their living-room window. Within seconds, he was running towards Theresa and Sutcliffe. When Sutcliffe saw him, he ran off into the darkness of the night. Theresa miraculously survived the brutal attack. After spending several weeks in hospital, she returned home but was never the same again. She was now afraid of men; her whole personality had changed, and she was quick to flare up in anger over the smallest thing. Sutcliffe had left his mark on yet another family.

On the night of 17 November 1980, Sutcliffe again was in the Headingley district of Leeds as he ate at the Kentucky Fried Chicken shop. He sat looking out of the window, and at 9.23pm he saw student Jacqueline Hill get off a bus. He began to follow Jacqueline after she passed the Kentucky Fried Chicken shop. He was behind her as she entered the dimly lit Alma Road towards the Lupton Flats, where she had recently moved. She was almost home when Sutcliffe struck her on the back of the head. He dragged her lifeless body onto some vacant land, which was hidden from view by trees and bushes, and stabbed her repeatedly. He stabbed her in the eye that had stared up at him accusingly as her tore at her clothes and slashed her naked body. When he had finished, he left her body and headed for home. However, he forgot that her handbag and glasses still lay on the pavement in Alma Road where she had dropped them when he initially attacked her. The bag was found by a member of the public and, due to blood spots found on it, handed to the police. They carried out a search of the area but failed to find the body. It was not until daybreak that the body was found where Sutcliffe had left it.

By now the public response was overwhelming and one report the police received came from the friend of Peter Sutcliffe, Trevor Birdsall. He actually named Peter Sutcliffe to the police, telling them that Sutcliffe was a lorry driver from Bradford. When police had still not questioned Sutcliffe two weeks later, Birdsall went to Bradford police station, where he repeated his allegations to the officer on the reception desk. The report was fed into the system but Peter Sutcliffe continued to roam free. Trevor had been suspicious of Peter for some time before he went to the police, even as far back as Olive Smelt's attack, but Peter was his friend and he didn't like to think he was capable of killing. The police insistence that the Yorkshire Ripper was from Sunderland and spoke with a Geordie accent had allayed Trevor's suspicions for a long time. When Birdsall heard nothing more from the police, he assumed that they had followed up his allegations but that he had been wrong about Sutcliffe. What he didn't know what that his letter had never reached the murder incident room. It had been lost under a mountain of uncollated paperwork.

On Friday, 2 January 1981, Peter Sutcliffe decided to go to Sheffield; it was the first time he had ventured this far away from home in search of prostitutes. He was in his own car and was armed with his hammer. It was not long before he came across another unsuspecting prostitute. Twenty-four-year-old Olivia Reivers had met with another prostitute, Denise Hall, 19, to ply her trade in Sheffield's red-light district. It was around 9pm when Denise met her first potential client, Peter Sutcliffe. He was driving his brown Rover 3500 and had pulled up to the kerb, but there was something about his eyes that had disturbed her. Despite his good looks, with a neatly trimmed beard and dark wavy hair, he had frightened her, so she declined his offer of £10.

Sutcliffe continued to cruise the area and an hour later came across Olivia Reivers. When Olivia looked into Peter's eyes she did not see what her friend Denise had seen. Sutcliffe offered her £10 and she got into his car. They drove a short distance to a quiet location where Olivia had often taken her clients. After attempting to have sex, Sutcliffe had been unable to become aroused, despite Olivia's many attempts to help him, so they had sat and talked for a while. She did not know that he had a hammer and a knife in his pocket.

Olivia Reivers was saved from an attack by Sutcliffe by the arrival of two uniformed police officers on patrol who had seen the parked car and decided to check it out. They pulled up behind the Rover and questioned the couple sitting in the car. Sutcliffe said his name was Peter Williams. Reivers said she was his girlfriend. One of the officers remembered her face and believed she was a convicted prostitute. He told her to get into the police car. Sutcliffe told them he needed to go to the toilet. He wanted to dispose of the hammer and the knife, and walked further along the dark driveway. There was an oil storage tank nearby. It was behind this tank, well out of view of the policemen, that Sutcliffe disposed of his hammer and knife; he hoped that the police had not seen or heard him.

In the meantime, one of the officers did a check on Sutcliffe's car and found that the registration number on his vehicle belonged to a Skoda and not a Rover 3500. The officers examined closely the plates on Sutcliffe's car, which were held on with black tape. They found the correct plates underneath. Sutcliffe confirmed this and admitted that his real name was Peter William Sutcliffe and that he lived at Garden Lane, Heaton, Bradford. He said he had lied because he didn't want his wife to find out that he had been with a prostitute.

Both Sutcliffe and Reivers were taken to the local police station. They were placed in separate interview rooms. Sutcliffe told them that he had stolen the plates from a car in a scrapyard in another police district, Dewsbury, which meant he should be taken back to the district where the crime was committed. The police, however, failed to make a thorough search of him when he arrived at the police station and so didn't notice that he was still in possession of a second knife. He asked to go to the toilet, where he hid the knife in the cistern. When Sutcliffe was stripped of his clothing at the police station, he was discovered to be wearing a V-neck sweater under his trousers; the arms had been pulled over his legs, so that the V-neck exposed his groin; the elbows were padded to protect his knees as, presumably, he knelt over his victims' corpses. The sexual implications of this outfit should have been obvious, but the police did not pick up on it at that time.

A routine call to the Dewsbury police was made from the incident room because of a recent directive that any man found with prostitutes in suspicious circumstances was to be reported. At 8.55am, Peter Sutcliffe arrived at Dewsbury police station, where he was transferred to the station's interview room. Just after 9am, Sonia called and was told that her husband was being interviewed in relation to the theft of car number plates. In the interview room, Sutcliffe chatted with officers about his work as a lorry driver and his love of cars. They noted that he had dark frizzy hair, a beard and a gap between his teeth.

The officers were familiar with the five points of reference for the elimination of suspects in the Yorkshire Ripper case but were not fazed by the lack of a Geordie accent. Peter Sutcliffe lived in Bradford in the heart of Ripper country and had told them that he had driven to Sunderland many times in his work as a lorry driver. The list of possible cars did not include the brown Rover that Sutcliffe was driving at the time of his arrest, but he had told them about his white Corsair with the black roof. While being questioned, Sutcliffe openly admitted that he had been questioned on a number of other occasions in relation to the Yorkshire Ripper case. Detective Sergeant Des O'Boyle, an officer working on the murders and well versed in the Yorkshire Ripper case, had left for Dewsbury at lunchtime on Saturday, 6 November, to question Sutcliffe himself. During the afternoon, a blood test revealed that Sutcliffe was of the rare B group. That night, Sutcliffe remained in the police cells at Dewsbury.

Back in Sheffield, one of the arresting officers Police Sgt Robert Ring came back on duty at 10pm. He was told that Sutcliffe was still being held at Dewsbury police station and being questioned by Yorkshire Ripper squad officers. This officer then made a decision that had a momentous impact on the Yorkshire Ripper investigation. Sutcliffe had left his car to go to the toilet; maybe he had left something at the scene – the officer recalled hearing a clinking noise. So he returned to the driveway on Melbourne Avenue to have a look around. When he shone his torch on the ground by the wall behind the oil storage tank, Sgt Ring found the hammer and knife that Sutcliffe had left there the night before.

The police now believed they might have finally caught the Yorkshire Ripper. They executed search warrants at Sutcliffe's house, and recovered a number of tools, including hammers. Sonia Sutcliffe accompanied them back to Bradford where she was extensively questioned for 13 hours. The officers attempted to obtain as many details of Sutcliffe's movements at the times of the attacks as possible. At the same time, officers behind the scenes were working to gain as much information about Sutcliffe's movements over the past five years as they could, including visits to past employers and making other enquiries in the Bradford area.

By early Sunday afternoon, Sutcliffe knew that he should not have been detained for the length of time he had been on a minor theft charge, and when the police questioned him about his movements on the night of Theresa Sykes's attack on 5 November 1980, he began to lose the incredible calmness that he had shown throughout the 48-hour detention. Sutcliffe told them that he was positive he had arrived home by 8pm. Sonia's recollection was different. She distinctly remembered Peter arriving home at 10pm.

Later that day, during another interview, Sutcliffe was told about the discovery of the hammer and knife as they continued to question him about the attack on Theresa Sykes. It was then that Peter Sutcliffe sat back in his chair and calmly admitted that he was the Yorkshire Ripper. Over the next 26 hours, Sutcliffe, calmly and with little display of emotion, told police officers the gruesome details of the last five years of death and mutilation. The only emotion he showed was when discussing the murder of 16-year-old Jayne McDonald. He did, however, deny the murder of Joan Harrison. Sutcliffe told police that in 1967, at the age of 20, he had heard the voice of God speak to him as he worked at Bingley cemetery. He claimed that he had first heard that voice while digging a grave. He stated that the voice had led him to a cross-shaped headstone upon which were written some Polish words. He said it was this same voice that had ordered him to kill prostitutes. Police were satisfied from what Sutcliffe had told them that he was mentally ill, suffering from paranoid schizophrenia and insane. However, there was some doubt about this later.

Following his confession, Peter Sutcliffe had one request. He wanted to be the one to tell his wife Sonia. She was immediately driven from Bradford police headquarters to the Dewsbury police station. Sutcliffe sat at a small table across from Sonia as he calmly told her his shocking story. When Sonia emerged from the interview room, she appeared to be calm, not revealing any emotions. With regard to the question of him being insane, Sutcliffe had been overheard telling his wife that he might be able to reduce his sentence to as little as ten years if he could convince everyone that he was mad. In any event, Sutcliffe would face trial for murder and it would be for a jury to decide whether he was insane or not.

THE EVIL WITHIN

On 5 May 1981, Peter Sutcliffe stood trial for 13 murders. During the trial, the insanity issues surrounding Sutcliffe were put before the jury. On one side, the prosecution put forward their case to show that Sutcliffe was not insane and, on the other side, his defence attempted to convince the jury of the opposite. On Friday, 22 May 1981, Peter Sutcliffe was found guilty of all of the murders; the jury believing him not to be insane but, in fact, an evil and sadistic murderer. He was sentenced to life imprisonment with a recommendation that he serve a minimum of 30 years before parole could even be considered. This recommendation meant that Sutcliffe was unlikely to be freed until at least 2011 at the age of 65.

Sutcliffe was later sent to Broadmoor, a high-security mental hospital, after being diagnosed as a paranoid schizophrenic. In 1983, while at Broadmoor, he was viciously attacked on several occasions by other inmates. One such attack resulted in him losing the sight in his right eye. He also developed diabetes. His wife Sonia divorced him in 1994.

Over the years, Sutcliffe's sentence and the question of future parole have been considered by two different Home Secretaries and, despite Sutcliffe being given a whole-life tariff by them, he could still be released from custody if the parole board were to decide that he is no longer a danger to the public. The European Court of Human Rights and also the High Court have since declared the system under which his tariff was increased illegal. The main point of conflict is that the continued detention of Sutcliffe and other life prisoners in England has in recent years been reviewed. Recent government legislation has now set out new guidelines in respect of convicted persons serving life sentences. All offenders convicted of murder need to have a minimum term set. This is the minimum time that the offender will serve before eligible for parole. Up until November 2002, the Home Secretary set the minimum term, but this practice ceased following the decision in *Anderson v Secretary of State* [2003] that declared the practice unlawful. As a consequence, all prisoners who had already been notified of a minimum term by the Home Secretary had the right to ask the High Court to review it. The High Court could confirm it or lower it, but not increase it.

It also meant that between 25 November 2002 and 18 December 2003 no minimum terms were set, and offenders were sentenced to life imprisonment without knowing their earliest date of release. This resulted in approximately 700 serving life prisoners who had not had a minimum term set. Those cases were referred back to the High Court by the Home Secretary for a minimum term to be set administratively by a High Court Judge. These provisions now apply to all cases where the date of offence is on or after 18 December 2003. For offences dated before 18 December 2003, complex transitional arrangements apply.

In accordance with section 269 of the Criminal Justice Act 2003 all courts passing a mandatory life sentence are required to order the minimum term the prisoner must serve before the Parole Board can consider release on licence, unless the seriousness of the offence is so exceptionally high that the early release provisions should not apply – in other words, a 'whole life order'. Sutcliffe did then make a further appeal in 2010 to the High Court who dismissed the appeal, confirming that he would serve a whole life tariff and would never be released from imprisonment.

The West Yorkshire Police were heavily criticised for being inadequately prepared for an investigation on this scale. The case was one of the largest-ever investigations by a UK police force and pre-dated the use of computers in criminal cases. Information on suspects was stored on handwritten index cards at various incident rooms across the county, making it a case of the left hand not knowing what the right was doing. Beside the logistical difficulties in storing and accessing such a mountain of paperwork, it was even more difficult for officers to overcome the information overload of such a large manual system. Sutcliffe was interviewed nine times, but all information the police had about the case was stored in paper form, making cross-referencing a difficult task. This fact was compounded by the television appeal for information, which generated thousands more documents to process. The police were also criticised for being too focused on the tape and letters from Sunderland, using them as a point of elimination rather than as a line of enquiry, which allowed Sutcliffe to remain at large for longer, as he did not fit the profile of the sender of the tape or letters. The official response to these problems ultimately led to the implementation of a computer program known as HOLMES, which stands for Home Office Large Major Enquiry System. This is now used for all major incidents and allows documents to be cross-referenced efficiently.

In addition, a judicial enquiry was ordered by the government to look into the whole Yorkshire Ripper case. Sir Lawrence Byford, HM Inspector of Constabulary, conducted this. His report was made public on 1 June 2006. Referring to the period between 1969, when Sutcliffe first came to the attention of police, and 1975, the year of the murder of Wilma McCann, the report stated: 'There is a curious and unexplained lull in Sutcliffe's criminal activities and there is the possibility that he carried out other attacks on prostitutes and unaccompanied women during that period.' In 1969, Sutcliffe, described in the Byford Report as 'an otherwise unremarkable young man', came to the notice of the police on two occasions in connection with incidents involving prostitutes. The report said that it was clear on at least one occasion that he had attacked a Bradford prostitute with a cosh. Also in 1969, he was arrested in the red-light district of the city in possession of a hammer. However, rather than believing Sutcliffe might use the hammer as an offensive weapon, the arresting officers assumed he was a burglar and he was charged with 'going equipped for stealing'.

Sir Lawrence Byford went on to state: 'We feel it is highly improbable that the crimes in respect of which Sutcliffe has been charged and convicted are the only ones attributable to him.

This feeling is reinforced by examining the details of a number of assaults on women since 1969, which, in some ways, clearly fall into the established pattern of Sutcliffe's overall *modus operandi*. I hasten to add that I feel sure that the senior police officers in the areas concerned are also mindful of this possibility but, in order to ensure full account is taken of all the information available, I have arranged for an effective liaison to take place.' Police identified a number of attacks that matched Sutcliffe's MO and tried to question the killer, but he was never charged with other crimes. Sir Lawrence described delays in following up vital tip-offs from Trevor Birdsall, an associate of Sutcliffe's since 1966. On 25 November 1980, Birdsall sent an anonymous letter to police, the text of which ran as follows: 'I have good reason to now [sic] the man you are looking for in the Ripper case. This man as [sic] dealings with prostitutes and always had a thing about them ... His name and address is Peter Sutcliffe, 6 Garden Lane, Heaton, Bradford. Works [sic] for Clarke's Transport, Shipley.' This letter was marked 'Priority No 1'. An index card was created on the basis of the letter and a policewoman found Sutcliffe already had three existing index cards in the records. But 'for some inexplicable reason', said the Byford Report, 'the papers remained in a filing tray in the incident room until the murderer's arrest on 2 January the following year. Birdsall visited Bradford police station the day after sending the letter to repeat his misgivings about Sutcliffe; he added the information that he had been with Sutcliffe when Sutcliffe got out of a car to pursue a woman with whom he had had a bar-room dispute in Halifax on 16 August 1975. This was the date and place of the Olive Smelt attack. A report compiled on this visit was lost, despite a 'comprehensive search' that took place after Sutcliffe's arrest, according to the report. Sir Lawrence said: 'The failure to take advantage of Birdsall's anonymous letter and his visit to the police station was yet again a stark illustration of the progressive decline in the overall efficiency of the major incident room. It resulted in Sutcliffe being at liberty for more than a month when he might conceivably have been in custody. Thankfully, there is no reason to think he committed any further murderous assaults within that period.'

Following Sutcliffe's arrest and conviction, the search for 'Wearside Jack', who sent police the letters and tape, continued. On 18 October 2005, it was reported that a suspect had been arrested. A West Yorkshire Police spokesman stated: 'Officers from West Yorkshire this afternoon travelled to the Sunderland area where they arrested a 49-year-old local man on suspicion of attempting to pervert the course of justice. This relates to the hoax letters and tape that were sent to police during the Yorkshire Ripper murder investigation. He is currently being transported to a West Yorkshire police station for interview.' The 49-year-old man would have been aged 22 or so back in March 1978.

On 19 October 2005, further information about the investigation and the suspect was disclosed. The man arrested was John Humble of the Ford area of Sunderland. Humble was separated from his wife and lived with his brother. Police confirmed that the two-bedroom council house where he lived was being searched by police officers. It was reported that neighbours said that he had lived there for approximately five years. Apparently, a man claiming to be the nephew of the arrested man said that the voice on the tape was not the voice of his uncle, and that his uncle was born near where he currently lived and had no association with the Castletown area where it is believed the man on the tape was from.

It was reported that the reason for the arrest was that a DNA profile had been obtained from the saliva used to seal the envelopes of the letters. The envelopes had been reported as missing as far back as 1999 when a request for them, to test for DNA, was made to the West Yorkshire police during the making of the documentary *Manhunt: The Search For The Yorkshire Ripper*. Furthermore, in July 2005 an ongoing audit, which had been under way for the previous 12 months, had discovered that the original hoax letters and cassette tape had also gone missing. It appears that the envelopes were eventually found and tests conducted.

On 20 October 2005, John Humble appeared at Leeds Magistrates Court charged with perverting the course of justice. The charge against him was read by a clerk at the court, who stated: 'You sent a series of communications, namely three letters and an audiotape, to West Yorkshire police and the press, claiming to be the perpetrator of a series of murders that at that time was the subject of a police investigation.'

During the four-minute hearing, John Humble confirmed his name, date of birth and place of residence. There was no plea entered by the defendant. District Judge Christopher Darnton remanded Humble in custody and no application for bail was made. It was also reported that John Humble might also face questioning by the Lancashire police in relation to Joan Harrison, whose murder was included in one of the hoax letters.

On 21 March 2006, having pleaded guilty at a previous hearing, John Humble appeared before Judge Norman Jones QC for sentencing on the four charges of perverting the course of justice in relation to the Wearside Jack hoax. The judge told Humble: 'You arrogantly set out to send the investigation away from the path of the true killer. You did that with an indifference to the potentially fatal consequences, which was breathtaking, and this sets you in the most serious category of offending of this type. The Ripper attacked without mercy and police were baffled for five years and he remained undetected. I'm satisfied one of the factors that may well have contributed to his remaining at large for so long was you sending the letters and the tape ... You took on his persona. Your letters comprised a mixture of taunts and threats and were well researched. Then you sent a tape recording of you pretending to be the Ripper. It was cleverly constructed and your delivery was sinister ... Police were persuaded that the hoaxer was the killer and you must have appreciated the way the police were being led astray. At no time did you have the courage to come forward and confess.'

Judge Jones said that while it could not be said that Humble's actions of sending the letters and tape caused or directly led to the murders of three women and the attacks on two other women who survived, it had moved the focus of the police investigation to Sunderland. In addition, it could not be said that the murderer might have been caught any earlier, but that when Peter Sutcliffe was arrested he told police the hoax letters and tape had given him 'confidence'. 'What can be said is there would have been a better chance of those women not being attacked had the letter and tapes not been sent and Sutcliffe himself might have been given a higher priority ... You are a man with a dislike of the police and it gave you pleasure to make fools of them. What is unforgivable is that you failed to put the record straight when you realised the damage you were doing. Had that tape not been sent, the deployment to Sunderland, whether wise or not, would simply not have occurred.' Following his address he sentenced John Humble to six years' imprisonment for each of the three letters he sent and eight years for the infamous hoax tape, all sentences to run concurrently.

On 13 July 2006, John Humble was granted the right to appeal the length of his eight-year sentence for the Wearside Jack hoax. On 24 October 2006, Humble lost his appeal. Humble was not present for the ruling by the Lord Chief Justice, Lord Phillips, who was sitting with two other judges. Delivering the ruling of the court, Mr Justice Calvert-Smith said that the case was 'uniquely serious and had possibly fatal consequences', and that 'the offence called for a very severe sentence ... Although the sentence was indeed severe, it cannot be said it was wrong in principle or excessive.' It was also stated that 'issues of personal mitigation and passage of time lose much of their influence'.

Parallels have been drawn between the Yorkshire Ripper and Jack the Ripper, despite the murders being more than 100 years apart. In the case of Sutcliffe, he targeted mainly prostitutes, rendering the majority of them unconscious before setting about killing and mutilating the bodies of some of the victims. Jack the Ripper did the same. Attempts by this author to contact Sutcliffe to pursue this theory and request an interview were unsuccessful. On two separate occasions I wrote to him at Broadmoor Hospital, the high-security psychiatric facility where he has been held since March 1984, enclosing a copy of my book, *Jack the Ripper: The 21st Century Investigation*. Twice I received a reply from a forensic psychologist declining my request and returning the book.

On 16 July 2010 Sutcliffe made an appeal to the High Court for a specific minimum life sentence to be set in order for him to be given a chance of parole. The appeal was considered by Mr Justice Mitting.

The judge considered the key issue of 'diminished responsibility'. The jury at the original trial in 1981 rejected the proposition that Sutcliffe's paranoid schizophrenia diminished his responsibility for the killings.

Having considered the appeal, the judge stated that he could not override the jury's decision, and so was not able to take that issue into account in setting Sutcliffe's minimum term. He stated: 'This was a campaign of murder which terrorised the population of a large part of Yorkshire for several years. The only explanation for it, on the jury's verdict, was anger, hatred and obsession. Apart from a terrorist outrage, it is difficult to conceive of circumstances in which one man could account for so many victims.'

The High Court decided that Peter Sutcliffe would never be released from prison. Various psychological reports describing Sutcliffe's mental state were taken into consideration, as well as the severity of his crimes. Not content to accept the court ruling, Sutcliffe's defence team launched a further appeal, this time to the Court of Appeal. The hearing for this appeal began on 30 November 2010 and was rejected on 14 January 2011. Sutcliffe's defence team launched a further appeal to the

Supreme Court. However, the Court of Appeal rejected Sutcliffe's application.

As things stand, Sutcliffe will spend the rest of his life in Broadmoor Hospital without hope of release. His lawyers have one final option – to appeal to the Criminal Cases Review Commission arguing that the original trial amounted to a miscarriage of justice. The issue of diminished responsibility would again be central.

FREDERICK AND ROSEMARY WEST

Frederick West was born into a poor family of farm workers in 1941. He left school at the age of 15 and began work as a casual labourer. He was a prolific petty criminal as a teenager. He moved from his parents' rural home to live with an aunt until he moved with his family to Gloucester, where he took a job in an abattoir. In April 1961, he was fined for the theft of watches and in October the same year he was also fined for stealing tools from a building site; these were his first convictions. A few months later, he was accused of impregnating a 13-year-old girl who was a friend of the West family. Fred West was surprisingly uncooperative and didn't see that there was anything wrong with molesting girls. 'Well, doesn't everyone do it?' he was heard to say.

This attitude and the ensuing scandal caused a serious rift with his family. West was ordered to find somewhere else to live. Distanced now from his family, he went to work on construction projects. It wasn't long before he was caught having sex with young girls. At his trial for having sex with the 13-year-old girl, his doctor claimed that he was suffering from epileptic fits. Consequently, he got off without a jail sentence. At the age of 20, Fred West was already a convicted child molester and petty thief and a disgrace to his family.

In November 1962, he married Catherine (Rena) Costello, a prostitute, and they moved to Glasgow. She gave birth to a girl, Charmaine, in March 1963. Charmaine's father, however, was a

Pakistani bus driver. A second child, Anne-Marie, was born to the couple on 6 July 1964. She was West's child. Soon after this, they separated.

When his wife returned to the area in 1966, Fred was living with another woman, Ann McFall. In early 1967, Ann McFall became pregnant with West's child. She was trying unsuccessfully to get West to divorce Costello and marry her. West responded to the stress of her demands by killing her and burying her near a caravan park sometime in July. Not only did he kill his mistress and their unborn child, he slowly and methodically dismembered her body and buried her along with the foetus. He cut off her fingers and toes, which were missing from the gravesite. This was to be his ritualistic signature in future crimes. West's wife Catherine returned to live with him and their children for a short time before leaving again for an unknown destination.

In late 1968, West met 16-year-old Rosemary Letts (b. 1953). She became pregnant by him, something she concealed from her parents until West was serving a short prison sentence for unpaid fines. She left her family home and moved in with West in Midland Road, Gloucester. She gave birth to a girl, Heather, on 17 October 1970 and, as a result, often neglected the older children. West's daughter Charmaine died in mid-1971 while West was still in prison, apparently murdered by Rose. Since West was in jail when Charmaine was murdered, when he came out he had to bury her body under the kitchen floor of their home in Midland Road where it would remain undiscovered for the next 20 years. Before he buried Charmaine, he cut off her fingers, toes and kneecaps. Fred would hold this murder over Rose for the rest of her life.

Rose used to invite many West Indian men over to their house on Midland Road to have sex with her, either for cash or fun. Fred, a voyeur, encouraged this behaviour and watched through a peephole. As over-sexed as he was, Fred was not at all interested in ordinary sex. It had to involve bondage, vibrators and acts of sadism or lesbianism to get him going.

Fred took erotic photos of Rose and ran them as ads in magazines for swingers.

When Rose murdered Charmaine, she created both a problem and an opportunity for Fred regarding his first wife, Rena. It was just a matter of time before Rena would come round looking for Charmaine. In fact, in August 1971, Fred saw that he had no choice but to kill Rena. He got her drunk and then strangled her at the house in Midland Road. He then dismembered her body and mutilated it in the same way that he had Ann McFall's body: he cut off her fingers and toes. Then he put her remains into bags and buried her in the same location where he had buried Ann McFall.

He later married Rose on 29 January 1972. She gave birth to a girl, Mae, in June 1972 and they moved to a new home at 25 Cromwell Street. Fred had plans for the cellar and said that he was either going to make it into a place for Rose to entertain her clients or he would soundproof it and use it as his 'torture chamber'.

The first occupant was to be his eight-year-old daughter, Anne-Marie. He and Rose undressed her and told her that she was lucky that she had such caring parents who were making sure that when she got married she would be able to satisfy her husband. Anne-Marie's hands were tied behind her and a gag put in her mouth. Then, while Rose held the girl down, her father raped her. The pain was so severe that the girl could not go to school for several days. She was warned that she would be beaten if she ever told anyone about the rape. On another occasion, Anne-Marie was strapped down while her father raped her in what he called a 'quickie' during his lunch hour.

In late 1972, Fred and Rose picked up a 17-year-old girl named Caroline Owens and hired her as a nanny. They promised Caroline's family that they would watch out for her while she lived with them. Caroline was very attractive, so much so that Rose and Fred competed with each other to seduce her. However, Caroline found the Wests repugnant and told them she was leaving. The couple abducted, stripped and raped her. Fred told her that if she didn't do what he wanted, 'I'll keep you in the cellar and let my black friends have you and when they are finished, we'll kill you and bury you under the paving stones of Gloucester.' Terrified, she believed him. When her mother saw her bruises, she got the truth from her and called the police.

Charges were brought against the Wests and the hearing took place in January 1973. Fred was 31 and Rose a mere 19 and pregnant once again. Fred was able to convince the magistrate to believe that Caroline had been a willing partner. Despite Fred's criminal record, the magistrate did not believe the Wests were capable of violence and let them both off with a fine.

For some time, the Wests had been carrying on a friendship with a seamstress, Lynda Gough. Eventually, Lynda moved into 25 Cromwell Street to take care of the children. Something went amiss in the relationship, though, and Lynda was murdered. Fred dismembered her and buried her in a pit in the garage. As before, he then removed her fingers, toes and kneecaps. When Lynda's family came looking for her, they were told that she had stayed there but had since left. A hideous pattern was emerging. Young women would come to stay at 25 Cromwell either as lodgers or friends or nannies, but so few ever made it out with their lives. The house was slowly becoming a monument to the depravity of its inhabitants.

In August 1973, Rose gave birth to their son Stephen, but this did not stop their desires to kill. They abducted 15-year-old Carol Ann Cooper in November and kept her a prisoner, subjecting her to sexual abuse. When they tired of her, she was strangled, dismembered and buried with the other bodies at 25 Cromwell Street in the cellar, which Fred had by now made larger.

Almost one month later, university student Lucy Partington had gone home to her mother's house to spend the Christmas holiday. On 27 December, she went to visit her friend and left to catch a bus shortly after 10pm. She had the misfortune to meet up with the Wests, who abducted her. Like Carol Ann Cooper, she was tortured and sexually abused for approximately a week and then murdered, dismembered and buried in the cellar. Also like Carol Ann Cooper, she was reported missing, but there was nothing to tie the two girls to the Wests.

Over the next 12 months, three more girls would meet the same fate at the hands of Rose and Fred West. Their next victim was Shirley Hubbard, aged 15, followed by Juanita Mott, aged 18. Bondage was becoming a major thrill for Fred and Rose. Shirley's head had been wrapped entirely with tape and a plastic tube was inserted in her nose so that she could breathe. Juanita was subjected to even more extreme bondage; she was gagged with a ligature made from two long, white nylon socks, a brassiere and two pairs of tights, one within the other. She was then trussed up with lengths of plastic-covered rope of the type used for washing line. The rope was used in a complicated way, with loops tied around her arms and thighs, both wrists, both ankles and her skull, horizontally and vertically, backwards and forwards across her body until she could only wriggle like a trapped animal. The West's produced a 2yd length of rope with a slip-knot end forming a noose. This was used to suspend Juanita's body from the beams in the cellar.

In 1976, the Wests enticed a young woman to the house. Her real name was never made public and she would later appear in court as a prosecution witness against the Wests. She came from a home for wayward girls. At Cromwell Street, she was led into a room with two naked girls who were prisoners there. She witnessed the torture of the two girls and was raped by Fred and sexually assaulted by Rose. One of the girls that she saw was probably Anne-Marie, Fred's daughter, who was a constant target for the couple's sexual sadism. As if Fred's rape and torture of his daughter were not enough, he brought home his friends to have sex with her.

In 1977, the upstairs of the house had been renovated to accommodate lodgers. One of them was Shirley Robinson, 18, a former prostitute with bisexual inclinations. She developed relationships with both Fred and Rose. Shirley became pregnant with Fred's child after Rose became pregnant by one of her black clients. While Fred was pleased that Rose was carrying a mixed-race child, Rose was not comfortable with Shirley carrying Fred's child. Shirley foolishly thought that she could displace Rose in Fred's life and, in the process, jeopardised her own existence. Rose made it clear that Shirley had to go.

In December 1977, after Rose gave birth to Tara, Shirley met her fate and was murdered in Cromwell Street. By now, the cellar was full of bodies. Shirley was buried in the back garden along with her unborn child. This time, Fred dismembered Shirley and their unborn baby.

In November 1978, Rose and Fred had yet another daughter whom they named Louise, making a total of six children in this bizarre and unwholesome household. Fred also impregnated his daughter Anne-Marie, but the pregnancy was ectopic and had to be terminated.

Several months later, the Wests continued their murdering. Their victim this time was a troubled teenager named Alison Chambers; she was murdered after they had raped and tortured her. Like Shirley, Alison was buried in the 'overflow' cemetery in the back garden.

As the Wests' children became older, they were aware of some of the goings-on in the home. They knew that Rose was a prostitute and that Anne-Marie was being raped by her father. When Anne-Marie moved out to live with her boyfriend, Fred instead focused his sexual advances on Heather and Mae. Heather resisted her father and was beaten for it. In June 1980, Rose gave birth to Barry, Fred's second son. Then in April 1982, Rose gave birth to Rosemarie Junior, who was not Fred's child. In July 1983, Rose gave birth to another daughter, whom they named Lucyanna. She was half-black, like Tara and Rosemarie Junior. Rose became increasingly irrational and beat the children without provocation. The stress of so many children in the household took its toll on Rose's already bad temper.

THE EVIL WITHIN

In 1986, the wall of family silence that had protected the Wests was broken. Heather told her girlfriend about her father's advances, her mother's affairs and the beatings she had received. The girlfriend told her parents, who were friends of the Wests, and Heather's parents soon murdered her. They told the rest of the children that she had left home. Fred asked his son Stephen to help him dig a hole in the back garden, where Fred later buried Heather's dismembered body.

Rose built up her prostitution business by advertising in special magazines. She and Fred were on the lookout for women who they could get to participate in their various perversions as well as prostitute themselves under Rose's direction. One such woman, Katherine Halliday, became a fixture in the West household and saw first-hand the black bondage suits and masks that they had collected, plus the whips and chains. With good reason, Katherine became alarmed and quickly broke off her relationship with them.

As time went on, Fred and Rosemary became increasingly concerned about creating a minimum façade of respectability, not because they cared what people thought of them, but because they were concerned that knowledge of what had gone on in their house would jeopardise their freedom.

The Wests' long run of luck was coming to an end, though. One of the very young girls who Fred had raped with Rose's assistance told her girlfriend what happened. The girlfriend went to the police and the case was assigned to a very talented and persistent detective constable named Hazel Savage. Hazel knew Fred from his days with his first wife and remembered the stories that she had told her about Fred's sexual perversions.

Following up the complaint on 6 August 1992, police arrived at 25 Cromwell Street with a search warrant to look for pornography and evidence of child abuse. They found mountains of pornography and arrested Rose for assisting in the rape of a minor. Fred was arrested for rape and buggery.

Due to the nature of the charges they both now faced, their

younger children were taken into care. Fred was remanded in custody and Rose took an overdose of pills but was saved by her son Stephen. Luck was again on their side when the trial collapsed due to the witnesses choosing not to give evidence. Still, the police had their doubts about the missing Heather and the rumour that she was buried under the patio. As a result, on 25 February 1994, police obtained a warrant to search the Cromwell Street house and garden. The nature of the search and the logistics of all the digging needed would be very expensive and was certain to attract attention from the media. The search would continue right up until March 1994.

Following the extensive search, bones were found buried in the garden but at that time the police could not identify who they belonged to. Fred and Rose West were questioned and confronted with the findings. Fred soon confessed to killing his daughter. When Rose was informed of Fred's confession, she claimed that Fred had sent her out of the house the day Heather disappeared and had no knowledge of Heather's death. The police set about the grim task of digging up the whole garden. Fred had been released on bail without charge and, back home, he watched the police dig up the garden. He knew it was a matter of time before they found Heather and the others he had buried in the garden.

Finally, the police found the remains of a young woman, dismembered and decapitated. Then another victim was found. Fred West was again taken back into custody and questioned. To protect Rose, he claimed responsibility for the murders himself. He was charged with the murders of Heather, Shirley Robinson and the as-yet-unidentified third woman. Furthermore, an investigation was opened into the disappearance of Rena and Charmaine. Fred decided to confess to the police about the bodies of the girls buried in his cellar. He admitted to murdering them, but would not admit to raping them first. He maintained they all consented to sex with him.

As West talked to the police about his murders, they were still unsure of the number of actual victims as identification was proving difficult. The police had unearthed nine different sets of bones and did not know whose they were. West was not much help, since he could not remember the names and details of some of the women he had picked up. Considering the many women who go missing every year, extensive work had to be undertaken to match up the missing persons reports with the remains.

As the investigation continued, Rose was arrested in April 1994. She abandoned Fred to save herself. She tried to position herself as the victim of a murderous man, but she was not convincing and the police worked tirelessly to link her to the murders. The bodies of Rena, Ann McFall and Charmaine were found as Fred West continued to cooperate with the police. With regard to the disappearance of Mary Bastholm, West for some reason decided not to cooperate and her body was not found.

On 13 December 1994, Fred and Rose West were jointly charged with the murders of 12 girls. At their first court appearance, Fred attempted to console Rose, but she avoided his touch. She had told the police he made her sick. Their partnership in crime was definitely over, but was this an act to place all the blame on Fred? They were both remanded in custody for a date to be set for their trial at a higher court. However, Fred would escape justice and never paid for his crimes. He was sent on remand to await trial to HMP Winson Green, Birmingham, where on 1 January 1995 he committed suicide by hanging himself, using strips of cloth from a bed sheet.

Despite the lack of direct evidence linking her to the murders, Rose West went to trial on 3 October 1995, charged with the murders of 10 girls. A number of witnesses, including Caroline Owens, the woman previously referred to as Miss A, and Anne-Marie testified about Rose West's sadistic sexual assaults on young women.

Her defence team tried to suggest that evidence of sexual assault was not the same as evidence of murder and that, furthermore, she did not know what Fred was doing when he murdered the girls and buried them. However, they made a grave error in allowing Rose to give evidence. Her defiance came through very clearly to the jury. Furthermore, the prosecution learnt to extract damaging testimony from her by making her angry. She left the jury with entrenched beliefs that she had treated the children badly and that she was completely dishonest. Finally, the defence played the recordings of Fred West describing how he had murdered the victims when she was out of the house. Unfortunately for Rose, Fred was shown to be lying on key issues, which cast a doubt over his entire statement.

The most dramatic evidence was given by Janet Leach, who was called as the 'appropriate adult' (witness) to Fred West's police interviews. Confidentially, Fred had told her that Rose was involved in the murders and that Rose had murdered Charmaine and Shirley Robinson without him but that he made a deal with his wife to take all the blame on himself. Janet was so stressed by this confidential confession that she suffered a stroke. It was only after Fred's death that she felt that she could tell the police what he had said to her. After her testimony, she collapsed and had to be taken to the hospital. Her evidence was to be the final nail in the coffin as far as Rose West was concerned. The jury found Rose West guilty of all the murders. The judge sentenced her to life imprisonment on each of 10 counts of murder.

Following several failed appeals, Rose West has indicated her intention to spend the rest of her life in prison and plans no further appeals, despite being eligible for parole in 2019, when she will be 66 years of age.

IAN BRADY AND MYRA HINDLEY, AKA THE MOORS MURDERERS

Myra Hindley was born in Manchester in 1942 and raised by her grandmother; she was regularly beaten by her alcoholic father, despite having an IQ of 107, being able write creatively and considered a responsible and sporty girl. She left school in 1957 and, after working in different jobs, on 16 January 1961 she started work as a typist for a chemical firm called Millward's. It was there that she met Ian Brady, a man four years her senior with a history of violence and a string of burglary convictions. Brady was the stock clerk, having worked there since February 1959.

Ian Stewart (he later took his stepfather's surname) was born in 1938 and grew up in an economically deprived area of Glasgow. His mother gave him up for adoption at birth. Early on, Brady showed troubling signs of dysfunctional behaviour and moodiness. When he could not have his way, he would throw violent tantrums that made him unpopular with local children. At school he was lazy and struggled to apply himself, and misbehaved. He started smoking and virtually gave up schoolwork.

Ian developed a fascination with Nazi pageantry and Nazi symbolism. He often asked other boys for souvenirs that their fathers brought back from the war and, when playing roughhouse war games, he would insist on being 'the German'. It was at this time that Ian also became known for perverse and sadistic tendencies, including bullying smaller children and torturing animals in a variety of grotesque ways.

As a teenager Ian was arrested for burglary and housebreaking. On the first two occasions he was given probation, but on the third he was deemed incorrigible and the court ordered him to leave Glasgow and live with his adopted mother. She had since moved to Manchester and had married an Irish labourer named Patrick Brady. In November 1954, two months before his 17th birthday, Ian travelled down to join his mother and her new husband. Although he did not get along with Mr Brady, Ian took his stepfather's name and used it as his own.

Brady started to collect books about torture and sadomasochism, domination and servitude. He also began drinking heavily and gambling, so often found himself in need of extra spending money to support these new habits. He soon resorted again to thieving and, after being convicted several more times, he was sentenced to two years training at a borstal school as well as a term of imprisonment in Strangeways prison.

While incarcerated, Brady learnt other criminal methods for acquiring money from other prisoners, and dreamt of becoming a big-time criminal, pulling off lucrative bank robberies. He also studied bookkeeping. Following his release, he moved from job to job and in 1961, while employed at Millward's, he met Myra Hindley, although it would be almost 12 months before they would actually form a long-lasting relationship. It would ultimately lead to them becoming the most publically reviled criminals of their era.

It was at the firm's Christmas party that Brady asked Hindley for their first date. This was to be her initiation into his secret world. That first night, he took her to see the hour-long film *The Nuremberg Trials*. As the weeks went by, he played her records of Hitler's marching songs and encouraged her to read some of his favourite books – *Mein Kampf*, *Crime and Punishment* and De Sade's works. Hindley happily complied – after her tough upbringing, she had waited so long for something different. Her inexperience and hunger left her incapable of distinguishing the new experiences that were healthy from those that were dangerous.

Brady became Hindley's first lover and she was soon totally besotted with him, soaking up all of his distorted philosophical theories. Her greatest desire was to please him. She even changed the way she dressed for him – Germanic-style with long boots, miniskirts and bleached hair. She allowed him to take pornographic photographs of her and of the two of them having sex. With such a devoted audience, Brady's ideas became increasingly paranoid and outrageous, but Hindley lacked the necessary skills and experience to discern good from bad – and bad from evil. When he told her there was no God, she stopped going to church, and when he told her that rape and murder were not wrong, that in fact murder was the 'supreme pleasure', she did not question it. Her personality had become totally fused with his.

Early in 1963, Brady put Hindley's blind acceptance of his ideas to the test. He began planning a bank robbery and needed her to be his getaway driver. Immediately, Hindley started taking driving lessons. He made her join the Cheadle Rifle Club and purchased two guns. The robbery was never carried out, but Brady's purpose had been fulfilled. Myra had shown herself willing. Brady knew she was ready to cement their relationship.

On the night of 12 July 1963, Ian Brady and Myra Hindley claimed their first joint victim, 16-year-old Pauline Reade. She was on her way to a dance at the Railway Workers' Social Club when she disappeared. Originally, she had planned to go with three girlfriends, but at the last minute they did not go, so Pauline decided to go alone. At 8pm Pauline, dressed in her prettiest pink party dress, left home. What Pauline didn't know was that her girlfriend Pat and another friend, Dorothy, had seen her leave. Curious to see whether she would really have the nerve to go to the dance alone, Pat and Dorothy followed her. When they were almost at the club, the two girls decided to take a short cut so they could arrive at the club before Pauline. They waited for her but she never arrived. She had been enticed by Hindley into her minivan. Hindley drove off, with Brady following behind on his motorcycle. They drove up to Saddleworth Moor, where Hindley asked Pauline to help her look for a lost glove. They were busy searching the moors when Brady pounced on Pauline and raped her. He then smashed her skull in with a shovel and slashed her throat so violently that she was almost decapitated. Brady then buried Pauline's body on the moor, where it would remain for the next 20 years.

When Pauline did not arrive home by midnight, her parents went out to look for her. They called the police the next morning when the night-long search had failed to find any trace of their daughter. A police search also proved negative; it seemed that Pauline had disappeared into thin air. The second child victim disappeared on 11 November 1963. Twelve-year-old John Kilbride and his friend John Ryan had gone to the local cinema for the afternoon. When the film finished at 5pm, they went to a local market to see if they could earn some pocket money helping the stallholders pack up. Ryan left Kilbride standing beside a salvage bin near the carpet dealer's stall to go and catch his bus home. It was the last time that anyone saw Kilbride alive.

As before, Hindley lured the unsuspecting victim into her vehicle from the market place and drove him to Saddleworth Moor. Brady was waiting there and ordered Hindley to wait for him in a nearby village in the Ford Anglia he'd hired to drive to the moor. While Hindley waited, Brady raped and attempted to stab the boy with a knife, but the weapon was too blunt. Brady lost his temper and strangled him to death with string before burying the body in a shallow grave. When John did not return home for dinner, his parents called the police. For the second time, a major search was conducted, with police and thousands of volunteers combing the surrounding area for any clue as to John's disappearance.

On 16 June 1964, 12-year-old Keith Bennett left to go to his grandmother's home to spend the night. As his grandmother's house was only a mile away, he walked there by himself. His mother watched him over the crossing and onto Stockport Road, and then left him to go in the opposite direction. Again, Brady and Hindley enticed him into their car and drove to Saddleworth Moor. Hindley stood and watched from the top of an embankment while Brady raped Keith in a ravine before strangling him to death with a piece of string and burying his body. When Keith didn't arrive at his grandmother's house, she assumed that his mother had decided not to send him. Keith's disappearance was not discovered until the next morning when his grandmother arrived at her daughter's home without Keith. Again the police were called and again a search was conducted; again another child had disappeared without a trace. Keith Bennett's body has never been found.

THE EVIL WITHIN

Six months passed before a fourth child, 10-year-old Lesley Ann Downey, disappeared. It was on the afternoon of 26 December 1964. Lesley had gone with her two brothers and some of their friends to a local fair only 10 minutes away. They had not been there long before they'd spent all of their money and become bored. All but Lesley left for home. A classmate last saw her, at just after 5.30pm, standing alone next to one of the rides. Brady lured her from the fairground into his car. He took nine obscene photographs of her, showing her naked, bound and gagged (these would later be found in a suitcase in a left luggage locker). Hindley recorded the child's rape and torture by Brady on audiotape. The tape clearly identifies the voices of Brady, Hindley and the child, who is heard to scream and protest and ask to be allowed to go home and pleading for her life. It is believed that Brady then killed her. The following morning, Brady and Hindley drove Lesley's body to Saddleworth Moor, where it was buried in a shallow grave.

When Lesley had not returned home, her mother began to search for her. She called the police when she could find no sign of Lesley. The countryside was searched, thousands of people were questioned and missing posters were displayed but no new leads were discovered. It would be another 10 months before the gruesome truth was uncovered.

On 6 October 1965, the couple claimed their fifth and final victim, 17-year-old Edward Evans. They enticed him from Manchester Central railway station to their house in Hattersley, where Hindley's 18-year-old brother-in-law David Smith was visiting. Smith heard a long, loud scream. Hindley called to him from the living room. When Smith first entered the room, he saw Brady holding what he initially thought was a life-size rag doll. As it fell against the couch, no more than 2ft from him, the realisation dawned on him that it was a young man, and not a doll at all.

As the young man lay sprawled, face down on the floor, Brady stood over him, his legs apart, holding an axe in his right hand.

The young man groaned. Brady lifted the axe into the air, and brought it down on the young man's head. There was silence for several seconds and then the young man groaned again, only it was much lower this time. Lifting the axe high above his head, Brady brought it down a second time. The young man stopped groaning. The only sound he made was a gurgling noise. Brady then placed a cover over the youth's head and wrapped a piece of electric wire around his neck. As he repeatedly pulled the wire tighter, Brady kept saying, 'You fucking dirty bastard,' over and over again. When the young man finally stopped making any noise, Ian looked up and said to Hindley, 'That's it, it's the messiest yet.'

Hindley then calmly made them all a cup of tea. She and Brady joked about the look on the young man's face when he had struck him. They laughed as they told David about another occasion when a policeman had confronted Myra while they had been burying another of their victims on Saddleworth Moor. Brady had told David that he had killed some people before, but David thought it was just a sick fantasy. This was real. He was horrified and scared for his own safety. He decided that the best thing he could do was to keep calm and go along with them. He helped them to clean up the mess, tie up the body and put it in the bedroom upstairs. It was not until the early hours of the morning that he was able to escape, promising to return in the morning to help dispose of the body. Safely back at home, he was violently sick. He then went to a public phone box to call the police.

The police at first did not know whether to believe this bizarre story. However, when they went to 16 Wardle Brook Avenue, the home address of Brady and Hindley, their doubts were put aside. At the house, they first spoke to Hindley, who reluctantly gave them a key to the upstairs bedroom, the only room in the house that was locked, where the body of Edward Evans was still wrapped in a grey blanket. The axe described by Smith as the murder weapon was found in the same room. Brady was then formally arrested.

Brady, when questioned at the police station, told police that there had been an argument between himself, David Smith and the victim. A fight had ensued that had quickly got out of control. Smith had hit Evans and kicked him several times. There had been an axe on the floor, which Brady said he had used to hit Evans. According to Brady, he and Smith alone had tied up the body and Hindley had had nothing to do with Evans's death.

Hindley was not arrested until four days later after police had found a three-page document in her car that described in explicit detail how she and Brady had planned to carry out the murder. When questioned, she corroborated Brady's story, describing how she had been horrified and frightened by the ordeal. The police investigation would probably have gone no further if Smith had not told police of Brady's claim that he had buried other bodies on Saddleworth Moor and the fact that numerous photos of the moors were found in their home.

Once the area where Brady and Hindley frequented was pinpointed, the digging began. Police believed that the bodies of four children who had mysteriously disappeared over the past two years might have been buried in the moors. They were proved right on 10 October 1965 when the naked body of 10-year-old Lesley Ann Downey was found in a shallow grave, with her clothing at her feet, but the police had nothing but hearsay and circumstantial evidence to connect Brady and Hindley to her death. They needed much more. A more thorough search of the house at Wardle Brook Avenue on 15 October gave them the evidence they needed.

They found a left-luggage ticket inside a prayer book, which led them to a locker at Manchester Central station. Inside were two suitcases filled with pornographic and sadistic paraphernalia. In among these were nine semi-pornographic photographs of Lesley Ann Downey, showing her naked, bound and gagged, in a variety of poses in Myra Hindley's bedroom. A tape recording was also found. The voice of a girl could be heard screaming, crying and begging for her life. Two other voices, one male and one female, could be heard threatening the child. Police were able to identify the adult voices as belonging to Brady and Hindley, but they needed Ann Downey's assistance to identify her child's voice. She listened in horror to her daughter in the last moments of her life. Even with such damning evidence against them, Brady and Hindley denied murdering Lesley. As in the case of Edward Evans, they attempted to implicate David Smith. They claimed that Smith had brought the girl to the house so Brady could photograph her. The tape recording was of their voices as they attempted to subdue the girl so they could take the pictures. Hindley protested that she had only used a harsh tone with the girl because she had been concerned that neighbours would hear her. As far as they were concerned, Lesley Ann had left their house, unharmed, with Smith, suggesting that Smith must have murdered her later.

As the search of Saddleworth Moor continued, 11 days after the discovery of Lesley Ann Downey the body of John Kilbride was found, also in a shallow grave. The evidence linking Brady and Hindley to his murder was mainly circumstantial and not overwhelming, but the police believed it was sufficient to charge them. They found the name 'John Kilbride' written, in Brady's handwriting, in his notebook and a photograph of Hindley on John's grave at the moors. It was also found that Hindley had hired a car on the day of John's disappearance and returned it in a muddy state. Also, according to Hindley's sister, Brady and Hindley shopped at Ashton market every week, where John had disappeared. Despite all their efforts, the police were unable to find the bodies of the two other missing children or any evidence to link Brady and Hindley to their disappearances. They had to content themselves with prosecuting them both for the murders of Edward Evans, Lesley Ann Downey and John Kilbride.

On 27 April 1966, Hindley and Brady were brought to trial at Chester Assizes, where they pleaded not guilty to all charges. Throughout the trial, they continued their attempts to blame David Smith for the murders, a cowardly stance that deepened public hatred of them. At no time during the trial did they show any remorse for their crimes or any sorrow towards the families of their victims. To those who were present at the trial, the accused appeared cold and heartless. Despite protestations of their innocence, Ian Brady was found guilty of the murders of Lesley Ann Downey, John Kilbride and Edward Evans. Myra Hindley was found guilty of the murders of Lesley Ann Downey and Edward Evans and for harbouring Brady in the knowledge that he had killed John Kilbride. They escaped the death penalty by only a couple of months as the Murder (Abolition of the Death Penalty) Act 1965 had come into effect just four weeks before their arrest. They were both sentenced to life imprisonment. In 1965, this murder investigation was unique. It was the first time in British legal history that a woman had been involved in a killing partnership that had involved the serial sex murders of children. The public could not comprehend how any woman could take part in such a horrific crime; her involvement made the crimes seem even more evil and unforgivable.

The trial judge spoke of his doubt that Brady could ever reform, describing him as 'wicked beyond belief' and effectively giving him little hope of eventual release. Successive Home Secretaries have agreed with that decision, while Lord Lane (the former Lord Chief Justice), set a 40-year minimum term in 1982. In 1990, Brady was told by the then Home Secretary David Waddington that both he and Hindley should never be freed. His successor Michael Howard agreed with this judgment in 1994 and told Brady so. Although in the UK Home Secretaries can no longer decide the minimum length of a life sentence, Brady has always insisted that he never wants to be released. He went on hunger strike in September 1999 and had to be force-fed, after the High Court refused him the right to starve himself to death. In early 2006, Brady was hospitalised and wanted to be allowed to die. He is, at the time of writing, still alive and is being held at Ashworth Hospital in Liverpool.

One question that has been asked many times since his arrest is, 'were there any more victims?' In 1987, Brady contacted the BBC and gave incomplete information about five other murders. They included a man from Manchester and a woman whose body was allegedly thrown into a local canal. At the time, police were unable to find out more and Brady would not elaborate further.

However, in 2008, this same question was asked again when a statement was issued by a lawyer representing another female murderer, Linda Calvey, who was known as the Black Widow. Calvey was serving a sentence for murdering an ex-lover and had made a statement that Hindley had told her (while they were in the same prison) how she and Brady had picked up a girl in her teens hitchhiking to Kilburn, north London. After murdering her they disposed of the body, which had at that point not been found. To date, police officers refute this and are of the belief that there were no more victims other than those already known. A young girl who did disappear in similar circumstances on 30 December 1964 and could not be traced thereafter has, after 43 years, now been traced and is alive and well.

Following her conviction, Hindley was sent to Holloway prison and quickly won many friends, who claimed that she had reformed. Although Hindley and Brady wrote to each other during their first few years in prison, and at one stage were refused a request to marry each other, in May 1972 Hindley broke off all contact with Brady, as she realised she would never see him again, and that doing so would increase her chances of parole. A year later, Hindley attempted to escape with the help of Pat Carnes, a prison officer said to have fallen in love with the murderer. The attempt was unsuccessful, and Hindley was transferred to Durham, Cookham Wood and then to Highpoint.

In November 1986, more than 20 years after the crimes, Brady and Hindley finally confessed to the murders of Pauline Reade and Keith Bennett. It is thought that the initiative came from Brady. Shortly afterwards, they returned to the moors, under heavy guard, to help police look for the dead children's burial places. Pauline Reade's body was discovered the following July. Keith Bennett's was never found. Brady and Hindley were never charged in connection with these murders.

Following her conviction Hindley was told that she would spend 25 years in prison before being considered for parole. The Lord Chief Justice agreed with that recommendation in 1982, but in January 1985 Home Secretary Leon Brittan increased her tariff to 30 years. By that time, Hindley claimed to be a reformed Roman Catholic. Campaigners who opposed her release regularly gave television and newspaper interviews whenever the subject was raised.

In 1990, then Home Secretary David Waddington imposed a whole life tariff on Hindley, after she confessed to having a greater involvement in the murders than she had previously admitted. Hindley was not made aware of this until 1994, when a Law Lords ruling obliged the Prison Service to inform all life sentence prisoners of the minimum period they must serve in prison before being considered for parole. In 1997, the Parole Board ruled that Hindley was low risk and should be moved to an open prison. She rejected the idea and was moved to a medium security prison. The House of Lords ruling left open the possibility of later freedom. Between December 1997 and March 2000, Hindley made three separate appeals against her life tariff, claiming she was a reformed woman and no longer a danger to society, but each was rejected by the courts.

When in 2002 another life sentence prisoner challenged the Home Secretary's power to set minimum terms, Hindley and hundreds of others whose tariffs had been increased by politicians, looked more likely to be released from prison, with plans made by supporters for Hindley to be given a new identity. Home Secretary David Blunkett instructed Greater Manchester Police to find new charges against her, to prevent her release from prison. The investigation initially looked at charging Hindley with the murders of Pauline Reade and Keith Bennett, but the advice given by government lawyers was that because of the

DPP's decision taken 15 years earlier, a new trial would probably be considered an abuse of process.

On 15 November 2002, at the age of 60, Hindley died in West Suffolk Hospital after a heart attack. She had spent 37 years in custody. During that time, she had gained an Open University degree and claimed to have returned to Roman Catholicism, to which she had ostensibly converted at the age of 15. She was Britain's longest detained female prisoner and was given the last rites before she died. While incarcerated, she wrote her autobiography, which remains unpublished.

Her lawyers told the press that Hindley had been truly sorry for what she did. She had portrayed herself as a remorseful sinner, but knew that few people were willing to forgive her, though it was not impossible to find people with sympathy for Hindley as a reformed character. Those who felt that one purpose of the prison system is to extend the possibility of reform, rehabilitation and redemption to convicted criminals – even those who have committed such evil acts as Mira Hindley – suggested that in the last decade of her life she had shown sufficient remorse and was no longer a threat to the public, and therefore qualified for parole. Lord Longford, for example, risked derision from the public and popular press in his campaign to secure the release of certain criminals. He described Hindley as a 'delightful' person and said 'you could loathe what people did but should not loathe what they were because human personality was sacred even though human behaviour was very often appalling'. Those who campaigned for her release said that she should not have ended her life behind bars.

None of Hindley's relatives, not even her elderly mother, were among the dozen or so mourners at her funeral at Cambridge City Crematorium on 20 November 2002. Apart from one woman from nearby Soham (a community that had only recently endured the Soham murders) who left a sign reading 'Burn in Hell' at the crematorium entrance, the public stayed away from the funeral, which had tight police security. Hindley was cremated and her ashes scattered at an undisclosed location. At an inquest into her death, it was revealed that she had asked doctors not to resuscitate her if she stopped breathing. Ironically, Myra Hindley could have been freed under a Law Lords ruling that came just two weeks later.

Three days after Hindley's death, Greater Manchester Police revealed that they had been considering bringing charges against her for the murders of Pauline Reade and Keith Bennett, to which Hindley had confessed, but for which she had not been charged. The police believed that a successful prosecution for these murders would have kept her in prison no matter how long she had lived.

DENNIS ANDREW NILSEN

Dennis Nilsen was born in Scotland in 1945. His mother was Scottish and his father Norwegian. His father was an alcoholic and his parents divorced when he was four years old. His mother remarried and sent Dennis to live with his grandparents, but after a couple of years he was sent back to his mother again.

Nilsen would later claim that the first traumatic event to shape his life came about when he was a small child, when his beloved grandfather died. His mother insisted that he view the body before burial. Whether this incident, or his mother's and stepfather's lectures on the 'impurities of the flesh', helped shape him into what he was to become, no one really knows.

In 1961, Nilsen joined the army and became a cook. He left the army in 1972 and served briefly as a police officer. From the mid-1970s, he worked as a civil servant in a job centre. During this time, he formed a number of casual relationships with men.

It was not until 1978 that Nilsen would turn to murder. On 30 December he met 14-year-old Stephen Holmes in a gay bar. They both went back to Nilsen's house where they continued to drink, and eventually, after having sex together in bed, both fell asleep. Nilsen woke up at dawn and realised that his new friend was going to leave. He ran his hand over the young boy's body, becoming aroused. His heart pounded and he began to sweat. He watched the youth sleep and looked over at the pile of clothing they had both discarded. He spotted his tie, so he got out of bed to retrieve it. Nilsen raised himself up and slipped the tie around the boy's neck, pulling it tight. Immediately, the boy woke up and started to struggle. They fell onto the floor and Nilsen retained the grip with the tie around his throat, finally rendering the boy unconscious. Nilsen then ran into the kitchen and filled a plastic bucket full of water in order to drown Holmes. Nilsen lifted him onto some chairs, draping his head back, pushed it into the bucket and soon the boy died.

Nilsen sat there shaking, barely cogniscant of what he had done and what he now faced as a result. He calmly made himself a cup of coffee and smoked several cigarettes, trying to think what to do. He removed the tie from the dead boy's neck and just stared at him. Then he got up and carried the body into the bathroom. Gently, Nilsen put him into the bath, ran the water and washed the boy's hair. He struggled to get him out of the tub and dry him off. Then he took him back into the other room and put him in the bed. His new friend was not going to leave him now. He ran his hand over the still-warm flesh, noticing the slight discoloration of the lips and face. He pulled the bedclothes over the body and sat on the bed, still trying to think what to do next.

Nilsen was not at all appalled by the sight of the body; in fact, he thought it quite beautiful. He had no idea why he had killed the young man. He just had not wanted him to leave. He had spent Christmas alone and did not want to do the same for New Year. Now he had someone to spend it with. Later that day, he went to the shop to buy an electric knife and a large pot, but he could not bring himself to cut the body up this way. Instead, he took some new underwear and re-dressed the body. That was when he decided to try to have sex with the dead boy. He got into bed, but could not sustain the erection he had had moments earlier, so he pulled the body off the bed and laid it on the floor. He used a curtain to cover it. He got up, made dinner and watched television with the body still lying there on the floor.

He knew he couldn't leave the body where it was so he took up some of the floorboards and tried to push the body under the floor, but rigor mortis had set in, preventing him from lowering it down. He decided to wait until the stiffness passed. Finally, he was able to get the body under the floor.

After a week, Nilsen grew curious, so he lifted the carpet and opened up the floor once again. The corpse was dirty, so Nilsen carried it back into the bathroom to wash it. Then Nilsen washed himself in the same water. When he carried the body back to the living room, he was so aroused that he knelt down and masturbated onto the corpse's stomach. Rather than stuff him beneath the floor again, he trussed him up by the ankles. Eventually, he put the body back under the floorboards. It would remain there for seven and a half months, until Nilsen took it out and burnt it on a bonfire. He added rubber to the fire to mask the smell of burning flesh.

Following this murder Nilsen attempted a second. His intended victim was Andrew Ho, a student he had met in the Salisbury public house in St Martin's Lane. Ho went home with Nilsen. The young man wanted to try some bondage play. Nilsen put a tie around his neck and told him he was playing a dangerous game. Ho managed to escape from the house and went to the police. Nilsen was questioned by police; however, the student decided he did not want to testify and Nilsen was released without charge.

Not put off by his failed murder attempt, on 3 December 1979 Nilsen met another young student, 23-year-old Kenneth Ockendon, a Canadian. They met at lunchtime at a pub. After drinking together for several hours, they ended up in Nilsen's flat. Nilsen enjoyed Ockendon's company, but he felt desperate at the thought that the Canadian was flying home the following day. When Ockendon fell asleep Nilsen strangled him with an electrical cord. He then removed Ockendon's clothing and dragged him into the bathroom to clean him up. Once finished, he placed the body in bed and slept with it for the rest of the night, caressing it frequently. In the morning, Nilsen placed the body in a cupboard and went to work.

Nilsen left the body until the following day, before taking it out. He cleaned the body, which he then dressed and placed in a chair, taking photos of it in various positions. When he was finished with that, he took the body into his bed and positioned it, spreadeagled, on top of him. He spoke to the body as if it could hear. Then he crossed the corpse's legs together and had sex with it between the thighs. Following this, Nilsen hid the body beneath the floorboards. However, he did not just leave the body there; from time to time he would take it out, placing it in a chair so he could watch television with the body close to him. The body remained under the floorboards until Nilsen's subsequent arrest.

On 13 May 1980, Martin Duffy, a 16-year-old homeless boy, accepted Nilsen's invitation to go home with him. They sat drinking and then went to bed. Nilsen climbed on top, trapping Duffy's arms under the covers, and strangled him. He went limp, but was still alive. Nilsen carried Duffy into the kitchen and drowned him by pushing his head into a sink full of water. Then he took the body to the bathroom and got into the bath with him. He sat talking to the body in the bath. Nilsen then took the body to the bedroom and kissed it all over, and then he sat on the stomach and masturbated. Finally, Nilsen put the body in the cupboard before later hiding it under the floorboards.

Nilsen's fifth and sixth victims were both male prostitutes whom he met in bars, one from the Far East and the other from Ireland. Neither was ever formally identified. Nilsen's seventh victim was a starving 'hippie type' he had found sleeping in a doorway in Charing Cross. Victim eight Nilsen could not recall anything at all about, except that after killing him he kept him under the floorboards of his flat until removing the corpse and cutting it into three pieces which he then put back again. He burnt the corpse one year later. Victims nine and ten were both young men, picked up in gay bars in Soho. All suffered the same fate. His eleventh victim was a skinhead Nilsen picked up in Piccadilly Circus who had a tattoo around his neck saying, 'Cut here'. He had boasted to Nilsen how tough he was and how he liked to fight; however, once he was drunk he proved no match for Nilsen, who strangled him when asleep and then hung his naked body in his bedroom for 24 hours before burying it under the floorboards.

Sometime during the period when Nilsen was committing the murders of victims five to 11, he had another brush with the law when David Painter, a young man whom Nilsen had met through his work, claimed that Nilsen had taken pictures of him while he was asleep. Painter was so incensed that he required hospitalisation as a result of their confrontation. Nilsen was brought in for questioning about the incident, but was subsequently released without charge. On 10 November 1980, he befriended another intended victim, a Scottish barman called Douglas Stewart, whom he met at the Golden Lion in Dean Street. He took Stewart back to his home address and, as with the previous victims, tried to strangle him while he was asleep. However, Stewart woke up while being strangled and was able to fend off Nilsen and escape. Although Stewart called the police almost immediately after the attack, the police, who considered the incident to be a domestic disagreement, took no action.

Nilsen's next victim was Billy Sutherland, a 26-year-old male prostitute who went back to Nilsen's house. During a sex session, Nilsen strangled Sutherland with his bare hands, disposing of the body in his usual way.

Nilsen's twelfth victim, on 18 September 1981, was Malcolm Barlow. Nilsen found Barlow sleeping rough in a doorway not far from his own home, took him in and called an ambulance for him. When Barlow was released the next day, he returned to Nilsen's home to thank him and was pleased to be invited in for a meal and a few drinks. Nilsen then strangled him. The following day, he placed Barlow's body in a cabinet under the kitchen sink. Nilsen now had six other bodies awaiting disposal. Some of them he had kept in bed with him for sexual purposes for as long as a week. Having control over these men thrilled him and the mystery of a dead body that would not respond fascinated him. He felt that he appreciated them more deeply than they had ever been appreciated before.

Nilsen sprayed his rooms twice a day to be rid of flies that were hatching. Another tenant mentioned the pervasive odour, but Nilsen assured her it was the decay of the building. To get rid of the bodies, he would put his dog and cat out in the garden, strip down to his underwear and cut the bodies up on the stone kitchen floor with a kitchen knife. Sometimes he would boil the flesh off the head in the pot he had bought for the first victim. He had learnt how to butcher, so he knew how best to cut up a body, and he placed the organs in a plastic bag. Then he would place the whole package under the floor until the next step. At one point, there were two entire bodies beneath the boards and one dismembered one. He also put body parts in the garden shed or down a hole near a bush outside. Internal organs he pushed into a gap between the double fencing in his yard. A few severed torsos he stuffed into suitcases. When he could, he dragged the bags and suitcases out to the yard and burnt the bodies a few feet from the garden fence. On one occasion, he spotted a skull in the centre of the burnt embers and crushed it into ash. Then he raked the remains of six men into the earth. When he prepared to move to a new house, he checked around and nearly forgot that he had placed the hands and arms of Malcolm Barlow near a bush.

In November 1981, after moving to a new house in Muswell Hill in London, Nilsen met Paul Nobbs, a student, and invited him back to his new home. The student awoke the following morning with little recollection of the previous evening's events, and later went to see his doctor because of some bruising that had appeared on his neck. The doctor revealed that it appeared as if the student had been strangled and advised him to go to the police. However, afraid of disclosing his sexual orientation, Nobbs decided not to do so.

Following this attempted murder, Nilsen met Carl Stotter, a drag queen also known as Khara Le Fox, at the Black Cap in Camden Town. Again he took the intended victim back to his house and proceeded to strangle him. However, after passing out from the strangulation, Stotter regained consciousness while Nilsen was trying to drown him in a bath of cold water. He managed to fight off his attacker and hurriedly left.

John Howlett was the first victim to be murdered in Nilsen's Muswell Hill home, in December 1981. Nilsen had taken a disliking to him and was determined that he should die. They had previously met once in a pub and had engaged in a long conversation. Then, on this day, Nilsen was drinking alone when Howlett walked in and recognised him. They chatted and then decided to go to Nilsen's place where, after drinking awhile, Howlett got into Nilsen's bed. Nilsen tried to get him to leave, but he refused to go. Nilsen then found a length of loose upholstery strap on an armchair and used it to strangle Howlett. At one point, he feared he would be overpowered so he tightened his grip as Howlett fought for his life. Then he struck his head, and soon Howlett went limp. Nilsen kept the strap on him until he was sure he was dead and then went shakily into the other room. However, he soon became aware that Howlett was still alive. Nilsen looped the strap around his neck again and held it for two or three minutes. Even then, Howlett's heart was still beating, so Nilsen dragged him into the bathroom to drown him, leaving him there for the rest of the night. Then he put the body in a cupboard as he contemplated how to get rid of it.

He made a decision to cut the body up into small pieces and flush it down the toilet. This process took much longer than he anticipated so he was forced to improvise. He boiled the head, hands and feet in pots in his kitchen and then separated the small bones, which he put in the dustbin. The large bones he threw over the garden fence into a waste area; other bones he put into a bag sprinkled inside with salt and stored it in a tea chest.

The next victim Nilsen murdered at this new address was Archibald Graham Allan, another homeless man whom Nilsen befriended. After taking Allan home and feeding him, Nilden proceeded to strangle him. He then placed the body in the bath and left it there for three days. He cut it up in the same way as his previous victim.

Nilsen's final victim was a drug addict called Stephen Sinclair. On 1 February 1983, they met in Oxford Street and Nilsen suggested that they go back to his place. They sat and listened to music and Sinclair fell asleep. Nilsen went into the kitchen and found some thick string. The string was too short so he attached it to a tie. He draped the ligature over the sleeping man's knees and poured himself a drink. Then he sat and contemplated all the pain in Stephen's life and decided to stop it for him. He went over, made sure he was still asleep and then used the string and tie to strangle him. Nilsen then bathed him and put him into the bed. He placed two mirrors by the bed and removed his clothes so that he could look at the two of them naked together. Nilsen experienced a feeling of oneness and thought that this surely was the meaning of life and death. He talked with Stephen as if he were still alive. He turned the young man's head towards him and kissed it. He had no idea that this body would later be his undoing and subsequent downfall. Nothing was further from the mind of Nilsen as he set about dismembering the body and disposing of the body parts in the same way as he had with the last two victims.

The house where Nilsen now lived was divided into flats. During the first week of February, one of the other tenants noticed that the downstairs toilet was not flushing properly. He tried to clear the blockage with acid, to no avail. Other toilets seemed not to be functioning properly either. A plumber arrived to investigate, but could not rectify the problem and called in a specialist.

Nilsen now believed that his own activities might be at the heart of the problems downstairs, so he stuffed the rest of Sinclair's body into plastic bags, along with the partially boiled head. He locked the remains in the wardrobe and stopped flushing the toilet. Two days later, other plumbing engineers arrived to examine the blockage. Deciding it was underground, one of the engineers went into a manhole by the side of the house. He noticed a peculiar smell. He spotted sludge about 8in thick on the floor of the sewer and found that it was composed of 30–40 pieces of flesh, and had come from the pipe leading from the house. The engineer reported the find to his superiors. The tenants gathered around him as he phoned, including Nilsen, and he mentioned that they might have to call the police. First, however, he would do a better analysis by daylight. He then took Nilsen and one of the other tenants back outside with him to see the pile of rotting flesh.

Nilsen returned at midnight to remove the particles of flesh and dumped them over the fence. He thought about replacing them with pieces of chicken and then pondered suicide. Instead, he sat alone in his flat and drank, surrounded by the body parts of three men. However, one of the downstairs tenants had noticed his movements. When the engineer returned and found the sewer cleaned out, undeterred he went deeper into the sewer and pulled out one piece of what looked like foul-smelling meat but turned out to be human flesh and bone. The police were then called. They waited outside until Nilsen returned home from work. As Nilsen entered the building, the police officers identified themselves to Nilsen and explained that they had come about his drains. As they entered Nilsen's flat, they immediately smelt rotting flesh. Nilsen queried why the police would be interested in his drains, so the officer told him they were filled with human remains. 'Good grief, how awful!' exclaimed Nilsen. One of the officers said to Nilsen, 'Don't mess about, where's the rest of the body?' Nilsen responded calmly by saying it was in two plastic bags in his wardrobe. He was then arrested and cautioned on suspicion of murder and taken to the police station. On the way back to the station, Nilsen was asked how many bodies they were talking about and he told them 15 or 16.

The police then conducted a detailed search of Nilsen's flat and his previous address. They found three heads in a cupboard in the flat and evidence of 13 more bodies at 195 Melrose Avenue, Cricklewood, Nilsen's previous address. When interviewed, he made a full and frank confession to all the murders. However, as he talked the police realised that they had been given clues over the past four years about his conduct and that, had they acted differently, many lives could have been saved.

Nilsen was charged with six murders and two charges of attempted murder. The prosecution would be seeking to prove that Nilsen had killed in full awareness of what he was doing and should be found guilty of murder. The principal evidence was from Nilsen's lengthy statement to the police, while the defence relied on psychiatric analysis to prove the opposite. The trial began on 24 October 1983. The charges were read and Nilsen pleaded not guilty to each one.

After hearing all the evidence and legal arguments, the jury retired on Thursday, 3 November. The following day, the judge said that he would accept a majority verdict, since there were two dissenters on every issue, except one of the attempted murder charges. At 4.25pm the jury delivered a verdict: guilty on all counts. The judge sentenced Dennis Andrew Nilsen to life in prison. He would not be eligible for parole for 25 years. In the interim period Nilsen had continued to challenge the legality of his sentence. His minimum term was set at 25 years by the trial judge, but the Home Secretary later imposed a whole life tariff, which meant he would never be released. In 2006, he was denied any further requests for parole.

ANTHONY HARDY, AKA THE CAMDEN TOWN RIPPER

Anthony John Hardy was born in 1951 in Burton-on-Trent, Staffordshire, the son of a coal miner. From an early age, Hardy yearned to escape the lower middle-class lifestyle in which he was raised. He worked hard in school and excelled academically. Ultimately, he was accepted at London's Imperial College to study engineering.

During the mid-1970s, Hardy met and married Judith Dwight, with whom he attended university. The couple moved to Tasmania, Australia, where they raised their two boys and two girls. However, it seemed that from as early as 1982, Hardy displayed symptoms of mental illness. It has been suggested that, around that time, Hardy tried to kill his wife by bludgeoning her over the head with a water bottle, before trying to drown her in the bath. Hardy was never charged; he simply checked himself into a psychiatric clinic in Queensland following the incident. He remained there for several weeks before discharging himself and returned to Britain.

The couple divorced in 1986. His wife secured custody of the children and, like Hardy, moved back to Britain to begin a new life. Shortly after returning to England, though, Hardy began stalking his ex-wife. This led to her obtaining a restraining order against him. He subsequently broke the order and as a result was imprisoned for a short time. Following his release, Hardy sought psychiatric help at outpatient clinics. He was diagnosed with peripheral neuropathy, a disorder that is known to cause depression. He was also diagnosed with manic depression and prescribed medication to reduce the symptoms. In the early and mid-1990s, Hardy became homeless and spent much of his time living in various hostels throughout London. During that time, he took to taking drugs and drinking heavily, which further exacerbated his psychological problems. He was arrested on several occasions for theft and served several short custodial sentences. In 1998, Hardy was arrested for indecent assault after a prostitute claimed he had raped her, but the charges were later dropped and he was released. Police also investigated him as a suspect in three other rape cases, but there was insufficient evidence to connect them with him.

In 2000, Hardy moved into a one-bedroom public housing flat on Royal College Street in Camden, a short distance from King's Cross, an area frequented by prostitutes. It was a location deliberately chosen for that very reason. The neighbourhood would become his hunting ground.

In January 2002, Hardy was again arrested after having been caught pouring battery acid through a neighbour's letterbox. That incident led police to a gruesome find at Hardy's flat. When police went to his flat, the bedroom door was locked. When they broke it open, they found the body of a young woman lying naked on his bed. She appeared to have cuts to her head and her body was covered in bite marks and bruises. The police suspected that she had been murdered. However, pathologists claimed that she had died of a heart attack rather than foul play.

The woman was later identified as Sally Rose White, 38, a prostitute from the King's Cross area, who was known to have an addiction to crack and suffered from brain damage and behavioural problems caused by a birth-related spinal cord injury. It was believed that her condition, which had worsened with age and lack of treatment, coupled with her addiction to drugs, had resulted in her heart attack. However, her death from 'natural causes' would later be questioned.

On 30 December 2002, a gruesome discovery was made in rubbish bins behind a public house in Royal College Street. A vagrant was foraging in the rubbish bin looking for food when he came across several black bin liners. In one of the bags he found human remains, including severed sections of two legs. Instead of calling the police, the man took the remains with him to a nearby hospital where the police were contacted. They went and searched the rubbish bins and found more bags containing various body parts. On widening the search, police found the torso of a young woman in another rubbish bin about 100yd from the original discovery.

The body parts were taken to St Pancras mortuary, where pathologists examined them. The causes of death were difficult to establish because the heads and hands of the victims were still missing. However, pathologists were able to determine that the remains were those of two different women, who had probably been murdered sometime over the Christmas holidays. DNA tests were conducted in the hope that it would help investigators uncover the identity of the women.

A crime scene examination revealed a trail of blood, which led police to Hardy's ground-floor flat, located a short distance from where the bodies were discovered. They promptly obtained a warrant. Hardy was not at home and the police forcibly entered and searched his flat. They found a hacksaw with what appeared to be human skin still attached to the blade. They also found an electric jigsaw power tool and pornographic magazines scattered about the flat. A woman's black stiletto shoe rested on the windowsill. Traces of blood were found in the bathroom and a devil's mask lay alongside a note on a table, reading 'Sally White RIP'. However, the most gruesome evidence found at Hardy's apartment was a woman's torso wrapped in bin liners.

Following the discovery, a massive search was launched to find Hardy, who had been missing for several days; it was suspected that he had absconded. However, a CCTV camera caught him on 1 January trying to obtain a prescription for his diabetic medication at a London hospital. He had shaved off his beard in an attempt to alter his appearance, but police now knew he was still in the immediate area. After his details were circulated on television, a member of the public came forward to say they had seen Hardy with a young woman named Kelly Anne Nicol, 24, shortly after the Christmas holidays. Family members and police were concerned for her safety, fearing that she might have become a victim. However, their fears were alleviated when she contacted her parents to let them know she was safe. Even though she had contact with Hardy, who repeatedly tried to persuade her back to his apartment, she did not allow herself to be influenced by him, and this had surely saved her life.

On 2 January, a member of the public contacted the police

after spotting Hardy at Great Ormond Street Hospital for children in central London. Police surrounded the area and he was promptly arrested.

Police had by now been able to identify the two victims whose remains had been discovered at his home and in the rubbish bin as Elizabeth Selina Valad, 29, and Brigitte McLennan, 34. Both were prostitutes and dependent on drugs. It was Elizabeth Valad's torso that had been found at Hardy's flat and her legs that had been discovered by the vagrant in the rubbish bin. It was difficult for investigators to identify her initially because her hands and head were never found. However, they were able to obtain a positive identification on her by processing the serial numbers found on her breast implants. McLennan was identified by conventional DNA techniques.

Hardy was interviewed by the police and made no comment to all questions put to him about the actual murders. He did, however, tell police that he had never intended to kill anyone and that the women had died as a result of the use of 'excessive force in the course of otherwise consensual but extreme sexual activity'.

However, when he appeared in court he pleaded guilty to three charges of murder, in fact making an admission in court to the murder of Sally White who, according to medical experts, had died of natural causes. The prosecution suggested that Hardy had lured all the women to his apartment with the offer of money. He had then engaged in extreme sex with the women before strangling them, and had dismembered the bodies with a hacksaw in the bath. It was suggested by the prosecution that the motive for the murders was that he had decided to kill these women in order to photograph them in various positions, which he had arranged when they were dead. Hardy had been in the process of preparing White to be photographed when police found her naked body.

Hardy was sentenced to three life sentences for the murders. Before passing sentence the judge, Mr Justice Keith, said: 'Only you know for sure how your victims met their deaths but the unspeakable indignities to which you subjected the bodies of your last two victims in order to satisfy your depraved and perverted needs are in no doubt.'

Hardy is also suspected of committing other undetected murders. In February 2000, boys fishing in Regent's Canal at Camden retrieved a bag from the murky water, which was found to contain body parts from a human female.

Police carried out a search of the area and, during a sweep of the canal, found approximately six further bags containing various body parts wrapped in bin liners. Bricks had been used to weight down the bags. Despite these finds, not all of the woman's body was recovered.

The woman was later identified as Paula Fields, 31, of Liverpool, who had lived in the Highbury Grove area for a couple of years before her death. She was a mother of two who worked as a prostitute to support her drug habit. Paula had last been seen getting into a red car on 13 December. The police believed that a hacksaw had probably been used to dismember her body.

On 17 December 2000, the dismembered body of prostitute Zoe Parker, aged 24, was found floating in the River Thames. To date, these crimes are still unsolved, but Anthony Hardy remains the prime suspect. Hardy was later sent to Rampton mental hospital for assessment between April and July 2003, and it was subsequently decided that he was sufficiently sane to be held within the general prison population rather than at a secure mental institution. Hardy is currently deemed a category-A prisoner and is held at Wakefield prison, where he claims to have found God and rediscovered Catholicism and has also become a vegan. He does not expect ever to be released from prison, following a 2010 ruling by a High Court judge. Mr Justice Keith, sitting in London, said: 'This is one of those exceptionally rare cases in which life should mean life.'

STEVE WRIGHT, AKA THE SUFFOLK STRANGLER

The naked body of prostitute Gemma Adams, aged 25, was discovered in a stream at Thorpes Hill, near Hintlesham, Suffolk, at 11.50am on Saturday, 2 December 2006. Gemma disappeared after leaving home on Wednesday, 15 November, to go to work. She was reported missing by her boyfriend, and a member of the public discovered her body. A post-mortem was carried out, but the cause of death could not be confirmed and further tests were carried out. Police later confirmed that Gemma had not been sexually assaulted.

A second body – that of another prostitute, Tania Nichol, 19 – was found on Friday, 8 December, near Copdock Mill, by police divers. Tania had disappeared on 30 October. She left to go to work in the Ipswich red-light district about 10.30pm and was not seen again. Tania was reported missing on Wednesday, 1 November, by her mother after she hadn't seen her for two days. Her naked body was discovered in the same stream as Gemma Adams's. Gemma and Tania had known each other and frequently worked the same 'patch'. Their bodies were found about two miles apart.

On Sunday, 10 December another naked body was discovered by a passing motorist in woods near Nacton, close to Ipswich. On Tuesday, 12 December, Suffolk police confirmed that the body was that of Anneli Alderton, aged 24, from Colchester, Essex, also a known prostitute. She had been strangled and was three months pregnant at the time of her death.

On that same day, police confirmed that at 3.05pm, following a call from a member of the public, a fourth body had been discovered along Old Felixstowe Road. The body was that of a naked woman, roughly 6yd from the roadside. About 40 minutes later, at 3.48pm, the police helicopter spotted a further body only a few hundred yards from the first. Suffolk police said that although they had no evidence to support their belief, they strongly believed these bodies to be connected to the first, making a total of five victims. The two new victims were later identified as two women previously reported missing: Annette Nicholls, aged 29, and Paula Clennell, aged 24, again both prostitutes.

On Thursday, 14 December, police confirmed the identity of the fourth victim as Paula Clennell. Paula had been reported missing, and had last been seen at about at 12.20am on Sunday, 10 December, on Handford Road near its junction with Burlington Road in Ipswich, Suffolk.

The police now had a total of five victims, all prostitutes, and all had apparently been strangled while under the influence of drugs and stripped naked before being dumped by the killer. The police were in no doubt that all the victims had been killed by the same hand. There was one unusual feature in the case of Anneli Alderton and Annette Nicholls – their bodies had been laid out in the shape of a crucifix, with their arms outstretched and their hair combed out behind their heads.

More than 500 officers were involved in the enquiry and a team of five investigating officers, one for each of the dead women, assessed and evaluated the evidence on the killings. Sifting this evidence proved to be fraught with difficulties, though. The victims were all known prostitutes and may have been with several men each night, and may also have been driven away from the district to other places to have sex; therefore there could be DNA from a number of different men found on their bodies and at the places where they were dumped. The police also believed that the victims were not killed where their bodies were found; as the locations were so close to each other they were looked on as deposition sites.

Police officers were also trying to establish whether the murders of the five women in Suffolk were linked to the murders or disappearances of other women and teenage girls, including six in East Anglia over the past 15 years.

These victims included:

- Diane McInally, aged 23, from Glasgow. She vanished in October 1991. The prostitute and drug addict's naked body was found dumped near bushes in a wood behind the Burrell Collection in Pollok Park, Glasgow. She died from compression to the neck.

- Natalie Pearman, aged 16, from Norwich, Norfolk. She disappeared in November 1992. Her body was found at Ringland, Norfolk, near Norwich. She had been strangled and was found partially clothed.

- Karen McGregor, aged 26, of Glasgow, Scotland, was found in the bushes of a car park in Glasgow in 1993. She had been badly beaten, sexually assaulted and strangled.

- Johanna Young, aged 14, from Watton, Norfolk. She was reported missing on 23 December 1992. She was found in a nearby frozen pond, half-naked, on 26 December.

- Mandy Duncan, aged 26, from Woodbridge, Suffolk. She disappeared in 1993 in Ipswich. Her body has never been found.

- Victoria Hall, aged 17, from Trimley St Mary, Suffolk. She vanished on 19 September 1999. Her body was found five days later 25 miles away in a river. A local businessman was later tried and acquitted of her murder.

- Kellie Pratt, aged 29, from Norwich. She disappeared in 2000 in Norwich. Her body has never been found.

- Michelle Bettles, aged 22, from Norwich. She was reported missing on 28 March 2002. She was found dead three days later near Dereham in woodland. Her body was found fully clothed.

Police in Suffolk acted quickly and arrested Tom Stephens, a former part-time Special Police Constable, at 7.20am on Monday, 18 December 2006. Stephens was a supermarket worker at Tesco in Martlesham. Police arrested him at his home at Jubilee Close, Trimley St Martin, near Felixstowe; the village is close to the A14 road between Ipswich and Felixstowe. The police stated that Stephens had been questioned earlier in the investigation, and that items had been removed from his house at that time. They had taken his mobile phone and laptop computer. It was believed that Stephens knew all five of the dead girls.

However, following lengthy questioning, he was released without charge on police bail for further enquiries to be carried out. Due to the public outcry over the murders, Stephens was forced to go into hiding, despite not having been charged. His bail was later cancelled and he was exonerated from any involvement in the murders, although police would later suggest that the man they finally arrested who was charged and later convicted may have had an accomplice.

At 5am on Tuesday, 19 December 2006, a second man, Steve Wright, aged 48, a forklift truck driver from London Road, Ipswich, was arrested on suspicion of murder. His house and car were subjected to intense forensic examinations. He underwent a lengthy interrogation, which consisted of ten separate interviews during which he chose not to answer any questions. However, following the results of the forensic examinations, which gave the police sufficient evidence to connect Wright to the murders, he was formally charged with the five murders.

The trial of Steve Wright started at Ipswich Crown Court on Monday, 14 January 2008, before Mr Justice Goss. Wright entered a plea of not guilty to all five murders. The prosecution was represented by Mr Peter Wright QC who, in his opening speech, outlined the case to the jury, which was told that the backbone of the prosecution case revolved around DNA evidence linking Wright to three of the five victims. DNA from Wright was found on the breast of Anneli Alderton, as were other fibres that matched fibres found at his home, inside his gardening gloves and on his clothes. Wright's DNA was also found on the victim Annette Nicholls along with matching fibres from his car, and her blood was found on a reflective jacket he sometimes wore.

Wright's DNA was also found on the body of Paula Clennell, along with matching fibres from his sofa, his lumber jacket, tracksuit and trousers. Her blood was also found on the same reflective jacket.

The jury was told that no DNA was found on either Gemma Adams or Tania Nichol but the prosecution would suggest that this was due to the fact that the bodies had been immersed in water for several weeks before being found, thereby destroying any DNA evidence that might have been present. However, fibres from Wright's car were found embedded in the hair of Gemma Adams and Tania Nicol, suggesting a 'forceful or sustained contact' with the carpet of the car. No other DNA relating to any other person was found on any of the victims.

In addition to the DNA evidence, the police enquiry had shown that Wright regularly cruised the red-light district of Ipswich, picking up prostitutes. On the night Tania Nichol disappeared, Wright's Ford Mondeo was captured on a police camera heading out of town towards the location where her body was later found. A car matching Wright's was also seen in the same area on the nights Gemma Adams and Anneli Alderton disappeared.

Steve Wright was represented by Timothy Langdale QC who, in his opening speech, told the jury that Wright would be denying the murders and had regularly picked up prostitutes, some of these being the victims, thereby suggesting that the DNA evidence was transferred through these meetings and not as a result of him murdering the women. Furthermore, he would state that he had also had sex with one of the other victims where there was no DNA evidence against him.

The majority of the prosecution evidence was unchallenged by the defence team representing Wright. After the prosecution closed its case, Wright took the witness stand. He told the court that he started to pick prostitutes up in the red-light district in the third week of October 2006. He stated that he could have been with all five women on the nights they vanished. He told Ipswich Crown Court that he had had sex with four of the women and was intending to have sex with the fifth, Nichol, before changing his mind after she had got into his car and he had seen her face was covered in acne. This had put him off so he told her to get out. He denied the murders, stating that he had been the victim of a series of coincidences. He said he recalled having sex in his car with Adams either late on 14 November or early on 15 November. Wright said he could not remember when he had picked up Nichol but it might have been on 8 December 2006, when she was last seen alive. Her blood was found on a reflective jacket belonging to him. But he could not account for this; he had not injured her during sex. Blood from Clennell, whom he also admitted picking up around the time of her disappearance, was also found on the same reflective jacket. He could not explain how this had got there, but said she had told him that she had 'bit her tongue' while lying down on a sofa in his home. Wright said that he had used the jacket as a blanket on the floor of his bedroom where he had taken the women, after spending time in his car.

After a trial lasting six weeks, on Thursday, 21 February 2008, the jury finally retired to consider their verdicts. It took them just eight hours to return with unanimous guilty verdicts against Wright on all five counts of murder. The judge deferred sentence until the following day.

On Friday, 22 February 2008, Mr Justice Goss sentenced Steve Wright to the maximum sentence of life imprisonment. The judge said, 'This was a targeted campaign of murder. It is right you should spend your whole life in prison ... Drugs and prostitution meant these women were at risk. But neither drugs nor prostitution killed them. You did. You killed them, stripped them and left them ... Why you did it may never be known.'

Wright sat emotionless as prosecutors asked the judge to ensure that he would never be allowed out of jail. The judge said, 'the case met the legal requirements for a whole life sentence because the murders involved a "substantial degree of premeditation and planning"'.

Wright's defence team said they would be considering whether there were grounds for an appeal, but said this was routine in all criminal cases.

UNITED KINGDOM

At the time of writing, police had undertaken to check the outstanding cases previously mentioned to see whether there could be links to Wright. Despite the lengthy investigation conducted by the police, they were never able to put forward a clear motive for Wright killing the five victims. Could Wright have killed before? This should not be discounted, as it is unusual for someone to suddenly become a serial killer at the age of 40.

On 25 February 2009 Wright made an application to the Court of Appeal for leave to challenge his conviction on the grounds that his trial was unfair and therefore the conviction was unsafe. The appeal was heard by Lord Justice Hughes, who sat with two other judges. After careful deliberation the judges rejected the appeal. Lord Justice Hughes, when announcing the decision of the court, said Wright had raised 'no arguable grounds of appeal'.

EPILOGUE

As you will have seen from reading about all of the aforementioned crimes, there have often been questions asked as to whether some of the murders could have been prevented, often by the families of the victims.

These questions tend to suggest that, in some cases, the police did not act quickly enough to arrest the offender or offenders. Others suggest that police departments were blinkered in their approach as they collected, assessed and evaluated evidence. It is worth bearing in mind, though, that many of the serial killers discussed here committed their crimes long before DNA technology, coupled with new investigative methods, became available. Had all of these been available to law enforcement officers at the time, perhaps these monsters would have been apprehended and brought to justice much sooner and more lives could have been saved. The sad fact is that there are mothers and fathers out there who still do not know what fate befell their missing sons and daughters. Many murders remain unsolved and the bodies of some victims have never been recovered. Serial killers, for various reasons, very rarely confess to all their crimes. Despite the police often having strong suspicions about other

EPILOGUE

murders individuals may have committed, without supporting evidence or a full confession they are powerless to prosecute. One can only hope that, at some time in the future, some of the serial killers already convicted will choose to unburden their consciences further.